A con

ific   tion.

Designed by Tim Larsen
Cover art by Lars Justinen
Cover design by Brian Gray

All Scripture texts are from the New Century Version unless other-wise indicated.

Additional copies of this book are available by calling toll free 1-800-765-6955 or visiting http://www.adventistbookcenter.com

Library of Congress Cataloging-in-Publication data:

Thomas, Jerry D., 1959-
    Messiah: a contemporary adaptation of the classic work on Jesus' life, The desire of ages / Jerry D. Thomas.
        p. cm.
    ISBN: 0-8163-1978-2
        1. Jesus Christ. I. White, Ellen Gould Harmon, 1827-1915.
Desire of ages. II. Title.

    BT301.2 .T475 2003
    232.9'01—dc21
    [B]   2001036668

03 04 05 06 07 • 5 4 3 2 1

"It would be well for us to spend a thoughtful hour each day in contemplation of the life of Christ. We should take it point by point, and let the imagination grasp each scene, especially the closing ones. As we thus dwell upon His great sacrifice for us, our confidence in Him will be more constant, our love will be quickened, and we shall be more deeply imbued with His spirit. If we would be saved at last, we must learn the lesson of penitence and humiliation at the foot of the cross."

The Desire of Ages, page 83

To my father:
Hagar Thomas

for the person he was,
the person he taught me to be,
and the Messiah he taught me to follow.

CONTENTS

GOD BECOMES ONE OF US

" 'They will name him Immanuel,' which means 'God is with us' "
(Matthew 1:23).

From the days of eternity, Jesus has been with His Father. They are both God. Both are full of glory and majesty greater than anything we can imagine. Jesus came to our world to show and to share that glory. He came to our dark, sinful planet to shine the light of divine love—to be "God with us." That's why the Bible writer said, "They will call him Immanuel."

Jesus came to this earth to show both humans and angels what God is really like. In fact, He was the word of God—God's thoughts spoken out loud, so we can hear them.

It wasn't just for His children on this planet that Jesus became a human being and demonstrated God's love. He did it for all created beings. Our world is now the textbook of the whole universe.

The purpose behind God's grace, the mystery of a love deep enough to save lost humans, will be studied by angels forever. Those who are saved, plus the beings from unfallen worlds will also sing about and study Jesus' life and death. They will find the glory that shines from Jesus' face is the glory of selfless love. Jesus' sacrifice on Calvary shows that the law of selfless love is the law of life for earth and heaven. This selfless love comes straight from the heart of God.

In the beginning, nature reflected God like a mirror. Jesus Himself rolled out the heavens and laid the foundation of the earth. With His own hands, He hung the worlds in space and fashioned the flowers of the field. He filled the earth with beauty and the sky with song. Upon all these things, He wrote the message of His Father's love.

Today sin has spoiled God's perfect creation. But the handwriting of God's love is still there. Even now, all created things—except for the selfish human heart—reflect in some way God's law of love. Every bird that takes flight, every animal that moves and breathes, has a part in helping other creatures survive. Even the leaves and blades of grass have their ministry. The oxygen they give supports all living creatures. Animals return to them the carbon dioxide they need to grow and survive.

All of nature lives to give. Flowers share their fragrance and beauty. The sun gives its life-sustaining light. The ocean, source of all water on earth, returns the water it is fed by rivers and streams in the rain and snow that fall on the earth.

In the same way, angels find their joy in giving. With great love, they watch over weak and sinful humans. Into this dark world, they bring the light of heaven; with gentle patience, they work to show humans the love of God and bring them into a relationship with Jesus.

In Jesus we see God most clearly. He shows us without doubt that His Father's greatest joy—His greatest glory—is to give. God's life flows out to the universe in His ministry for all created beings. It flows out through His beloved Son, and through His Son it returns in praise and joyful service. It becomes a great wave of love, flowing back to the Source of life. Through Jesus, the circle of life and love is complete.

SELFISHNESS IN HEAVEN

The law of selfless love was broken in heaven itself. Sin began as selfishness. Lucifer, the brightest and mightiest angel, wanted more. He wanted to be the most important being in heaven. He tried to gain control of the other angels by breaking their loyalty to God. He wanted the angels looking at him.

He began implying that God was demanding worship and loyalty. He painted God as a self-centered dictator who tolerated no questions and no doubts. With these suggestions, Satan deceived the angels. With the same ideas, he would deceive humans. He led them to doubt God's word and to question His goodness. He tricked them into seeing a God of justice and awesome majesty as cruel and unforgiving. By misreprenting God's character, Satan pulled humans into his rebellion. The long dark night of earth's history began.

In Jesus, we see God most clearly of all.

The only way to lighten the shadows was to show that Satan's description of God was wrong. This couldn't be done by force. Force has no place in God's plans. He wants only a response of love, and love does not happen on demand. Love cannot be forced or ordered of anyone. Love is returned only when love is offered.

To know God is to love Him. So the way to lead humans back to God was to show humans what God was really like. This could be done by only one Being in the universe. Only Jesus, who knew the limitless love of His Father, could make that love clear to all others.

The plan to save humans was not an afterthought. It was in place before Adam and Eve sinned. The plan was a natural result of the law of selfless love. God's throne and the operation of the universe was founded on this principle. From eternity, God and Jesus knew of Lucifer's fall and that his lies would lead humans to rebel also.

God didn't create sin. He did not want it to exist. But He knew that it would happen and made a plan to deal with that most critical emergency. His plan revealed the great love He had for this world and humanity. He promised to give His one and only Son, " ' . . . that whoever believes in him may not be lost, but have eternal life' " (John 3:16).

Satan in his selfishness wanted to be more important, more honored. He wanted to become a god. Jesus, in His selfless love, did not care about glory or honor. He became a human being.

A VOLUNTEER FOR THE SACRIFICE

Jesus volunteered to make this sacrifice. He could have stayed at His Father's side in the glory of heaven, worshipped and honored by the angels. Instead He chose to step down from the throne of the universe to bring light and life to a dark world.

Two thousand years ago in heaven, Jesus announced fulfillment of the plan that had been hidden from eternity. " 'You do not want sacrifices and offerings, but you have prepared a body for me.... "Look, I have come. It is written about me in the book. God, I have come to do what you want." ' " (Hebrews 10:5, 7). Jesus was ready to visit our world and become a human.

Humans could not have lived in the glory of His normal appearance. Only the specially prepared body made it possible for Him to walk among us. His divinity was covered with humanity; His invisible glory was hidden by His visible human body.

While the Israelites wandered in the desert, Jesus lived among them in the sanctuary He commanded them to build. Now He came to live among humans again, to teach us the truth about God's character and His love.

Since Jesus came to live as a human, we know that God understands our trials and sympathizes with our troubles. Everyone can see that our Creator is the Friend of sinners. Throughout Jesus' life on earth, every act of love, every promise of joy, every teaching of grace showed God living with us.

Satan claimed that God's law of love is a law of selfishness, impossible to obey. He blamed God for the sin of Adam and Eve and all the suffering that has happened since that day. He led humans to think that God and His law are the reason that sin, suffering, and death exist.

Jesus came to show that Satan was wrong. As a human, He would show that the law could be kept. He had to face all the temptations that any human would face. If anyone had to bear a trial that Jesus did not, then Satan would claim that God's power was not strong enough for us. Because of this, Jesus endured every trial that we face. He used no power that God does not offer freely to anyone.

As a human, He faced temptations with the strength given to Him by God. He went about doing good and healing those who suffered. He showed the truth about God's law and what it means to serve God. Jesus' life proves that it is possible for us also to obey God's law.

Jesus bound Himself to humanity with a tie that will never be broken.

By His humanity, Jesus reached humans. By His divinity, He kept hold on the throne of God. As the Son of man, He gave us an example of living by God's law. As the Son of God, He gives us the power to do the same. He is our Guarantee that sin can be overcome. Through His power, heaven's laws can be obeyed.

Jesus gave up honor and glory to become a human. He showed that His character is just the opposite of Satan's. But Jesus went even further. He didn't just become a human. He became a sacrifice to save humans.

TREATED AS WE DESERVE

Jesus was treated as we deserve to be, so that we can be treated the way He deserves. He was condemned for our sins, which He had nothing to do with. This was so we can be saved by His righteous goodness, which we have nothing to do with. He suffered our death, so that we can be given His life. "We are healed because of his wounds" (Isaiah 53:5).

With His life and His death, Jesus did more than just restore the damage caused by sin. Satan tried to separate humankind from God forever. But because of Jesus, we are more closely tied to God than if we had never fallen into sin. By becoming one of us, Jesus bound Himself to humanity with a tie that will never be broken.

When God "so loved the world" that He gave His Son, He gave that Son to humanity forever. God has adopted human nature in the person of His Son. Through Him, God carried that nature into heaven.

It is the "Son of humanity" who shares the throne of the universe. In Jesus, the family of earth and the family of heaven are bound together. He is our Brother.

Through the work of Jesus, God's rulership over the universe stands justified. The all-knowing God is shown to be the God of unending love. Satan's accusations are proven false, and his evil character becomes obvious to all. Rebellion against God can never rise again. Sin can never again arise anywhere in the universe. All beings everywhere are safe. By love's self-sacrifice, the inhabitants of heaven and earth are bound to their Creator in bonds that can never be broken.

The work of saving the lost will be complete. Where sin seemed to be so powerful, God's grace was much more powerful. The planet on which the battle was fought will be given a place of honor above all others. Earth where the King of glory lived and suffered and died, will be made new. Here God Himself will live with His people.

Through time that never ends, the saved will walk in the light of their Lord. They will praise Him for His gift of love beyond understanding—Immanuel, "God with us."

CHAPTER 2

THE CHOSEN PEOPLE

"He came to the world that was his own, but his own people did not accept him" (John 1:11).

For more than a thousand years, the Jewish people waited for the arrival of the Savior, the Promised One, the Messiah. Their brightest hopes rested on this promise. Songs, prophecies, temple services, and household prayers all called out His name. Then, when He did arrive, they didn't even recognize Him.

God chose the nation of Israel as the ones who would remember His laws and the symbols and prophecies that pointed to the coming Savior. God wanted them to be fountains of information about Him in the world. Abraham had done this when he wandered the land. Joseph had spoken for God in Egypt. Daniel was a light for God in the courts of Babylon. The Hebrew people were to do the same among the nations of the world. They were to tell others about the true God of heaven.

God promised Abraham that through him, all the families of the earth would be blessed. Abraham's descendants—the nation of Israel—were given the same promise. But the Israelites could not see past the lure of worldly greatness. From the time they entered the land of Canaan, they ignored God's laws and followed the lifestyle of the heathen around them. God sent prophets to warn them, but it did no good. Neither did being conquered by other nations.When they did try to repent and follow God, the change never lasted.

If Israel had only followed God faithfully, He would have made them the most honored, the most admired nation in the world. Because of their stubborn unfaithfulness, His plans had to be worked out through hardship and suffering.

Eventually, the nation was conquered by Babylon and the people were scattered through many lands. In this time of trouble, many of them began to follow God again. The light of truth shone out from them. Information about Him began to spread. Many sincere followers of heathen religions learned of the true God and had faith in the promised Savior.

Many of the faithful exiles in heathen lands were persecuted. Some were killed because they refused to honor heathen festivals instead of the Sabbath. But many times, when idol worshippers moved to destroy the faithful, God brought His followers face to face with kings and other rulers so they could witness for Him. Over and over, the great rulers were led to admit the supreme power of the God of the Hebrew captives.

The Israelites who finally were allowed to return to their land were cured of the worship of carved idols. After further invasions they eventually became convinced that their only hope for prosperity was to obey the law of God. But with most, this was not an obedience of love. Their motives were selfish. They served God because that would keep their nation strong. Instead of becoming the light of the world, they shut themselves away from other nations to avoid temptation.

They used God's instructions through Moses about avoiding association with the heathen as an excuse to build a wall to separate themselves from all other nations. The Jews considered Jerusalem to be their heaven. The last thing they wanted was God's showing mercy to any heathen Gentile nation.

HOW THEY TWISTED THE TEMPLE SERVICES

After their captivity in Babylon, the Jews got serious about religious instruction. All across the country, synagogues (local churches) were built and priests and scribes taught the law of God. Schools were opened to teach religion as well as arts and sciences. But these schools were quickly corrupted. Many of the strange, heathen ideas and customs they had seen being practiced while in captivity were now brought into their own religious services.

As the Jews drifted farther from God, they mostly lost sight of the meaning of the rituals and services in the temple. Jesus Himself had started that service and every part of it was a symbol of Him. But the Jews were only going through the motions. They trusted the sacrifices and rituals instead of trusting the God to whom those rituals pointed. To make up for the lost meaning, the priests and rabbis added more and more rules of their own. The more rules they had, the more judgmental they became, and the less they showed of God's love. They considered themselves holy, but pride and hypocrisy filled their hearts.

Great rulers were led to admit the supreme power of the God of the Hebrew captives.

With all their minute, nit-picky rules, it became impossible to keep the law. Those who wanted to follow God faithfully—who tried to follow the rules of the rabbis—carried an extremely heavy burden. They were never free from guilt.

In this way, Satan discouraged the people, lowered their understanding of God, and made the religion of Israel a hated thing. Satan hoped to prove the point he started with in heaven—that God's laws were unjust and could not be obeyed. Even God's own people, Israel, couldn't do it.

THEY EXPECTED THE WRONG MESSIAH

In spite of all this, the Jews did look forward to the promised Messiah. But they misunderstood His mission. They weren't looking to be saved from sin—they wanted to be saved from the Romans. They looked for a Messiah to come as a conquering hero, driving the hated Romans from their land and making their nation the dominant force in the world. When the Savior did appear, they were well prepared to reject Him.

At the time of Jesus' birth, the nation was grumbling against its Roman rulers. Arguing and fighting among the Jewish religious and political power groups was getting worse. The Jews had their own government, but there was no denying that the Romans were in charge. The Romans reserved the right to appoint or remove the nation's high priest. The position was often acquired by fraud, bribery, or sometimes even murder. The priests became very corrupt. Still they carried great power, and mostly used it for selfish reasons.

They had studied the prophecies, but they did not understand what God meant.

It was the people who suffered. In addition to the demands of the priests were the heavy taxes of the Romans. Popular rebellions popped up frequently. Greed, violence, and a lack of interest in spiritual things were eating the heart right out of the nation.

The people, in their dark despair, and the rulers, in their thirst for revenge and power, both longed for the day when the Messiah would appear and restore the kingdom of Israel. They had studied the prophecies, but they did not understand what they read. So they overlooked the scriptures that pointed out the humble nature of Jesus' first coming. And they misapplied those scriptures that speak of the power and glory of His second coming. Pride blurred their vision. They interpreted prophecy to fit into their own selfish plans.

CHAPTER 3

AT EXACTLY THE RIGHT TIME

"But when the right time came, God sent His Son who was born of a woman and lived under the law" (Galatians 4:4).

he first promise of a coming Savior was given in the Garden of Eden. Adam and Eve heard that promise and looked for it to be fulfilled soon. Part of the joy at the birth of their first son was the hope that this child might be the promised Savior.

Adam, Eve, their children, and their children's children lived and died without seeing the Messiah. From Enoch to Abraham, Isaac, and Joseph, the promise was passed on, but the waiting continued. The vision given to Daniel predicted the time of Jesus' first coming, but not everyone understood the message. Century after century of time went by, leaving many to wonder if the promise would ever be kept.

Like the endless movement of stars and planets, God's plans are not rushed or delayed. In heaven, the hour for the coming of the Messiah had been set. And when the great clock of time pointed to that moment, Jesus was born in Bethlehem.

It was exactly the right time. God had directed the actions of the nations until the world was ripe and ready for the promised Savior. Many nations were united under one government and one language was widely spoken.

From all over the world, Jews regularly returned to Jerusalem for the yearly feasts. As they returned to their homes, they could easily spread the news of the Messiah around the world.

At this same time, many were losing faith in their heathen belief systems. People, long tired of complicated stories and fables, were searching for a religion that would meet the needs of their hearts. While God's truth seemed to have faded from the earth, many were searching for light. They were searching to know the true God and for some hope of life after death.

MANY PEOPLE WERE HOPING FOR A MESSIAH

As the Jews had failed to follow God, the light they could have spread was reduced to a flicker. Few people had any faith or hope for a future life. To the vast majority, death was a mystery of uncertainty and gloom. They longed for Someone to explain it, to give them hope.

Outside the Jewish nation, some predicted that a divine teacher would appear. They were searching for truth and God gave them what they could understand. These teachers rose up like stars in a night sky as their words gave hope to thousands in the Gentile world.

For hundreds of years, the Old Testament Scriptures had been available in Greek. Since Greek was spoken throughout the Roman Empire, people were becoming familiar with the Word of God. The hope of the coming Messiah was understood and shared by many Gentiles.

Some of these people had a better understanding of the Scripture's prophecies of the Messiah than did the Jewish priests. Many were eager to learn more from the traditions and rituals of God's people. But in their prejudice, the Jews had as little to do with outsiders as possible. They were most concerned with keeping the walls of separation in place. A new Teacher, a true Teacher, would have to come and explain it all.

God had been speaking to the world in many ways: through nature, through symbols, and through His prophets and leaders. Now it was time to speak more clearly, in a language all could understand.

Jesus must come, and when He did His life and His words would show the truth about God and the plan of redemption to the whole world.

There were still faithful believers among the Jews. Many expected to see the promises made to their ancestors fulfilled. They knew what the Scriptures said: a Prophet, an Anointed One, a Mighty Prince was coming to save their people. Jacob, the father of their nation, had promised on his deathbed that the Savior would come to deliver them. Since their nation's power had almost disappeared under the iron rule of Rome, they knew the Messiah must come soon. Few understood the true purpose of Jesus' mission. Most expected a mighty warrior and king who would free Israel and make it the mightiest nation on earth.

> *He wanted God to abandon earth and give up on humans forever.*

SATAN ALMOST SUCCEEDED

They were right about this: the time had come. For ages, Satan had been working to keep earth and heaven separate. With his lies, he enticed humans to sin, hoping to wear out God's patience, to extinguish God's love for them. He wanted God to abandon earth and give up on humans forever. Satan worked to keep humanity from knowing any truth about God. And after all this time, his workplan to control earth seemed almost completely successful.

It is true that God had faithful followers in every generation. Even among heathen nations there were people through whom Jesus worked to lift up humans from their sad, evil lives. But those people were despised and hated. Most of them died violently. The dark shadow Satan had cast over the world grew deeper and deeper.

Through the many ignorant and savage religions of the world, Satan had turned people away from God. But his greatest victory was in perverting the religion of God's people in Israel. By worshipping things they created with their own hands, the heathen had lost any knowledge of God and had become more and more evil. Sadly, the same thing happened in Israel. The idea that humans can save themselves by their own works is at the foundation of every heathen religion. Now, through Satan's efforts, it was the center of the Jewish religion as well.

By trying to keep their religion away from others, and only for themselves, the Jews robbed God of His glory and cheated the world with a counterfeit gospel. They refused to surrender themselves to God to help save the world. Instead, they became agents of Satan to destroy it. The people whom God had called to be the source of truth were doing Satan's work. They were distorting the people's understanding of God, making the world see God as a heartless tyrant.

But instead of destroying the world, God sent His Son to save it.

Even the priests who ministered in the temple no longer saw the meaning of the services they performed. They carried on as if they were only actors in a play. Instead of leading people to God, the temple services now closed people's minds and hardened their hearts. God could no longer reach people through symbols and ceremonies.

JESUS STEPS IN

The Son of God saw the suffering and misery that sin was causing. He saw how humans had become victims of satanic cruelty—corrupted, murdered, lost in sin. Confused and deceived, they were moving in a hopeless march toward eternal ruin—death with no hope of life, night with no hope of morning.

The bodies of human beings, made to be God's dwelling place, had become the homes of demons. With supernatural skill, human senses and passions were perverted causing people to do the most degrading things. Demon eyes looked out through human faces.

This is what the world's Savior saw when He looked down upon His children. What a heartbreaking sight! Sin had become a science and evil was now a part of religion. Without God, there was no hope for humanity.

Other worlds watched with intense interest to see if the God of heaven would sweep the earth clean of humanity. Satan watched as well, ready with a plan to win the loyalty of heavenly beings. He had declared that the principles of God's government made forgiveness impossible. If humans were destroyed, Satan would have trumpeted this as proof that he was right and then spread his rebellion to the other worlds.

But instead of destroying the world, God sent His Son to save it. At the very moment when Satan seemed about to win, the Son of God came with proof of divine love and grace. When exactly the right time came, God poured out a flood of healing grace that will never stop flowing until the plan of salvation is complete.

Jesus came to throw out the demons that control us, to lift us up from the dust, to reshape our character into His image, to make us beautiful with His own glory.

CHAPTER 4

A SAVIOR
IS BORN

"I bring you good news of great joy that will be for all the people"
(Luke 2:10, NIV).

he King of the universe gave up all of His power and honor to become a human. He left the glory of heaven to live in wood-and-stone houses and walk on dirt roads. His supernatural splender was buried deep, so that no one would follow Him because of it. He wanted nothing to do with looking good or being popular. He wanted only the appeal of truth—real, heavenly truth—to grab people's interest. He wanted people to accept Him because they recognized Him from the words of Scripture.

The angels were amazed at this plan to save humankind. They watched to see how those who claimed to follow God would accept God's Son, when He looked just like one of them. Many angels came to visit the land of the people specially chosen to know and follow God. Without being seen, they watched the priests of the temple and those who studied and taught the Holy Scriptures.

An angel had already appeared to Zachariah as he ministered in the Holy Place of the temple to announce that the Messiah was coming soon. Zacharias's son had been born, just as the angel had promised. And everyone had been told that this special son was going to

This chapter is based on Luke 2:1-20.

announce the coming Messiah and prepare people to meet Him. Yet the priests and people of Jerusalem were not preparing to welcome their Savior.

The angels couldn't believe it! How could these people—the ones God had chosen to tell the world about Him—not even care about the arrival of Jesus? God had spared the Jewish nation so they could witness that Jesus would indeed be born from the family of Abraham and King David. It was almost time for Jesus' birth but God's people didn't know.

God used Caesar Augustus's decree to bring Mary to Bethlehem at just the right time.

At the temple, the priests sacrificed a lamb every morning and evening. These services pointed to the day when Jesus, the Lamb of God, would come to save His people. Yet none of the priests in the temple were preparing to meet Him.

Not even the priests and teachers knew that the most amazing event of history was about to take place. They said prayers they didn't mean; they went through the motions of worship only to impress others. Since they cared only about riches and honor, they weren't ready for the coming of Jesus, the Messiah, the Promised One.

Across the whole land, people seemed to care only about getting more of what they wanted. None of the joy of heaven reached them. Only a few people waited and hoped that the Messiah would come soon. To those people, God sent angels with a message.

Some of the angels traveled with Joseph and Mary from their home in Nazareth to Bethlehem. The Roman emperor was forcing everyone to make a trip to their home city, to the place where their ancestors had lived. That way the Romans could count every family and charge them taxes.

God had a plan. He used Caesar Augustus's decree to bring Mary to Bethlehem at just the right time. Because Mary was a descendant of King David, she had to travel to David's city, Bethlehem, to be counted. Many years before, the prophet Micah had foretold that the Messiah would be born in Bethlehem. And now, thanks to the Romans, He was going to be.

In the city of their royal ancestor, Joseph and Mary were lost in the crowds. No one noticed them or cared about them. Tired and homeless, they wandered down the long narrow street from one end of the city to the other searching for a place to rest that night. There was no room for them at the crowded inn. Finally, in a shelter full of animals, they found a spot to rest. And there, the Savior of the world was born.

Humans didn't know it, but the news filled heaven with joy. Angels gathered in the sky over the hills around Bethlehem, waiting for the signal to announce the happy news to the world. If the leaders of God's people had been waiting and watching for the Messiah, they could have joined in announcing Jesus' birth. But they were passed by. Instead, God searched for those who were faithfully waiting and watching.

ONLY THE SHEPHERDS WERE READY

In the same fields where King David as a boy had watched over his sheep, shepherds were keeping watch over their flocks that night. Through the long hours, they talked about the promise that a Savior was coming. They prayed that the Heir to King David's throne would come soon.

Then it happened. "An angel of the Lord appeared to them, and the glory of the Lord shone around them, and they were terrified. But the angel said to them, 'Do not be afraid. I bring you good news of great joy that will be for all the people. Today in the town of David a Savior has been born to you; he is Christ the Lord' " (Luke 2:9-11, NIV).

The shepherds told everyone they met about the angels and the baby.

When they heard these words, the shepherds began to imagine what this would mean. Finally, their country would have its long-awaited king! He would bring power and glory! He would free them from the Romans!

But the angel knew that Jesus was a different kind of king. He helped the shepherds begin to understand by telling them where to find Him. " 'This will be a sign to you: You will find a baby wrapped in cloths and lying in a manger' " (Luke 2:12, NIV).

With great kindness, the angel had quietly explained how to find Jesus. He had given the shepherds time to get used to their glory. But now the angels could not hold back their joy and glory any longer. It flashed out and lit up the hills and plains for miles around. Earth was silent, and heaven leaned down to listen to their song: " 'Glory to God in the highest, and on earth peace to men on whom his favor rests' " (Luke 2:14, NIV). The music and message of their song would carry to the whole earth and linger to the end of time.

Then the angels disappeared, the light faded away, and the shadows of night fell once more on the hills of Bethlehem. But the shepherds couldn't forget what they had seen and heard. No humans had ever seen a more astounding sight.

The shepherds said to each other, "Let's go and see this amazing thing that God has told us about." They hurried to town and found Mary and Joseph, and the Baby in the manger just as the angel had said. When they left, they were too happy to be quiet. They told everyone they met about the angels and the baby and everything they had seen and heard.

Heaven and earth are no farther apart today than they were on that night when shepherds heard the angels' song. In those days, God sometimes sent angels to speak to people as they worked in the fields. He is just as close to us today. As we go about our work, as we live according to His will, angels are with us every step of the way.

The story of that night in Bethlehem will never grow old. How can that kind of love be measured? By coming to this earth to be our Savior, Jesus traded His throne and all the angels in heaven for a manger and a barn full of animals. And this was only a small part of what He gave up.

For the Son of God to become a human like Adam and Eve—perfect, before sin entered the world—would have meant giving up more than we can imagine. But what Jesus did was even more amazing. He became one of us after thousands of years of sin had made humans weak. Like all the children of Adam and Eve, Jesus had to live with the weaknesses He inherited from His ancestors. But He came anyway to share our pain and our problems. He came to give us an example of a life fully dedicated to God, a life without sin.

Even before he was thrown out of heaven, Satan hated Jesus. He hated Jesus all the more because Jesus had promised to save the lost humans of earth. Yet into this world where Satan claims ownership, God allowed His Son to come as a helpless infant to meet life's dangers just like every other human. He allowed His Son to fight the battles that every person must fight, at the risk of failing and losing His eternal life.

Every father worries over his children. Looking into their faces, he can't help but tremble at the dangers of life. There is nothing he would like more than to protect those children from Satan, to keep them safe from harm and temptation. Yet God sent His only Son into this world to meet even greater dangers, to take even greater risks so that our children could be forever safe someday.

Only love could do such a thing, a love beyond the understanding of humans, a love that amazes even the angels of heaven.

CHAPTER 5

THE
DEDICATION

"For unto us a child is born, unto us a son is given"
(Isaiah 9:6, KJV).

bout forty days after Jesus' birth, Joseph and Mary took Him to Jerusalem. As all Jewish families did—it was required by Jewish law—they took their first-born Son to the temple to present Him to the Lord and to offer a sacrifice. Even as a child, Jesus lived by the code of Jewish law.

For a new mother, Jewish law required two sacrifices: a year-old lamb for a burnt offering, and a young pigeon or dove for a sin offering. However, if the parents were poor, it was acceptable to offer two pigeons or two doves.

Each bird or animal used as an offering was to be perfect—not scarred or blemished in any way. These offerings were symbols of the coming Messiah, and in the same way His body was strong and healthy. His physical structure had no defects. All through His life, He lived by nature's laws. Physically as well as spiritually, He was an example of what God had designed all humans to be.

Since the earliest times, with God's promise that the Firstborn of heaven would be given to save sinners, the firstborn son of Hebrew families had been dedicated to God and to serving Him. Because of this, pre-

This chapter is based on Luke 2:21-38.

senting firstborn sons was very meaningful. What an amazing thing it was when the Baby Jesus was presented at the temple! How sad that the priest who conducted the ceremony had no idea what child he held. Day after day, he assisted parents and their newborn sons, paying little attention to either unless the family appeared to be wealthy or important. Clearly, Joseph and Mary were neither. Their humble clothes marked them as Galileans; their offering showed that they were poor.

In the simple temple service, the Son of God was dedicated to the work He had come to do.

The priest went through the motions. He took the baby in his arms and held it up before the altar. Then he handed the baby back to Mary and wrote the name "Jesus" on the list of firstborn sons. Little did he think, as the baby lay in his arms, that he was holding the Majesty of Heaven, the King of glory, the reason behind all the Jewish ceremonies.

This sleeping baby was the Promised One, the Messiah. To Moses, He called Himself "I AM." He was in the pillar of clouds and fire that led the Israelites through the desert. For centuries, prophets had spoken of Him: the Offspring of David, the Morning Star, the Desire of all nations. He was the hope of fallen humanity. In the simple temple service, the Son of God was dedicated to the work He had come to do. The priest didn't see or feel anything special, but God's act in giving His Son to the world was seen. Someone did recognize the Messiah.

SIMEON RECOGNIZES THE MESSIAH

At that moment, a dedicated believer named Simeon entered the temple. He was old, but he had been told by the Holy Spirit that he would not die until he had seen the Messiah. He saw the poor family presenting their firstborn Son and the Holy Spirit spoke to his heart. To the amazement of the priest, he took the baby from Mary's arms and held Him up to God. With a joy beyond any he had ever felt before, he said, " 'Now, Lord, you can let me, your servant, die in peace as you said. With my own eyes I have seen your salvation, which you prepared before all people. It is a light for the non-Jewish people to see and an honor for your people, the Israelites' " (Luke 2:29-32).

Turning to Mary and Joseph, who stood amazed at what he was saying, Simeon blessed them. He said to Mary, " 'God has chosen this child to cause the fall and rise of many in Israel. He will be a sign from God that many people will not accept so that the thoughts of many will be made known. And the things that will happen will make your heart sad, too' " (Luke 2:34, 35).

Just then, another believer named Anna, who was also a prophet, came in. She confirmed Simeon's words. As he spoke, her face lighted up with the glory of God. She also poured out heartfelt thanks that she had been allowed to see the Messiah.

These two humble worshippers had studied the prophecies of the Messiah and had opened their hearts to God. But the priests and rulers in Israel—with the same prophecies to study—did not follow God with all their hearts. Their eyes were closed to the miracle that happened right before them.

And it still happens today. Events that are the center of attention in heaven go unnoticed by Christians on earth. Religious leaders talk about the Jesus of history and ignore His call to help the poor and suffering. The call to do His work in spite of poverty or criticism is as ignored today as it was 2,000 years ago.

As Mary looked at the baby in her arms, she remembered the words of the shepherds of Bethlehem. Those words and the prophecy of Simeon filled her heart with joy and hope. The words of the prophet Isaiah came to her mind:

"For unto us a child is born, unto us a son is given: and the government shall be upon his shoulder: and his name shall be called Wonderful, Counsellor, The mighty God, The everlasting Father, the Prince of Peace" (Isaiah 9:6, KJV).

MARY DIDN'T UNDERSTAND IT ALL

Mary looked forward to the day when her Son would rule as king of Israel. She didn't see the suffering that lay ahead for Him. Simeon's words had foretold His difficult life. Through Simeon's words to Mary, "the things that will happen will make your heart sad, too," God was trying to help prepare the new mother for the sorrow she would bear.

Simeon's prophecy called for the Child to cause the "fall and rise" of many and "a sign ... that many people will not accept." This was a sign that the Jews, like all of us, needed to drive "self" off the throne of their hearts before they could be lifted up by Jesus. Many Jews did let go of their false beliefs about the Messiah. Many more never could and they blinded themselves to the work of their Savior.

As Simeon also said, the arrival of Jesus caused "the thoughts of many [to] be made known." His life revealed the hearts of all, from the Creator to the prince of darkness. Satan had painted God as selfish, demanding all and giving nothing. But the gift of Jesus showed the true heart of God. His hate for sin is as strong as death. His love for sinners is even stronger.

With the treasures of the universe at His fingertips and infinite power at His command, the Father places all in the hands of Jesus. "All this is for humans," He says. "Use these gifts to convince them that there is no greater love than Mine in heaven or earth. They will find the most happiness in returning that love."

PEOPLE WILL JUDGE THEMSELVES

Satan's thoughts would be fully revealed at the Cross. There, love and selfishness would stand face to face. Jesus lived only to bless others. By putting Him to death, Satan showed the depth of his hate. He made it clear that the real purpose of his rebellion was to pull God down from the throne of the universe and to destroy the One through whom God's love was shown.

From the manger to the Cross, Jesus' life was a call to selflessness. It exposed the real purposes of people. Jesus came with the truth of heaven. Those who listened to the voice of the Holy Spirit were drawn to Him. Those who worshipped self, whether they knew it or not, were Satan's followers. By their attitude toward Jesus, all

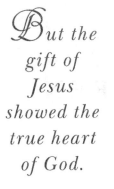

But the gift of Jesus showed the true heart of God.

who met Him showed which side they were on.

All who hear of Him today judge themselves in the same way. In the final judgment, the Cross will be clearly seen and understood by all. All who are lost will understand that they rejected Jesus. When every excuse has been swept away, it will be clear that God is not to blame for evil and that God offered a way to escape it.

When the thoughts of all people are revealed at last, those who chose to follow God and those who rebelled will agree that God's plans and His decisions were fair and just and right.

CHAPTER 6

"WE HAVE SEEN HIS STAR"

*"They came to the house where the child was and saw him
with his mother" (Matthew 2:11).*

ow when Jesus was born in Bethlehem of Judaea
in the days of Herod the king, behold, there came
wise men from the East to Jerusalem, saying, Where
is he that is born King of the Jews? for we have seen
his star in the East, and are come to worship him" (Matthew 2:1, 2, KJV).

These wise men from the East were philosophers and scholars.
They were some of the most wealthy and best educated people of their
land. Some of their fellow "magi" were little more than magicians who
fooled naïve people for their own profit. But these men were honored
for their wisdom, kindness, and integrity.

As these wise men studied to understand the stars of the heavens, they were impressed that a mighty Creator must exist. Wanting to know more, they studied the Hebrew Scriptures. They knew
of the Scriptures because Balaam, once a prophet of God, had
been a magician or wise man in their land. Inspired by the Holy
Spirit, Balaam had foretold the success of Israel and the appearing of the Messiah. His words had been handed down century
after century.

This chapter is based on Matthew 2.

When they read the Old Testament Scriptures, the wise men found more promises of the Messiah. To their joy, they determined that His coming was near and that it would change the world with a new understanding of God.

These men had seen a mysterious light in the heavens on the night that God's glory had flooded the hills around Bethlehem. And as that light faded, a bright star appeared. It was not a star or a planet, but it remained visible in the same spot each night.

This "star" was actually a company of brilliantly shining angels, but the wise men didn't know that. It did seem that the star had a special meaning for them. They spoke to priests and philosophers and searched the oldest scrolls in the land. Balaam's prophecy claimed, " 'A star will come from Jacob; a ruler will rise from Israel' " (Numbers 24:17).

These wise men from the East were philosophers and scholars.

Was the strange star a sign that the Promised One had arrived? These wise men believed the truth when they discovered it. Now God rewarded them. In a dream they were told to go and find the newborn Prince. Because it was their custom to give gifts to newborn royalty, they took with them the most valuable things they owned. The richest treasures of their land were brought as an offering to the One who would bless every family on earth.

TRAVEL BY NIGHT

Following the star meant that the wise men had to travel at night. Through the long dark hours they repeated the prophecies and sayings that they knew. At every rest stop, they searched the Scriptures again and felt even more strongly that God was leading them. The star was a visible sign to follow, but their hearts carried the message just as strongly. The long journey went quickly because of their hope and joy.

Finally they arrived in the land of Israel. As they walked down the Mount of Olives toward Jerusalem, the star stopped above the temple and slowly faded from view. The wise men hurried on, certain that everyone they met would be talking about the Messiah's birth. But when they asked, no one knew what they were talking about. They found their way to the temple, where to their amazement, no one knew anything about a newborn king. Worse still, rather than causing joy, their questions brought them looks of fear and contempt.

Even the priests—the teachers of Scripture and prophecy—had no interest in their questions. These priests looked down on them as heathen—non-Jews who were no better than the Romans or Greeks. But in God's eyes, the wise men stood closer to heaven than the tradition-bound priests.

KING HEROD'S SUSPICIONS

News of the wise men's arrival spread quickly through the city. Their strange search created a stir of excitement that reached all the way to King Herod's palace. The talk of a new king concerned Herod. Being a foreigner in the land of Israel, he knew he was hated by the people he ruled. His only security was the Romans. A new prince born in the kingdom would have a stronger claim to the throne.

Herod suspected that the priests were plotting with the strangers to stir up the people and throw him off the throne by force. He said nothing of his suspicions, though. Instead he called the chief priests and scribes to the palace and questioned them about the prophecies in the Scriptures. He wanted to know what was said about where this Messiah would be born.

The Jewish teachers and leaders were offended at being questioned by their foreign king—especially because of the heathen strangers. But their lack of interest about find-

> *The Jewish priests were not as ignorant about the birth of the Messiah as they pretended to be.*

ing answers to his questions made Herod angry. He thought they were trying to hide something from him. With threats of violence, he forced them to search their prophecies to find answers.

The Messiah will be born " 'in the town of Bethlehem in Judea,' " they reported. " 'The prophet [Micah] wrote about this in the Scriptures: "But you, Bethlehem, in the land of Judah, are important among the tribes of Judah. A ruler will come from you who will be like a shepherd for my people Israel" ' " (Matthew 2:5, 6).

Hearing this, Herod then met privately with the wise men. Inside he was boiling with anger and fear, but his face was calm. Politely he asked when the star had appeared. He acted joyful to hear the news of the Messiah's birth. "Search for this child," he said to his visitors, "and when you find him, come and tell me. Then I can go and worship him also." Herod then sent them on their way to Bethlehem.

The Jewish priests were not as ignorant about the birth of the Messiah as they pretended to be. The story of the angels' visit to the shepherds had been told in Jerusalem, but the rabbis had treated it as unworthy of their attention. They themselves could have gone and found Jesus. They could have been ready to lead the wise men to His birthplace. But instead, it was the wise men who called their attention to the birth of the Messiah.

If people believed the stories of the shepherds and wise men, it would lead them to doubt the role of their leaders. It would prove that the priests and rabbis were not the only source of the truth from God. These proud teachers would not stoop to be instructed by those whom they thought of as heathen. It was not possible, they said, that God would bypass them to speak to ignorant shepherds or heathen Gentiles. The Jewish leaders showed how they felt about the stories that were exciting King Herod and the people of Jerusalem. They would not even bother to go to Bethlehem. Instead, they told all who would listen that only foolish fanatics would be interested in the stories of Jesus' birth.

This was the beginning of their rejection of Jesus. From then on, their stubborn pride grew into jealous hatred. While God was opening a door of light to the rest of the world, the Jewish leaders were closing the door to themselves.

Night was falling as the wise men rode alone out through the gates of Jerusalem. Disappointed by the attitude of the Jews, they left feeling less sure that God was leading them. Unlike the shepherds, angels had not directed them to the Baby King. But now to their great joy, the star appeared again and led the way to Bethlehem.

NO ROYAL GUARD FOR THE KING

In the tiny town, they found no royal guard defending a newborn King. They found no priests, no scholars, no presidents. Only a baby, cradled in a manger, and His simple peasant parents. Could this really be the One of whom the Scriptures spoke? Could this be the One who would raise the nation of Israel and be a light that would shine to the ends of the earth?

> *Beneath the appearance of a small helpless baby, they recognized the presence of God.*

"They came to the house where the child was and saw him with his mother, Mary, and they bowed down and worshiped him" (Matthew 2:11). Beneath the appearance of a small helpless baby, they recognized the presence of God. With remarkable faith, they knelt and gave their hearts to their Savior, then laid their gifts at His feet—gold, frankincense, and myrrh, a precious spice.

With their journey complete, the wise men prepared to return to King Herod in Jerusalem and tell him what they had seen. They didn't know that he intended to harm the baby. In a dream, they were told to avoid King Herod, so they took a different road home.

Joseph had a similar dream warning him to leave Bethlehem and take his family to Egypt. The angel said, " 'Herod is starting to look for the child so he can kill him. Stay in Egypt until I tell you to return' " (Matthew 2:13). Leaving after dark for greater safety, Joseph wasted no time getting his family out of town.

God used the wise men to draw the attention of the Jews to the birth of His Son. Their questions in Jerusalem, the jealousy of

Herod, the actions of the priests—all these things led many to consider the prophecies about the Messiah. It made them think that something great might have happened right before their eyes.

Satan was determined to shut out God's light from the world, to destroy the Savior. But the God who never sleeps was watching over His Son. He gave Mary and the baby Jesus a hiding place in Egypt. The gifts of the wise men paid for the journey and their expenses while they were there.

HEROD ORDERS A MASSACRE

Back in Jerusalem, King Herod waited impatiently for the wise men to return. When they did not, he became suspicious. It seemed to him that the priests and rabbis who had tried to avoid telling him where the Messiah was to be born had figured out his plans and warned the wise men away. The longer he waited, the angrier he became. Finally, he decided that if he couldn't trick them, he could always use force. He could make an example of this baby king and teach the Jews what they could expect if they tried to force him off the throne.

In a jealous rage, Herod sent soldiers to Bethlehem with orders to kill all children two years of age and under. The horror and heartbreak in the city of David was the sad fulfillment of prophecy: " 'A voice was heard in Ramah of painful crying and deep sadness: Rachel crying for her children. She refused to be comforted, because her children are dead' " (Matthew 2:18).

If the Jewish people had been faithful to God, He would have protected them. But they had separated themselves from Him and rejected their only shield from evil—the Holy Spirit. They had not studied the Scripture in order to learn more of God and His will for them. They had studied only for prophecies that could be understood to predict glory for Israel and that seemed to indicate how God despised all other nations. They proudly boasted that the Messiah would come as a conquering king who would destroy his heathen enemies.

Of course, this caused their rulers—like Herod—to hate them and their promised Messiah. In this way, they created the feelings that led to the slaughter in Bethlehem. Satan tried to use the Jews' pride to destroy Jesus. But instead of injuring Him, their twisted words came back to hurt them and their children.

Herod's act of cruelty in Bethlehem was one of his last. Soon after his slaughter of the innocent children, he was forced to face his own horrible death. At that time an angel spoke to Joseph who was still hiding his family in Egypt. It was time to go home. Joseph wanted to make their home in Bethlehem, the city of David, since Jesus was the Heir to the throne of David. But Herod's territory had been divided by his sons when he died and Archelaus was the ruler in Judea, where Bethlehem was located. Joseph was afraid that Archelaus would try to do as his father had.

Once again, Joseph was led to a safe place. He took the family back to Nazareth, his former home. There, young Jesus lived and grew up, fulfilling the prophecy that He would be called a "Nazarene." Galilee, the region where Nazareth was located, had a much larger mix of foreign people than the region of Judea. Because of this, there was less interest in things that concerned only Jews. The claims about Jesus were not likely to concern those in power there.

There seemed to be no place of safety for the infant Savior when He came to earth. God could not trust His beloved Son with humans even while He was carrying out His plan to save them. He sent angels to be with Jesus to protect Him until He accomplished His mission on earth—until He was killed by the ones He came to save.

CHAPTER 7

AS A CHILD

"Jesus became wiser and grew physically. People liked him, and he pleased God" (Luke 2:52).

esus didn't grow up in a wealthy home or attend an elite school. His childhood was spent in the little mountain village of Nazareth. In the sunlight of His Father's smile, Jesus grew taller, stronger, and wiser. He was a child that people liked and His actions and attitude pleased God. Like every other child, His mind and body developed gradually as the years went by.

As a child, Jesus had a kind personality, patience that never ran out, and honesty that never wavered. Although firm about right and wrong, He was always unselfish and polite.

Mary watched carefully as Jesus grew and developed. She saw the perfection in His character, His attitude, and behavior. It was a joy to encourage His learning and thinking. Through the Holy Spirit, she was given wisdom to cooperate with heaven in her boy's development, her boy who could claim only God as His Father.

In the days of Jesus, the teaching of religion to children was very formal. Tradition had become more important than Scripture. The Jewish teachers emphasized the ceremony—the actions of be-

This chapter is based on Luke 2:39, 40.

ing "holy"—and did not teach the basics of serving God or of understanding His law.

The students were given no quiet time to spend with God or to hear His voice speaking to their hearts. In their search for knowledge, they were turned away from the Source of wisdom. Under the training of the rabbis—the Jewish teachers—the minds of the young became cramped and narrow.

As a child, Jesus was not taught in the synagogue schools. His mother was His first teacher. He learned of God and of heaven from her words and from the words of Scripture; including the very words that He had spoken to Moses for Israel. Even as a teenager, Jesus did not turn to the rabbis for His education. He did not need their instruction, for God was His Teacher.

STUDYING SCRIPTURE AND NATURE

Jesus learned the same way we do. His deep understanding of the Scripture shows how much time He spent studying God's Word. He also spent long hours in the library of God's creation. How amazing that the One who wrote lessons in the earth, sea, and sky, was now gathering scientific facts from nature!

From His earliest years, Jesus had one purpose: He lived to bless others. His studies of nature helped Him in doing this. New ideas flashed into His mind as He studied plants and animals. In life around Him, He was constantly searching for illustrations that would make it easier to share the truth about God. The parables He used later in His ministry show how open He was to nature and how its study can open a person to spiritual truths.

Jesus began to understand the importance of the word and works of God. Angels were with Him always, and He was continually in prayer and meditation. From the time of His earliest thoughts, He grew in grace and in His understanding of truth. Every child can learn the way Jesus did. When we try to learn more about our heavenly Father through the Bible, angels come near, our minds are strengthened, and our character is lifted up. We become more like our Savior.

When the grandeur and beauty in nature strikes a person, his or her soul is refreshed and inspired. When we come in contact with the work of His hands, our hearts go out to God. Spending time with God in prayer strengthens us mentally and morally.

From His earliest days, Jesus' life was in harmony with God. When He was a child, He thought and spoke like a child. But no trace of sin scarred the image of God in Him. Not that He escaped temptation—the people of Nazareth were well known for their wicked ways. It was often said, "Can anything good come out of Nazareth?"

Jesus was in a place where His character was tested. He had to be on guard constantly against sin. Having faced the same kinds of conflicts we all face, He is an example to children, young people, and adults.

From His earliest years, Jesus had one purpose: He lived to bless others.

Satan never slowed in his effort to overwhelm the child Jesus. Even though Jesus was guarded by angels from the day of His birth, His life was one long struggle against the powers of darkness. The devil tried everything to trap Jesus.

Jesus' parents were poor. They worked hard every day to make a living. Jesus' simple life helped keep Him safe. In His busy day there were no idle moments that might lead to temptation. No empty hours opened the way to corrupting friendships. As far as possible, He kept the door to temptation closed. Nothing—not pleasure, not the applause or jeers of others—could influence Him to do a wrong act. He was wise enough to recognize evil and strong enough to resist it.

Jesus—the only sinless Person who ever lived on earth—lived for thirty years with the wicked people of Nazareth. No person has an excuse to sin because of where or how he or she lives.

HARD WORK IS A BLESSING

The One who had been the Commander of angels in heaven now served faithfully and cheerfully in a peasant's home. With His own hands, He worked in Joseph's carpenter shop as a loving, obedient son. Like any other worker, He wore simple clothes as He walked to and from the carpenter shop. He never used His divine power to make His day easier or His workload lighter.

The mind and body of Jesus were strengthened as He worked. He was not physically reckless, but kept in good condition and in good health so that He could do His best. Even at skills such as handling tools, He wanted to make no mistakes. He was just as perfect as a worker as He was in character. By His example, He taught that it is our duty to be good workers in whatever we do, even as children. Hard work is honorable and should be done faithfully and well. God created work to be a blessing. True joy in life only comes to those who work faithfully at whatever they do. God lovingly approves of children and youth who cheerfully help their parents in the home. Children like that will go on to become valuable members of society.

During His life on earth, Jesus did not avoid work or responsibility even though many who claim to be His followers do. Many with great talent are weak or useless when difficulties come because they have not had the discipline of hard work. The same energy, positive attitude, and strength of character that Jesus had are to be developed in us. We, too, can face life with the same grace and cheerfulness that He did.

Jesus lived His whole life among the poor. He shared their cares and their hardships. No one who truly understands His teachings and His life can believe that there are different classes of people, that the rich are more valuable than the poor.

JESUS THE SINGER

The joy in Jesus' heart often came out in songs. When His weary neighbors heard His voice praising God, their own hearts were lightened. His songs seemed to fill a place with fragrance like incense, and to drive away evil.

Through all those years in Nazareth, Jesus' life flowed out in sympathy and tenderness. The elderly, the sad, those with heavy burdens, playing children, little creatures in the trees, the donkeys and oxen at work; all of them were happier when He was around.

The One who set the planets in place would stop to help a wounded bird.

As Jesus grew both taller and wiser, He was loved by God and was better liked by the people around Him. The atmosphere of hope and courage that surrounded Him made Him welcome in every home. Often, in the synagogue on the Sabbath, He was asked to read the lesson from the prophets. When He did, the hearts of all who heard were moved by new thoughts from the familiar words.

The joy in Jesus' heart often came out in songs.

But Jesus avoided the spotlight of attention and popularity. Not once in all His years in Nazareth did He perform a miracle. His quiet and simple life—shown by how little the Bible tells us of His early years—teaches us an important lesson. The more quiet and simple a child's life is— the more free from artificial excitement, the more in tune with nature—the more favorable it is to physical, mental, and spiritual strength.

Jesus is our Example. Many who study with interest His years of public ministry pass over the teaching of His early years. But it is in His home life that He is the example for all children and young adults.

The Savior lowered Himself to poverty so that He could teach how closely we who have little status or influence can walk with God. He lived to honor, and glorify His Father in the common things of life. He was doing God's work just as much when laboring in the carpenter shop as when working miracles for the crowds. And all young adults who follow Jesus' example of faithfulness and obedience in His simple home can know that God sees them also and delights in their service.

CHAPTER 8

THE
PASSOVER VISIT

"Didn't you know that I must be in my Father's house?"
(Luke 2:49).

y Jewish custom, at age twelve a child becomes an adult. At the end of his twelfth year, a Hebrew boy was expected to attend the sacred feasts and holy day services. So in the year of His twelfth birthday, Jesus joined His parents in their yearly trip to Jerusalem to celebrate the Passover feast.

All men of Israel were expected to attend three yearly feasts in Jerusalem—Passover, Pentecost, and the Feast of Tabernacles. Many Jews traveled in from other countries for the feasts, especially for Passover. From all areas of Palestine, large crowds headed to Jerusalem. The journey from Nazareth in Galilee took several days. Large groups traveled together for safety and the chance to socialize. Women and old men rode oxen or donkeys over the steep, rocky roads. The stronger men and young adults like Jesus walked.

Passover comes in spring—late March or early April—and that year the land was painted bright with flowers and filled with the songs of birds. All along the road to Jerusalem, the travelers passed spots rich with Israel's history. At these places, parents retold stories to their chil-

This chapter is based on Luke 2:41-51.

dren—stories about the miracles God had performed for His people in years gone by.

The observance of the Passover began at the very beginning of the Hebrew nation. It happened on their last night as slaves in Egypt.

> *The sacrificed lamb, the unleavened bread, and the first fruits of the harvest were symbols of the Messiah.*

Even though there seemed to be no hope of escaping their Egyptian masters, God told them to get ready to leave. He also warned Pharaoh of one final judgement to come upon the Egyptians.

God also told the Hebrews to gather their families in their houses. He instructed them to kill a lamb and sprinkle a little of its blood on the doorposts of the house. Then they were to roast the lamb and serve it with flat, unleavened bread and bitter herbs.

At midnight, the angel of death passed through the land. All the Hebrews who had followed Moses' directions were safe. But all the firstborn sons of the Egyptians died. Then Pharaoh sent the Hebrews a message: "Get out of Egypt and go serve your God."

So the Hebrews left Egypt as an independent nation. And God commanded them to celebrate a festival of the Passover every year. "This way," God said, "when your children ask, 'What does this service mean?' you will answer, 'This ceremony reminds us of the last night in Egypt when our homes were passed over, but the Egyptians died.'"

The Passover ceremonies were followed by the seven days' feast of unleavened bread. On the second day of the feast, the "first fruits" of the harvest—a sheaf of barley—was offered to God as a sacrifice. All the ceremonies of the feast were symbols of Jesus, the coming Savior. The deliverance from Egypt was a lesson in salvation. The sacrificed lamb, the unleavened bread, and the first fruits of the harvest were symbols of the Messiah.

By the time Jesus came, most people had forgotten the meaning of the services and were just going through the motions. But imagine how much it all meant to the Son of God, to twelve-year-old Jesus!

As Jesus saw the temple for the first time, He saw the white-robed priests performing their sacred services. He saw the bleeding lamb on the altar. With the other worshippers, He bowed in prayer while the cloud of incense rose up to God.

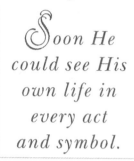

Soon He could see His own life in every act and symbol.

Every day, He witnessed the services and rituals and saw their meaning more clearly. Soon He could see His own life in every act and symbol. As new thoughts raced through His mind, the mystery of His mission became clearer. Jesus needed time to be alone. When the services were over, He stayed in the temple courts. As the worshippers left the temple and the city, Jesus was left behind.

On this trip to Jerusalem, Joseph and Mary wanted Jesus to meet the great teachers at the temple. While He was obedient in every way to God's Word, Jesus was not so careful to follow the rules and teachings of the rabbis. His parents hoped that in Jerusalem, He would learn to respect the rabbis and listen to them.

But Jesus had been taught by God. While at the temple, He began to teach the things He had learned.

At that time, an apartment connected to the temple was being used as a school, a place where leading rabbis met with their students. Finding a seat at the feet of the rabbis, Jesus listened to their teachings. Soon He began to ask questions about the prophecies of the coming Messiah and about current events that pointed to the Messiah's appearance.

Jesus appeared to be someone who was searching to know God. His questions were lessons in vital truths, long forgotten. They showed how the teachings of these rabbis had become narrow and shallow. When the rabbis explained how the coming of the Messiah would make Israel a great nation, Jesus asked about the prophecies of Isaiah, which predicted the suffering and death of the Messiah, the Lamb of God.

The teachers began to question Him and were amazed at His answers. With the humility of a child, Jesus repeated words of Scripture, giving them meaning that the teachers had never imagined. If they had accepted the truths He suggested that day, it would have sparked a new interest in spiritual things. The whole nation would have been touched, and when Jesus began His ministry, many would have followed Him at once.

The rabbis knew that Jesus had not been taught in their schools. Yet He understood the prophecies much better than they did. They saw great potential in the thoughtful Galilean boy and wanted to take charge of His education. They believed that a mind as original as His should be under their influence.

Jesus' age and childlike grace reached these teachers. His words touched their hearts as no other person's words had ever done. In their pride, they would never admit that anyone could teach them. They told themselves that they were teaching Him, or at least testing His knowledge of the Scriptures. God reached out to them in the only way they would listen. Without realizing it, their minds were open and the Holy Spirit spoke to their hearts.

For the first time they saw that the Messiah they expected was not the One promised by the prophecies. Their dreams of power and glory for Israel were hard to give up. They couldn't admit that they had misunderstood the Scriptures. So they asked each other, "How can this boy know anything, since we didn't teach him?"

Meanwhile, Joseph and Mary had finally panicked. There had been much confusion when their big caravan left the city. Having lost track of Jesus when they left Jerusalem, they didn't realize that He had stayed behind. Rather, they assumed Jesus was with their group and had spent the day enjoying the journey with His friends.

When the caravan stopped for the night, Jesus did not show up to help them. They began to worry. By the time they had searched the whole group without finding Him, they were almost frantic with fear. Now all they could think of was how Herod had tried to kill Jesus as a baby. How could they have left Him to face that kind of danger alone!

They raced back to the city and kept searching. By the next day, their search had led them to the temple. There as they mingled with the other worshippers, a familiar voice caught their attention. Only one voice could sound so serious and so full of joy—it had to be Jesus.

They found Him with the rabbis. As happy as they were to see Him safe, they could not forget their fear and worry. His mother asked, "Son, why did You do that to us? Your father and I have been worried sick. We searched everywhere for You."

"Why were you searching for Me?" Jesus asked. "Didn't you know I had to be doing My Father's business?" When they seemed confused, He pointed up toward heaven. His face glowed with a wondrous light. His divinity was flashing through His humanity.

His human parents were almost overwhelmed. They had heard some of His discussion with the rabbis and were astonished by His words. Somehow they had lost sight of who He really was and of their honor in raising Him. For an entire day they had lost sight of the One they should not have forgotten for a moment. And being human, when they finally found Him, they blamed Him for being lost.

It was only natural that Jesus' parents saw Him as their own child. In many ways, He was just like any other child. It was easy to forget that He was the Son of God. But after the events of this day, they would not soon forget the sacred responsibility they had been given.

Jesus' answer to His mother showed for the first time that He understood His relationship to God. But for now, nothing changed between Jesus and His earthly parents. He returned home with them and worked for them as He had before. The mystery of His mission stayed hidden in His heart as He waited patiently for the right time to begin His work. For eighteen years after He knew that He was the Son of God, He honored His obligations at home in Nazareth as a son, a brother, a friend, and a citizen.

On the way home to Nazareth that day, Jesus wanted some quiet time to think about His mission. With the Passover service, God called His people away from their everyday work to remind them of their deliverance from Egypt. He wanted them to see that as the blood of the lamb saved them on the Passover night, now the blood of their Messiah would save them from sin. God wanted the services to lead the people to prayerful study and meditation. But in the excitement of travel and socializing with friends, most quickly forgot what they had seen and heard.

It would be good for us to spend an hour every day thinking about the life of Jesus.

JESUS AND HIS MOTHER

On the way home with just His parents, Jesus hoped to help them understand His mission and the suffering it would bring. His mother would be with Him at the cross, and He wanted to help her be strong enough to face it. It would be much easier on her then if she would only see now what the Scriptures said must happen.

One day of neglect cost Joseph and Mary three days of anxious searching. The same thing can happen to us. One day of gossiping, criticizing others, and neglecting prayer will separate us from Jesus. And it may take many days to feel His peace in our hearts again.

We should be careful in our busy lives not to forget Jesus. When we become so caught up in everyday things that we don't even think of Jesus, we separate ourselves from Him and His angels. Angels cannot stay where Jesus isn't wanted or where a person doesn't even notice He is missing. This is why many who claim to be followers of Jesus are discouraged so much of the time.

Many feel blessed and refreshed when they attend church, but the feeling doesn't last and soon they feel more stressed or depressed than before. Sometimes it seems as if God has been hard on them or overlooked them. But it's their own fault. By separating themselves from Jesus—by not remembering to pray and study—they shut themselves off from the Source of peace and joy.

It would be good for us to spend an hour every day thinking about the life of Jesus. We should use our imagination to put ourselves in each story, especially the stories from the last week of His life. The more we think about His great sacrifice for us, the more confidence we'll have in Him, and the more love we will feel. The more we study and think and talk about Jesus, the more like Him we will become.

CHAPTER 9

DAYS OF CONFLICT

"I have taken your words to heart so I would not sin against you"
(Psalm 119:9).

he life of a Jewish child was controlled by the rules of the rabbis. Young Jews were taught strict laws by the synagogue teachers and they were expected to keep each one. But Jesus was different. From the time He was a child, He did what He thought was right and paid little attention to their rules. Because He was always reading the Scriptures, He often explained, "This is what God says."

As He began to understand society around Him, He saw that its demands were in direct conflict with the teachings of God. Most people had lost sight of God's Word and were following traditions that meant nothing. The services that were supposed to help them understand God brought them no help, no peace. They did not know the freedom of truly serving God.

Jesus had come to show what it means to worship God. He wanted no part of mixing human tradition with God's law of selfless love. He did not attack or condemn the synagogue teachers; He just didn't follow them. When He was criticized for His own simple habits, He pointed to God's Word to explain.

In His gentle, caring way, Jesus tried to help every person He met. Because He was so gentle and quiet, the teachers assumed that He would be easily influenced. They pushed Him to accept the traditions and rules handed down from rabbis of ages long past.

Jesus had a simple reply: "Show Me where it says so in the Scriptures." He would listen to anything from God's Word, but He wasn't interested in human inventions. Jesus seemed to know the Scriptures from beginning to end. The rabbis knew that their traditions were not taught by Scripture. They could see that Jesus understood spiritual things better than they did. Even so, they refused to be taught by a child.

"It is our place to explain Scripture, and your place to accept what we say," they claimed. They were annoyed that He would not accept their authority. When they could not change His mind, they complained to Joseph and Mary. Again, Jesus would be in trouble.

At a very young age, Jesus had begun to think for Himself. Nothing, not even His love and respect for His parents, could keep Him from obeying God's Word. But the rabbis made His life miserable. Even as a young adult, He learned to endure quietly and patiently.

Jesus' brothers—the sons of Joseph—agreed with the rabbis that traditions should be followed as if required by God. When Jesus stubbornly obeyed the Scriptures only, it made them very angry. Knowing that Jesus had never been formally educated, they were surprised at how well He answered the rabbis.

JESUS CARED FOR EVERYONE

Jesus offended the Pharisees also. This group of priests and elders were among the leaders of Israel. To them, true religion was too holy for everyday life. Holiness meant being separate from others, and superior to them.

Instead of hiding away to show His holiness, Jesus mingled with people, helping those in need. He showed that real religion is not only for special occasions. In all times and places, He showed that He cared about others. This made the Pharisees look bad. Their devotion to themselves was not true holiness. As time went by, they grew to hate Jesus as they tried to force Him to obey their rules.

Every time Jesus saw someone in need, He did something to help. He had very little money, but He would often place His own meal in the hands of a hungry person. When His brothers spoke harshly to poor, sinful men and women, Jesus took time to find them and encourage them. He spoke to people about God's love as He helped them, and they never forgot His words.

In His gentle, caring way, Jesus tried to help every person He met.

These things greatly annoyed His brothers. Being older than Jesus, they felt that He should obey them. They decided that He thought He was better than they were. In fact, they accused Him of thinking He was wiser and better than their teachers, priests, and rulers. When they threatened and harassed Him, Jesus endured it quietly.

JESUS' FAMILY PROBLEMS

Jesus loved His brothers and always treated them with kindness. But they were jealous of Him and treated Him with contempt. They didn't understand Him. It's no wonder—His life contained great contradictions.

He was the Son of God and a helpless child. He was the Creator and owner of the earth, but financially poor every day of His earthly life. He had a dignity and self-awareness that was completely different from human pride. He did not want praise or greatness—He was happy to serve.

All this left his brothers confused and angry. They could not understand how He could be calm when He faced so many trials. Jesus was misunderstood by His brothers because He was not like them. The brothers had chosen to follow their rabbis instead of God. And the rituals and ceremonies they kept did not have the power to change their lives. They paid attention to the smallest details of ritual and ignored major things like justice and mercy.

Jesus' life was an endless irritation to them. He hated only one thing in this world—sin. Just seeing a wrong act caused Him pain. Because Jesus' life condemned evil, He was opposed wherever He went. People sneered at His unselfishness and called Him a coward for His patience and kindness.

Jesus tasted all of the bitterness of life. Many cruel people pointed at Him and whispered rumors about His birth—that His mother had been pregnant before she married Joseph. If He had responded even with an impatient word or look, He would have failed to be the perfect example He was born to be. He would have failed to follow the plan to save us. If He just agreed that there could be even one excuse to sin, Satan would have won and the world would be lost forever.

Because of this possibility, Satan made life as difficult as possible for Jesus. But every time He was tempted, Jesus had the same answer: "God's Word says . . ."

When His brothers called Him a coward for refusing to join them in doing something wrong, His answer was, "God's Word says, 'The fear of the Lord is wisdom; to stay away from evil is understanding' " (Job 28:28).

Some people just felt better when He was around, but many avoided Him since His life made them look bad. Sometimes, His young friends urged Him to join them in their fun. Usually they liked to have Him around, but they called Him strict and strait-laced. His answer to that: "God's Word says, 'How can a young person live a pure life? By obeying your word. I have taken your words to heart so I would not sin against you' " (Psalm 119:9, 11).

Jesus was happiest spending time alone in the fields or forests talking with God.

Often He was asked, "Why do you want to be so different from us all?"

"God's Word says," He answered, " 'Happy are those who live pure lives, who follow the Lord's teachings. Happy are those who keep his rules, who try to obey him with their whole heart' " (Psalm 119:1, 2).

Jesus didn't fight for His rights. Often His work was made more difficult because He was so willing and didn't complain. He didn't get discouraged or strike back when people hurt Him. He seemed to live in a different place, a place where God was with Him all the time. Again and again He was asked, "Why do you let people treat you like that—even your brothers?"

His answer? "God's Word says, 'My child, do not forget my teaching, but keep my commands in mind. Then you will live a long time, and your life will be successful. Don't ever forget kindness and truth. Wear them like a necklace. Write them on your heart as if on a tablet. Then you will be respected and will please both God and people' " (Proverbs 3:1-4).

JESUS WAS DIFFERENT

From the day Jesus' parents found Him in the temple, His behavior was a mystery to them. He seemed very different. He was happiest spending time alone in the fields or forests talking with God. In the early morning, often He was in a quiet place meditating, reading the Scriptures, or praying.

Jesus always treated His mother with love and respect. Mary believed in her heart that her child was the promised Messiah. But she didn't dare say this to others. All through His life, she suffered when He did. She saw how He was treated and was often caught in the middle trying to defend Him. She believed that the home life and the care of the mother was very important in forming a child's character. She worried about how Jesus' character was being formed in her home. Joseph's sons and daughters knew this and tried to use her worry as a way to control Jesus.

Mary often urged Jesus to follow the rabbis' rules. But even she couldn't persuade Him to give up His time with God in nature or to stop helping people and animals whenever He saw them in need. Mary became very upset when the rabbis expected her aid in controlling Jesus. When He explained His actions by showing her scriptures, peace filled her heart.

At times, her faith in Jesus wavered because His brothers didn't believe He was the Messiah. But the evidence was there. She saw Him sacrificing Himself for others. His presence made their home and their town a better place. He walked every day with people who were rude, thoughtless, and sometimes evil. He dealt with soldiers, Samaritans, and peasants. He helped carry their heavy burdens, spoke words of encouragement, and told them what He had learned about God's love and kindness.

He taught people that they had been given precious talents. His own life showed that every moment has lasting results. Every moment is a treasure to be spent making someone's life better and heaven more real. To Jesus, no human was worthless. He gave hope to the roughest, most unpromising people, assuring them that they could become gentle, obedient children of God. When He met those who had fallen completely under Satan's control with no hope of escape, He offered help with gentle kindness. He encouraged those He found bravely fighting against Satan and evil, promising them that the angels fighting beside them made victory certain. The people He helped learned that they could trust Him completely.

Jesus didn't just heal people's minds and spirits. He often healed their bodies as well. No one could say that He had performed a miracle, but His kind words and gentle attention had a soothing, healing effect. The healing power of love went out from Him to the sick and injured. In this quiet way, He reached out and helped people from the time He was a child.

But as a child, a teenager, and a young adult, Jesus walked alone. Faithful and pure, He carried the weight of knowing that He was the only hope for the human race. He knew that unless people chose to make real changes, they would all be lost. No one else could see or understand this burden. Determined to save men and women at any cost to Himself, Jesus continued on with the mission of His life.

CHAPTER 10

THE VOICE IN
THE WILDERNESS

*"Change your hearts and lives because the kingdom of heaven
is here" (Matthew 3:2).*

hile many seemed to have lost interest in God's
plans, there were faithful believers in Israel who
were waiting and watching for the Messiah.
Among these was an older priest named Zechariah
and his wife, Elizabeth. They lived quiet, holy lives
and their faith shone like a star in the darkness of those days. This
faithful couple was promised a son who would prepare the way for
the Messiah.

Zechariah lived in the hills of Judea but he was in Jerusalem serving in the temple. Twice each year he was required to spend a week at
the temple. This time, he was chosen to burn the incense at the golden
altar in the Holy Place of the temple's sanctuary. As the incense burned,
a cloud of sweet smoke rose up before God. According to the ceremony, the prayers of Israel with the incense.

As Zechariah ministered, he suddenly felt a supernatural presence—an angel stood at the side of the altar. For years Zechariah had
prayed that the Messiah would come—now an angel was here to announce that his prayers were answered. Amazed but terrified,
Zechariah cowered away from the altar.

This chapter is based on Luke 1:5-23, 57-80; 3:1-18; Matt. 3:1-12; Mark 1:1-8.

The angel said to him, " 'Zechariah don't be afraid. God has heard your prayer. Your wife, Elizabeth, will give birth to a son, and you will name him John. He will bring you joy and gladness, and many people will be happy because of his birth. John will be a great man for the Lord' " (Luke 1:13-15).

The angel said that the baby would be filled with the Holy Spirit from the time he was born. Specific instructions were given on how this child should be raised. And he was given a special mission. Speaking with the power of Elijah, he was to prepare people for the coming of the Messiah.

ZECHARIAH DOUBTS

Zechariah asked, "How can I be sure of this? I am an old man, and my wife is old too." Zechariah was having a moment of weakness. He knew the story of Abraham. In his old age, Abraham became a father because he believed when God said it would happen. Zechariah forgot that when God promises something, He makes it happen.

God had given John the most important work ever given to a human.

The birth of Zechariah's son, like the birth of Abraham's son, has a lesson for us all. It teaches a great spiritual truth: by ourselves we are not capable of anything good. But the things we cannot do can be done if we have faith in God's power. By faith, Abraham could believe that a promised child would be born. Through faith, we can believe that we are reborn to obey God's law and follow Jesus' way.

The angel answered Zechariah, " 'I am Gabriel. I stand before God, who sent me to talk to you and to tell you this good news' " (Luke 1:19).

Five hundred years earlier, this same angel had explained the prophecy of the coming Messiah to Daniel. Zechariah had studied those prophecies. He knew that the time was near. He had been praying for that day to come soon. Now the same angel who gave the prophecy returned to announce that the time had come—the Messiah would soon appear.

Outside the temple, a crowd of people waited for the priest's blessing. Zechariah had been inside for so long they began to be afraid. "Maybe God is angry," they whispered, "at the priest or at us. Maybe Zechariah is dead."

When Zechariah stepped out of the Holy Place, his face was glowing with the glory of God. The people thought he had seen a vision. Zechariah opened his mouth to pray and bless them, but no words would come out. Because Zechariah had doubted the angel's words, Gabriel had taken away Zechariah's ability to speak until the baby was born. Eventually, Zechariah made the people understand what he had seen. Silently he finished his days of work at the temple, then went home.

Soon the promised child was born, and Zechariah could speak again. He praised God that the Messiah was coming and that his son John would help prepare the way. His friends and neighbors heard him say these things and repeated the words to others. Soon everyone in the hill country of Judea was wondering, "What kind of person will John be?" This made them think about the coming Messiah, since John was supposed to prepare the way for Him.

"And so the child grew up and became strong in spirit. John lived in the desert until the time when he came out to preach to Israel" (Luke 1:80). God had given John the most important work ever given to a human. He was to share a message that would change people's lives. He was to give them a glimpse of God's holiness, an understanding of what God expects.

To carry this message, he would need to be holy. The Holy Spirit would have to live in his heart. He would need to be strong physically, mentally, and spiritually. He must be so strong, so much in control of himself, including his appetite and passions, that no matter what happened he could stand as firm as the rocks and mountains of the desert he grew up in.

In Israel in those days, most people were focused on getting rich and living in luxury. Their endless search for sensual pleasure, their excessive partying and drinking was making them weak and sick. It was numbing their minds to spiritual things and making sinful things seem more acceptable.

John was to be a reformer. This is why the angel gave his parents such specific instructions. By his simple life and plain clothes, by refusing to drink wine or other alcoholic drinks, he spoke against the lifestyle of the day.

Self-control and self-discipline are important lessons to learn during childhood and the teen years. More than any personality or talents, the habits formed during those early years will determine whether a person will succeed or fail at the battle of life. The seeds sown during childhood and the teen years will determine the harvest a person reaps—both in adult life and for eternity.

John prepared people for Jesus' first appearance. He is an example of those who will work to prepare people for Jesus' second coming. Today's world is filled with errors and lies. Satan's traps for destroying souls are everywhere. All who choose to pursue holiness, obedience, and respect for God must learn self-control. They must be stronger than any addiction or craving. This kind of self-control gives the mental strength and spiritual power to understand and obey God's Word.

Before Jesus could heal people's hearts, they had to realize that they had been wounded by sin.

Normally, Zechariah's son would have been taught and trained to be a priest like his father. But that kind of education would have prevented him from doing his work. Instead, God called John to the desert to learn from nature.

JOHN'S UNUSUAL EDUCATION

John lived in a lonely area among rocky caves and steep canyons. He chose to give up an easy, entertaining life to live in the wilderness. The setting made it easier for him to develop discipline and learn self-denial. Away from the noise of the world, he studied the lessons of nature and of the Scriptures. He learned about God.

John's parents often repeated to him the words of the angel. And John accepted the mission he had been given. He didn't resent his lonely life. To him, the quiet desert was a welcome escape from the hopeless, faithless, evil lives of many in society. He knew better than to trust his own power to resist temptation, so he avoided the sinful life as much as possible. He didn't want to lose his sense of how bad sin was, or how much it hurt people.

John did not spend his life just worshipping by himself. At times, he mingled with people and watched what was happening in society. He watched people and with the help of the Holy Spirit he began to understand how to reach their hearts with the message of heaven. Then he returned to the desert to meditate and pray and prepare himself for his work.

Even in the desert, John was tempted to sin. But as far as possible, he cut off every path Satan used to reach him. He developed a strong character and spiritual insight. As He learned to depend on the Holy Spirit, he was able to resist Satan's power.

Like Moses in the mountains of Midian, John lived in a wilderness that spoke of God's strength and power. The wastelands also spoke of Israel's failure. God's people, the vineyard of the Lord, had become a spiritual desert. The skies above John's desert were still bright and beautiful. As a rainbow above dark, menacing clouds, the promise of a coming Messiah brightened Israel's future.

With quiet excitement, he searched the scrolls of Scripture for information about the Messiah—the Promised One who was to appear while there was still a king on David's throne. Since a Roman ruler sat in the palace, John concluded the Messiah must already be born.

PICTURES OF THE MESSIAH

John studied the pictures of the Messiah in the book of Isaiah: a Branch from Jesse's family tree, a King of righteousness, a great Rock throwing a welcome shadow in a weary land. Isaiah described how Israel would again be a nation God delighted in.

John saw this coming King in Isaiah's words and knew that he was not worthy to announce His arrival. But he would not hesitate to share his message. He was not afraid of humans, because he had seen a glimpse of God. He could stand fearless before earth's kings, because he had bowed before the King of heaven.

Not fully understanding the Messiah's mission, John expected Israel to be freed from the Romans. His greatest hope was that the Messiah would be a righteous king who would lead Israel to be a holy nation.

John saw that his people were deceived, satisfied to live their sinful, unhappy lives. He wanted more for them. The message God had given him to share was designed to shake them up and bring them face to face with their wickedness. Before the seed of the gospel could grow, the soil of the heart would have to be plowed up. Before Jesus could heal people's hearts, they had to realize that they had been wounded by sin.

God doesn't send messages to flatter sinners. He speaks to wake up their consciences, to force them to face their true situation. When angels point to God's judgments, it makes humans realize their need. It leads them to ask, "What can I do to be saved?" And when they ask, the same hand that pointed out their sin can lift them up to a new life.

THE EDGE OF A REVOLUTION

When John began his work, the nation was on the edge of a revolution. Archelaus, the local king, had been removed from office, and Judea was under the direct control of Rome. The cruel Roman governors were determined to fill Judea with Roman ideas and customs. This fueled years of armed resistance from the people that ended in the deaths of thousands of the bravest Jews. More than ever, the nation hated their Roman rulers and longed to be free from their power.

In the middle of all this pain and hatred, a new voice rang out—a voice both startling and stern, but full of hope. John began to share his message: "Change your hearts and lives because the kingdom of heaven is here" (Matthew 3:2).

With a strange power, the voice moved people. Prophets had always spoken of the coming of the Messiah as a distant future event. But this voice announced that it was happening now!

John reminded those who heard him of the ancient prophets—especially of Elijah. With the spirit and power of Elijah, John declared that the nation had fallen into sin. With his simple, convincing words, he denounced the popular sins of the day. The whole country was stirred up. Crowds came from all over to hear him.

John announced that the Promised One was coming. He insisted that people repent. Those who did give up their sins, he baptized in the Jordan River. Their baptism was an object lesson that taught that even the chosen people of God were sinful. Unless sin was washed out of their hearts and lives, they could not join the Messiah's kingdom.

John didn't hesitate to speak to all those who were insincere.

Princes and rabbis, soldiers and peasants came to hear the prophet. At first, the solemn warning from God alarmed them. Many repented and were baptized. Even other Pharisees and religious leaders came confessing their sins and asking for baptism. They had claimed to be better and more holy than ordinary people. Now their guilty secrets came to light.

But the Holy Spirit impressed John that many of these men had no real sense of their sins and no intention of changing their lives. They wanted to be seen as friends of the prophet, hoping that it would impress the coming Messiah. They were certain that being baptized by the popular young preacher would give them more influence with the people.

JOHN POINTS OUT THE HYPOCRITES

John didn't hesitate to speak to all those who were insincere: "You snakes! Who warned you about what is coming? If you've truly repented, it will show in your actions. Don't think that you're safe because you are children of the family of Abraham. God can make children of Abraham out of rocks!"

The Jews had misunderstood God's promises that Israel would always be His chosen people. They assumed that because they were genetic descendants of Abraham, that this promise applied to them. Because God had blessed them in the past, they excused their sins. They considered themselves better than other people, uniquely worthy of God's blessings.

John told those leaders and teachers that their pride and selfishness made them—like snakes—a curse to their people. Because God had given them so much, they were worse than the heathen people to whom they felt superior. They forgot where they came from—God had called Abraham out of a heathen nation and He could call others.

John reminded them that a fruit tree is valued for its fruit, not its name. If it produces no fruit, the fact that it is a fruit tree will not keep it from being cut down and replaced. John made it clear that what a person claims to be means nothing. If the life and character are not in harmony with God, they are not His people.

Many who heard him were convinced by his words. They asked, "What can we do then?"

He told them that by the changes in their lives it would be obvious who was truly following the Messiah. Justice and honesty would be seen. With kindness and compassion, they would defend the weak and help the needy.

John baptized them in water, but promised that the Messiah was coming to baptize them with fire—with the Holy Spirit. That fire was a symbol of how Jesus would burn away the sin in their lives. But if they refused to turn loose from sin, the fire would someday consume them also. This is how the lost are destroyed at the end of time when Jesus returns for His people. The light of God's glory burns up all sin and all people who choose to keep it in their hearts.

In the days of John the Baptist, Jesus was ready to appear and show what God was really like. In Jesus' presence, people would not be able to hide their sinful habits. Only if they were willing to give up their sins could they truly follow Him.

So John announced God's message to Israel. Many listened, believed, and gave up everything they owned to obey him. Large crowds followed him everywhere. Many hoped that he was the Messiah.

But John always pointed them to the Promised One, the One who was coming. Soon.

CHAPTER 11

THE BAPTISM
OF JESUS

" 'This is my Son, whom I love, and I am very pleased with him' "
(Matthew 3:17).

ews of the desert prophet and his amazing announcement spread throughout Galilee—to the peasants in the small hill towns and the fishermen by the sea. It reached Nazareth and was repeated in the carpenter's shop. When Jesus heard John's message, He laid down His tools, said goodbye to His mother, and followed the crowds to the Jordan River.

Although Jesus and John were cousins, they didn't know each other. Jesus grew up in Nazareth, while John lived far away in the desert of Judea. Since they had never met, no one could suggest that they had plotted their claims as prophet and Messiah together.

John knew the story of Jesus' birth. He had been told what happened when Jesus visited the temple as a boy. He knew of Jesus' apparently perfect life, and believed that Jesus was the Promised One. But as the years went by, and Jesus remained quietly in Nazareth, doubts began to arise.

Still John waited in faith, believing that God would help him understand it all in His own time. He had been shown that the Mes-

This chapter is based on Matt. 3:13-17; Mark 1:9-11; Luke 3:21, 22.

siah would come to him to be baptized, and that a divine sign would be given at that time. This would allow John to introduce the Messiah to the people.

When Jesus arrived at the Jordan River and asked to be baptized, John immediately saw that He was different. John had seen many people weighed down by sin, but Jesus was pure—sinless, with a perfect character. The very air around Him seemed holy.

This was just what John had been shown about the coming Messiah. But he felt he could not do what Jesus asked. How could he, a sinner, baptize the Sinless One? And why would a sinless person need this symbol of repentance? "Why did You come to me to be baptized?" John asked. "I need to be baptized by You."

With gentle authority, Jesus answered, "It needs to be this way. This is the right way to follow God's plan."

SINLESS, BUT BAPTIZED AS AN EXAMPLE

So John led the Savior into the Jordan River and dipped Him under the water. When Jesus came up out of the water, He saw the heavens open and the Spirit of God coming down like a dove.

Jesus was not baptized because He needed to repent or confess. He did it to put Himself on the side of sinners—on our side— taking the same steps that we must take. On this day, and all the days of His life, He lived as an Example to us.

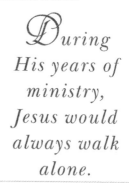

During His years of ministry, Jesus would always walk alone.

Stepping out of the water, Jesus knelt at the riverbank and prayed. Finally, it was time. Time to begin His public work. Time to begin the fight of His life. Like a drawn sword, His appearance would create conflict and friction on every side. His kingdom would be just the opposite of what the Jews were looking for. Even though He had spoken the Ten Commandments on Mt. Sinai, He would soon be condemned as a lawbreaker. Even though He came to break the power of Satan, He would be called a demon.

His mother and brothers did not understand His mission. Even His disciples didn't understand Him. No one on earth had ever really understood Him. Jesus had always been with His Father, but during His years of ministry He would always walk alone.

Being one with us, He shared the burden of our guilt and shame. Every sin, every action of anger or lust was torture to His pure spirit. He laid aside His divinity—together with His power and glory—and accepted the weakness of humanity. But in spite of the pain it caused Him, He didn't waver. The salvation of the human race was on His shoulders, and His hand was firmly in the grasp of His Father's.

With eyes that seemed to penetrate to heaven, Jesus poured out His heart in prayer. He knew how sin had hardened the hearts of humans. He knew how difficult it would be for them to understand Him and accept the gift of salvation. He pled with His Father for power to reach their hearts and free them from Satan's chains. Then He asked for proof that God had embraced the human family along with His Son.

The listening angels had never heard such a prayer. They waited eagerly for the opportunity to carry their Commander a message of comfort. But this was not their message to deliver. The Father Himself answered His Son's prayer. A dazzling beam of glory shone from the throne of the universe. The sky opened and a dovelike form of pure light descended on Jesus' head.

Only a few in the crowd at the river besides John saw the heavenly miracle. But a sense of a divine presence settled on the people, and they stood silently watching Jesus. The light of heaven surrounded Him and His face glowed like no man they had ever seen. A voice from heaven said, " 'This is my Son, whom I love, and I am very pleased with him' " (Matthew 3:17).

REMEMBERED AND ACCEPTED BY GOD

These words were spoken to inspire faith in the people and to strengthen Jesus for His mission. It didn't matter that He now stood with sinful humans. The voice from heaven declared that He was still the Son of God.

John was deeply moved to see Jesus pleading as He prayed. When the glory of heaven surrounded Jesus and the Voice spoke, John recognized the sign he had been promised. He knew that he had baptized the Savior of the world. With the Holy Spirit filling his heart and mind, he pointed to Jesus and cried, "This is the Lamb of God, who will take away the sins of the world."

No one there, not even John, understood the true meaning of the words, "the Lamb of God." Many of the Israelites saw the sacrifices as the heathen nations did—as offerings to appease God. Instead, God wanted to teach them that He would give them the gift—the sacrifice—that would bring them back to Him.

When God said, "This is My Son, whom I love," He included every human being. With all our sins and weaknesses, we are still treasured by our Creator. The light that shone down on Jesus is a promise not only of God's love, but of the power of prayer. We can be sure that our voices are heard in heaven when we pray for help. Sin had cut earth off from heaven, but Jesus connected it again. The light that shone down on Jesus will shine on us when we pray for help to resist temptation. The Voice that spoke to Jesus speaks to each of us, saying, "You are My child, whom I love, and I am very pleased with you."

Our Savior has created a way for the most sinful, the most needy, the most hated humans to come to the Father. All are welcome to go home to the mansions Jesus is preparing in heaven.

CHAPTER 12

TEMPTATION IN THE DESERT

"A person does not live by eating only bread, but by everything God says" (Matthew 4:4).

mmediately after His baptism, Jesus walked out into the desert, led by the Holy Spirit. He went to be alone, to think deeply about His mission. He spent His time in prayer, not even eating as He prepared Himself for the painful road He must travel.

But Satan knew where Jesus had gone. He decided that this would be the best time to approach Him and try to turn Him from His mission. After he successfully tripped Adam and Eve into sinning, Satan claimed this world as His own. He declared to the universe that the human race had chosen him as their ruler. Since he controlled humanity, he was now the prince of the planet.

As the Son of humanity, Jesus came to show that Satan did not control the human family. By staying loyal to God as a human, Jesus showed that Satan's claim was false—all who chose to be free of Satan's power could be free.

Since the beginning, Satan had known that he was not in complete control of the world. Always, there were some who stood against him. With intense interest, Satan watched the sacrifices offered by Adam and his sons. He saw that this was a meaningful symbol of

This chapter is based on Matt. 4:1-11; Mark 1:12, 13; Luke 4:1-13.

their relationship with heaven, and worked to destroy it. He distorted their understanding of God and of the symbols of the coming Savior. Over time, humans began to be afraid of God, and to offer their sacrifices to keep Him from destroying them.

When God's word was written in the Scriptures, Satan studied the prophecies pointing to the coming Messiah. As the centuries passed, he worked to confuse God's people, so that when the Messiah arrived, they would reject Him.

When Jesus was born, Satan knew that his claim to earth was being contested. He knew who Jesus was, and was astounded that the Son of God would come to earth as a human. Humans could only imagine the glory and joy of heaven, but Satan, formerly called Lucifer, the covering cherub, knew it well. His selfish soul could not understand that kind of love. Since he lost heaven, he made it his mission to make others share his fate.

SATAN IS DETERMINED TO TRAP JESUS

From the time Jesus was a baby in Bethlehem, He was constantly under attack. Satan's evil angels dogged Jesus' every step. No human had ever escaped his power, and he was determined that Jesus would fall as well.

Satan witnessed the baptism at the Jordan River. He heard the voice of God the Father. Satan had hoped that God's hatred of evil would separate the earth from Him forever. Until then, the Father had only communicated to humans *through* Jesus. Now He Himself spoke to humanity *in* Jesus. The connection between God and humans had been restored.

> *Satan saw that he must either destroy Jesus or be destroyed.*

Satan saw that he must either destroy Jesus or be destroyed. He would fight this battle personally, and all the weapons of hell would be used.

Some may think that this desert battle between the Savior and Satan means little to us. But the same battle is fought in each of our hearts. The temptations Jesus faced are the same ones we find so hard to resist. With the weight of the world's sins on His shoulders, Jesus faced the same tests that Adam had failed—the same ones that we fail.

JESUS TOOK ALL OF HUMANITY'S WEAKNESSES

Satan pointed to Adam's sin as proof that God's law was not fair and could not be obeyed. As a human, Jesus must keep that law. While Adam faced the test as a perfect human being in the Garden of Eden, Jesus would face it like the humans of His day, weakened physically, mentally, and morally by four thousand years of sin.

Many have claimed that it was impossible for Jesus to fall into sin. If that were true, then He was not facing the same situation Adam had. If we have to face more difficult temptations than Jesus did, then He would not be able to save us. Jesus was born with all of humanity's weaknesses. He could have chosen to rebel against God. He faced the same temptations that we face, with the same opportunity to fail. Actually, His temptations were stronger than any we face.

When Jesus entered the desert, He was communing deeply with His Father. Jesus didn't think of food or rest for days. Then the glorious presence of the Father left Him. Suddenly, the hazards of His mission seemed overwhelming. Weak with hunger, worn from mental agony, Jesus was close to collapse.

Satan saw his opportunity. The words of God still rang in his ears: "This is My Son." Satan plotted to make Jesus doubt those words. If he could get Jesus to lose confidence in His mission, Satan would win. If, in His hunger and depression, Jesus lost faith in His Father, the plan of salvation would be broken.

TEMPTATION TO DOUBT

Suddenly, there in the desert, as if an answer to His prayer, someone who looked like an angel from heaven appeared before Jesus. It seemed that an angel had been sent to save Him.

But only if Jesus could prove that He was truly who He claimed to be. Pointing to the scattered desert rocks, the angel said, "If you are the Son of God, tell these stones to become bread."

If. The angel's words suggested doubt. "Would God really treat His own Son this way? Leave Him in the desert, hungry and alone? Surely God never meant for His Son to suffer this way. So if you really are the Son of God, turn the stones to bread."

Jesus struggled with the temptation to explain His mission or prove His identity. But there was no reason for Him to do that. No miracle, no proof would have changed Satan's heart. Jesus could not—must not—use His divine power for Himself. He had come to earth to face life and temptation as a human, to show us an example of faith and loyalty to God. Not once in His life on earth did He do a miracle for His own benefit.

Jesus, even in His weakness, refused to doubt His Father. He didn't argue or explain. He simply quoted from Scripture: " 'It is written in the Scriptures, "A person does not live by eating only bread, but by everything God says" ' " (Matthew 4:4). End of discussion.

Satan was blocked. He went on to tempt Jesus from another angle. There are lessons here for us to learn.

The strongest temptations struck Jesus when He was weakest. This is the way Satan had succeeded in tempting the strongest, most faithful humans. When they were exhausted, when their will power was at its weakest—this is when he struck. At times like that, when their faith in God seemed far away, even the strongest believers stumbled and fell.

Satan has always taken advantage of the weakness of humans. He still does today. Whenever someone faces hard times—poverty, sickness, pain, or depression—Satan is there to tempt. He attacks our weaknesses, whatever they are. He tries to shake our confidence in a God who would allow such things to happen. We are tempted to distrust God, to question His love for us. If Satan can discourage us and break our hold on God, he wins. If we face him as Jesus did, with no discussion or explanation, with only the promises and commands of the Word of God, we can escape his temptation.

When Jesus said, "A person does not live by eating only bread, but by everything God says," He was repeating words that He had spoken to the Israelites more than 1,400 years earlier. Jesus had provided His people with manna, the miracle food, to show that He would not abandon them if they would only trust and follow Him. Now Jesus practiced the same lesson He had taught. He knew that God had led Him into the desert and that God would provide food when it was needed. To the watching universe, Jesus showed that it was better to suffer with whatever happens than to move from God's plans for us.

Satan is working to destroy the mental and moral powers God gave each of us.

Sometimes a Christian will face a situation where it may seem that a decision to obey God will result in losing a job or an income. Satan will suggest that our beliefs are not worth starving for. If like Jesus, we learn the power of God's Word, we won't need to follow Satan's plan to save our jobs or our lives. Our only questions will be "What does God expect?" "What does He promise?" Then we will follow the first and trust in the second.

In the last days, those who are loyal to God will lose everything: jobs, homes, and possessions. When they refuse to obey their government instead of God, they will not be allowed to buy or sell anything. But those who follow God faithfully have the promise that He will provide for them.

CONTROLLING OUR APPETITES AND DESIRES

The most important lesson we can learn from Jesus' temptation is the importance of controlling our appetites and desires. Temptations that appeal to the physical needs of our bodies have always led humans into the worst and most degrading actions. Satan is working to destroy the mental and moral powers God gave each of us. He wants to make it impossible for us to appreciate things that have eternal value. By appealing to our need for stimulation and excitement, Satan is trying to blot out from our hearts our most precious gift—our likeness to God.

As we approach the end days of earth, the uncontrolled appetites and desires of humans will have led us to a time when people's thoughts are always selfish and evil. It will be as bad as it was in the time before the Flood and in the days of Sodom and Gomorrah. Our only hope of salvation is to place our appetites and desires under the control of God and His plan for our lives.

By our own strength, it is impossible for humans to resist the call of our fallen nature. Satan knows this. Our appetites and desires almost overwhelm us. The weaknesses that all humans have inherited make us easy prey.

Jesus changed that. Anyone who is struggling with appetites and desires should learn from Jesus in the desert. He faced the same temptations, yet not even by a thought did He respond to those temptations. He was able to do this not because He was God but because He had surrendered His life completely to His Father. The Holy Spirit filled Him.

Jesus came to make us like Him. Joining with our fallen nature, He offers us His divine nature so sin is no longer stronger than we are. We can stand and face temptation because Jesus lives within us by faith. We can have perfect characters by holding on by faith to the One sent by God to be our Savior.

Jesus showed us how to deal with temptation. He used the Word of God as a shield and it protected Him. By using the same words with the same faith, we can overcome temptations the same way. God's Word is filled with promises given to shield us from the enemy.

Every promise found in the Bible is ours to depend on. When temptations strike, don't look for excuses because of the situation or because of your weaknesses. Look at God's Word. "I have taken your words to heart so I would not sin against you" (Psalm 119:11).

CHAPTER 13

JESUS GETS THE VICTORY

" 'Go away from me, Satan! It is written in the Scriptures, "You must worship the Lord your God and serve only him" ' " (Matthew 4:10).

hen the devil led Jesus to the holy city of Jerusalem and put him on a high place of the temple. The devil said, 'If you are the Son of God, jump down, because it is written in the Scriptures: "He has put his angels in charge of you. They will catch you in their hands so that you will not hit your foot on a rock" ' " (Matthew 4:5, 6).

This time, Satan—still pretending to be an angel of heaven—started by quoting Scripture. He claimed that he had only been testing Jesus the first time, and complimented Him on His faithfulness. "You've shown your trust in God. Now prove that you trust Him with your life."

But once again, the temptation came marked with doubt. "If you are the Son of God." Jesus was tempted to answer that "if" but He refused to even discuss the possibility of doubting God. He would not risk His life or His mission to try to prove anything to Satan.

Satan tried to take advantage of Jesus' humanness by pushing Him to assume God's protection. But all Satan could do was suggest. He couldn't throw Jesus off the tower—God would certainly step in and save Jesus' life. He couldn't force Jesus to throw Himself off. Unless Jesus agreed to Satan's suggestion, He could not fall.

This chapter is based on Matt. 4:5-11; Mark 1:12, 13; Luke 4:5-13.

The same is true for us. Satan cannot force anyone to do evil. He cannot control a person's mind unless that person gives him control. People must give up their faith in God and surrender their will to Satan before he can use his power over them. Every sinful desire we indulge, every choice we make to follow our own way instead of God's, is an open invitation for Satan to step in to tempt and destroy us. Every time we fall, Satan uses it to blame Jesus.

Notice that when Satan quoted the promise, "He has put his angels in charge of you," he left out the words, "to watch over you wherever you go." These words imply "wherever you go by God's leading."

Jesus refused to go anywhere or do anything outside of God's plan. He trusted His Father perfectly and would not knowingly put Himself in a situation where God had to step in to save His life. He would not fail to give humans an example of trusting and surrendering to God.

Satan cannot force anyone to do evil.

Jesus responded to Satan. " 'It also says in the Scriptures, "Do not test the Lord your God" ' " (Matthew 4:7). This is what Satan was tempting Jesus to do, to test God and force Him to act. God had already spoken and stated that Jesus was His Son. There was no need to demand proof. It would be like asking God for something He has not promised. We shouldn't make requests of God to try to *prove* that He is listening and that He loves us. We should make our requests *because* He is listening and He loves us.

Faith is not the same as assuming that even if we disobey God, He will do for us whatever we want. Faith is claiming God's promises and seeing our lives change with His power. Assuming also claims God's promises, but uses them like Satan did, as excuses to continue doing wrong. True faith would have allowed Adam and Eve to trust God's love and to obey His rules. But they assumed that His love would save them from the results of breaking His law. Faith doesn't claim that we belong in heaven without following God's provided path to get there. Assuming is the counterfeit of faith.

When Satan fails to break our trust in God, he often succeeds in leading us to assume. If he can get us to place ourselves in the path of temptation by assuming that we can handle it, he can trap us every time. God protects those who follow Him obediently, but when we stray from that path, we are sure to stumble and fall.

We shouldn't be discouraged when we are tempted. Sometimes we doubt that the Holy Spirit has been leading us when we find ourselves in a difficult situation. But remember, the Holy Spirit led Jesus into the desert to face Satan's temptations.

When God brings us face-to-face with temptation, He has a reason. He has a purpose, a plan that will make us better, stronger, and more faithful to Him. Jesus didn't search for temptations but He wasn't discouraged when they appeared. Neither should we be.

RICHES AND SELFISHNESS

So Jesus faced the second temptation and won. Finally, Satan stopped trying to hide his identity and faced Jesus as himself. He didn't appear as a devil with horns and bats' wings. He showed his true self—a mighty but fallen angel who claimed to be the leader of a great rebellion and the ruler of earth.

Satan took Jesus to the top of a mountain and showed Him all the kingdoms of the world—the wondrous cities, the stunning palaces, the fertile fields, and fruit-filled orchards and vineyards. The effects of evil were hidden. To Jesus, who had been in the dry, barren desert for so long, the scene was overwhelmingly rich and beautiful.

Then Satan made his offer. "All this I will give you, if you will bow down and worship me."

Consider this offer from Jesus' point of view. His mission to save this world could only lead to suffering. Before Him lay years of sorrow, hardship, and conflict, ending in a painful, shameful death. He would have to carry the sins of the whole world. He would be separated from His Father's love. Now Satan offered to give Him the world without the pain, without the suffering. Jesus could save Himself from His dreadful future by just bowing down and recognizing that Satan was the real ruler of this world—the ruler of all humans, including Jesus.

If Jesus did this, the great controversy would end with Satan's victory. Satan had rebelled in heaven because he wanted to be greater than Jesus. If Jesus bowed to him now, he would have won.

It was only partly true that Satan stood as ruler of this world. He had taken Adam's place when Adam sinned, but Adam had not been the independent ruler of earth. The earth was God's, and Adam served under Jesus' rule. In spite of Satan's power, he could do only what God permitted. So when Satan offered Jesus the kingdoms of the world, he wanted Jesus to give up His true kingship of earth and become subject to Satan.

Jesus could not be bought with the riches of this world, or even with the possibility of escape from suffering. He had come to set up a kingdom of righteousness and love, and He would not give that up.

How sad that the very people Jesus had come to save would gladly have accepted an offer of ruling the world. The Jews were looking for a Messiah who would defeat the Romans and make Israel the strongest nation on earth. They wanted power and glory.

Satan often makes this offer to humans. He says, "If you want to be rich or powerful or famous in this world, you must serve me. Don't get carried away with noble ideas like honesty or self-sacrifice. Ignore your conscience and think of yourself first."

Many people are deceived. They agree to live only for their own pleasure, which serves Satan completely. Satan offers them a world, which isn't his to give, and by accepting his offer, they lose their right to inherit that world as children of God.

Jesus did not even consider Satan's offer. He said, " 'Go away from me, Satan! It is written in the Scriptures, "You must worship the Lord your God and serve only him" ' " (Matthew 4:10). Again, Jesus used the words of Scripture to turn Satan away. But this time, He did more. Satan had asked for proof that Jesus was the Son of God. This time, he got proof.

SATAN IS DISMISSED

When Jesus said, "Go away from me, Satan!" the power of divinity flashed through Jesus' human form. Satan was forced to leave. Angry and humiliated, he turned and fled from the Savior of the world. Long before in Eden, Adam had failed completely. But Jesus was completely victorious.

There are lessons here for us as we resist temptations. We can force Satan to leave us also. Jesus won because He had surrendered His life to God and held on to His faith. In the book of James, Jesus tells us, "Give yourselves completely to God. Stand against the devil, and the devil will run from you. Come near to God, and God will come near to you" (James 4:7, 8).

We can't stand up to Satan ourselves—he is stronger than humans. If we try to stand alone, he will overcome us. But Satan runs in fear from the weakest person who hides behind the name of Jesus.

Angry and humiliated, Satan turned and fled from the Savior of the world.

After Satan fled, Jesus fell to the ground exhausted and nearly dead. The angels of heaven had been watching the battle, watching their beloved Commander as He suffered to make a way for humans to escape. He had survived a test greater than any that humans could endure. Now those angels brought Him food and water along with a message of His Father's love. They assured Him that heaven rang with joy over His victory.

As His strength returned, His amazing heart of love went out again to the humans He had come to save. He set out to complete His mission, refusing to rest until the enemy was finally defeated and the fallen human race was redeemed.

The price of our salvation will never be fully understood until we stand with Jesus before the throne of God in heaven. There, when the overwhelming glory of heaven bursts over our senses, we will remember that Jesus left all this for us. Not only did He leave heaven for us, He took the risk of failing and never returning to His Father's love.

When we finally understand, we will throw our crowns at His feet and sing, " 'The Lamb who was killed is worthy to receive power, wealth, wisdom, and strength, honor, glory, and praise!' " (Revelation 5:12).

CHAPTER 14

"WE HAVE FOUND THE MESSIAH"

"Look, the Lamb of God, who takes away the sins of the world!"
(John 1:29).

t this time, John the Baptist was preaching and baptizing people at Bethabara on the far side of the Jordan River. John's preaching had made such an impact on the people that it drew the attention of the religious leaders. Because there was always the possibility that the Jews would launch a rebellion, the Roman rulers were suspicious of every crowd that gathered. So whatever might arouse the suspicions of the Romans excited the fears of the Jewish rulers.

John had not asked for the approval of the Jewish leaders, the Sanhedrin, before beginning his preaching. In fact, he regularly criticized the rulers and people alike. Yet the people listened to him eagerly. Interest in his work seemed to be constantly increasing. Even though he hadn't asked their approval, the Sanhedrin decided that since he was teaching and preaching in public, he was their responsibility.

When Israel was an independent nation, the Sanhedrin was the supreme court of the land. It had authority to make and enforce laws in religious and civil matters. Now it was subject to the Roman rulers and laws, but it still spoke with strong authority to the Jews. This court

This chapter is based on John 1:19-51.

was made up of members chosen from the nation's priests, leaders, and teachers. The high priest was usually the president of this body.

At this point, they felt forced to investigate John's work. Some remembered the story of what had happened to John's father, Zechariah, at the temple. Zechariah's prophecy pointed to John as the proclaimer of the Messiah.

Centuries had passed since Israel had heard the voice of a prophet and many years since a true revival had begun among the people of the nation. John's demand that sin be confessed seemed new and startling. Many of the leaders would not go and listen to his messages. They feared that they might confess the secret sins of their own lives.

John's preaching was a sign that the Messiah was coming.

John's preaching was a sign that the Messiah was coming. It was well known that the seventy-week prophecy of Daniel that predicted the Messiah was nearly ended. Most expected the Messiah to arrive at any time and were eagerly waiting the glory and power their nation would experience then.

The people were so excited about John's messages that the Sanhedrin would soon be forced to either endorse his words or announce that he was a fraud. Already, their influence over the people was weakening. Soon many would not care what their leaders said or did. Finally, they sent a delegation of priests and rabbis to meet with John and discuss his mission.

When the delegates arrived, they found a great crowd listening to John. With an air of authority designed to impress the people and humble the prophet, these rabbis pressed forward. With a sense of respect, even fear, the people stepped back and let them pass. Eventually these great men, proud of their own positions and power, stood in their rich robes before the prophet of the desert.

"Who are you?" they demanded.

John knew what they were thinking. "I am not the Messiah," he answered.

"Who, then?" they asked. "Elijah?"

"I am not," John stated.

"Are you that prophet, Moses?"

John shook his head. "No."

The rabbis pressed for an answer. "Then who are you? We need an answer to take back to those who sent us. What do you say about yourself?"

John answered with the words of the prophet Isaiah. " 'I am the voice of one calling out in the desert: "Make the road straight for the Lord" ' " (John 1:23).

In ancient times, when the king would visit remote areas of his kingdom, a team would be sent ahead to smooth the road for his chariot. Holes would be filled in and bumps would be smoothed out. In the same way, when the Holy Spirit touches human hearts, it cuts down pride and the love of pleasure and power. It increases humility and self-sacrificing love. John's mission was the same: to prepare the hearts of people for the coming King, so that they would be ready to accept Him.

The rabbis kept asking questions. "Why are you baptizing people then, if you aren't the Messiah, you aren't Elijah, and you aren't the prophet Moses?"

When John began his ministry, some had speculated that he might be Moses brought back to life since he knew so much about the prophecies and the history of Israel. Many also believed that before the Messiah arrived, the prophet Elijah would personally appear. John had already denied being Elijah. But his words had a deeper meaning. Jesus later said that John had come as Elijah for those who were willing to listen to him. John came in the spirit and power of Elijah to work as Elijah did.

MANY PEOPLE FAIL TO SEE JESUS

Many of the people at the river that day had been present when John had baptized Jesus. But most had not seen or heard the miraculous sign from heaven. These people had listened to John for months but had never repented or changed their lives. Their eyes had never turned to God in faith, so they never saw His glory that day. Their ears had never tuned to His voice, so they heard none of the words from heaven.

It happens the same way today. Many times, Jesus and His angels are present when believers worship together. Some feel His presence and are blessed, comforted, and encouraged. But many others never know it. They sense nothing special or unusual.

The rabbis still demanded an answer to their question, "Why are you baptizing?" John stared out into the crowd in silence for a moment. Then his face lit up and his body tensed with emotion. "I baptize with water, but Someone stands among you whom you don't know. He is the One whose shoes I am not worthy to untie."

This was an unmistakable message to take back to the Sanhedrin. There was no doubt who John was talking about—the Messiah was among them! The astounded rabbis glanced around, hoping to see the One John spoke of. But Jesus was lost in the crowd.

While His manner was gentle and unassuming, there was a sense of power hidden inside.

At the baptism, John pointed to Jesus as the Lamb of God. This opened the way for a new understanding of the Messiah's work. John remembered the words of Isaiah: "He is brought like a lamb to be slaughtered." In the following weeks, John studied the prophecies again along with the sacrificial services. He didn't understand the two parts of Jesus' work—both as a sacrifice who would suffer and a king who would rule—but He saw that there was more to the Messiah's coming than the priests or people understood.

John saw Jesus in the crowd after He returned from the desert and watched for Him to give some sign of who He was. Almost impatiently, he waited to hear Jesus announce His mission. But nothing was said. When John announced Jesus to the rabbis, He just mingled with the other believers, saying and doing nothing to attract attention.

But the next day, when John saw Jesus approaching, something happened. The light of God's glory lit up John's face, and he pointed and announced, "Look! This is the Lamb of God who will take away the sins of the world. I tell you, this is the Son of God."

WAS THIS REALLY THE MESSIAH?

With amazement and wonder, the people stared at Jesus. This was the Messiah? The Son of God? They had listened faithfully to John day after day and were deeply touched by his messages. They believed that John had been sent by heaven. Could this Person be greater than John? Nothing about His appearance showed importance. He seemed simple and poor—like themselves.

Some had seen Him at His baptism with the glory of heaven shining in His face. Now that face was so pale and worn that they didn't recognize Him. But as they watched His face, they saw something more. His eyes expressed great love and compassion. He seemed surrounded with a refreshing, spiritual air. While His manner was gentle and unassuming, there was a sense of power hidden inside. Could this be the One for whom the nation had waited?

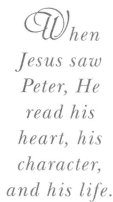

When Jesus saw Peter, He read his heart, his character, and his life.

Jesus came as a poor and humble person so that He could be our example as well as our Savior. If He had appeared as a king, how could He teach humility? How could He preach about serving others with love?

Many in the crowd were confused and disappointed. How could the person John pointed to be the Messiah? They were waiting for a king who would drive out the Romans and reestablish the kingdom of Israel. They could not accept Someone who came only to create a kingdom of righteousness and peace in their hearts.

JOHN'S DISCIPLES FOLLOW JESUS

The next day, two of John's disciples were standing nearby when John saw Jesus in the crowd. Again the prophet's face lit up with divine glory. "Behold the Lamb of God!" he cried.

John's words thrilled his disciples even though they didn't understand what he meant. The two—Andrew and John—left the prophet and went to find Jesus. Drawn by an impulse they could not resist, they followed Him. Although they were anxious to speak to Him, they were overwhelmed into silence by the thought, "Is this the Messiah?"

Jesus knew they were following Him. These two were the first to respond to Him and it brought joy to His heart. But respecting their freedom to choose, He only turned and asked, "What are you looking for?"

Now His presence overwhelmed them. They could only ask, "Teacher, where do you live?" A brief moment by the roadside could not give them the answers they longed for. They needed to be alone with Jesus, to sit at His feet and listen to His words.

Jesus answered, "Come and see." So they went with Him and stayed with Him all day.

If John and Andrew had come to Jesus with the same attitude as the priests and rulers, if they had come to judge His words and worthiness, they would have missed a precious opportunity. But they didn't. They first responded to the Holy Spirit in the preaching of John the Baptist. Now they recognized that spirit in the voice of Jesus. To them, His words were full of freshness, truth, and beauty. They shone a divine light on the teachings of the Old Testament and opened up old truths in new ways.

John the disciple was a man of deep thoughts and deep affections. He had begun to get a of glimpse of what the Messiah was to be—not the power and prestige he had been taught to hope for, but the glory of the Son of God, full of grace and truth.

Andrew could only think of sharing the joy that filled his heart. He left to find his brother, Peter. "We have found the Messiah!" he cried. Peter didn't wait to be told twice. He believed the preaching of John the Baptist and hurried to the Messiah.

When Jesus saw Peter, He read his heart, his character, and his life. He saw Peter's impulsive nature, his loving heart, his ambition and self-confidence. Jesus saw Peter's future—his betrayal and repentance, his lifework and death. Jesus said, "You are called Peter, the son of Jonas, but you will be known as a rock."

The next day, Jesus traveled into Galilee. There He found Philip and said to him, "Follow Me." Philip did, and immediately began to work for Jesus. It was Philip who found Nathaniel.

Nathaniel had been in the crowd when John the Baptist pointed to Jesus as the Lamb of God. Seeing Jesus, Nathaniel was disappointed. How could this poor, humble man be the Messiah? But Nathaniel couldn't reject Jesus, because John's words had touched his heart.

NATHANIEL'S SECRET PRAYERS ARE ANSWERED

When Philip found him, Nathaniel was resting in a quiet grove of trees, meditating on John's announcement and the prophecies of the Messiah. He prayed that if this was indeed the Promised One, God would show him that it was true. Immediately through the Holy Spirit, God assured him that it was true.

Philip looked for his friend in the quiet place under a fig tree where they had often prayed together. "Nathaniel," he said, "we have found Him—the One Moses and the prophets wrote about." It seemed like the answer to Nathaniel's prayer. Philip then expressed a suggestion of doubt. "He is Jesus of Nazareth, the Son of Joseph."

Nathaniel's doubt and prejudice leapt to the surface. "Nazareth? Has any good thing ever come from Nazareth?"

Philip didn't argue. "Come and see for yourself," he said.

When Jesus saw Nathaniel, He said, "Look! An Israelite whose heart holds no deceit."

Surprised, Nathaniel asked, "How do you know me?"

Jesus answered, "Before Philip found you under the fig tree—I saw you."

That was enough for Nathaniel. The Spirit that had spoken to him as he prayed now spoke to him in the words of Jesus. Though torn by doubt and prejudice, Nathaniel had come to Jesus with an honest desire for truth. And he found it. His faith grew stronger than Philip's. "Rabbi," he said, "You are the Son of God. You are the King of Israel."

If Nathaniel had depended only on the rabbis and teachers to guide him, he would never have found Jesus. It was by seeing and judging for himself that he became a disciple. Many today put too much trust in others to guide them. Like Nathaniel, we need to study God's Word for ourselves. We need to pray for the light of the Holy Spirit. The One who saw Nathaniel under the fig tree will see us as we pray. Angels are always with those who are searching for guidance from God.

The calling of these five—John, Andrew, Peter, Philip, and Nathaniel—was the beginning of the Christian church. Two of these were sent to Jesus by John the Baptist. One was called to Jesus by his own brother. When Philip was called, he went immediately to find his friend.

These examples show us how important it is to reach out in a personal way to our families, friends, and neighbors. Many have spent their whole lives claiming to be Christians without ever making a personal effort to bring someone to Jesus.

OUR GREATEST INFLUENCE

Philip did not ask Nathaniel to take his word for it, but to come meet Jesus for himself. We can do the same today by not just telling people about Jesus but showing them what He is like in our own lives. Our greatest influence on people is not in what we say but in what we are. People may challenge our logic, they may decline our invitations, but a life of selfless love is an argument they can't resist.

Our greatest influence on people is not in what we say but in what we are.

The Word of God, shared by someone whose life has been changed by it, has a powerful effect on those who hear it. When someone is struck by the love found in God's Word, he or she will want to share that love. Their testimony will speak with more power and meaning than any other. Sharing always brings a blessing of joy. We share Jesus' joy—the joy of seeing others saved by His sacrifice—when we share His work.

Nathaniel's words of faith, "You are the Messiah," fell like music on Jesus' ears. He said to Nathaniel, "Because I said I saw you under the fig tree, you believe? You will see greater things than this."

With real joy, Jesus looked forward to His work—preaching the good news, healing those who were sick in mind and body, freeing those in slavery to Satan. He said, "Truly I tell you, soon you will see heaven open with angels coming and going through Me."

Jesus wanted them to see that He had opened the world to Heaven. As their faith in Him strengthened, they would see that Heaven's relationship with humans would never be the same.

The angels of God had always moved between heaven and earth carrying prayers to the Father and bringing blessings to His human children. Now, as never before, earth would see evidence of these angels. The miracles Jesus performed were done by God's power through the work of angels. In fact, every blessing we receive comes through Jesus by the ministry of His angels.

By becoming human, Jesus grasped hands with the sons and daughters of Adam. By remaining divine, He holds tightly to the throne of God. Jesus is the connection between God and humanity.

CHAPTER 15

MIRACLE AT THE MARRIAGE FEAST

"Do whatever he tells you to do"
(John 2:5).

esus did not begin His ministry with a miracle before the religious leaders of the Sanhedrin in Jerusalem. Instead, He used His power to add to the joy of a wedding feast in a small Galilean village. By doing this, He showed His interest in people and in their happiness.

When He left the Jordan River, Jesus went to Cana, a small town near Nazareth where relatives of Joseph and Mary were planning a wedding. Jesus and His disciples were invited. At the wedding, Jesus met His mother, whom He had not seen in some time. She had heard about His baptism. The story of the Voice from heaven had spread to Nazareth. It brought back many memories that had long been hidden in Mary's heart.

Like all of the people of Israel, Mary was deeply moved by the words of John the Baptist. She remembered the prophecies given when he was born to her cousin. Now his connection to Jesus reawakened her hopes. From the day the angel appeared in her home, Mary had treasured every sign that her Son was the Messiah. His sweet, unselfish attitude in life reassured her, but she also had doubts and disappointments. She longed for the day when His identity would be revealed.

This chapter is based on John 2:1-11.

Only Joseph shared her experience of the mystery of Jesus' birth. After he died, she had no one with whom she could share her hopes and fears. The two months since Jesus had left home had left her more lonely than ever before. She missed Him very much.

When they met at the marriage celebration, she found Jesus to be the same gentle Son she had raised. But something was different. In His eyes, she saw traces of pain from His battle with Satan and a new look of dignity and power showed on His face.

The young men whose eyes followed Jesus with looks of reverence called Him Master. They told Mary what they saw and heard at the baptism and elsewhere. They believed He was the Messiah. Their words reassured Mary that her long-hidden hopes were not dreams. And she would have been more than human if her joy was not mingled with a mother's fond pride.

There was a sense of excitement as the guests gathered. In small clusters they whispered, gestured, and stared at the source of so many rumors—Jesus. Mary saw them and wished that Jesus would prove to them that He really was the Messiah. She hoped that He would find a reason to work a miracle.

It was the custom in those days for marriage celebrations to last several days. But before this feast ended, the hosts ran out of wine. They were mortified, afraid that the guests would see this as an insult or an attempt to get them to leave.

As a relative, Mary had helped with the arrangements for the feast. She found Jesus and said, "They are out of wine," suggesting that He could supply the drink.

Jesus answered, "Woman, what do I have to do with this? My time has not yet come."

This answer may seem rude to us, but it was a respectful answer in that culture. Jesus addressed His mother in the same tender way from the cross when He left her in the care of His disciple John. Both times, He spoke the words with love.

As He had after His boyhood visit to the temple, Jesus was reminding His mother of His mission. There was a danger that Mary would feel that being Jesus' mother gave her a special claim on His time and on the focus of His mission. Jesus had been her loving and obedient

Son for thirty years, and His love for her hadn't changed. But now He was doing His Father's business. No earthly ties could keep Him from His mission or alter His actions. He had to be free to do the will of God. In the same way, we should not allow earthly attractions or relationships to turn us from the path on which God is leading us.

Mary hoped that He would find a reason to work a miracle.

Like all other sinful humans, Mary's only hope for salvation was through Jesus, the Lamb of God. Her relationship with Him did not give her special advantages or holiness. By saying, "My time has not yet come," Jesus answered Mary's unspoken thoughts. She hoped He would reveal Himself as the Messiah and take the throne of Israel.

But every act of Jesus' life on earth was happening according to a plan that was in place before creation. As He walked among humans, He was guided step-by-step by His Father's will. He never hesitated to act when the time was right. And now—with perfect patience—He waited for the right moment.

MARY'S FAITH IS REWARDED

Although Mary didn't understand Jesus' mission, she trusted Him completely. To honor her trust and to strengthen the faith of His disciples, Jesus performed His first miracle.

The disciples needed the faith these early miracles would bring them. They believed the prophecies pointed to Jesus as the Messiah. They repeated Jesus' wonderful words to everyone and added their own confidence in His mission. But to their amazement and bitter disappointment, the priests and rabbis showed suspicion and prejudice toward Jesus.

Back at the wedding, Mary was not discouraged by Jesus' words. She told those serving the tables, "Do whatever He tells you."

Six large stone water jars stood by the door. Jesus told the servants to fill them with water. As soon as this was done, He said, "Pour it and serve it to the host of the feast."

To this point, neither the host nor the guests were aware that the wine had run out. When he tasted from his newly filled cup, the host found that the taste was better than what he had drunk earlier. In fact, it was better than any wine he had ever tasted.

He turned to the groom and said, "Usually a person puts out the good wine at the beginning of a feast and then when much has been drunk, brings out the inferior wine. But you kept the best for last!"

The things of the world may seem beautiful and fascinating yet in the end, they don't satisfy the heart. The "wine" turns bitter and the happiness fades to a dull ache. What begins as songs and laughter ends up sadness and boredom. The things Jesus gives always bring peace and joy to our hearts. If we follow His way, the rich gifts of today are promises of a richer, more joy-filled tomorrow.

Jesus was guided step-by-step by His Father's will.

The miracle was also a symbol of baptism and Jesus' death. The jars were filled with water by human hands, but Jesus' words gave that action new meaning. The same is true of the religious symbols pointing to Christ's death. Humans can offer the right words and actions, but it is only the power of Jesus that gives them meaning to change lives.

Jesus did not turn the water into an alcoholic beverage. The Scriptures warn against the dangers of allowing wine or "strong drink" to control our actions. Satan tempts humans to the kind of drinking that clouds their minds and numbs their hearts. Jesus invites us to give those urges and addictions to Him to control. It was Jesus who planned for John the Baptist to avoid alcoholic drinks. Through His prophet Habakkuk, He said that the person who encouraged his neighbor to drink would be cursed. The unfermented grape juice Jesus created was a refreshing and wholesome drink.

Before long, the servants were questioned about the excellent new drink and they told about the miracle. The guests were astounded! By the time they began to ask about the Person who had performed the miracle, Jesus had slipped away unnoticed.

So the guests turned to the disciples for answers. For the first time, they had the opportunity to publicly express their faith in Jesus. And when they told what they had seen and heard at the Jordan River, hope grew in the hearts of those who listened.

News of the miracle spread until the priests and rulers in Jerusalem heard it. With new interest, they searched the prophecies that pointed to the Messiah.

The humble attitude of this new Teacher was a real contrast to the Jewish rabbis. Their lives centered around formal tradition and their fear of being "defiled" or touching someone or something that was unholy.

Jesus started His ministry by coming close to people. While He showed great respect for God's law, He rebuked the showy holiness of the Pharisees. He wanted to free the people from the senseless rules that bound them. He wanted to break down the barriers of society to bring all humans together as children of one family. Attending the wedding feast was Jesus' first step toward that goal.

Also, by attending the wedding feast, Jesus honored the holy institution of marriage. Over and over, Scripture uses marriage as an illustration of the relationship God wants with His people. To Jesus, the joy of the wedding was a symbol of the joy on the day that He would bring His bride—the saved people of earth—home to His Father.

Jesus was a social person. He visited the homes of rich people and poor people. He spoke with the educated and the ignorant, trying to lift their thoughts beyond everyday life to spiritual and eternal matters. Jesus did not join in sinful or foolish pleasures. Instead, He found real joy in scenes of innocent happiness like the marriage celebration in Cana.

No matter where Jesus met a person, He saw them as someone who must be invited to join His kingdom. He touched people's hearts by mingling with them as someone who actually cared. On the streets, in their homes, on boats, in the synagogues, by the lakeshore or at wedding feasts, Jesus met people and showed interest in their everyday lives. At their work and in their homes, His sympathy with their concerns won their hearts.

When Jesus retreated to the mountain to pray alone, it was only to prepare Himself for His work. Refreshed by time spent with His Father, He would return to heal the sick, teach the ignorant or misinformed, and break the chains of those in slavery to sin and Satan.

Jesus touched people's hearts by mingling with them like someone who actually cared.

As Jesus ministered to people's needs, He taught His disciples to do the same. He took them with Him as He walked through the cities and villages. Sometimes they sat together on a mountainside or by the sea as He explained the mysteries of God's kingdom. He didn't command them to do one thing or another. Instead, He said, "Follow My way." He took them with Him on His journeys so they could see how He taught people.

All who preach God's Word or who live as witnesses to His love should follow Jesus' example. We should not isolate ourselves or avoid nonbelievers. If we wish to reach people, we must meet them where they are—at home, at work, and at social gatherings. Church is not the only place where God's truth is to be shared. If we try to preserve our religion by hiding it behind church walls, we'll lose many social opportunities to help others and influence them for Jesus.

We can show the world that we are not selfishly focused on ourselves, that our religion does not make us unsympathetic or judgmental. If we claim to be following Jesus' way, then we will minister to others as He did.

Too many have the impression that Christians are gloomy, unhappy people. Jesus' followers are not statues—they are living men and women who have felt divine love in their hearts. The light that shines there from Jesus is reflected to others in actions that glow with the love of Heaven.

CHAPTER 16

CORRUPTION IN THE TEMPLE

"Take these things out of here! Don't make my Father's house a place for buying and selling!" (John 2:16).

fter He left Cana, Jesus and His disciples joined His mother and brothers in a large group that was traveling through Capernaum to Jerusalem for Passover. This important Jewish festival drew great crowds every year.

Because He had not publicly announced His mission as the Messiah, Jesus mingled unnoticed with the crowd. As they walked, there were frequent discussions of the promised Messiah. Since John the Baptist had begun announcing the Messiah's arrival there was great hope that their nation would soon be free from its Roman rulers. Jesus knew they were destined to be disappointed. Their hope was based on a misunderstanding of the Scriptures. He explained the prophecies to those who would listen and encouraged a deeper study of God's Word.

During the Passover week, Jews from all over Palestine and from many other lands filled the temple courts to have a part in the rituals and sacrifices. Each one was to bring an animal sacrifice to offer in the ceremony that pointed to the Messiah—the one great Sacrifice.

Many travelers could not bring their offering, so animals were bought and sold in the outer court of the temple. People of all classes gathered there to purchase an offering.

This chapter is based on John 2:12-22.

The animal sellers took advantage of the people by demanding terribly high prices for the animals they sold. Since the worshippers had been taught that they must offer a sacrifice or risk losing the blessing of God on their family and lands, they were trapped. Having traveled so far, they could not return home without offering a sacrifice. So they paid the awful prices and the sellers divided the profits with the temple priests.

The money-changing had also turned criminal. In the outer court, foreign money was exchanged for temple shekels. Each Jew was required to pay a half shekel yearly to support the work of the temple. Shekels were also used for offerings. Because no other coin was accepted by the priests, the people were forced to exchange far more than the temple shekels were worth. Here also, the priests collected a share of the profits.

HOLY GROUND BECOMES A CRUEL MARKETPLACE

A great number of sacrifices were offered during the Passover week and sales in the temple court were large and loud. The noise sounded more like a cattle market than the sacred temple of God. Between the sounds of hard bargaining and angry arguments came the bleating of sheep, the lowing of cattle, the cooing of doves, and the clinking of many coins. The uproar and confusion was so loud that worshippers inside the temple couldn't hear the prayers of the priests.

What a tragically odd thing for the Jewish people, who were so proud of their temple and so careful in performing its ceremonies. All the grounds of the temple should have been considered sacred. But the love of money had blinded them to how far they had fallen from God's intended purpose for the temple service.

The priests and rulers, of course, should have been the ones to stop this abuse of the temple and of the people. They should have been ready to help those who arrived needing an offering, and should not have taken advantage of them. But greed hardened their hearts, and all they could see was the money and the power.

Many who came to this feast were suffering—the blind, the lame, the deaf, those too poor to give offerings or even to buy food. They came begging for help, believing that their sins could not be forgiven without an animal to offer as a sacrifice. The priests had no sympathy for them. They were ignored or turned away.

The noise sounded more like a cattle market than the sacred temple of God.

As Jesus stood on the steps of the temple court, He saw the unfair bargaining and the heartbreak of the poor. He saw that holy ground had become a cruel marketplace. Something had to be done. The worshippers had come to offer sacrifices without understanding what these sacrifices represented. The whole service was pointing to the One who stood among them—and they didn't even recognize Him. Jesus could see that the priests had no connection to God. His work to create a completely different kind of worship would begin here.

As He stood and stared, His eyes flashed with power, with authority, with righteous anger. One by one, people turned toward Him. The crushing sounds of the bustling marketplace faded until the silence was painful. The corrupt merchants froze, their eyes locked on His face. Some tried to hide, as if those piercing eyes were reading their guilt from their faces.

A sense of awe overwhelmed the crowd. It was as if they were standing in the judgment room of God Himself. And in a sense, they were. As they stared at Jesus, divinity flashed through His human form. He seemed to loom above them with commanding dignity and His whole body shone with a divine light.

He spoke and His clear, ringing voice echoed through the arches of the temple. It was the same voice that spoke the Ten Commandments on Mt. Sinai—the commandments these merchants were breaking. Slowly descending the steps into the courtyard, Jesus raised a whip made of cords in one hand and pointed with the other. "Take these things out. Do not make my Father's house a marketplace."

Then with an intensity He had never shown before, Jesus began knocking over the tables of the moneychangers. The coins clattered across the marble floor, but no one stooped to pick them up. No one even attempted to defy His authority. He didn't strike anyone with the whip, but to the guilty it seemed as frightening as a sword of fire. The merchants and traders raced from the courtyard along with their cattle and sheep. Priests and temple officers ran with them, thinking only about escaping from His presence.

Panic swept over the crowd as they felt the power of His divinity. Hundreds of voices cried out in terror. Even the disciples trembled with awe at Jesus' words and actions. Before long, the sellers and their merchandise were far from the temple and a solemn silence fell over the courtyard. The presence of the Lord now made His temple holy.

By cleansing the temple of its unholy traffic, Jesus announced His mission as the Messiah. That temple, built to be the home of God among humans, was designed to be a living lesson for Israel and for the world. It was God's plan that every created being—from angels to humans—would be a temple where God would always reside. Because of sin, the human heart was no longer a temple for God. But in Jesus, God could again live among the humans He loves. By His saving grace, their hearts could again become His temple.

Even the disciples trembled with awe at Jesus' words and actions.

God planned for the temple in Jerusalem to show what was available to every human. But the Jews didn't open their hearts to the Holy Spirit. The noisy courtyard of the temple with its unholy activities was too real an example of human hearts filled with sensual desires and unholy thoughts.

By cleansing the temple, Jesus also announced His mission to cleanse our hearts from sin, from the selfish desires and evil habits that overwhelm us. We cannot drive the evil out of our own hearts. Only Jesus can cleanse the soul temple. But He will not force His way in. He says, " 'I stand at the door and knock. If you hear my voice and open the door, I will come in.' " (Revelation 3:20) His presence cleanses the heart and makes it a holy temple—a place where God can live.

JUDGED BY GOD

Overwhelmed with terror, the priests and rulers ran from the temple court, from the searching eyes that read their hearts. Jesus saw them as a symbol of the whole Jewish nation that had been scattered because of their faithlessness and wickedness.

And why did they run? Why didn't they stand their ground against this carpenter's Son, this poor Man from Galilee? Why did they leave their stolen money and run from Someone who appeared to be so powerless?

Because Jesus spoke with the authority of a king and they could not resist the power of His voice. When He spoke, they saw clearly that they were really hypocrites and thieves. When divinity flashed through Him, they saw more than just Jesus' anger; they saw how serious His words were. They felt as if God had judged them for eternity. For a time, they were certain that He was a prophet—many of them even thought He was the Messiah. The Holy Spirit worked in their hearts, reminding them of the prophecies that had come to pass. Would they accept Jesus and turn from their selfish lives?

They would not. They knew they were guilty. Now they were also humiliated in the eyes of the people, people who would see Jesus as a hero. Slowly and thoughtfully, with hatred in their hearts, they returned to the temple to challenge Him and His authority.

But the scene in the courtyard had changed. The poor and needy had not run at the sight of Jesus raising a whip. They had not seen anger in His eyes—they saw love and hope. They turned to this Rescuer and cried, "Master, bless me!"

Like a mother bending to help her children, He reached out to those who suffered. Each one was healed—the dumb spoke words of praise, the blind wept at the sight of their Savior's face. Voices again filled the temple with echoing sound. But this time the voices were filled with thankfulness and praise. Young and old, fathers and mothers, friends and onlookers were filled with joy and hope. And they spread that hope as they returned to their homes, telling the story to everyone they met along the way.

Those who were healed here didn't join in the shouts of "Crucify Him" when Jesus was killed. They had felt His power. They knew He was their

Savior. They listened to His apostles and began to spread their stories about His love and the salvation He offers.

The crowd that had run from the temple was now making its way back. When they saw and heard what Jesus had done, they were astounded. Most felt sure that Jesus must be the Messiah.

The priests were responsible for what the temple had become. The people were largely innocent. Years of religious training told them that the priests must know best. What right did Jesus have to interfere with the temple market that the priests allowed? With thoughts like these, they quieted the voice of the Holy Spirit and refused to follow Jesus.

THE BEGINNING OF THE REJECTION

Of course, the priests and rulers should have been the first to see that Jesus was the Messiah. They held the scrolls that told about His mission and His work. They knew that something more than human power had cleared the temple of wrongdoers. But the thought of losing their power over the people and their income from temple selling made the hate in their hearts grow stronger.

They were still afraid that Jesus might be a prophet sent by God. With respect that grew from fear, they asked, "What sign will you show us to prove that you have the right to do these things?"

Jesus had already shown them a sign. Light had flashed into their hearts and they could see and hear the healed people. Both were signs of their promised Messiah. So He answered them with a parable, a riddle that showed that He had read the hatred in their hearts. "Destroy this temple," He said, "and in three days I will build it again."

The priests were offended. "It took forty-six years to build this temple, but you can rebuild it in three days?!" In their minds, this ridiculous claim convinced them that they were right to reject Him as the possible Messiah.

But Jesus' words had more than one meaning. First, He was referring to His own body. These Jewish leaders had already discussed having Him killed because they considered Him a troublemaker. Jesus knew that no one, not even the disciples understood His meaning. He also knew that the priests would remember these words and throw them back in His face at His trial and at the Cross.

But if He tried to explain them now, His disciples would be overwhelmed. They weren't ready to learn that He would suffer and die. And His explanation would prematurely show the Jewish leaders the end of the path they were walking.

Like a mother bending to help her children, He reached out to those who suffered.

Jesus spoke the words for those who would believe in Him. Because it was Passover, they would be repeated to thousands of people and carried to all parts of the world. After He rose from the dead, all those people would understand what He had meant and their faith would grow. To many, these words would prove that He was the Son of God.

His words also referred to the temple and to the services held in it. Those sacrifices and services were symbols of Jesus and His sacrifice to save the world. When Jesus was killed, the meaning and purpose of the temple and its rituals were destroyed. The Jewish leaders did destroy the temple, by having Jesus put to death.

When Jesus died, the inner curtain of the temple was torn from top to bottom, showing that the great final sacrifice had been made and the system of sacrificial offerings was forever ended. But when He rose three days later, Jesus became not only our Savior but also our High Priest in the great temple in heaven.

Now people could focus on the true sacrifice for the sins of the world. Even though the heavenly sanctuary and our High Priest were not visible to human eyes, the disciples never felt separated from Jesus' love and power. When Jesus ministers in the sanctuary above, He still ministers on earth through His Holy Spirit. This fulfills His parting promise: "I will be with you always, even to the end of the world." Jesus is still with His church.

CHAPTER 17

NICODEMUS
AT NIGHT

" 'I tell you the truth, unless one is born again, he cannot be in God's kingdom' " (John 3:3).

icodemus was strangely stirred by the teachings of this humble man from Nazareth. Although he was rich, educated, and honored as a teacher and leader himself, the truths Jesus taught had greatly impressed him and he wanted to learn more.

Most of the priests and rulers hated Jesus after He cleared them from the temple that day. Such a bold move by a nobody from Galilee could not be tolerated. They were determined to put an end to His work, but at the same time, they were afraid of His power.

Not everyone agreed that His work should end. To some, it was very clear that the Spirit of God was working in Jesus and they had no wish to oppose that. Their history was filled with stories of prophets who were sent by God only to be killed by the leaders of Israel. In their minds, it was clear that Israel was under the rule of Rome because the nation had rejected other warnings from God. Would plotting against Jesus be a path to more disaster?

When the Sanhedrin discussed Jesus, Nicodemus suggested caution. If Jesus really was a prophet sent by God, he warned, it would be disastrous to reject Him and His messages. The priests could not

This chapter is based on John 3:1-17.

argue with that, so for a time they did nothing openly against Jesus.

Nicodemus anxiously studied the prophecies of the Messiah. The more he studied, the more he was convinced that Jesus was the Promised One. He was in the temple courtyard the day Jesus cleansed it. He saw the divine power; he saw the sick healed and the poor comforted; he heard their shouts of joy and praise. He could hardly doubt that Jesus was the promised Messiah.

" You don't need more knowledge about truth. You need a new heart. "

Nicodemus wasn't ready to approach Jesus openly. It would be too humiliating for a ruler like himself to be seen with a nearly unknown teacher like Jesus. And if others in the Sanhedrin found out, they would certainly criticize him. So he decided on a secret meeting. After learning that Jesus was spending the night at the Mount of Olives, Nicodemus waited until dark, then went there to find Him.

Face to face with Jesus, Nicodemus felt nervous but he tried to hide it under a mask of confidence and dignity. "Teacher, we know you must have been sent by God, because no one can do the miracles you do unless God is with him."

Nicodemus thought by complimenting Jesus' teaching and His ability to perform miracles, he would make Jesus think that he was on His side. Actually, he was showing that he didn't believe. He didn't call Jesus the Messiah, just a teacher from God.

Jesus didn't respond to Nicodemus's words. He looked Nicodemus in the eye and saw into his heart. He saw that Nicodemus was sincerely searching for truth. So He said kindly and quietly, " 'I tell you the truth, unless one is born again, he cannot be in God's kingdom' " (John 3:3).

Nicodemus thought he had come to discuss the idea of truth, but Jesus cut straight to the heart. He told Nicodemus, "You don't need more knowledge about truth. You don't need answers to questions. You need a new heart. You won't understand heavenly things until you have a new life from above. Until you have this new heart, there is no real benefit in discussing My power or My mission."

Nicodemus was shocked. He had heard John the Baptist preach about repenting and being baptized. He agreed that there was too much prejudice and too little interest in spiritual things among his people. He just didn't think it applied to him. He was a strict Pharisee who took pride in his good deeds and his good life. He couldn't imagine that there was something he wasn't holy enough to be a part of.

> *The human heart is naturally evil. And there is no human cure for the problem.*

The idea of being born again was not new to Nicodemus. People from other countries who joined the Jewish faith were often referred to as newborn children. He just couldn't imagine that he—an Israelite—would need that kind of change. His pride as a Pharisee struggled against his honest search for truth.

Surprised and irritated that Jesus would speak to him that way, Nicodemus responded to what he thought was a ridiculous statement with a ridiculous question. "But if a person is already old, how can he be born again?"

Jesus didn't argue with him. He raised his hand and said quietly, " 'I tell you the truth, unless one is born from water and the Spirit, he cannot enter God's kingdom' " (John 3:5).

Nicodemus knew that Jesus was talking about being baptized in water and being touched by the Holy Spirit. Now he was convinced that this was the One whom John the Baptist had spoken about and pointed to.

BEING BORN AGAIN

Jesus went on. " 'Human life comes from human parents, but spiritual life comes from the Spirit' " (John 3:6).

The human heart is naturally evil, and there is no human cure for the problem. Anyone who tries to qualify for heaven by keeping the law is trying the impossible. A Christian life is not a change or improvement from the old life—it is a complete change of heart. The old life dies and a new life is given by the Holy Spirit.

With Nicodemus still confused, Jesus used another example. " 'The wind blows where it wants to and you hear the sound of it, but you don't know where the wind comes from or where it is going. It is the same with every person who is born from the Spirit' " (John 3:8).

You can hear the wind rustling the leaves of the trees, but you can't see it. It's the same with the work of the Holy Spirit on a person's heart. One may not be able to tell the exact time or place when the heart was changed. But through the Holy Spirit, Jesus is working with each of us each moment of each day, whispering an invitation to come closer to His kingdom. Impressions are made as we read the Scriptures for ourselves or hear the word explained by a preacher. There may be an unforgettable moment when our heart is flooded with love for Him and we surrender to Jesus, but it is the result of the long, patient work of the Holy Spirit.

The effects of the wind can be seen and felt. In the same way, when the Holy Spirit has touched a life, sinful thoughts and actions are left behind. Love, humility, and peace replace anger, jealousy, and fighting. When a person surrenders to God, a new being is created in His image. We experience here just the beginning of salvation—the results will be seen in eternity.

NICODEMUS SEES THE LIGHT

The truth was beginning to penetrate to Nicodemus's mind. The Holy Spirit was working on his heart. But he did not yet understand. "How can this happen?" he asked.

"Jesus said, 'You are an important teacher in Israel, and you don't understand these things?' " (John 3:10). Nicodemus might have been offended, but the look of love on Jesus' face kept him listening. As Jesus explained that His mission was to create a spiritual kingdom, not an earthly one, He could see that Nicodemus was troubled. He said, " 'I have told you about things here on earth, and you do not believe me. So you will not believe me if I tell you about things of heaven' " (John 3:12).

The priests who ran from the temple that day worked hard to appear holy, but there was no holiness in their hearts. They guarded strictly the letter of the law and completely violated the spirit of it. They needed exactly what Jesus was explaining to Nicodemus—a new heart.

The idea shouldn't have been new to them. Their great king David had prayed, "Create in me a pure heart, God, and make my spirit right again" (Psalm 51:10). And God had offered through their prophet Ezekiel, " 'I will put a new way of thinking inside you. I will take out the stubborn hearts of stone from your bodies, and I will give you obedient hearts of flesh' " (Ezekiel 36:26).

Nicodemus had read these scriptures but only now began to understand them. He saw now that strictly obeying the exact words of the law wouldn't earn anyone a place in heaven. By human standards, his life and behavior were practically perfect. But standing next to Jesus, he felt unclean and unholy.

Nicodemus was drawn to Jesus and the new life He offered, but he still didn't understand. Before he even asked, Jesus answered with an illustration that Nicodemus understood. " 'Just as Moses lifted up the snake in the desert, the Son of Man must also be lifted up. So that everyone who believes can have eternal life in him' " (John 3:14, 15).

Nicodemus knew the story. During the years that the children of Israel wandered in the desert, they faced a time when poisonous snakes swarmed into the camp. Each person who was bitten was sure to die. When they cried to God for help, God told Moses to make a brass snake, put it on a pole and lift it up into the air. Then all were told that anyone who looked at the snake would live.

They knew that the brass snake had no magic or power to save them. It was a symbol of the Promised One, the Messiah. The image, made to look like the snakes that were killing them, healed them. In the same way, Jesus came looking like sinful humans, to save humans. Whether to have their snake bites healed or to have their sins forgiven, they could do nothing but show faith in God's gift. Those who were bitten were not given explanations of how the brass snake would heal them. They could choose to look at it, or die. The temple and its sacrifices played the same role. They had no power in themselves. They pointed people to the Savior.

Nicodemus understood. He began to study Scripture in a different way—not to have more knowledge for more discussions, but to fill his own soul with God's love and His saving power. He began to listen to the Holy Spirit.

Many today need to learn the same lesson that Jesus taught to Nicodemus. By faith we receive God's gift of salvation, but faith is not our savior. It doesn't earn us anything. Faith is the hand we use to take hold of Jesus—the cure for sin. We can't even repent without the help of the Holy Spirit. The desire to be forgiven comes from Jesus as much as the forgiveness itself.

> *The desire to be forgiven comes from Jesus as much as the forgiveness itself.*

How are we saved then? The love of God—shining from the Cross—draws us to Him. If we don't resist it, it leads us to the foot of the Cross to repent for the sins that put Jesus there. Then the Holy Spirit changes us. Our thoughts and desires begin to come under the control of Jesus. Our hearts and minds are recreated to be like His. Then God's law is written in our hearts and minds.

In His talk with Nicodemus, Jesus explained the plan to save humans and His mission to the world. Never again did He explain so clearly the step-by-step work that must be done in the hearts of all who would join His kingdom. Here, at the very beginning of His ministry, He showed the truth to a member of the Sanhedrin, a respected teacher of the people. But the other rulers didn't welcome His new thoughts. Nicodemus kept what he had learned to himself.

Still, Jesus' words were not wasted. Nicodemus watched Him and studied what He taught. He worked to stop plans to destroy Jesus whenever they were discussed in the Sanhedrin. When Jesus was finally sentenced to die and lifted up on the cross, Nicodemus remembered the story of the brass snake and recognized Jesus as the world's Savior.

After Jesus had risen from the dead and returned to heaven, when the disciples were in hiding to escape arrest, Nicodemus stepped up to help. The one who had been so quiet and cautious now spent his entire fortune keeping the young church alive as it began to spread the story of Jesus to the world. He was hated and persecuted by those who had honored him before.

Nicodemus shared this story with John, who wrote it down in his history of the life and teachings of Jesus. The truths Jesus taught that night are still as important as they were when a Jewish ruler heard them from the humble Teacher of Galilee.

CHAPTER 18

JOHN'S EXAMPLE

"He must become greater, and I must become less important"
(John 3:30).

For a time, John the Baptist was the most powerful man in Israel. If he had declared himself the Messiah and led a revolt against Rome, the people and priests would have rushed to join him. Satan held out the temptation of power and glory. But John turned away from it. He took the attention that was focused on him and directed it to the coming Messiah—to Jesus.

As Jesus began His ministry, John saw his popularity begin to fade. The attention and interest of the people began to shift to Jesus. When Jesus traveled from Jerusalem to the area of the Jordan River, crowds flocked to hear Him. Many now came to Jesus to be baptized. While Jesus Himself did no baptizing, He allowed His disciples to baptize.

John's disciples were jealous of Jesus' growing popularity. They argued that Jesus' baptisms were different from John's. They insisted that Jesus' disciples had no right to baptize. They came to John and said, "Teacher, the man who was with you at the Jordan, the one you pointed out of the crowd—he's baptizing and everyone is accepting him instead of you."

This chapter is based on John 3:22-36.

John was human. He could have been jealous. He could have created a serious problem for Jesus' ministry, but he didn't. John had been touched by divine love. He welcomed the change, welcomed the ministry of the Messiah to whom he had pointed people. He told his disciples, "You all heard me say that I was not the Messiah, that I was sent to prepare the people for Him. The bridegroom gets the bride, but the groom's best man shares in the joy. He must become greater, and I must become less important."

Seeing Jesus' success brought John nothing but joy. With his faith in the Messiah, John showed complete selflessness.

John saw himself as the friend who acted as a messenger between an engaged couple. When the wedding was over, the friend's work was done and he was happy for them. Seeing Jesus' success brought John nothing but joy. With his faith in the Messiah, John showed complete selflessness. He was happy to fade away so that everyone's eyes would turn to Jesus.

This is how is should be with all Christians. When we give up on self-importance and surrender all of our thoughts to Jesus, we can be filled with the selfless love that John showed. All who do this are promised the unlimited blessings of the Holy Spirit.

The priests and teachers in Jerusalem heard the same reports that John did. They were already jealous that so many people had left their synagogues to hear John the Baptist in the desert. Now even more people were leaving to hear Jesus. And these leaders didn't have John's attitude about Jesus—they were determined to put an end to this new Teacher's work.

JESUS SHOWS HOW TO AVOID MISUNDERSTANDINGS

Jesus knew the religious leaders would do everything they could to cause conflicts between His disciples and John's. To avoid any misunderstandings or problems, He stopped His work there and returned to Galilee. When a situation threatens to cause problems and divide people, we should follow the example set by Jesus and John.

Since John gave a powerful call to reform and return to God, those who followed him faced the danger of focusing too much on him and his work. It was easy for them to lose sight of the fact that John was only an instrument used to point people to Jesus. John wasn't called to begin the Christian church. He finished his work so that Jesus' mission could begin. But his disciples didn't understand this. When Jesus took over the work, they were jealous.

The same thing can happen today. God calls a person to do a certain work and when it has been carried as far as that person can, He brings in others to carry it further. But jealousy can arise when some feel that the success was because of the worker rather than because of God. This is where we need the spirit of John the Baptist. His example of stepping aside so that God's plan could go forward should be an example and an inspiration to all who follow God today.

CHAPTER 19

THE WOMAN
AT THE WELL

" 'Everyone who drinks this water will be thirsty again, but whoever drinks the water I give will never be thirsty' " (John 4:13, 14).

s they traveled toward Galilee, Jesus and His disciples passed through Samaria. At noon, they reached the beautiful Shechem valley and stopped to rest at Jacob's well. Tired from the long morning's walk, Jesus waited at the well while the disciples went into town to buy food for their meal.

The Jews and the Samaritans were bitter enemies. They avoided dealing with each other as much as possible. By the teachings of the Jewish leaders, a Jew could not borrow anything from a Samaritan or accept anything from one—not even a bit of food or a drink of water. One could buy from them only what was absolutely necessary. No socializing or mingling with them was allowed.

As Jesus waited in the hot sun, His hunger and thirst grew. Even though He was waiting by a well of cool, refreshing water, He had no rope or jar to lower into the deep well to reach it. Like any other human would have to do, He waited, thirsty, for someone with a jar to come and draw out water.

A woman from the Samaritan town walked up. She didn't appear to notice Jesus, but lowered her pitcher into the well and drew out her

This chapter is based on John 4:1-42.

water. As she turned to go, Jesus asked her for a drink. The King of heaven, the One who created the oceans and controls the rivers and streams, was dependent on a stranger's kindness for a drink of water.

Those who try to quench their thirst with what the world offers will be left unsatisfied.

It was not a request she could deny. In that culture, providing a drink to a thirsty traveler was a sacred responsibility. Because of the hate between the Samaritans and the Jews, she couldn't offer Jesus a drink. But He was looking for a way to her heart. By asking for a favor instead of offering one, He started to build trust with her.

The woman saw that Jesus was a Jew. She was so shocked that He would speak to her that she forgot to give Him a drink. She could only ask, "Why would you ask me for a drink, since you're a Jewish man and I am a Samaritan woman?"

Jesus answered, "You're surprised that I would ask for something so small as a drink of water from this well. If you had asked Me, I would have given you a drink of the water of eternal life."

She didn't understand what Jesus meant. She saw Him as just another dusty, thirsty traveler. "Sir, this well is deep and you don't even have a jar to draw water out. How could you have given me any water? Are you a better person than our ancestor Jacob who dug this well?" She didn't realize that the One Jacob had looked for—the Messiah—was right in front of her. How many people today, thirsty for eternal truth, are searching everywhere but in the Bible on their bookshelf?

Jesus didn't argue with her. He didn't even answer her question. He said, " 'Everyone who drinks this water will be thirsty again, but whoever drinks the water I give will never be thirsty' " (John 4:13, 14).

Those who try to quench their thirst with what the world offers will be left unsatisfied. People everywhere are searching for something that meets the needs of their hearts. Only Jesus can do that. The grace He can give is like living water—it purifies, refreshes, and strengthens the soul. Jesus wasn't saying that only one drink of His living water was needed. Anyone who experiences His love will be back for more. He was saying that nothing else—not riches, fame, or pleasure—would attract them the same way. The heart will constantly cry for more of His love. And more is always available. We can drink and drink again.

The woman stared in amazement as Jesus spoke. She knew He wasn't talking about the water in the well beside them. She drank it every day and always had to return for more. "Give me this water, sir," she asked, "so I'll never be thirsty and never have to come to this well again."

HER DARK SECRETS

But Jesus knew she wasn't ready for the gift He offered. First, she needed to understand her need and recognize her Savior. He said, " 'Go get your husband and come back here' " (John 4:16).

She quickly answered, "I have no husband," hoping Jesus would not ask any more questions.

But Jesus went on. " 'You are right to say you have no husband. Really you have had five husbands, and the man you live with now is not your husband. You told the truth' " (John 4:17, 18).

The woman must have stepped back as she trembled. How could this stranger know all the dark secrets of her life? Would he condemn her next? Her mind flashed back to scenes where others had judged her and to the future when God would judge her. She didn't deny the truth. But she did try to change the subject. With real respect, she said, "Sir, you must be a prophet." Then she tried to steer Him into a religious argument. "Our ancestors worshipped here on this mountain. But you Jews say that all people must worship in Jerusalem."

Patiently, Jesus listened. He knew the history of her question. Samaria had once been a part of Israel, but because the people there refused to follow God's way, the country had been overrun by another nation. Over many generations, those Jews mingled with the people of that heathen nation and picked up some of their religion of worshipping idols.

When the Jews rebuilt the temple in Jerusalem in the days of Ezra, the Samaritans wanted to help. But the Jews refused to accept them or their help. This was when the hatred between the two nations began. The Samaritans eventually built their own temple on Mount Gerizim. There they followed the same rituals and sacrifices as those in Jerusalem, although they didn't completely abandon idol worship.

But the Samaritans seemed to be cursed. Their country suffered one disaster after another. An enemy nation invaded and destroyed their temple. Still, the people held on to their traditions and their worship rituals. They refused to believe that the Jewish temple was the house of God or that the Jewish religion was better than theirs.

> *People do not reach heaven by searching for a holy mountain or a sacred temple in which to worship.*

Jesus said, " 'Believe me, woman. The time is coming when neither in Jerusalem nor on this mountain will you actually worship the Father. You Samaritans worship something you don't understand. We understand what we worship, because salvation comes from the Jews' " (John 4:21, 22).

He had shown that He had no hate for the Samaritans. Now Jesus wanted her to give up her hatred of the Jews. She had to recognize that the Jews had the Holy Scriptures that held the truth about God and the promise of a coming Savior. He wanted to raise her thinking past the arguments of where and how worship should be conducted. Jesus said, " 'The time is coming when the true worshipers will worship the Father in spirit and truth, and that time is here already' " (John 4:23).

People do not reach heaven by searching for a holy mountain or a sacred temple in which to worship. To serve God, we must be reborn by the Holy Spirit. True worship means joyfully obeying His laws because the Holy Spirit has changed us. Whenever people reach out to God, the Holy Spirit works to show them God's love.

The woman was impressed with Jesus. No one had ever said such things to her. Remembering the sins of her past had made her aware again of how much was missing from her life. This conversation had made her realize that she had a desperate need for God's love in her life. Even though Jesus knew the dark secrets of her life, she could still feel His friendship, His love for her. His purity condemned her sins, but He did not condemn her. An amazing thought came to her mind. Could this Person be the Promised One, the Messiah? "I know the Messiah is coming," she said. "And when He is here, He will explain everything to us."

And Jesus said, " 'I am he—I, the one talking to you' " (John 4:26).

As she heard the words, the hope in her heart turned to faith. She never doubted Him. The Holy Spirit had been working with her and now she was ready to learn and understand more about Scripture, about God's love, and about the Messiah's mission. Jesus' living water flooded her heart.

The plain, outright claim Jesus made to this woman could not have been said to the arrogant Jews. He had to be much more careful when He spoke to them. Because of her faith, Jesus could tell her much more than the Jews were ready to accept. He knew she would use everything He said to explain to others about the Messiah and His love.

> *All she could think about was telling other people about this remarkable Man and His message.*

FOOD AND WATER FOR JESUS' HEART

When the disciples returned from town with food, they were more than a little surprised to find their Teacher talking to a woman. They could see that He hadn't had a drink, and He didn't stop His conversation to eat. When the woman left, Jesus sat silently, His face glowing with joy. The disciples were afraid to disturb Him, but they knew He was weak and hungry and finally begged Him, "Teacher, eat something!"

Jesus answered, "I have eaten food that you don't know about." When the disciples wondered who brought Him food, He explained, " 'My food is to do what the One who sent me wants me to do and to finish his work' " (John 4:34).

To help someone who was honestly searching for truth, to see the faith in the Samaritan woman's eyes, was enough to make Jesus forget about things like eating and drinking. This is what He lived for. This is why He came to earth. To Him, it brought the same kind of joy that a mother feels the first time her child smiles at her.

The woman was almost overwhelmed with joy and hope. She ran back to the city, leaving her water jar at the well. Jesus knew why she left so quickly. She forgot why she had come to the well and forgot to give Jesus the drink of water He had asked her for. All she could think about was telling other people about this remarkable Man and His message.

She went straight to the leaders of the city. "Come and meet a man who knows everything I've ever done. He must be the Messiah!" It was the look on her face as much as her words, but their hearts were touched. They had to meet the Man who could make such a change in this woman.

Jesus still sat beside the well, looking out over green fields of grain waving in the bright sunshine. Beyond them, He could see the crowd of people coming out from the city. Pointing to the grain, He said to His disciples, "Would you say that there are still four months until harvest time? I say, look closer—these fields are ripe and ready to harvest."

Jesus could see that the words He had spoken were seeds that would quickly bring a harvest of believers. He also knew that most of the seeds He planted in His ministry would be harvested at a later time by His disciples. It would be their privilege to be there when the Holy Spirit overflowed on the Day of Pentecost and thousands were converted in one day.

A HARVEST OF SAMARITANS

Even though the Jews were not ready to accept Jesus, the Samaritans were. Following the woman back to the well, they crowded around Him, listened to Him, and believed. He answered their questions and explained things they had never understood before. It was as if a bright ray of light had burst into their dark world. They begged Jesus to come back to their city, to speak to their friends and families, to teach them more.

Jesus stayed with them for two more days and many more Samaritans believed in Him. In Israel, the Pharisees despised Jesus' simple, humble life. They ignored His miracles and demanded proof that He was the Son of God. But the Samaritans didn't demand any proof. Jesus performed no miracles for them, except in telling the woman at the well her life's secrets. But many of them believed. They told the woman, "Now we believe that He is the Messiah—the Savior of the world—not because of what you told us, but because we heard Him ourselves."

With this visit to Samaria, Jesus began to break down the walls between Jews and Gentiles. Even though He was a Jew, He cared nothing about the Pharisees' customs. He ignored their prejudice and accepted the hospitality of the despised Samaritans. He slept in their homes, ate at their tables, taught in their streets, and treated them with kindness and courtesy. The temple in Jerusalem had a low wall in the courtyard that only Jews could go past. But Jesus—the Creator and Reason for the temple—brought His salvation out to the Gentiles, to the rest of the world.

Jesus' time in Samaria was designed to be a blessing to His disciples. They felt that being loyal to their own country meant being enemies with the Samaritans. They were amazed at Jesus' actions. Because they had to follow His example, they kept their prejudice under control during those two days. But none of this changed their hearts. At least, not yet.

After Jesus returned to heaven, after the Holy Spirit fell on them all, the disciples remembered their days in Samaria and Jesus' kindness and respect for their enemies. When Peter went to preach in Samaria, he went with the same kind of love. When John was called to Ephesus and Smyrna, he remembered those days and their divine Teacher, who knew what was ahead and gave them an example to follow.

When Jesus sat down to rest at Jacob's well, He had come from Judea where His work had not affected many. The priests and teachers rejected Him. Even the people who followed Him didn't really understand who He was. He was weak and tired, but He didn't hesitate when the opportunity came to speak to a woman in need—a stranger, an enemy of Israel, and a sinner with a bad reputation. Those who claim to be Christians sometimes shun the outcasts of society. But no social shame, no race or nationality, no circumstances in life, can keep Jesus' love from any person no matter how sinful. The gospel is for everyone.

Jesus never waited for a crowd to gather.

Jesus never waited for a crowd to gather. Often He began to teach with only a few people around. But one by one, people passing by heard His words and stopped to listen. Before long, a crowd was captivated by the words of God spoken by this Teacher from heaven. Anyone speaking for Jesus can speak as easily to a small group as to a large crowd. Even if only one person hears the message, who knows how far it may reach or how many may be changed by hearing it?

The Samaritan woman was a more effective missionary than the disciples—she brought a whole city to hear Jesus. But every disciple is born into God's kingdom as a missionary. Whoever drinks the living water becomes a fountain for others. The grace of Jesus in a person's heart is like a stream in the desert, refreshing all and saving those who are dying of thirst, eager for the water of life.

CHAPTER 20

THE JEWISH
OFFICER'S SON

" 'You people must see signs and miracles before you will believe
in me' " (John 4:48).

hen the people of Galilee returned home from
the Passover festival, they carried stories of Jesus
and the miracles He performed. The fact that
the rulers in Jerusalem disapproved of His actions made Him more popular in Galilee. Many of
the people there resented the arrogant attitude of the priests and
what they had turned the temple into. They hoped this Man who
had chased the priests from the temple would be the Promised One.
They were delighted to hear the rumors that He was claiming to be
the Messiah.

But the people of Nazareth didn't believe that the young man who
grew up in their town could be the Messiah. Jesus told His disciples
that even a prophet isn't respected in his own hometown. People judge
others by their own standards. The narrow-minded people of Nazareth
could only see Jesus' poor home and His peasant clothing. They
couldn't see His pure heart or His selfless love. So Jesus didn't stop in
Nazareth as He traveled back to Cana, where He had turned the water
into wine at the wedding.

The news of His return spread through the countryside, bringing

This chapter is based on John 4:43-54.

hope to many of the sick and suffering people. In the town of Capernaum, a Jewish officer of the king heard about Jesus. This officer had a son who was sick; in fact, the doctors had given up on the boy and left him to die.

When the father heard about Jesus, he decided to go to Cana and ask Jesus to help his son. Pressing through the jostling crowd, he saw only a plainly dressed man, as dusty from walking the roads as he was himself. With a breaking heart, he almost lost faith that this common-looking person could do anything to help. But since he was there, he went ahead with his plan. Asking for a chance to speak to Jesus, he explained his need. "My son is dying. Please, you must come with me and heal him."

But Jesus already knew about the sick child. Before the officer had even left his home, Jesus had seen the painful situation. He also knew that the father had decided that he would not accept Jesus as the Messiah unless Jesus healed his son.

The narrow-minded people of Nazareth could only see Jesus' poor home and His peasant clothing.

With all the stories of Jesus' miracles being told all around him, this man would believe in Jesus only if a miracle happened for him. Jesus must have shaken His head as He remembered the simple faith of the Samaritans who asked for no miracles. It hurt to think that His own people, who had been given the Holy Scriptures, could fail to hear the voice of God speaking to them through His Son.

Jesus said to the man, " 'You people must see signs and miracles before you will believe in me' " (John 4:48). Jesus wanted to do more than just heal the child. He wanted to bring the family a true understanding of God's love and His plan to save them. He wanted them to be a light in the darkness of Capernaum, a city where Jesus would soon be teaching and healing.

When he heard Jesus' words, the man suddenly saw his lack of faith clearly. In an instant, he saw that he was in the presence of

Someone who could read his thoughts, Someone who had the power to answer any request. With a stab of pain, he realized that his doubt might cost the life of his son. He fell to his knees and begged, "Sir, please come with me! Please don't let my son die!"

Jesus recognized his new faith and his love for his child. He couldn't turn from someone in such great need. He said, " 'Go. Your son will live' " (John 4:50).

The officer left, feeling more peace and joy than he had ever experienced before. Not only did he believe that his son was healed, now he believed that Jesus was the Messiah, the Savior.

At that same moment back in Capernaum, something happened. Those who were watching the sick child saw his fever fade, his eyes light up, and his strength return. Looking healthy and happy, he fell into a deep, restful sleep. The rest of the family were amazed and beside themselves with joy.

Cana was not too far from Capernaum. The officer could have rushed and made it home that same

> *It was the exact moment when Jesus spoke the words, "Your son will live."*

night after he spoke to Jesus. But he didn't hurry. When he left Capernaum to find Jesus, his heart was heavy. The sunshine that day seemed cruelly bright and the songs of the birds seemed to mock his pain. But today, everything was different. As he traveled toward home, all of nature seemed to be praising God with him.

When he was still some distance from home, his servants rushed to meet him. They were anxious to tell him the wonderful news. "Your son is alive and well!" they must have shouted.

But he wasn't surprised to hear it. He asked, "When did my son begin to get well?"

"Yesterday, at the seventh hour," they answered.

It was the exact moment when Jesus spoke the words, "Your son will live."

Suddenly in a great hurry, the father rushed home to his son. As he held the child next to his heart, he thanked God again and again.

Now the officer wanted to know more about Jesus. In the following months, when he heard Jesus teach, he and his whole family became followers of the Messiah. As the story of their miracle was told and retold, the city of Capernaum was prepared to meet Jesus, to listen to His teachings, and to follow Him.

Many times, we turn to Jesus when we want something. But Jesus wants to give us something greater than what we ask for—He wants to share a true friendship, one that doesn't wait for a crisis or a selfish request before we speak with Him.

Like the officer from Capernaum, we need to learn to believe God before He answers our prayers. We can trust His promises. When we ask for God's blessing, we can believe we have it and thank Him for it, knowing that it will come when we need it most.

CHAPTER 21

HEALING ON
THE SABBATH

" 'My Father never stops working, and so I keep working, too' "
(John 5:17).

ear the sheep market in Jerusalem was a pool
called Bethesda. At certain times of the year, the water in this pool moved for no apparent reason. Many
believed that some supernatural force was stirring the
water. They also believed that the first person that
stepped into the pool after the water was stirred would be healed of
any disease.

Hundreds visited the pool hoping to be healed, and when the waters moved, the crowd rushed forward, trampling men, women, and
children alike. Many never got near the water. Many nearly reached it
only to be crushed under the press of the crowd.

Shelters had been built around the pool so that the sick could be
protected from the sun during the day and from the cold during the
night. Some of the sick people slept in these porches, crawling to the
edge of the pool day after day, hoping to be cured.

Jesus was walking alone in Jerusalem, praying and thinking, when
He came to the Bethesda pool. He saw the sick, sad people waiting
and watching for what they thought was their only hope of ever being
well again. He ached to heal every one of them. But it was the Sabbath

This chapter is based on John 5.

day, and healing all those people on the Sabbath would cause trouble.
It would create so much criticism and hatred among the Pharisees
and leaders that His work might be stopped.

Jesus ached to heal every one of them.

Under one of the porches was a man who had
been crippled for thirty-eight years. Since the disease had been caused by his own lifestyle, most
saw his fate as punishment from God. With no
friends or family to help him, the man had spent
long years feeling alone and cursed by God.

At the times when the water was expected to
ripple, some that had pity on him would carry him
to the porch by the pool. But when the waters
moved, there was no one to help him get into the pool. He had seen
the rippling water, but with the crowd around him, others always
pushed to the pool first. Jesus just couldn't walk away from this man.

As the sick man lay on his mat—lifting his head occasionally to
stare at the water—a kind, caring face appeared above him. A voice
said, "Do you want to be well?"

For a moment, hope filled the man's heart. Then reality came crash-
ing back. With a sigh, he answered, "Sir, I have no one to help me to the
pool when the water ripples. Someone else always gets there first."

Jesus didn't ask for a show of faith. He didn't ask the man to believe in Him. He simply said, "Stand up. Pick up your bedding and
walk."

The man didn't ask any questions. He didn't hesitate. He just
moved to stand up and as he did, his muscles responded. With strength
and energy they hadn't felt in years, his arms and legs came to life and
he leaped to his feet.

THE SECRET OF HEALING

Jesus hadn't promised that God would heal him. The man could
have doubted and never been healed. But he believed Jesus' words
and by responding when they were spoken, he was healed.

With the same kind of faith, we can be spiritually healed. Sin may
have cut us off from God and left us with withering hearts. By our own

power, we can do no more to live a holy life than that sick man could move himself to the water. We can see our helplessness. We desperately want to live as we should and we're struggling hard to make it happen. And all the while, our Savior is leaning over us asking, "Do you want to be well?" Don't wait to feel healed—believe God's promise to heal you and go forward. Like the man by the pool, you will be given the strength you need. Whatever sin or evil thing is holding down your heart or your body, Jesus is able to heal you.

The healed man bent to pick up the mat and blanket he slept on. Then he stretched his new muscles with delight and turned to thank the Man who healed him. But Jesus had already disappeared into the crowd.

Not even certain that he would recognize his Healer, the man hurried away, praising God. As he enjoyed each healthy step, he met several Pharisees and told them what had happened. To his surprise, they listened with cold silence. With scowling faces, they interrupted him to ask why he was carrying his bedding on the Sabbath. "Surely you remember that it is wrong to carry such things on God's day."

Overjoyed at being healed, the man had forgotten that it was Sabbath. But he didn't feel guilty—he was obeying Someone whom God had given the power to heal him. He told the Pharisees, "The One who healed me said, 'Pick up your bedding and walk.' So I did."

"Who healed you?" they asked. He couldn't tell them. But they knew. Only one Person had shown the power to perform this kind of miracle. But they wanted proof that it was Jesus so they could condemn Him as someone who broke the Sabbath laws. In their minds, not only was Jesus breaking the Sabbath laws by healing someone, He had made it worse by telling someone to break the Sabbath by carrying his bedding.

MEANINGLESS RULES

The Jews had twisted God's laws badly, especially the law about Sabbath keeping. The Pharisees and teachers added hundreds of rules that spelled out exactly what could and could not be done. They made Sabbath a pain instead of a joy.

A Jew was not allowed to light a fire—even a candle—on the Sabbath. So they depended on non–Jewish people around them for many of the services they needed. Since they thought that only Jews could be saved, there was no harm in the others doing this work—they had no hope anyway. But God didn't give any commandments that can't be kept by all people.

Jesus talked about God as a caring Father instead of a harsh judge.

The healed man later went to the temple to give an offering of thanks. Jesus saw him there and spoke to him again. "See, you are well now. Stay away from that sinful lifestyle so nothing worse happens to you."

The man was excited to see Jesus again. Not understanding their hate for his Healer, he pointed out Jesus to the Pharisees. Then the Pharisees charged Jesus with breaking the Sabbath. Many of them wanted Him dead for ignoring the law.

Jesus was forced to appear before the Sanhedrin. If the Jews had been free to rule their own country, the Sanhedrin could have enforced a death sentence for Sabbath breaking. But the Romans were in power and they didn't allow capital punishment for breaking the Jewish Sabbath. What the Pharisees really wanted was to discredit Jesus in the eyes of the people. In spite of everything they had said and done, He was gaining influence with the crowds and the Pharisees were losing it.

Many who were not interested in the critical lectures of the Pharisees listened to the teachings of Jesus. They could understand the words He used. He talked about God as a caring Father instead of a harsh judge. He showed what God was like by His own actions. By His works and His words, Jesus was breaking the power of the old traditions and man-made commandments. He was showing a true picture of the love of God.

PEOPLE LOVED JESUS' WORDS

And the people were responding to Him. If the priests and teachers had not interfered, Jesus' teaching would have started a revival that would have changed history.

But in order to keep their power, the Jewish priests and leaders worked to discredit Jesus. By forcing Him to appear before the Sanhedrin, they could make people doubt Him. The people still had great respect for their leaders, and if they publicly charged Jesus with breaking their laws, many would turn away from His teachings.

The priests tried to paint Jesus as not only guilty of ignoring the laws of their religion, but also guilty of treason to their country. They suggested that Jesus was trying to undermine the customs of the nation, to create division among the people so that the Romans could step in and completely control the nation.

These plans didn't come first from the Sanhedrin. After Satan failed to trip up Jesus in the desert, he made plans with his fallen angels to blind the minds of the Jews so that they wouldn't recognize Jesus as their Messiah. By leading the Jewish leaders to reject Jesus and make His life and work as painful as possible, Satan hoped to discourage Jesus into giving up His mission.

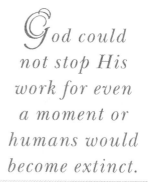

God could not stop His work for even a moment or humans would become extinct.

Jesus came to build up the importance of God's law, not to weaken it. He came to free the Sabbath from all the unnecessary rules that made it a curse instead of a blessing. He could have healed the crippled man on some other day of the week. He could have healed him without telling him to carry away his bedding. But Jesus was looking for a chance to challenge the way His people thought about the Sabbath.

Standing before the Sanhedrin, Jesus told them that helping the sick was very much in harmony with Sabbath laws. He said that it was doing the same work that God does in helping all humans each moment of their lives. Does God stop working on Sabbath? Does the sun stop shining or the grass stop growing? Do the planets stop in their orbits or the oceans' waves stand still? Jesus said, " 'My Father never stops working, and so I keep working, too' " (John 5:17).

God could not stop His work for even a moment or humans would become extinct. We also have a work to do on the Sabbath day. The sick must be cared for and those in need must be helped. God's holy rest day was made for humans. He doesn't want any person to suffer who could be helped on the Sabbath.

The Sabbath law says that work to make a living should stop along with other efforts for worldly pleasure or profit. Just as God rested from creation on the seventh day, we should stop our daily work and save those holy hours for rest, worship, and work to help others.

The Pharisees ignored Jesus' words about the Sabbath and focused on His words about God. They could not argue with the scriptures He quoted—they could only try to turn people against Him. "First he breaks the laws about Sabbath and now he's claiming that God is his Father. He thinks he's equal with God."

Now they were nearly beside themselves with rage. If Jesus had not been so popular with the people, they would have killed Him on the spot.

Jesus of course denied their charges of blasphemy—of falsely claiming to be God. "My right to do the things I do," He told them, "is that I am the Son of God. I am cooperating with Him in His work."

Then the humble Man from Nazareth showed His true identity. There He stood—the One who is worshiped by angels—the Son of God, One with the Master of the universe. No human had ever spoken as He was now doing or held himself with such majesty. His words were unmistakable as He announced His authority in the world:

" 'The Father judges no one, but he has given the Son power to do all the judging so that all people will honor the Son just as much as they honor the Father' " (John 5:22, 23).

The priests thought they were judging Jesus, but the opposite was happening. Because Jesus identifies with humans, understands humans, and because He faced Satan and won, because He would die to offer them salvation, Jesus was qualified to judge all humans. But He didn't come to this world to judge it—He came to save it.

JESUS PROMISES ETERNAL LIFE

" 'I tell you the truth, whoever hears what I say and believes in the One who sent me has eternal life' " (John 5:24). As His final proof to them that He was the Messiah, Jesus promised that God would call the dead to life through Him.

The priests and leaders refused to see it. Jesus had broken their traditions and ignored their authority, so they would not believe in Him. They criticized Jesus for doing exactly what He came to do—His Father's work. They felt no need to depend on a Higher Power, but Jesus had surrendered His will to His Father and depended on Him completely. He didn't make any plans for Himself. Instead He followed the plans His Father unfolded each day.

We should completely depend on our Father in heaven. He gives us work and the ability to do it. As long as we surrender our will to God and trust His strength and wisdom, we'll be guided to do our part in His plan. Depending on our own wisdom and power will separate us from God and place us on the side of Satan.

The Sadducees—the other major religious party in the Sanhedrin—taught that there would be no resurrection after death. But Jesus told them that one of His Father's greatest works was to raise the dead. He said, "The time is coming when the dead will hear the voice of the Son of God and live again." These people would witness the truth of the resurrection and the power of God. That same power can also give new life to those trapped in sin. Faith in that power will keep our souls free and pure.

Jesus didn't apologize for His healing and He didn't explain His reasons to them. He turned their charges around and scolded them for having such closed minds and for being ignorant of the Scriptures they claimed to study. " 'You carefully study the Scriptures because you think they give you eternal life. They do in fact tell about me, but you refuse to come to me to have that life' "(John 5:39, 40).

Every page of the Old Testament—every story, every prophecy, every sermon—pointed to God's plan of salvation, to the coming Messiah. From the promise given in the Garden of Eden, down through the ages, God's words to humanity promised that the Savior was coming. Every sacrifice in the temple showed His death.

THEY PLAN TO KILL JESUS

The Jews' leaders had studied what the prophets said about the kingdom the Messiah would set up. But they only looked for words that supported their hopes of defeating the Romans and having their own kingdom again. When Jesus didn't come as the Messiah they expected, they wanted nothing to do with Him. The more directly He spoke to them, the more they resisted His words.

They criticized Jesus for doing exactly what He came to do—His Father's work.

They would have accepted someone who wanted glory for himself because that person would have flattered them. But Jesus taught selfless love and they would not accept it. The same thing happens today. Many people—even religious leaders—reject God's Word so they can keep their own traditions.

Jesus knew that the priests and rabbis were determined to have Him killed. Still He gave them a clear picture of His relationship with the Father and His mission to the world. It left them in fear of the power of His presence and of His words. Their guilty feelings became an even heavier burden to bear. Instead of causing them to change their attitudes, it made them even more bitter. They knew they had no excuse to oppose Jesus but they hated Him anyway.

Their plan had failed to undermine His authority or His popularity with the people; so they began to plot to kill Him. They sent messengers around the country warning people that Jesus was a fake messiah. Their spies followed wherever He went, reporting everything He said and did.

The Savior of the world was now standing in the shadow of the Cross.

CHAPTER 22

THE DEATH OF
JOHN THE BAPTIST

*"Are you the One who is to come, or should we wait
for someone else?" (Matthew 11:3).*

ohn the Baptist had spent most of his time in the area
east of the Jordan River, an area ruled by King Herod
Antipas. Even Herod had listened to John's preaching and
had felt his call to repent and change his ways.

John hadn't changed his warnings to impress the king. He
spoke out against Herod's relationship with Herodias, the wife of
Herod's brother. For a time, Herod listened to John and tried to break
the chains of lust that tied him to her. But in the end, Herodias trapped
him even more tightly. Her revenge on John was to persuade Herod
to throw him into prison.

From the wide-open spaces of the desert where great crowds hung
on his every word, John became a prisoner trapped in the dungeon of
Herod's palace. As weeks went by in the quiet darkness and small space,
John experienced doubt and depression. His disciples were allowed
to visit and they brought news about Jesus and how the people were
flocking to Him. "If he is the Messiah," they asked, "why hasn't he
done anything to help you?" Satan enjoyed seeing their words bruise
John's heart. Too often, the friends of a good person speak words that
depress and discourage instead of strengthening faith.

This chapter is based on Matt. 11:1-11; 14:1-11; Mark 6:17-28; Luke 7:19-28.

Like Jesus' disciples, John the Baptist did not understand the Messiah's mission. He expected Jesus to drive out the Romans and take the throne. He had preached with the spirit of Elijah—he expected Jesus to show Himself as the God who speaks with fire from heaven.

John waited for Jesus to stand up for the poor and pitiful, to give them honor and power. All Jesus did was heal the sick, teach the crowds, and eat with tax collectors while the Romans dominated Jewish life and Herod and his wicked mistress partied.

COULD IT HAVE BEEN A MISTAKE?

John couldn't understand it. Through the long hours, he was tortured by a most frightening thought—what if Jesus wasn't the Messiah? Was it possible that he had made a mistake? And what did that mean about his own mission? Had he wasted his whole life?

He couldn't shake the thought. After all, if Jesus was the Messiah and if John had done his work well, why hadn't Jesus come to free him from his prison?

John didn't call fire down from heaven or raise the dead to life, but he did the work he was given.

In spite of his doubts, John didn't give up. He remembered the Voice from heaven, the power of the Spirit that had touched him when he announced Jesus, and the promises of the Scriptures. He sent two of his disciples to Jesus with a special mission.

When they found Jesus they asked, "Are you the Messiah or should we look for someone else?" Their question must have been bitterly disappointing to Jesus. If John, His faithful prophet, didn't understand His mission, how would anyone?

Jesus didn't answer them right away. As they stood nearby, waiting for His reply to John, other people were pushing their way forward to Jesus. Blind people groped their way through the crowd. The sick and crippled, often carried by friends, pressed closer, and Jesus healed them. When His voice reached the ears of the dying, they jumped to their feet like children. When His hand touched the blind, they saw the light of day for the first time. People possessed by demons found their sanity again at His command. But that wasn't all. As He healed the people, He taught them. He shared God's love with these poor peasants and workers that the priests and teachers wanted nothing to do with.

JESUS SHOWS THE EVIDENCE

All day long, John's disciples watched Jesus. Finally, He said to them, "Go tell John what you saw and heard here."

They carried the message and John understood. He began to realize that Jesus' kingdom was not about swords and armies, but about changing people's lives and hearts. He also saw that the Jewish leaders would never accept that kind of Messiah. He knew that his own prison sentence was a small taste of how Jesus would someday suffer. Once again, John surrendered himself—in prison or out, in life or death—to God's plan.

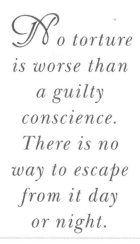

No torture is worse than a guilty conscience. There is no way to escape from it day or night.

Jesus' heart went out to John. After his disciples left, Jesus talked to the crowd about him. He didn't want people to think that God had forsaken him or that John had given up his faith. Jesus compared the rabbis, who criticized John's work, to "reeds shaken by the wind." But John had always stood firmly and spoken plainly—to the Pharisees, King Herod, soldiers, tax collectors, and peasants. Even in prison, his loyalty to God and commitment to his principles were firm as a rock.

Jesus said, "I tell you, no one has ever done greater work or been a greater person than John." How does heaven measure greatness? Not by wealth or fame or family name or intellect. God values love and purity—moral worth. John's greatness came from pointing to Jesus as the Promised One with no thought of himself.

John didn't call fire down from heaven or raise the dead to life, but he did the work he was given. Years later, people said, "John never did a miracle, but everything he said about Jesus was true."

Because so many knew and loved John, there was great unhappiness when Herod had him thrown in prison. But everyone knew that he wasn't guilty of anything, so they assumed he would soon be released.

JOHN'S FATE

Herod believed that John was a prophet and he intended to set John free quickly. But he was afraid of what Herodias would do, so he waited. Herodias hated John, but she knew that the king would never willingly agree to have him killed. So she plotted to force Herod's hand. The king's birthday was coming soon and all the officers and noblemen of the country would join him for a great party of feasting and drinking. Herodias planned to take advantage of the occasion.

When the birthday arrived and the party was in full swing, Herodias sent her daughter, Salome, in to dance for the king and his guests. Now, it was very unusual for a lady of the royal court to make an appearance at this kind of party. And to have her dance was a real compliment to the king and his guests.

Salome was young and beautiful and her sensual dance held the attention of every man in the room. Herod, drunk with wine and the girl's beauty, wanted to impress the important men in the room. He swore before all his guests to give the girl a present. "I will give you anything you ask for," he told her.

Salome ran to consult with her mother and quickly returned with her answer. "I want the head of John the Baptist on a platter."

At those words, the drunken laughter of the room faded to silence. Herod was shocked and horrified. But he had promised in front of these guests, and unless one of them insisted that he not do it, he would have to deliver what she asked. His guests had all heard John preach and knew that he wasn't guilty of any crime, but they were too drunk to think it through and speak up.

Herod couldn't see any way out. He ordered the execution. Soon the prophet's head was delivered as promised. Herodias celebrated her victory, but she failed to stop John's influence over the king. Herod was now tormented more than ever by guilt. No torture is worse than a guilty conscience. There is no way to escape from it day or night.

WHY JESUS DIDN'T RESCUE JOHN

Jesus couldn't rescue John without risking His own mission, but that didn't mean He didn't care. He felt the pain of John's death. Satan had failed to make Jesus sin, so he caused John's death to make Jesus suffer.

Many wonder why John was left to die in prison. His fate won't shake our confidence in God if we understand that John was honored to share the suffering Jesus went through to save humans. Everyone who follows Jesus will suffer in the war against Satan.

John wasn't forgotten. Angels kept him company, helping him understand the prophecies and promises of Scripture. John would be an example and an encouragement to the thousands through the centuries who would suffer in lonely prison cells, or die by the sword, by fire, or by torture. John's story would reassure them that God had not forgotten them either.

God never allows things to happen to His children that they would not choose for themselves if they knew the end from the beginning and could understand their part in His plans. Neither Enoch nor Elijah, both of whom went to heaven without dying, were greater than John the Baptist who died alone in a dungeon.

Of all the gifts heaven can give us, the heaviest trust and the highest honor goes to those who share Jesus' suffering to save the human race.

CHAPTER 23

THE
KINGDOM OF GOD

"The right time has come. The kingdom of God is near"
(Mark 1:15).

he news that the Messiah would soon appear was first heard in Judea. The province of Judea included Jerusalem, where the angel promised the birth of John the Baptist to his father, and where the temple-goers heard the testimony of Simeon and Anna about the Baby Jesus. It included Bethlehem, where the angels sang.

Jesus received His first disciples in Judea and spent most of His early ministry there. The flash of divinity when He cleared the temple, His miracles of healing, the truths that He taught, all made the same public claim—that Jesus was the Son of God.

If the leaders of Israel had accepted Jesus as the Messiah, they would have had the honor of carrying His message to the world. Instead, the jealousy and suspicion they harbored grew into hate. They worked to turn the people away from Jesus.

After the Sanhedrin rejected Jesus' message and decided to kill Him, Jesus left Jerusalem, the temple, the priests, and the people who thought they knew so much about God's law. He left Judea to find a different class of people with which to share His message.

He needed to find the ones who would carry the gospel to the whole world.

Just as Jesus was forced to turn away from the leaders of the Jewish religion, others have been forced to leave their churches to share the truth about God. The leaders of the Reformation didn't plan to leave the Catholic Church and start new churches. But when their church leaders wouldn't allow them to share new truths about God, they were forced to leave it. Even today, some people have to leave their own churches to follow truth as they learn it from Scripture.

So Jesus traveled to the province of Galilee. The teachers in Jerusalem considered the Galilean people rude and ignorant. They were different—they were more earnest and less prejudiced. They were more open to learning truth. Galilee was very crowded with more non-Jewish people living there than in Judea.

As Jesus walked through the countryside, teaching and healing, people from the cities and villages began to follow wherever He went. Others came from Judea and other provinces. The crowds got so large and so enthusiastic that Jesus often had to hide from people. At that time, it was dangerous for large groups to gather because the Romans considered every crowd a potential for revolt against them.

But the people wouldn't stay away. Never before had the world seen or heard anything like this. It was as if heaven had come down to earth. The love Jesus showed and taught was like a feast to people starving for truth—for an understanding of God.

DANIEL'S PROPHECY IS FULFILLED

The truth Jesus taught started with this: "The time has come, the kingdom of God is here. Repent and believe the good news."

When Jesus said, "The time has come," He was referring to the prophecy the angel had given Daniel when Israel was in captivity in Babylon many years before. "Seventy weeks are given to your people and your city," the angel told Daniel. Since a day in prophecy stands for a year (see Numbers 13:34; Ezekiel 4:6), the seventy weeks or 490 days represented 490 years.

The angel gave the starting date for this prophecy. "From the time of the command to return and rebuild Jerusalem until the Messiah arrives will be sixty-nine weeks." This command, which allowed the Jews to return to their land, was given by King Artaxerxes in the fall of 457 B.C. From that date, sixty-nine weeks or 483 years later takes us to the fall of A.D. 27. This was the time when Jesus was baptized in the Jordan River. Soon after, He began His ministry.

Never before had the world seen or heard anything like this. It was as if heaven had come down to earth.

That is why Jesus could say, "The time has come." At just the right time, the kingdom of God had arrived.

Then the angel also told Daniel that the gospel—the good news of the Messiah—would be preached to the Jewish nation for one week, or seven years. But in the middle of that seven years, the sacrifices and services in the temple would come to an end. In the spring of A.D. 31, Jesus became the True Sacrifice on the cross. At the moment He died, the curtain in the temple was torn from top to bottom. The purpose and meaning of the sacrifices and services in the temple came to an end.

For three and a half more years, the disciples continued to share the story of Jesus with their Jewish nation. But when Jesus' follower Stephen was stoned to death in A.D. 34, the disciples began to scatter and carry the gospel to other nations and peoples around the world. The seven years of the Jews came to an end.

Daniel's prophecies pointed out the time of Jesus' birth, the time of His ministry and of His death, and the time the gospel would be carried to other nations. The Jews had the opportunity to understand these prophecies and to see them fulfilled in Jesus' life. After His resurrection, Jesus explained these prophecies to His disciples.

The angel Gabriel, second-in-command in heaven after Jesus, brought those messages to Daniel. Jesus would later send Gabriel to John with the messages of Revelation, which tell us when Jesus will come the second time. As that book promises, God always blesses those who prayerfully study the prophecies in the Bible.

At Jesus' first coming, He introduced His kingdom of grace. At His second coming, He will introduce His kingdom of glory. And the Second Coming is predicted by prophecies just as the first coming was. Jesus Himself gave us signs to watch for and said, "Watch, pray, and be ready all the time." That period is here; Jesus is about to return.

The Jews misinterpreted the prophecies they were given. They were looking for a different Messiah—one who would bring them power and glory—so they rejected

> *If we let the cares of this world consume our thoughts, we will be as unprepared as the Jews were to meet Jesus when He returns again.*

Jesus and planned to kill Him. If we let the cares of this world consume our thoughts and ignore the prophecies or interpret them to suit ourselves, we will be as unprepared as they were to meet Jesus when He returns.

CHAPTER 24

"ISN'T THIS THE CARPENTER'S SON?"

"The Lord has put his Spirit in me, because he appointed me to tell the Good News to the poor" (Luke 4:18).

s Jesus was growing up, He worshipped with His neighbors in the synagogue in Nazareth. He had been away since He started His ministry, but the people of Nazareth heard all the stories about Him. They heard about all the miracles that He had performed.

Now that Jesus was traveling in Galilee, He visited Nazareth on Sabbath morning and joined His family at the synagogue. He sat among people who had known Him since He was a child, and they were all watching Him.

It was a typical service that morning. The local elder read a passage from the Scriptures and reminded the listeners of the signs that the Messiah was coming soon. He promised that the Messiah would appear in glory to lead the armies of Israel to victory over their enemies.

Any Israelite who visited a synagogue might be asked to read from the Scriptures. On this Sabbath, Jesus was asked to be a part of the service. He was given a scroll from the prophet Isaiah and He read:

"The Lord has put his Spirit in me, because he appointed me to tell the Good News to the poor. He has sent me to tell the captives they are free and to tell the blind that they can see

This chapter is based on Luke 4:16-30.

again. God sent me to free those who have been treated unfairly and to announce the time when the Lord will show his
kindness" (Luke 4:18, 19).

As Jesus explained the words He had read, He talked about the Messiah as Someone who would help them, heal them, and show them the
truth about God. His words, His expressions, His voice thrilled the listening people like nothing they had ever heard before. The Holy Spirit broke
down the barriers of their hearts and the idea that God cared so much
that He would send this Messiah left them praising Him out loud.

Then Jesus said, "Today, the One these Scriptures promised has
come to you."

In an instant, the mood in the synagogue changed. As the people
realized that Jesus was claiming to be the Messiah, their happiness
turned to anger. "Who does this Jesus think he is?" they asked. "How
can he claim to be the Messiah when we all know that he's just a
carpenter's son? We've known him since he was a baby! We watched
him grow up and become a man. Don't his brothers and sisters still
live here with us? Sure, Jesus is a good person, but the Messiah? I
don't think so!"

The more they thought about it, the angrier it made them. None
of His talk about the Messiah included driving out the Romans and
becoming the new power in the world. In fact, this Messiah sounded
like someone who would want to look in their hearts and change them.
This made them pull back from His deep, searching eyes. He intended
to heal them, as if they were not already the children of Abraham, the
people of God, the greatest people in the world! Unseen to their eyes,
Satan was working feverishly to turn them against Jesus.

Jesus then gave them proof of His divinity by reading their thoughts.
He reminded them of two stories from their history. "A prophet is never
accepted in his own country. There were many widows in Israel in the
days of Elijah. But when the famine came, God sent Elijah to stay with a
widow in another country. There were many lepers in Israel during the
days of Elisha, but only Naaman of Syria was healed."

Even though both prophets had given God's messages to the
people, very few believed them. So God worked with those who did

believe—wherever they were from—even if they didn't know as much about God as the Israelites did.

JESUS CUTS TO THE ROOT OF THE PROBLEM

Jesus' words cut like a knife to the root of the problem—the people's pride. It forced them to consider that maybe they had stopped listening to God, that maybe they were no longer His special people. The faith Jesus' words had stirred in their hearts turned to contempt. Their anger and jealousy allowed Satan to push them to violence. The congregation became an angry mob. They grabbed Jesus and rushed Him out of their synagogue, and out of their city.

"Who does this Jesus think he is?" they asked.

With shouts and curses, the crowd forced Jesus toward the edge of a nearby cliff, planning to shove Him off to die on the rocks below. There, in the middle of the angry mob, while some were grabbing rocks to hurl at His head, something unexpected happened.

Jesus disappeared.

The angels who stood by Him in the synagogue were still with Him in the middle of the angry mob. When His life was in danger, they spread their protecting wings around Jesus and led Him to a place where He would be safe.

Throughout earth's history, evil forces have threatened Jesus' followers. But armies of angels have protected them. Only in heaven will we learn how many times God's angels saved us from Satan's plans.

Jesus wanted to save the people of Nazareth. He wanted them to join His kingdom. But they would not listen. Near the end of His work in Galilee, Jesus visited His hometown one last time. Since His first visit, the stories of His teachings and His miracles in Galilee had been told everywhere. Not even the people of Nazareth could deny that He had more power than any human. Near them were whole villages where not one person was sick or hurt, because Jesus had passed through and healed them all.

And even though they had tried to kill Him, Jesus wanted to do the same for the people in His hometown. As He preached to them again, their hearts wanted to respond to His love. But they could not admit that this Man who had grown up with them was any better than they were. They would ask, "Where did he get the power to heal and the wisdom to speak like he does?" They would not believe that He was the Messiah.

Jesus' words cut like a knife to the root of the problem— the people's pride.

Because of this, Jesus could not do many miracles in their town. Only a few hearts were willing to be blessed by Him. Their sick loved ones remained sick; their crippled friends were not given the ability to walk. Finally Jesus left, never to return.

Just as the people of Nazareth and the Sanhedrin rejected Jesus, the nation of Israel finally made the same choice. They rejected the Holy Spirit and put Jesus on the cross. This led to the destruction of Jerusalem and the scattering of the Jews to nations all around the world.

Jesus wanted so much to show Israel the precious treasures of truth. But they desperately held on to their pointless laws and empty ceremonies. If they had honestly studied the Scriptures, the destruction of their city and nation could have been avoided.

Jesus' teachings also demanded repentance. They would have had to change their behavior and give up on their hopes of national greatness. They would be forced to go against the opinions of the great thinkers and teachers of their time.

The Jewish leaders didn't understand Jesus at all. Their spiritual pride led them to expect honor at every turn. Their jealousy protected their customs and ceremonies. But Jesus, with all His power, was so humble! If He was truly the Messiah, they argued, why didn't He want honor and glory and an army to destroy His enemies?

But for more than any of these reasons, the Jews rejected Jesus because His pure life of love showed up their sinfulness. They could live with disappointed plans for national glory, but they couldn't live with the spotlight of His purity shinning on their unclean lives.

CHAPTER 25

THE CALL
BY THE SEA

"Come follow me, and I will make you fish for people"
(Matthew 4:19).

s the sun rose over the Sea of Galilee, Jesus was
spending some quiet moments at the lakeshore. His
disciples—exhausted after fishing all night and
catching nothing—were still in their fishing boats on
the lake.

Jesus was hoping to rest from the crush of the crowds that followed Him every day. But there was no rest on this morning. As soon
as it was light, people began to gather around Him. The crowd grew
so quickly that Jesus was surrounded on every side and could barely
move.

Meanwhile, the disciples had brought their boats in to the shore.
Jesus stepped up onto Peter's boat and asked him to move it back just
a little way. Now He could be seen and heard by everyone in the crowd.
From Peter's boat, He began to teach the crowd on the beach.

What an amazing sight this was to the angels of heaven! Here was
their Commander, their glorious Leader, sitting in a fisherman's boat,
rocked by the waves as He shared the good news of salvation. The
King of heaven was teaching the truths of His kingdom in the open
air to the common people.

This chapter is based on Matt.4:18-22; Mark 1:16-20; Luke 5:1-11.

It was a perfect setting for His words. The lake, the mountains, the fields bathed in sunlight—all became illustrations of the truths He was teaching. Every lesson that He taught touched hearts and led people to accept Him.

The crowd onshore grew larger with each passing moment. Old men leaning on their canes, strong farmers from the hills, fishermen from their boats on the lake, businessmen and teachers—all came to hear His words. The rich, the educated, the young, the old, those bringing their sick loved ones, all crowded close to listen to this Teacher sent from God.

Jesus saw beyond the crowd on the shore of Galilee. Looking into the future, He saw His faithful followers as they struggled with life—in loneliness, in pain, in temptation, or in prison. He saw them as they celebrated, as they fought, as they sat confused and concerned. The words that He spoke were for each of them as well. Through the miracle of the Holy Spirit, the Voice speaking from the fisherman's boat that morning would bring hope, comfort, wisdom, and peace to human hearts until the end of time.

When He finished speaking, Jesus turned to Peter and said, "Take the boat farther out into the lake so you can drop your net and gather up some fish."

Peter was tired and discouraged. During his long hours of fishing the night before, he had been thinking of John the Baptist, who at that time was still locked in Herod's dungeon. How could Jesus succeed where John had failed—especially with the priests and rulers against Him? As the hours passed, even Peter's fishing was a failure. The future seemed dark and depressing.

Finally, he answered Jesus. "Master, we fished all night and caught nothing. But if You say so, I'll put out the nets."

It seemed pointless—everyone knew that night was the only time to catch fish in a lake as clear as Galilee. No one fished during the day. But because Jesus said to, Peter and his brother Andrew let the net out into the water. As they began to pull it back in, they were astonished to find the net so full of fish that it was in danger of ripping apart!

Quickly they called to James and John on the other boat for help. Together, they managed to bring in so many fish that both boats were nearly swamped!

A FISHER OF PEOPLE

Peter was no longer thinking about his boat or the fish. This miracle, more than any of the others he had witnessed, showed him true divine power. Now Peter saw Jesus as Someone who could control nature. And he saw his sinful, doubting self compared to Jesus' perfect holiness.

Suddenly, Peter was overwhelmed with real love for his Teacher and a new sense of his unworthiness to stand near the Son of God.

> *Now Peter saw Jesus as Someone who could control nature.*

While his friends took care of the fish, Peter threw himself down in front of Jesus and said, "Lord, stay away from me—I am too sinful to be near You."

Yet even as he said it, Peter grabbed on to Jesus' feet, wishing never to be separated from Him.

Jesus must have smiled. "Don't be afraid, Peter," He said. "From now on, you will fish for people." Now that Peter could see his weak self clearly and his need to depend on Jesus, he was ready for his "call"—his invitation—to work for Jesus.

Up to this time, none of the disciples had completely joined Jesus' work and ministry. They had seen His miracles and heard Him teach, but they still worked at their regular jobs. Now it was time for them to choose. When Jesus reached the shore, He gave Andrew, James, and John the same call He had given Peter. "Follow Me," He said, "I will teach you to fish for people."

THEY CHANGED THE WORLD

During the long, sad night on the lake, away from Jesus, the disciples were filled with doubts. Being near Him now reignited their faith and brought them joy and success. The miracle with the fish had shown them that God would take care of them and their families. Without a second thought, they left their nets and boats and followed Him.

It is the same with us. Apart from Jesus, our work seems meaningless and wasted. But when we work as He directs us, He inspires faith and hope, and His power is clear to see. The One whose words gathered fish can also touch human hearts and direct them to His followers—His fishers of people.

Jesus could have chosen the "wise" and educated men of His day to be His disciples. Education is a blessing when it is directed by God's love. But in their prejudice, they refused to be taught by someone like Jesus. Their pride kept them from caring about the suffering people around them. They disqualified themselves from the greatest education ever offered. The first thing workers for God must learn is not to trust their own hearts. Then they are ready to trust Jesus and learn His character and His way.

Jesus picked simple fishermen because they had little to unlearn. They had not been taught all the traditions and wrong customs of their time. These men had natural talent, but more importantly, they were humble and teachable. They were willing to follow Jesus and learn from Him. In everyday life around us, many people go about their work unaware that they have the ability—if it were called upon—to become honored and powerful leaders. All that is needed is the touch of a skilled hand. Jesus called men like this to work with Him. After their training, they became like Him. As a result, these simple men became preachers and teachers of such power that they went out and changed the world.

The more time we spend with Jesus in devotions and prayer, the more we will become like Him.

The people they became and the work that they did are a testimony of what God will do for all who are teachable and willing to follow His law and His way. There is no limit to what people can do if they are willing to open their hearts to the Holy Spirit and dedicate their lives to God. If we accept the needed discipline, God will teach us hour by hour and day by day. God takes people as they are and educates them for His service, if they surrender themselves to Him. The Holy Spirit, now invited into their hearts, will sharpen their minds and skills. Weaknesses can become strengths through dependence on God.

The more time we spend with Jesus in prayer and devotions, the more we will become like Him. We will have clearer insights and better judgment. Then we will do great things for God. Christians can always get the best education at the greatest school—they can sit at the feet of Jesus.

CHAPTER 26

DAYS AT CAPERNAUM

"He taught like a person who had authority"
(Matthew 7:29).

n the time of Jesus, Capernaum was a warm and beautiful city, filled with palm and olive trees. The streams flowing from the cliffs to the Sea of Galilee watered its orchards, vineyards, green fields, and bright flower gardens.

Capernaum sat on the shores of the deep blue lake called the Sea of Galilee, on the edge of the great plain called Gennesaret. Travelers from all over—from Damascus to Jerusalem, and Egypt to the Mediterranean—passed through its gates. The shores of the lake and the hills around it were dotted with towns and villages. From farms and fishing boats came the goods that were traded in the city market. It was a vibrant city, and full of life.

Jesus often stopped and stayed at Capernaum as He traveled back and forth across the land. It was a place where He could meet people from many countries as they paused to rest from their travel. Because of that, His teachings and the stories of His miracles were carried all over the known world. In many places, sincere people began to ask about the prophecies and about God's plans for this world.

In spite of the Sanhedrin's warnings about Jesus, people everywhere wanted to learn more about Him and His mission. The angels of heaven were busy working on people's hearts, leading them to the Savior. Nowhere was this truer than in Capernaum.

> *The angels of heaven were busy working on people's hearts, leading them to the Savior.*

The government official's son who was healed told everyone about Jesus' power. His family couldn't stop talking about their faith in Jesus. Whenever Jesus was in town, the whole place was in an uproar. Great crowds followed Him everywhere. On the Sabbath, the crowds that followed Jesus to the synagogue were so large that the building couldn't hold them all. Many had to be turned away.

Everyone who heard Jesus teach was amazed. The teaching they were used to hearing—from the scribes and elders—was very formal, very cold. But Jesus' words were full of life and power! The words He used were clear and understandable. His voice was like music to their ears after listening to the droning of the Pharisees.

JESUS' WORDS

The rabbis spoke cautiously when teaching the scriptures, as if they might be understood one way—or the exact opposite. Jesus taught Scripture with authority. He knew what it meant and He shared that in a powerful way. Jesus didn't get involved in the various arguments of the Jews. With a calm but serious voice, He shared the truth about God and showed how the stories and teachings of the Old Testament contained those same truths. People began to understand the Scriptures as never before.

Jesus' way was practical. He didn't ignore the importance of everyday life. He showed how following God prepares a person to deal successfully with life. Jesus used stories and illustrations taken from life around them—the birds, the flowers, seeds, the shepherd and the sheep. These simple stories carried real lessons that the people remembered every time they saw a bird, a sheep, or a flower. His words charmed those who were educated, but also were understood by those who had never studied in school.

Even with angry enemies all around Him, Jesus was surrounded by an atmosphere of peace. Love showed in the look on His face and was heard in the tone of His voice. It attracted people to Him. Those in trouble felt immediately that He was a friend they could count on. They wanted to know more about the truths He taught.

Jesus watched people's faces. He could tell when the truth struck home. When someone's eyes lighted up with understanding, He was filled with joy. When a face was hardened and a person turned away from truth, His heart nearly broke.

A DEMON-POSSESSED MAN

One day in Capernaum, Jesus was in the synagogue explaining His mission to set free those who were slaves of Satan. Suddenly, a wild-looking man rushed out of the crowd and started shouting. "Leave us alone! What do you want from us, Jesus of Nazareth? Are you here to destroy us? I know you are the Holy One from God!"

This man was possessed by a demon. He had spent his life chasing pleasure and sin, and when his nature was perverted enough Satan took control of his mind. He had been driven away from his family and friends to wander the land as a wild man, living in disgusting filth and frightening everyone that saw him.

But the human mind in chains sensed Jesus' presence and power. The man rushed into the synagogue to reach out to Jesus and beg for help, but the demon controlled his voice.

The people backed away from the shouting, demon-possessed man. Jesus didn't. He heard the unspoken prayer of a human He loved. He commanded the demon, "Be quiet and come out of this man." The demon fought to hold on to his victim and tossed the man to the ground. But at Jesus' words, it left the man without hurting him anymore. Eyes that had been glazed with insanity now overflowed with grateful tears.

The watching people were amazed. "What is this? When this Man speaks, even the evil spirits obey!"

The man had thought that his pursuit of pleasure was just harmless fun. When finally, he would have given anything to escape his sinful life, it was too late. Satan had taken complete control. It will be the same for all who surrender to evil—their search for thrills and pleasure will end in addiction, despair, and madness.

The same evil spirit that possessed this man also controlled the Jewish priests and leaders. Instead of driving them to run wildly through the countryside, Satan gave them a sense of godliness, as if they were holy and all others were unclean. They were even more hopeless than the possessed man, because they felt no need for Jesus at all. They could have found protection in the Scripture, but the way they twisted the words robbed them of their power against Satan.

The Jewish leaders twisted God's Word to say things God never intended.

During these years of Jesus' ministry, Satan worked furiously to control the bodies and minds of humans. Likewise in the future, at the time of the final conflict, as Jesus' followers take His message of love and hope to the whole world, Satan and his demons will work harder than ever to confuse and deceive humans.

The leaders and teachers in Israel neglected their only protection from evil spirits—the Word of God. Jesus used Scripture to defeat Satan in the desert. The Jewish leaders twisted God's Word to say things God never intended. They argued over trivial things and ignored important truths. So God's Word lost its power and evil spirits had their way.

History is repeating itself. Religious leaders today dissect God's Word and twist it with their own opinions until honest seekers turn away in disgust. Without the truths of God's Word to protect them, people are opening themselves to be controlled by demons. As spiritualism becomes more and more acceptable in our society and in our churches, many are being lured into contact with mysterious "higher powers or beings." As their defenses are broken down, they give up control of their own will.

But their situation is not hopeless—through faith in the promises of God's Word, anyone can be freed from the traps they have fallen into. No person is ever so trapped, so tied down by evil, that Jesus cannot set him or her free. The cry of a person in need—even unspoken—will always be heard.

HEALING AT PETER'S HOUSE

While the crowd in the synagogue was still buzzing, Jesus left for Peter's house to rest. But there was trouble at Peter's also—his wife's mother was sick with a serious fever. Jesus banished the sickness from her body. She felt completely well and got up to help serve dinner to Peter's guests—Jesus and the other disciples.

News about the man at the synagogue and about the healing of Peter's mother-in-law spread through the whole city. No one dared to come and ask for healing on the Sabbath—that would anger the

rabbis. But as soon as the sun disappeared below the horizon, it seemed as if everyone in the city headed toward Peter's house—for healing, for a blessing, for a chance to be near Jesus.

Hour after hour, families brought their sick loved ones through the door of Peter's house to be healed by Jesus. They kept coming, because no one knew if Jesus would still be there the next morning. It was a day unlike any Capernaum had ever seen—the city was filled with tears of joy, with shouts of praise, with a feeling that heaven had indeed reached down and touched their little piece of earth. Jesus took great joy in His power to give these people back their health and happiness.

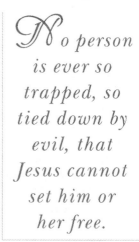

No person is ever so trapped, so tied down by evil, that Jesus cannot set him or her free.

It was very late before the crowds began to thin out. When the last sufferer left and Peter's home fell silent, Jesus, exhausted, rested for a time. But long before sunrise, while the city still slept, He left the house to find a private place to pray.

Jesus often sent His disciples to their homes to visit their families and to rest, but He didn't often take time out for rest Himself. In the early morning, or in the evening after working all day teaching and healing people, He would go to the mountains to talk to His Father. Often He would spend the whole night praying and meditating, and then return to His work at sunrise.

That morning, Peter and the other disciples followed Jesus to tell Him that people were already gathering and asking for Him. This was especially exciting to the disciples. They knew that the rabbis and leaders at Jerusalem wanted Jesus dead. They had seen the people of His own hometown try to kill Him. But here in Capernaum, the people loved Him. Maybe these liberty-loving people of Galilee would be the first ones to support the Messiah and the new kingdom.

His response surprised them. "Let's go on to other towns, so I can preach there also. That is why I came."

Jesus wasn't interested in becoming a famous miracle worker or healer. He knew that the people were eager to believe He had come to be their new king. He wanted to turn their minds away from earthly kingdoms and physical healing to spiritual things.

The applause and adoration of the crushing crowds jarred Jesus' spirit. The honor the world gives to the famous, the wealthy, or the talented was foreign to Him. Jesus didn't do anything to get attention or applause. Everything He did was according to the plans and will of His Father. God was revealed in the actions and teachings of His Son.

Jesus, the Sun of Righteousness, did not burst upon the world to dazzle the senses with His glory. Quietly and gently, like the dawn of a new day, He worked to push back the darkness and wake the world to a new life.

CHAPTER 27

HEALINGS
IN CAPERNAUM

"Stand up, take your mat, and go home"
(Matthew 9:6).

f all the diseases known in the Middle East in those days, none was feared as much as leprosy. It was contagious and incurable, a particularly horrible disease that left the body decaying as the sufferer lost feeling in all extremities. To make matters worse, the Jews considered leprosy a direct judgment from God. They called it "the finger of God."

A person who had leprosy was forced to leave home and family. Everything a leper touched was unclean. The air he or she breathed was infected. Anyone who was even suspected of having leprosy was forced to undergo inspection by the priests. Even if he were a king or a ruler, if the priests declared that man a leper, the law demanded that he stay away from all healthy humans.

As their bodies slowly disintegrated, these cursed people were expected to warn others of their presence. Everywhere they went, they shouted, "Unclean! Unclean!" as they shuffled along.

When the lepers of Galilee heard about Jesus and His miracles of healing, they felt a spark of hope. But only a spark, since no one had been healed of leprosy since the days of Elisha.

There was one man, however, who held on to that hope. He won-

This chapter is based on Matt. 8:2-4; 9:1-8, 32-34; Mark 1:40-45; 2:1-12; Luke 5:12-28.

dered, "Would Jesus heal me? How can I get near enough to ask Him? Would He even notice a leper like me? And if He does, will He just say that I deserve the curse from God?"

Of all the things he had heard about Jesus, one stood out in the man's mind—no one who asked for Jesus' help had ever been turned away. So this man decided to find Jesus. If he could cross paths with Jesus as He walked along a road or taught outside of a town, he could approach Him and beg for help.

No one who asked for Jesus' help had ever been turned away.

The leper was guided to where Jesus was teaching beside the lake. Even as far as he stood from the other people, he could hear a few of the words that Jesus spoke. He watched as Jesus healed people who were sick, blind, and crippled. When he heard those people praising God, the faith in his heart grew stronger. He forgot about the laws that kept him from coming near other people. He forgot how they ran from him in fear and disgust. He forgot everything but the hope of being healed.

As he rushed closer, people pushed back, terrified by his gruesome, decaying body. Some shouted for him to stop, to stay away, but he didn't hear or see anyone but the Savior. He threw himself to the ground at Jesus' feet and cried, "Lord, if You will, You can make me clean."

"I will," Jesus said. "Be clean." Then He reached out and touched the man. Immediately, the leper changed. His nerves were once again sensitive. His muscles were firm and strong. His skin became as pink and healthy as a child's. He was healed!

Then Jesus said, "Don't say anything to anyone—just go and show yourself to the priests and follow the cleansing rituals." Jesus knew that if the priests found out who had healed him, they might refuse to pronounce him clean and fit to rejoin society and his family. He wanted the man to show himself at the temple before the priests heard about the healing.

Jesus also knew that if the story of the healed leper were spread around, lepers from across the country would swarm Him. Then everyone else would keep away because of their fear of catching the disease.

He would be accused again of ignoring the religious laws of the Pharisees. Then His preaching, His ministry, His mission would be held back.

The cured leper didn't understand that his case would turn the priests and elders even more against Jesus. He thought Jesus was just being modest. So he told everyone what happened. He felt so good, so healthy, that he couldn't help praising the Person who had healed him. He went back to the same priests who had declared him unclean with leprosy and they pronounced him clean and welcome to return to normal life.

Jesus didn't miss any opportunity to reach out to the priests and teachers. By sending the cured leper to them, He was showing them His love for all humans, His respect for the law of Moses, and His power to save anyone from sin and death. While most of the priests reacted to Jesus with anger and hatred, after His death and resurrection a great many of them became followers of His way.

Because the cured man and the people who saw the miracle told the story everywhere, the crowds that came to see Jesus were so large that He was forced to stop His work for a while.

SIN IS LIKE LEPROSY

Healing and cleansing the leper shows us what Jesus wants to do with us and the sin in our lives. Jesus didn't become infected or unclean by touching the leper. His power drove the leprosy out. Sin in our lives is just as deadly as leprosy. Only Jesus has the power to drive it out, to make us clean and give us a new life.

Although this leper's healing was instant, at other times Jesus didn't answer a person's request immediately. When we pray and ask for a blessing, the answer may be for us to wait or God may give us something else than what we ask for. But when we pray and ask to be saved from our sins, the answer is always an instant "Yes."

THE PARALYZED MAN FROM CAPERNAUM

In Capernaum lived a man who was paralyzed. His disease was a direct result of his lifestyle of sin. Besides his pain and wasted life, this man was greatly troubled by regret. He asked the priests and doctors to help him, but they declared him incurable and cursed by God.

The paralyzed man sunk into depression and gave up all hope. Then he heard about Jesus. His friends encouraged him to believe he could be cured if he could see Jesus. But this man didn't want to be healed as much as he wanted to be forgiven. If he could be sure that God still loved him, dying wouldn't matter. He asked his friends to carry him to see this Jesus and they were happy to do it.

Now Jesus was teaching that day in Peter's house. His disciples were inside the house sitting around their Master, and nearby were a number of Pharisees and teachers who had come to spy on Jesus. Outside was an enormous crowd who had come to listen and watch for more miracles.

It was the same Voice that had given life to the dust of the earth in Eden. Now it recreated the body of a forgiven man.

The paralyzed man's friends tried to push their way through the crowd as they carried the stretcher, but they couldn't. As they began to give up hope, the man had an idea. "Carry me up to the roof," he suggested. "We can go through from there and find Jesus."

So that's what they did. The man's friends carried him up on top of the house, then broke through the roof and lowered his stretcher down until he was lying at Jesus' feet.

When Jesus saw the man's pleading eyes, He knew what he wanted. In fact, Jesus already knew about this man. He had seen the man's desire for forgiveness while he was still at his home, and had blessed him there. As the man planned and worked with his friends to find Jesus, the Savior had seen his faith grow. Now Jesus knew exactly what to say.

"Son," He said, "your sins are forgiven."

These words were music to the paralyzed man's ears. His depression and despair evaporated and peace filled his heart. His pain was gone. More than just healed, he was forgiven! His faith was rewarded and he lay there in joyful silence while the people looked on in amazement.

The rabbis who were there remembered this man and how they had given him no hope or sympathy. They had declared that he was cursed by God for his sins. Now they realized how they would lose their influence over the people who had watched Jesus forgive the man. They had to do something, and with a quick look to one another agreed on a plan. They would call it blasphemy—a sin that called for a death sentence—and remind the people that no one could forgive sins but God.

But Jesus was reading their faces and hearts. "Why are you thinking like that among yourselves?" He asked. "Which is easier, to say to this paralyzed man 'You are forgiven,' or to say 'Stand, pick up your stretcher and walk?' But so you will know that I have the authority to forgive sins, I will tell you," He said to the paralyzed man, "Stand, pick up your stretcher and go home."

It was the same Voice that had given life to the dust of the earth in Eden. Now it recreated the body of a forgiven man. He jumped up from the floor as nimble as a growing boy. Every organ in his body leaped to full life. With new, strong muscles he picked up the stretcher as if it weighed no more than a feather and walked out through the crowd.

Thousands today who suffer with disease are actually longing to hear those same words: "Your sins are forgiven." Only Jesus, the Healer of the soul, can give them health and strength again. Jesus still has the same power today to forgive sinners and heal the sick.

The people stepped back to give room for the sick man to walk out, and whispered to each other, "We have seen strange and wonderful things today." They could only praise God and say, "We have never seen anything like this before."

The Pharisees were amazed into silence. Defeated and shamed, they recognized the presence of a superior being. But it didn't change them. They left Peter's house determined to find a way to stop Jesus, to put an end to the Son of God.

When the formerly paralyzed man got home, his family and friends could hardly believe their eyes and could hardly stop weeping for joy. The body that was so shriveled now bounced with strength. The face that was so depressed now glowed with joy and peace. This man and his family were ready to lay down their lives for Jesus. Nothing could weaken their faith in the One who brought light and life back to their once dark home.

CHAPTER 28

MATTHEW:
A TAX COLLECTOR
BECOMES A DISCIPLE

"It is not the healthy people who need a doctor, but the sick"
(Matthew 9:12).

very Roman official in Palestine was hated. Their presence, and the taxes that the Jews were forced to pay to Rome, were daily reminders that Israel was not a free country. To make matters worse, the Roman tax collectors used their authority to cheat the people out of extra money, and then kept it for themselves.

The only officials hated more than the Roman tax collectors were the Jews who worked to collect the Roman taxes. They were considered traitors to their people—worse than criminals.

One such Jew was a man named Matthew. As he listened to Jesus, the Holy Spirit worked on his heart. He wanted to give up his cheating, sinful life and follow Jesus. But he knew what the other Jewish teachers and rabbis were like so he was sure that Jesus would want nothing to do with him.

One day as Matthew sat at his tax booth, collecting taxes from the Jewish businessmen, he saw Jesus walking straight toward him. To his astonishment, Jesus stopped right in front of him and said, "Follow Me."

So Matthew did. He got up and left everything and followed Jesus.

This chapter is based on Matt. 9:9-17; Mark 2:14-22; Luke 5:27-39.

He didn't hesitate or think it over; he didn't consider the money or the lifestyle he'd be losing. He just wanted to be with Jesus, to listen to His words, and to support His mission.

It was the same when Jesus asked Peter, James, and John to follow Him. They left their businesses and their income behind. They didn't ask, "What will I live on? How will I take care of my family?"

Matthew faced the same test that Andrew and Peter did. At a moment of great success—when the nets were full of fish—Jesus asked them to leave it all for Him.

Later, when Jesus asked, "Even though I sent you out without money or clothes or shoes, were you ever in need of anything?" they could truly answer, "No. Nothing."

At some point, every person is tested to see if he or she will sacrifice financial profits and success for a deeper friendship with Jesus. No one can successfully and happily follow Jesus and do His work unless the whole heart is dedicated to it. When people see the sacrifice Jesus made, they will give up anything to follow Him.

When Jesus invited Matthew to join His small group of disciples, it was a major scandal. It offended the religious leaders, those who saw tax collectors as criminals, and of course, the national pride since this man worked for the Romans. The Pharisees used the people's prejudices to stir up anger toward Jesus.

Meanwhile, Matthew planned a celebration dinner at his house. He invited all of his family and friends, other tax collectors, and social and religious outcasts. Suddenly, there was a lot of interest in Jesus from this group.

A LONG-LASTING DINNER

Matthew's dinner was given in honor of Jesus who was happy to be there. He knew that the Pharisees and leaders would be offended, and He knew that in some people's eyes He would be condemned for eating with those sinners. But Jesus didn't let that keep Him from doing what was right.

By sitting and eating with the tax collectors and their friends, Jesus showed that He recognized the value and dignity of all humans. In His presence those outcasts of society began to imagine a new life—a life with meaning. To Matthew, Jesus' example at that dinner was an inspiration that led him to a life of showing and telling others about God's love. Although most of the others did not become followers of Jesus immediately, they were among the thousands who joined His church after the Resurrection.

WHY WOULD JESUS DO THAT?

The rabbis seized this opportunity to try to drive a wedge between Jesus and His disciples. "Why is your Teacher eating with tax collectors and sinners?" they asked, trying to stir up prejudice against the outcasts.

Jesus heard the question, and He didn't wait for the disciples to answer. He said, "Healthy people have no need for a doctor—sick people do. I came to call sinners to repent, not righteous people."

By sitting and eating with the tax collectors and their friends, Jesus showed that He recognized the value and dignity of all humans.

The Pharisees claimed to be righteous and spiritually strong while they considered the tax collectors and Gentiles to be sick sinners. Didn't it make sense that Jesus would spend time with the ones who needed Him?

Then Jesus told the rabbis, "Go and study what the scripture means that says, 'I want kindness more than I want animal sacrifices.'" The rabbis claimed to study and teach the Word of God, but they did not understand its spirit of love.

Frustrated by their failure, the Pharisees next tried to turn the disciples of John the Baptist against Jesus. Not long before, they had criticized John for his simple life and clothes and tried to turn people against him. Now they pointed to him as an example of a holy man. In contrast, Jesus was known to eat and drink at gatherings with all kinds of sinners, so He must not be a righteous person at all!

They would not accept the idea that Jesus was eating with sinners so He could bring light into their dark lives or that His words were dropping into their hearts like seeds that would someday grow into fruit for God. They only wanted to turn John's disciples against Jesus.

At this time, John the Baptist was still in prison and his disciples were depressed and worried. They followed many of the rules the rabbis taught, including fasting, or going without food. According to the rabbis, a person should go without food at least once a week—the most dedicated ones went without food two days every week to gain religious merit. The rabbis raised the question, "We know John was sent by God. So why do Jesus and his disciples act so differently?"

One week, while they were going without food along with the Pharisees, John's disciples came to Jesus and asked, "Why don't your disciples give up food like we do?"

Jesus didn't try to correct their misunderstanding of the value of going without food for religious reasons. He only tried to help them understand His mission. Since John had once told them that Jesus was the Bridegroom while John was the Bridegroom's friend, Jesus tried to explain it this way, "Why would you make the Bridegroom's friends go without food while the Bridegroom is still with them?"

In other words, the Crown Prince of heaven was on earth with His people, sharing the truth of God's love and His plans. This was no time for mourning and going without food! This was a time for joy!

But Jesus knew that darker days were coming. "The day will come when the Bridegroom will be taken away," He said. When His disciples and followers saw Jesus betrayed, arrested, and killed, they would mourn and go without food.

They would have joy again when He rose from the dead, but even after He left them to return to heaven they could not spend their time mourning and not eat-

The Jewish leaders were stuck in a rut of ceremonies and traditions.

ing. There would be days of difficulty, and times that would be more appropriate to go without food, but the Holy Spirit would be with them to keep the joy alive in their hearts.

Whether He was eating with sinners or going without food in the wilderness, Jesus was giving His life to save the lost. True devotion isn't about going without food to make yourself more holy. It's about giving your life to serve others.

NEW WINE IN OLD WINESKINS

Jesus shared a parable with John's disciples as He explained. "No one takes a patch of cloth from a new coat to cover a hole in an old coat—the new coat would be ruined and the old coat would look odd." He wanted to tell them that trying to combine the rules and traditions of the Pharisees with the true faith of John would only show how different they really were.

Trying to combine the rules and traditions of the Pharisees with the teachings of Jesus was even worse. Jesus compared it to putting new wine in old leather bags.

In those days, wine was often stored in containers made of specially prepared watertight leather. When new, these leather containers were soft and flexible, but they got dry and brittle with age. Newly squeezed grape juice would ferment slowly as it aged and create gases that expanded and stretched the leather, causing it to burst if it was old and dry.

Jesus saw that the Jewish leaders with their traditions and rules had become like old brittle leather bags. He said, "If new wine is stored in old leather bags, the bags burst and the wine is spilled." Jesus knew there was no way to combine His teaching of faith and love with their rules and prejudices. The truth about God would burst the traditions and teachings of the Pharisees.

The Jewish leaders were stuck in a rut of ceremonies and traditions. Their hearts were like brittle leather bags. Satisfied with the religion they had, they could not accept real faith. Faith motivated by love that purifies the soul could not be a part of their dead beliefs. The living truth of Jesus would burst the old traditions of the Pharisees.

Jesus found His new leather bags among the uneducated fishermen, the tax collectors, and the Samaritans. They were happy to hear the truth of God's love and share that truth with the world around them.

Even though Jesus used the idea of "new wine" to illustrate His teaching, it really wasn't new at all. It was the same truth that had been taught since the Garden of Eden. The Pharisees thought that almost everything Jesus did and said was a new teaching, but that was because they studied their own traditions more than the Scriptures. They would never be able to understand or accept Jesus' teaching until they were willing to give up their old traditions and beliefs.

Many today leave themselves in the same trap. Rather than give up their long-held opinion that humans must in some way work to be saved, they reject the truth when they hear it. A religion based on legalism, on the idea that salvation can be earned, has no peace or joy. The idea of giving up food or praying in order to earn salvation offends God. Nothing we can do will save us. Only by giving up self as the center of our lives, and giving our hearts and lives to Jesus can we find what we are searching for. Then we can become the "wine in new leather bags" with a message to share as we reflect the love of Jesus to the world.

CHAPTER 29

JESUS
AND THE SABBATH

" 'The Sabbath day was made to help people; they were not made to be ruled by the Sabbath day' " (Mark 2:27).

t the end of the first week of earth's history—when the world and everything in it was created—God looked around at what He had made and said, "This is all very good." And on the seventh day of that first week, God rested. He blessed the seventh day and made it a holy day, a day for humans to remember God's love and power.

The Son of God—Jesus—did all this creating. So the Sabbath is a memorial in time to the love and power of Jesus. The hours of the Sabbath are to bring us close to Him. We can hear His voice in the songs of birds, in the swaying leaves of the trees, in the endless rhythm of the oceans. The Sabbath gives us the time to recognize the genius and the power behind the creation of a world like ours. It gives us the time to realize that the Person behind that genius and power loves us and wants to save us and be with us.

After Creation, God's people remembered His Sabbath and enjoyed the blessings that came with it. However, in time most forgot the truth about God and His ways. So the Sabbath was given again at Sinai along with the other Ten Commandments. And as the principles in those other commandments, the Sabbath was not just for the Israelites, but for everyone.

The Sabbath will continue to be a sign of the Creator's power and of the Savior's love as long as the earth revolves and the sun rises and sets. It will still be celebrated when sin is finally destroyed and the earth is recreated in perfection once more.

THE SABBATH TWISTED

Only a true follower of Jesus, who by faith has accepted His holiness, can truly keep the Sabbath. As the Jews drifted away from God's plan, they lost sight of what the Sabbath was supposed to be. Over the centuries, the Jewish leaders surrounded the Sabbath with laws and rules of behavior that made the day a burden to all who kept it.

By the time of Jesus, keeping the Sabbath had been twisted to show the pride and selfishness of men who judged others rather than showing the love of God. By adding burdens to the Sabbath, the rabbis made it seem that God had given laws that were impossible to obey. People began to see God as a cruel dictator. They could only assume that keeping the Sabbath made people cruel and critical.

Jesus came to share the truth about God and about the Sabbath. He kept the Sabbath according to the Scriptures and ignored the rabbis' laws and rules. This set the stage for many conflicts.

A LESSON ABOUT SABBATH KEEPING

One Sabbath day, Jesus and His disciples walked through a field of ripening grain. Some of the disciples were hungry, so they picked heads of grain off the stalks, rubbing them between their hands to separate out the grain to chew on.

On other days of the week, no one would have seen any problem with this. Anyone walking through a field or orchard or vineyard was free to pick for eating what he or she wanted. But on Sabbath, this was seen as breaking the law because it was considered harvesting the grain.

The spies who always followed along with Jesus immediately pointed fingers. "Look," they said to Jesus, "your disciples are breaking the

Sabbath law." When He had been accused of breaking the Sabbath law before, Jesus defended His actions by stating His relationship to God and His work. This time, when His disciples were accused, He defended them with stories from the Old Testament about things done on Sabbath by people who were serving God.

Jesus' answer implied that the Pharisees were ignorant of the Scriptures. "Have you never read what David did when he and those with him were hungry? David went into the temple and ate the holy bread, which only the priests are supposed to eat." And He used another example: "Have you never read that the priests who work in the temple are breaking the Sabbath, but are not guilty because of the work they do?"

> *The Sabbath gives us the time to recognize the genius and the power behind the creation of a world like ours.*

If it was right for David to eat the holy bread, set apart for use in the temple, when he was hungry, then it was right for the disciples to gather and eat grain on the Sabbath. The priests worked harder on the Sabbath than on any other day, but that was right because their work was to point others to the Lord of the Sabbath.

Jesus made it very clear. " 'The Sabbath day was made to help people; they were not made to be ruled by the Sabbath day' " (Mark 2:27). God's mission in this world is to save humans. So any work done on the Sabbath that is necessary to accomplish that goal does not break the Sabbath law.

Jesus' final point ended the argument. "I—the Son of man—am the Lord of the Sabbath." As the Judge, He declared that what the disciples had done was right and acceptable on His Sabbath day.

Like the sacrifices in the temple, the Sabbath was supposed to point people to the Savior. Going through the motions of the sacrifice without understanding their meaning offended God. In the same way, going through the motions of keeping the Sabbath without understanding its purpose or knowing its Lord offends Him as well.

JESUS HEALS TO TEACH A LESSON

On another Sabbath, Jesus was in a synagogue when a man with a crippled hand entered. The Pharisees watched to see what He would do. They wanted to trap Him, to prove that He was a lawbreaker. "Is it lawful to heal someone on the Sabbath?" they asked.

Jesus didn't even hesitate. He told the man to stand with Him in front of everyone, then asked, " 'Which is lawful on the Sabbath day: to do good or to do evil, to save a life or to kill?' " (Mark 3:4).

There was a saying among the Jews that failing to do good when you had the opportunity was the same as doing evil, that neglecting to save someone's life was the same as killing that person. So they knew exactly what Jesus was asking. But they didn't answer His question.

So Jesus asked, "If a sheep belonging to one of you fell into a pit on Sabbath, wouldn't you go down and lift it out? Isn't a person more valuable than a sheep? It is always lawful to do good for someone on the Sabbath."

The spies didn't dare answer any of His questions. They recognized the truth when they heard it. Jesus was right—to keep their rules and traditions, they would let a person suffer on Sabbath even when they would help an animal. Like all false religions, this kind of thinking starts with the human desire to be greater than God and ends with humans valued less than animals. Only the gospel teaches humans to care for the needs of others. It places a high value on human beings, for only they have been paid for by the blood of Jesus.

Finally, with anger and great sadness at their stubbornness, Jesus said to the crippled man, "Stretch out your hand." As the man stretched it out, his hand was healed.

The Pharisees continued to plan to have Jesus killed. What a difference they showed between themselves and Jesus—while they spent Sabbath plotting to kill, He spent it healing the sick and injured.

By healing the man's crippled hand, Jesus honored the fourth commandment and swept aside the pointless rules that the Jews had invented. Those who claim that Jesus abolished the Sabbath law when He died on the cross are making the same mistake the Jewish leaders did. They fail to see that by His death, He honored the Sabbath law by upholding the Ten Commandments of which it is a part. In both His life and death, Jesus restored the Sabbath to what God had intended.

It is always lawful to do good for someone on the Sabbath.

The Sabbath was made to be a blessing to all who take advantage of its hours to spend time with their Savior. It will be a time of joy for those who see it as a symbol of Jesus' power to create us, save us, and make us holy. Because they see Jesus in it, they find the Sabbath to be delightful. In the peace of the Sabbath they can see back to what Eden was, and forward to what heaven will be.

Because the Sabbath was made for people, it is God's day. Since Jesus created all things, He created the Sabbath and made it a reminder of creation. It points to Jesus both as our Creator and our Savior.

CHAPTER 30

MESSENGERS TO THE WORLD

"The next morning, Jesus called his followers to him and chose twelve of them, whom he named apostles" (Luke 6:13).

t was time to take the first step in organizing the church that would carry Jesus' message to the world after His mission on earth was finished. There was no expensive church or temple to gather His most faithful followers in, but Jesus took them to a place He loved—a mountainside not far from the Sea of Galilee.

Whenever He taught His disciples, Jesus left the hustle and hurry of the city and took them to the peaceful quiet of the fields and hills. Even when He was teaching and preaching to large crowds of people, Jesus loved to gather them under the blue sky on a grassy hillside or on the beach by the lake. With the beauty of nature around them, people were more open to the truths of God's kingdom.

When Jesus called His twelve apostles to meet with Him, He knew their weaknesses; He knew the pride, the anger, the misunderstandings they carried in their hearts. As they slept the evening before, Jesus spent the whole night praying for them. Then when the sun rose, He called them together.

This chapter is based on Mark 3:13-19; Luke 6:12-16.

"You will be my apostles, my messengers to the world," He said to the twelve men. He wanted them to travel with Him, to watch Him and learn from Him, then to go out and tell the world everything they had seen and heard. Their position—apostles—was the most important any human had ever held. It was second only to the position of Jesus Himself. They were to work with God to save humankind.

It is in John's writing that Jesus' love is revealed most clearly.

Of the Twelve, James, John, Peter, Andrew, Philip, Nathanael, and Matthew actually worked more closely with Jesus than the others. And Peter, James, and John spent the most time with Him. They witnessed all of His miracles and were there to hear everything that He taught.

Although Jesus loved them all, He was closest to John. John was younger than the other apostles and his youthful trust led him to understand and accept Jesus' real mission. He opened his heart to Jesus and understood the deep, spiritual, life-changing power of the gospel. It is in John's writing that Jesus' love and message are revealed most clearly.

Although Philip was the first one to whom Jesus said, "Follow Me," he was slow to believe that Jesus was really the Messiah. Even though he had heard John the Baptist announce that Jesus was the Lamb of God, and the voice from heaven had identified Jesus as the Son of God, Philip told Nathanael about "Jesus from Nazareth, the Son of Joseph."

Later, Philip doubted whether there was any way that 5,000 hungry people could be fed. Even when he had seen Jesus do many miracles, Philip doubted His power. Even up to the last hours before Jesus died, Philip showed doubt. Instead of accepting Jesus' words that in knowing Him they could know the Father, Philip asked that Jesus show them His Father. Jesus must have shaken His head when He said, " 'I have been with you a long time now. Do you still not know me, Philip?' " (John 14:9).

But Philip was a student in Jesus' school, and Jesus taught him with great patience. When the Holy Spirit was poured out on the apostles, Philip became a great evangelist, teaching many people about the Savior.

JUDAS THE APOSTLE

While Jesus was preparing His disciples for their work as apostles, one whom He had never called pushed himself forward to join that small group. Judas wanted to be in the inner circle of Jesus' friends, because he wanted a powerful position when Jesus threw out the Romans and set up His new kingdom.

Judas was intelligent and decisive. His personal charm and appearance led the other disciples to recommend to Jesus that Judas would be a real benefit to His work. If Jesus had turned Judas away, the others would have seriously doubted His wisdom. Of course, Judas's story shows the danger of using worldly standards to measure a person's readiness to work for God.

Judas was accepted in the group. He witnessed Jesus' unselfish love every day and felt the call to surrender his heart to the Savior. Although Jesus could read the selfishness in Judas's heart and see what, unless converted, it would lead him to do, He would never have sent Judas away while there was even the smallest chance to save him.

Judas had the same opportunities as the other disciples. But living God's way conflicted with his plans and desires. He would not surrender his will to God. With great tenderness, Jesus reached out to Judas day after day, even though He knew that Judas would betray Him. While protecting his privacy, Jesus showed Judas over and over that He could read his heart. He warned him about the dangers of greed and selfishness, but Judas would not let go of his selfish ways. He held on to his evil desires, his longing for revenge, and his dark thoughts until Satan completely controlled him.

If Judas had given his heart to Jesus, he might have been one of the leaders of the apostles and of the new church they would create. But his selfish ambition to have power disqualified him to do God's work.

BEING WILLING TO CHANGE

God takes people as they are and trains them to do His work, if they are willing to learn, surrender, and change. The more they learn about Jesus, the more they become like Him.

All of the disciples had faults when Jesus called them. James and John were called the sons of thunder because of their reputation for having violent tempers. From this background, John watched how Jesus treated people, and listened to His words about love and patience. He opened his heart to Jesus and was changed forever. Jesus corrected His disciples many times, but John and the others didn't leave. They shared Jesus' troubles and learned His lessons until the end. As they watched Jesus, their lives changed.

> *Judas was accepted in the group. He witnessed Jesus' unselfish love every day.*

The apostles were all very different people: Matthew, the tax collector; Simon the angry fanatic; impulsive Peter; mean-spirited Judas; Thomas—faithful, but frightened and shy; doubtful Philip, the outspoken, sometimes violent James and John, along with all the others. Mixed together, with the usual human tendencies to selfishness and evil, they should have exploded against each other. But they had Jesus in common and so they shared love and faith in Him.

In the years after Jesus was gone, they had differences of opinion, but with Jesus in their hearts they did not argue and fight. The closer they were to Jesus, the closer they were to each other, and the more they agreed.

Early that morning, after instructing them, Jesus gathered that small group close to Him. He knelt with them and placed His hands on their heads as He prayed and dedicated each one of them to His holy mission.

OUR WORK IN OUR WORLD

Jesus didn't choose angels to lead out in the work to reach fallen, sinful humans. He chose people who understood the struggle to surrender, people who showed in their lives what He had done in their hearts. As Jesus showed by becoming human, both the human and the divine are needed to bring salvation to our world. The human followers of Jesus must have His divine power in their hearts to bring His gospel to others.

The same One who called fishermen from Galilee is calling people to do His work today. However imperfect and sinful we are, Jesus offers to teach us and train us to become like Him. Connected to Him, we can do the works of God.

All around us are people who are filled with doubt, who don't have enough faith to understand and believe in Someone they cannot see. But we can be there for them. Each of us can be someone whose love they can see. We can connect their weak faith to Jesus.

> *The same One who called fishermen from Galilee is calling people to do His work today.*

God communicates to humans through humans. That is one reason Jesus became a human. With our lives surrendered to Him, angels can speak through our voices to share God's love.

CHAPTER 31

THE SERMON
BY THE SEA

*" 'Everyone who hears my words and obeys them is like a wise man
who built his house on a rock' " (Matthew 7:24).*

fter He prayed for His chosen apostles, Jesus led
them down to the Sea of Galilee. Even though it
was early morning, a crowd was gathering. Everywhere Jesus went, a crowd followed. Many were there
to hear His words but also there were people begging
to be healed. This morning, as every other morning, Jesus' heart
went out to those who suffered, and He healed every sick or crippled
person.

Before long, the narrow beach by the sea was so crowded that there
wasn't room for everyone, even with all of them standing. So Jesus led
them back toward the mountainside. There He found a nice level place
and sat down on the green grass. His disciples sat close around Him
while the crowd found places to watch and listen as well.

This sermon by the sea was especially for the newly chosen apostles,
to help correct their mistaken beliefs and understand what the kingdom of heaven was really like. They were eager to understand the
truths they were now to share with all people everywhere. But Jesus
rarely spoke to the disciples alone. He took every opportunity to encourage and educate everyone who would listen.

This chapter is based on Matt. 5; 6 ; 7.

The disciples were certain that Jesus was about to announce His kingdom—that He was ready to drive out the Romans and lead Israel to victory and freedom. The people in the crowd had the same expectations. They sat on the green hillside filled with dreams of national glory. The poor farmers and fishermen hoped to trade in their broken-down homes and simple food for mansions and feasts. Even the Pharisees and rabbis who were there to spy dreamed of the day when they would rule over the Romans and enjoy the riches of the world's greatest empire.

A DIFFERENT KINGDOM

But Jesus had a different agenda. He had come to promise them a different kingdom. He didn't explain what was wrong with their ideas about the Messiah and the kingdom of heaven. He simply explained what kind of people would be welcomed there and let them conclude what kind of kingdom that must be.

Jesus began by saying, " 'Those people who know they have great spiritual needs are happy, because the kingdom of heaven belongs to them' " (Matthew 5:3). Only the humble-hearted can accept the gift of salvation and nothing will keep God from reaching the person who feels a need and asks for help. The kingdom of heaven can belong to us if we recognize that Jesus paid the price and that He gives us the strength and will to follow His way. But God can do nothing to save a person until he or she surrenders to Him.

Then Jesus said, " 'Those who are sad now are happy, because God will comfort them' " (Matthew 5:4). He wasn't talking about depression or unhappiness over the results of making sinful choices. He was talking about the real pain believers feel when they realize that those sinful decisions put Jesus on the cross. It's the sadness we feel when the Holy Spirit causes us to understand that every time we choose not to follow His way, we wound Him. This kind of sadness is what leads people to turn away from sin and selfishness.

Jesus offers comfort here also for those who are sad because of pain, suffering, or loss. Through suffering, God shows us the weaknesses in our characters and offers His power to change. He is with us in these difficult times, and promises that something good can come from them. We don't need to lose our hold on Jesus because of anger or worry when troubles come. The way may seem dark and sad, but through it God is leading us to eternal joy.

Jesus said, " 'Those who are humble are happy, because the earth will belong to them' " (Matthew 5:5). If we have humility as Jesus did, we can overlook people's critical remarks or annoying habits. When we deal with other people's anger or meanness calmly, we allow God to show Himself through us. Even though others may scoff, true humility means knowing who you are—a child of God—and how important and valuable that makes you. Humility is the key to a successful Christian life.

> *If we have humility like Jesus did, we can overlook people's critical remarks or annoying habits.*

Next Jesus said, " 'Those who want to do right more than anything else are happy, because God will fully satisfy them' " (Matthew 5:6). Those who want more than anything to reflect the character of God will be able to do so. Learning to love will expand their hearts and minds, allowing them to understand more about God, love more like God, and become more like God.

Jesus said, " 'Those who show mercy to others are happy, because God will show mercy to them. Those who are pure in their thinking are happy, because they will be with God' " (Matthew 5:7, 8). Impure thoughts cloud our understanding of spiritual things. It is another form of selfishness, which always keeps us away from God. God forgives those who repent, but the soul is damaged. Until we stop putting self first, we can never understand God's love.

Jesus knew that in a sinful world, there would always be conflicts and wars. He said, " 'Those who work to bring peace are happy, because God will call them his children' " (Matthew 5:9). Human plans for peace will ultimately fail because they don't reach the heart. The only real power for true peace in this world or in our hearts is Jesus.

THE CROWD IS AMAZED

These words about true happiness amazed the crowd. They had believed that happiness came from being rich or famous or powerful. Jesus claimed that earthly honor was all such people would get. True happiness comes from following God. The rewards will come in heaven.

Then Jesus added some words just for His disciples and those who would follow them. " 'Those who are treated badly for doing good are happy, because the kingdom of heaven belongs to them' " (Matthew 5:10).

He knew they would be insulted, persecuted, imprisoned, tortured, and killed. Like God's messengers, the prophets, in times gone by, they would be rejected because bringing God's truth to the world exposes sin. They might suffer in the war against sin and Satan, but they would be cheerful, knowing that their reward was eternal life in heaven.

"You are like salt and light in this world," Jesus told them. In order to change the world, they would have to be a part of it—just as salt changes flavor by mixing with food. Without the presence of people who love and serve God, this world would destroy itself. Even the lives of evil people are blessed because of God's followers. But those who say they are Christians and don't act like Jesus are like salt that is no longer salty. They give God a bad name. And like sunshine, salvation belongs to the whole world. The truth about God shouldn't be trapped inside the pages of a book or inside the walls of a church—it belongs to everyone. Unwavering honesty, a giving spirit, a good example—these are all ways we spread light to the world around us.

As long as the sun is shining and the earth is solid beneath our feet, God's law will not change.

Jesus knew that Pharisee spies were there. Nothing He said conflicted with the Old Testament laws. He Himself had given those laws and He wouldn't speak against His own instructions.

But to the Pharisees, Jesus' words sounded like heresy—false teachings. He read their thoughts and said, " 'Don't think that I have come to destroy the law of Moses or the teachings of the prophets. I have not come to destroy them but to bring about what they said' " (Matthew 5:17). His mission was to strengthen and live by God's laws. If they could be changed, there would have been no need for His sacrifice. He came to explain those laws and teachings and to show their true meaning by His life.

FOLLOWING THE LAW PROTECTS US

God loves humankind, and that is why He gave us the law—the Ten Commandments. When we follow these laws, we are protected from the results of doing sinful things. The same Ten Commandments show us the holiness of God's character in contrast to our own sinfulness. When we see that, we accept Jesus and obey the law, we find true happpiness.

As long as the sun is shining and the earth is solid beneath our feet, God's law will not change. The ceremonial laws that pointed to the coming Messiah were abolished when Jesus died, but the Ten Commandments are as permanent as the throne of God.

Jesus' life proved that humans can keep God's law. Those who break God's commandments support Satan's claim that the law cannot be obeyed. To allow them into heaven would just bring rebellion and war to the universe again. No one who disregards even one of God's laws is safe to save.

The greatest error humans accepted in Jesus' day was that simply agreeing to truth made a person righteous or holy. Just knowing about truth does not change a person's life. History shows that those who claimed to know the most about God often were the cruelest and most evil. The beliefs of Pharisees—experts on religious teachings—led them to kill the Messiah. Anyone who claims to believe in the truth, but is not honest, kind, and patient is a curse to the world around them.

JESUS' PERFECT LIFE

Next, Jesus showed that the Ten Commandments reach deeper than just our actions. Because holding hate in your heart puts you on a path to kill, hating someone breaks the commandment against murder. It is not sinful for a Christian to be angry when God's name is disrespected or innocent people are repressed. But you can't be angry over every little thing and be in harmony with heaven.

God's dream for what His children can be is greater than we can even imagine. " 'So you must be perfect,' " Jesus said, " 'just as your Father in heaven is perfect' " (Matthew 5:48). This command is a promise. God's plan to save goes beyond just saving our lives—He plans to remake us to be like Him.

Being tempted is not an excuse for sinning. Every believing child of God can resist sin as Jesus did. Jesus is the ladder that Jacob saw in His dream connecting earth to heaven. He reaches us where we are. He took our nature and overcame sin so we can take His nature and also overcome. By faith in Him, we can be perfect like our Father in heaven.

Jesus also spoke about practical christianity. "Don't do good deeds or give to the needy just to impress others. Do these things secretly and only to help those who suffer. When you pray, talk to God, not to the people around who can hear you. When you go without food, do it privately."

God sees what is done secretly and He will reward us openly. The atmosphere of heaven surrounds people who live that kind of life— living as Jesus did—walking and working with God. For them, God's kingdom has already begun.

"No one can serve two masters," Jesus said. Worldly human plans and the values of Jesus' kingdom do not blend together like the colors of a rainbow. God draws a clear line between them. We can't find a compromise between them. We must choose whom we will serve.

Each person who chooses to serve God can be sure that He is watching over him or her. As Jesus spoke to His disciples and the crowd, He pointed to the birds flying past in the sky. "They don't plant or harvest food, but your Father in heaven feeds them. And you know that you are worth much more than birds."

God cares enough to paint the grass green, and the flowers in bright colors though they live only a short while. He must care so much more for humans who were created in His own image! In God's book of life, we each have a page that holds everything about our lives. We are never out of His thoughts.

So Jesus said, "Don't worry about tomorrow." God doesn't tell us everything we will need to know for our whole life's journey. He tells us just what we need to know for now. Strength and wisdom will be given when we need them.

God's plan to save goes beyond just saving our lives—He plans to remake us to be like Him.

Jesus added this warning. " 'Don't judge other people, or you will be judged' " (Matthew 7:1). Since we cannot know what is driving a person from the inside, what the reasons are for his or her behavior, we aren't capable of judging fairly. When we criticize another person, we are only passing sentence on ourselves.

A good tree bears good fruit. Good deeds—right actions and decisions—are the fruit of a life surrendered to Jesus. Our good deeds don't buy our salvation, but they are proof of the faith that is in our hearts.

With this sermon, Jesus explained the principles of His kingdom. He finished with a story: " 'Everyone who hears my words and obeys them is like a wise man who built his house on a rock' " (Matthew 7:24). When the wind and floods came, the house stood strong. Those who refuse to listen are like a foolish man who built his house on sand. When trouble comes, his house collapses. We must build our lives on the principles Jesus gave, not on selfishness or human theories.

CHAPTER 32

A SERVANT IS HEALED, A DEAD MAN COMES TO LIFE

"Then Jesus said to the officer, 'Go home. Your servant will be healed just as you believed he would'" (Matthew 8:13).

I n his years living among the Jews, a Roman army officer in Capernaum became convinced that there was truth in their religion. He gave up on the hate and prejudice that most Romans felt toward the people they had conquered. He became friends with his neighbors and supported their religion in the city.

Although the officer had never met Jesus, when he heard of His teachings, his whole heart responded. This was the truth about God that he had searched for. He believed that Jesus was Messiah. This officer had a desperate, personal request to make of Jesus, and he believed that Jesus had the power to answer it. But he was in such awe of Jesus that he didn't feel he should speak to Him in person.

The officer had a servant who was sick—in fact, nearly dead. For most Romans, the household servants were slaves who were bought and sold, and often cruelly abused. But this man had grown to love his servant, and couldn't bear to think of him dying. He was convinced by the stories he had heard that Jesus could heal his servant.

The officer begged the Jewish elders to ask Jesus for this miracle.

This chapter is based on Matt. 8:5-13; Luke 7:1-17.

He thought that since they knew this great Teacher, they would know best how to ask Him.

So as Jesus walked into Capernaum that day, the elders met Him. "Heal this man's servant," they asked. "He loves the Jewish people. He even donated enough money to build our synagogue. He deserves this favor."

Jesus began walking toward the officer's house, but with the crowd surrounding Him, He moved very slowly. When the officer heard what was happening, he sent a message: "Lord, I'm not worthy for You to enter my house." But Jesus kept going.

Jesus was amazed. "I have not seen this much faith anywhere— even in Israel."

Finally, the officer came out and met Jesus on the street. "You only have to command it, and my servant will be healed," he told Jesus. "I represent the power of Rome and my soldiers know it. When I tell them to do something, they do it. You represent the power of God. All created things know it and obey You. You can command the sickness to leave and it will obey. Just say the words, and I know my servant will be healed."

Jesus was amazed. "I have not seen this much faith anywhere— even in Israel," He exclaimed to the crowd. Then He turned to the officer and said, "Go home. Your servant is healed, just as you believed he would be."

The self-righteous Jews thought the officer deserved a favor for what he had done for them. The officer felt that he was not worthy to even ask for a favor. He didn't feel that he had earned this miracle— by faith, he trusted in Jesus.

When Satan tells you that you are a sinner and deserve nothing, tell him that Jesus came to the world to save sinners. We cannot save ourselves so our helpless situation means that we must trust Him to save us.

The Jewish leaders didn't think Jesus had anything to offer them. But this army officer—taught only about idols in Rome and surrounded by sometimes-hateful Jews—saw the truth that Jesus taught and lived. To Jesus, he was among the first of many from other nations who would recognize the truth and follow the Savior.

A DEAD MAN COMES TO LIFE

Jesus traveled next to the village of Nain, about a day's walk from Capernaum. All along the way, people brought the sick and injured to be healed. Then they followed along, hoping to hear Jesus announce His claim to be King of Israel.

As they neared the gates of the mountain village, a funeral procession was headed out toward the graveyard. With wailing cries, mourners followed along to show their sympathy. As was the custom of the time, the body of the dead man was being carried on a pallet at the front of the procession. The weeping mother staggered blindly behind, a widow who was burying her only son, her sole source of support, her last hope.

When Jesus saw the woman, He felt compassion for her. He walked up next to her and gently said, "Don't cry." Then He reached over and touched the pallet where the dead man was lying.

The men carrying the pallet froze in place. With a gasp, the crowd and the mourners pressed closer and everyone seemed to hold

The same Jesus who stood beside that grieving mother feels our pain when we lose a loved one.

their breath with hope. Was it possible? They had seen this Man command demons—could He also command death?

In a quiet voice that rang with power, a voice that even dead ears could hear, Jesus said, "Young man, I tell you, get up!"

The young man opened his eyes and blinked. Jesus took his hand and lifted him up—and into the embrace of his mother. For a moment, the young man's questions and his mother's tearful prayer of thanks were the only sounds as the crowd watched in astounded silence. They felt as if they were in the presence of God.

Finally, the crowd erupted to join the mother in praising God. "A great prophet has come to us," they said. "God has come to help His people." The funeral procession returned to Nain as a parade of joy.

The same Jesus who stood beside that grieving mother feels our pain when we lose a loved one. His words today have just as much power as they did when He spoke to the young man outside Nain. His power will someday raise the ones we have lost to death and lead them back to our arms and hearts.

In the same way, His words will save us from spiritual death. Satan cannot hold us as prisoners in sin if we have faith in Jesus' words of life. When He tells us to get up and leave our sinful lives, He gives us the power to do it.

Even though Jesus raised that young man to life, he would still suffer the pain and sorrow of life and eventually die again. But when He raises us all again in the resurrection, it will be to a joy-filled life with Him and love that never ends.

CHAPTER 33

FAMILY
PROBLEMS

*"My true brother and sister and mother are those who do what my
Father in heaven wants" (Matthew 12:50).*

esus' family and friends were worried about Him. They
heard that He stayed up all night praying, then spent all
day in the crush of crowds, teaching and healing without
even taking time to eat. They thought He was wearing Himself out. And since they didn't understand His attitude toward
the Pharisees and leaders, they were afraid that Jesus might have become mentally unbalanced.

Jesus' brothers—the sons of Joseph—did not support His mission.
They had never understood Him. Now they were angry because they
were being blamed for some of the things He said against the Pharisees.
They decided to go and convince Jesus to stop that kind of talk and the
kind of work that made the Pharisees angry. They persuaded Mary to
go with them. Hoping that His love for His mother might be enough to
make Him stop, they headed to the place where Jesus was teaching.

USING THE DEVIL TO DRIVE OUT DEVILS

One of the things that stirred up the brothers was the Pharisees'
claim that Jesus was using the power of Satan to drive demons out of

This chapter is based on Matt. 12:22-50; Mark 3:20-35.

people. Now, the Pharisees didn't really believe this. They had felt the stirring of the Holy Spirit in their own hearts when Jesus shared His teachings about God. When they stood in His presence, they could feel His holiness and their lack of it.

After announcing their rejection of His claim to be the Messiah, it would be too humiliating to admit that they were wrong. Instead, they argued with everything He taught. Since they couldn't prevent His miracles, they did everything in their power to make Him look bad. Still, the Holy Spirit—the strongest force known to the human heart—worked to draw them to the truth.

When the Pharisees claimed that the work of the Holy Spirit in driving out demons was actually the work of the devil, they were walking on dangerous ground. Jesus warned that they were close to committing an "unforgivable sin." Every sin can be forgiven, but it is the Holy Spirit that touches our hearts and leads us to want forgiveness. When the Pharisees rejected the Holy Spirit's work they were cutting off the channel that God could use to touch their hearts.

God doesn't blind people's eyes or turn their hearts against Him. He sends them light, or truth, to show them the true way. Each time a human rejects this light, they are blinded just a little, and the next ray of light is easier to reject. It's the slippery slope that leads a person away from God. The Jewish leaders were becoming more and more controlled by Satan.

> *When they stood in His presence, they could feel His holiness and their lack of it.*

Jesus also warned against using careless and evil words. Sometimes—with Satan's influence— we say things we don't really believe. Yet, when we hear the words, they seem more reasonable, more believable. Like the Jewish leaders, we may be too proud to admit that we were wrong and find ourselves trapped in sin. This is why it can be so dangerous to carelessly criticize the truth of God. From there it can be a short path to criticizing and rejecting the Holy Spirit, the power that draws us to God.

Jesus added a warning to those who had been freed from a demon. If they did not fill their hearts with God's love, that demon and others might return to possess them again. The same thing can happen to us today. If we find freedom from Satan by accepting God's love, but do not surrender ourselves daily to His will, we may find ourselves controlled by Satan again.

Our only defense against evil is Jesus living in our hearts. We might have the will power to stop bad habits for a short time, but without a real connection to God, we cannot resist selfishness and temptation. In the end, Satan will claim us as his own.

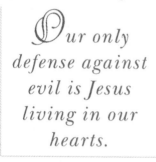

Our only defense against evil is Jesus living in our hearts.

By rejecting Jesus, the Jewish people committed an unforgivable sin. By refusing to accept Jesus and His truth, we could be making the same mistake. We dishonor Jesus before the whole universe when we refuse to listen to His messengers and listen to Satan's agents instead. If we keep doing this, we can't hope to be forgiven. Eventually, we will completely lose interest in God.

JESUS' REAL FAMILY

While Jesus was teaching, His disciples brought Him a message—His mother and brothers were outside and they wanted to see Him. But Jesus didn't go out to see them. Instead He asked, "Who is My mother and who are My brothers?" He pointed to His disciples. "Here is My family. Whoever does as My Father wishes is a brother, a sister, and a mother to Me."

When people accept Jesus by faith, that relationship is closer than if they were related to Him by family ties. Mary was more closely related to Jesus by her faith in His mission than she was by being His mother.

Of all the rejection Jesus felt from humans, the most painful was the rejection in His own home. His brothers didn't understand Him or His mission. They thought they could teach Jesus about God, not realizing that Jesus was God. They wanted Him to stop disagreeing with the Pharisees, and to stop claiming that God had given Him the right to do and say what He did. To them, it sounded crazy. They knew the Pharisees were looking for reasons to have Jesus arrested and killed—and it didn't surprise them.

Instead of a family that protected and comforted Him, Jesus had a family that criticized and hurt Him. It was so painful that often He was glad to be somewhere else. He loved visiting the home of Lazarus, Mary, and Martha. The atmosphere of faith and love there made it a place where He felt comfortable. But many times He could find true rest only when He was alone communicating with His Father.

Those who suffer through criticism and anger in their homes because of their faith can find comfort in the thought that Jesus faced the same thing. They can know that they don't face their pain alone; they are not orphans. Jesus invites them to call His Father their Father. He loves them more than any human parent could love a child.

In the Jewish society, if a person had to sell himself or herself as a servant to pay their debts, their closest relative could save them by buying back their freedom. To save us, Jesus became our closest Relative—closer than any father, mother, brother, sister, or lover. We can't understand His kind of love but we can know that it is real, and we can reveal it by loving others.

CHAPTER 34

"THE LOAD I GIVE YOU IS LIGHT"

" 'Come to me, all of you who are tired and have heavy loads, and I will give you rest' " (Matthew 11:28).

hen Jesus looked out at the hard-working people of Galilee, He longed to take away their pain and worry. He said, " 'Come to me, all of you who are tired and have heavy loads, and I will give you rest' " (Matthew 11:28). He saw that they were worn out by the cares of life. They were trying to fill their hopeless hearts with the pleasures and promises of everyday life. He offered them something more.

Jesus said, " 'Accept my teachings and learn from me, because I am gentle and humble in spirit, and you will find rest for your lives' " (Matthew 11:29). What was missing from their hearts and lives was God—an understanding of His love and His plan for them.

Jesus spoke those words for all human beings. Whether they admit it or not, all humans are carrying heavy burdens that only Jesus can take from them. The heaviest burden is the weight—the guilt—of sin. This weight alone would crush us if we were left to carry it. But Jesus—the Sinless One—came to carry the guilt of our sins and the burden of our worries and sorrows.

This chapter is based on Matt. 11:28-30.

Jesus stands now by the throne of the universe, but He still identifies with humans. He knows by experience our weaknesses, our desires, and the power of the temptations we face. He faced all the same temptations we do—but He won each battle. He never sinned. Today He offers His victory to us.

Whatever human weakness we find in ourselves, we can turn to Jesus for help. Whatever trial or problem we face, we can turn to Him and He will give us the strength to face it, the wisdom to accept it, and the endurance to get through it.

The heaviest burden is the weight—the guilt—of sin.

Jesus asks only one thing of us—to follow His way. He said, " 'The teaching that I ask you to accept is easy; the load I give you to carry is light' " (Matthew 11:30). He wants us to live by the law that He offers to write on our hearts. When we follow His way, we follow His will—that is, we live by what Jesus would do, rather than the sinful way we would choose for ourselves.

This is the way Jesus lived while He was on earth. He said, "I came from heaven to follow My Father's plan, not My own." In the same way, we can follow Jesus' way instead of our own.

WHAT CAUSES US STRESS AND PAIN

People create much of their own stress and unhappiness when they try to live by the rules and customs of the world around them. Pursuing possessions and power, they wound their own hearts and add regrets to the burdens they carry. But God wants us to give up our worries and burdens and trust Him. If we put honoring and serving God first in our lives, we will find that our heavenly Father has a thousand ways to care for us that we know nothing about!

When Jesus said, "Take my teachings and learn from me," He offered us a place in His school that will train us for heaven. It will free us from the wrong ideas, bad habits, or poor behavior that we have learned from Satan's school of death.

Jesus' heart was always at peace. He was not excited by praise or depressed by criticism. He kept His courage even in the face of danger or rejection. But many who follow Him are worried and anxious because they are afraid to trust God. God's peace can come only with complete surrender. The troubles of this world cannot destroy us when Jesus is with us.

When we are reborn, our minds will be like Jesus' mind. We won't be searching for glory or honor. We will want only to learn from Jesus. We will understand that the value of our efforts depends on the blessings of the Holy Spirit, not on us. When we surrender our will to Jesus, He shares our burdens—He takes our stresses and worries. Then we will have His peace. Nothing in this world can hold us down in depression when Jesus is in our hearts.

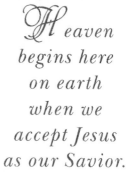

Heaven begins here on earth when we accept Jesus as our Savior.

Our lives may seem like a tangled mess at times, but when we surrender them to Jesus, He will weave the strands of experience into a pattern that shows His glory. Lives that reflect the glory and the character of Jesus will be at home in heaven. In fact, heaven begins here on earth when we accept Jesus as our Savior. As we learn to follow Him, to be like Him, we begin to experience the joy of eternal life. The more we know about God, the happier our lives will be. As we walk with Jesus here, we can feel His love. Heaven begins as we feel His presence here.

CHAPTER 35

THE STORM
ON THE SEA

"Why are you afraid? Do you still have no faith?"
(Mark 4:40).

It was the end of a long day of teaching and healing by the Sea of Galilee and Jesus was exhausted. For days He had ministered to the people, sharing His first parables, explaining His kingdom and how to be a part of it. Evening had come, but still the crowds didn't want to leave.

Jesus needed rest. After dismissing the people, He asked His disciples to take Him to a quiet, hidden place on the other side of the lake. They quickly pushed their boat away from shore and headed out into the lake, because already people were filling other boats to follow them.

As soon as the ship sailed, Jesus lay down in the back of the boat and fell asleep. What began as a calm, pleasant evening quickly turned into a stormy night. The wind suddenly began to howl, driving the little boat into wild waves that grew larger and stronger by the minute. Soon they were washing over the boat, filling it faster than it could be bailed out. The other boats that had chased them from the shore were caught in the same storm.

The disciples were experienced fishermen. They had guided their boats through many rough storms on this lake. But all their strength

This chapter is based on Matt. 8:23-34; Mark 4:35-41; 5:1-20; Luke 8:22-39.

and experience made no difference in the face of this angry storm. Their boat seemed about to sink and they were helpless to stop it.

Working so hard to save the boat and their lives, the disciples had forgotten that Jesus was on board. Now, certain that they were going to die, they remembered. Jesus was their only hope. "Master, Master," they shouted from where they held on for dear life. But the wind drowned out their voices and there was no response.

Now their doubts and fears got stronger. Was Jesus unable to help them? Did He not care enough to bother saving them? Again they called out to Him, but the only answer was the shrieking wind. With no hope, they stared into the black water that would soon be their grave.

Suddenly, a flash of lightning cut through the darkness, and to their astonishment, there was Jesus, still sleeping, undisturbed by the storm. "Master," they cried, "don't You care that we're all going to drown?"

This time Jesus heard them and opened His eyes. In the glare of the lightning, they saw peace on His face and love for them in His eyes. They shouted again, "Lord, save us! We're going to die!"

No one has ever cried out those words without being heard. While the disciples grabbed their oars for one last attempt to pull the boat out of the storm, Jesus rose to His feet. As the wind and waves tore at His robes, Jesus lifted His hands. "Quiet!" He said to the wind. "Be still!" He said to the waves.

Instantly, the wind stopped, the waves sank, and the clouds dissipated. The boat bobbed on quiet waters under a sky full of stars. As the disciples stared, Jesus asked, "Why were you afraid? Don't you have faith?"

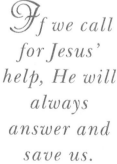

If we call for Jesus' help, He will always answer and save us.

The disciples were speechless. But the storm had brought the other boats near, and everyone witnessed the miracle. On those boats, people whispered, "What kind of man is this? Even the wind and the waves obey Him!"

When Jesus woke up to the fierce storm, He wasn't afraid. It wasn't because of His own power over nature—He had given up that power to come to earth. It was because He trusted His Father. Jesus had faith in His Father's love and it was His Father's power that quieted the storm.

The disciples could have had the same trust and the same peace in the face of the storm. But they forgot about Jesus and tried to handle the storm on their own. Only when they cried out to Him could He help.

Often we do the same thing when we face the storms of temptation. We try to battle the temptation alone, trusting our own strength of will until the attraction of sin is ready to sweep us away. But if we call for Jesus' help, He will always answer and save us.

Because of sin, the human heart is filled with passions that we cannot control. We are as helpless here as the disciples were on the lake. But no matter how strong those feelings are, those who cry out, "Lord, save me!" will be rescued. His grace will give us peace; His love will give us hope.

WILD MEN OF GERGESA

As the sun rose, Jesus and His companions came to shore on the other side of the lake. But instead of finding peace and quiet in the early morning light, they found something that seemed even more terrible than the storm.

Two wild men rushed out of the shadows, broken chains hanging from their arms and legs, their skin torn and bleeding. With wild eyes glaring out from under long, matted hair, they seemed more like animals than humans. Possessed by demons, they rushed at the group as if planning to tear them to pieces.

The disciples ran down the beach terrified. Eventually, they turned to look for Jesus and found that He still stood where they had left Him. When the wild men—screaming and foaming at the mouth—rushed at Him, He held up the same hand that had quieted the waves in the storm and they could not come nearer.

As Jesus commanded the demons to leave, His words reached through the darkness to the minds of these poor men. In some dim way, they realized that this Person could save them from the demons. But when they opened their mouths to beg for help, the demons spoke instead. "What do you want from me, Jesus, Son of the Most High God? I beg you not to torture me!"

"What is your name?" Jesus asked.

"My name is Legion," the demon answered, "because we are many spirits." Not far away on the mountainside was a great herd of pigs. The demons begged Jesus to let them enter the pigs. So Jesus allowed them to do it. Immediately the whole herd rushed off a cliff into the lake and drowned.

Meanwhile, a wondrous change had come over the wild men. They were once more in possession of their own minds, and the first thing they did was praise God.

Now the pig-herders saw everything that had happened and they rushed back to tell the owners and everyone else they met. In fear and amazement, the people of Gergesa rushed to meet Jesus. Those wild men had terrorized the whole countryside. Now here they were—clothed and in their right minds, listening to Jesus and praising Him for their healing.

But the local people weren't happy. In their minds, the lost pigs had more value than the men who had been freed from Satan. The owners of the pigs were more concerned about earthly profits than spiritual truths. Jesus wanted to break the spell of their selfishness so they could see the salvation He offered. But their financial loss blinded them to the Savior's mercy and grace.

MONEY OVER MIRACLES

All this supernatural power frightened the people of Gergesa. Who knew what other disasters might happen with this Stranger among them? The people who had crossed the lake during the storm shared their story and the miracle they had witnessed. But their story only frightened the local people more. They begged Jesus to go away, and so He did, leaving immediately to sail to the other shore.

The people of Gergesa were so afraid of losing money that they treated Jesus like an uninvited guest, even though they knew He was more powerful than demons. They refused to accept the Gift of heaven. Many today refuse to obey God's Word because it will cost them some profit. They drive the Holy Spirit away to keep from losing money.

The healed men wanted to stay with Jesus. They felt safe with Him near. As Jesus got back into the boat, they begged to go with Him. But

Jesus had work for them to do. He told them to go home and tell what had happened. In spite of their fear and of their difficulty adjusting back to normal life, they were ready to obey.

These two became the first missionaries Jesus sent to Gergesa and the area of Decapolis. They traveled around the whole area, telling everyone about Jesus and His power to save them. They had heard Jesus teach only for a few moments, but their own lives were evidence enough that Jesus was the Messiah. They could tell what they knew about the power and love of Jesus—as everyone can do whose heart has been touched by the grace of God. If we have been following Jesus, we will be able to share with others how He has led our steps and kept His promises.

> *They begged Jesus to go away and so He did, leaving immediately to sail to the other shore.*

Although the people of Gergesa rejected Jesus, He did not reject them. The matter of the drowned pigs got attention as nothing else could have in that region. So there was talk about Jesus. The healed men remained there as evidence of His power, channels of light and truth, as messengers of the Son of God. Through them, the door of truth was opened, and when Jesus returned to the area of Decapolis, thousands were ready to hear His message.

The demon-possessed men of Gergesa, living in a graveyard, wild and disgusting, show what all humans would be like if Satan were in control. Satan is constantly scheming to control the minds of humans and push them to violence and crime. Whenever people reject Jesus, they are giving themselves to Satan. This has caused the violence, crime, and moral decay in today's society. Satan will lead people to worse and worse habits and addictions until they lose their moral conscience completely.

It is clear to all—humans and angels—that Satan is humanity's enemy and destroyer while Jesus is humanity's Friend and Savior. This story gives us hope that even those who have been under Satan's control can be changed into messengers of the gospel as they tell what God has done for them.

CHAPTER 36

THE TOUCH
OF FAITH

"Jesus said to her, 'Dear woman, you are made well because you believed. Go in peace'" (Luke 8:48).

hen Jesus returned to the western shore of the Sea of Galilee, He found a great crowd waiting. He stayed there by the shore for a time, teaching and healing, then went to Matthew's house for a banquet with the tax collectors. While He was there, Jairus, the leader of the local synagogue, rushed in.

"My daughter is dying," Jairus told Jesus. "Please come and touch her with Your hand so she will live."

Jesus left immediately with Jairus. The disciples were surprised that Jesus would agree to help this arrogant rabbi, but they went with Him and a crowd of people followed. In fact, people crowded around Jesus from every direction so that He and His companions could only move slowly down the streets. Even though the worried father was impatient, Jesus stopped now and then to offer healing or comfort to someone in pain.

Among the crowd was a poor woman who had been suffering for twelve years with a condition that caused bleeding. She had spent all her money on doctors and cures, but nothing helped and she was pronounced incurable. She had no hope at all—until she heard about Jesus. She knew if she could only get to Him, she would be healed.

This chapter is based on Matt. 9:18-26; Mark 5:21-43; Luke 8:40-56.

She came to the shore where Jesus was teaching, but being weak and in pain, she couldn't force her way through the crowd. She followed Him to Matthew's banquet, but still couldn't come near Him. She was beginning to give up hope, when suddenly there He was coming toward her through the crowd!

Faith like that couldn't be passed by without notice.

In the crush and confusion, she couldn't speak to Him or even see Him clearly through all the people. Afraid of losing her one chance, she pushed forward saying to herself, "If I can only touch His coat, I know I will be healed."

As Jesus passed by, she stretched out her hand and touched just the edge of His coat with her fingers. All of her faith was focused into that one touch—and instantly, she was healed.

With a heart full of joy and gratitude, she tried to melt away into the crowd. But Jesus suddenly stopped. Looking around at the faces, He asked in a voice that carried over the noise of the street: "Who touched Me?"

It seemed like a strange question. Peter, always ready to speak up, said, "Master, the crowd is bumping and touching us from every side. What do You mean, 'Who touched Me?'"

Jesus could tell the difference between an act of faith and the casual touch of a careless gawker. He said, "I know someone touched Me, because I felt power go out to somebody." Faith like that couldn't be passed by without notice. He wanted to comfort the woman and those who would be inspired by her faith to the end of time.

Seeing that she couldn't hide, the woman came forward trembling. Through grateful tears, she told Jesus the story of her suffering and why she had touched Him. Jesus must have smiled as He said, "Daughter, you were healed because you believed. Go in peace."

While Jesus continued on His way, a messenger pressed through the crowd and told Jairus, "Your daughter is dead. Don't bother the teacher anymore."

Jesus overheard, and said to Jairus, "Don't be afraid—just believe." They pushed on to Jairus's home. Already the usual hired mourners and flute players were wailing. Jesus said, "Don't make such a fuss. Stop crying. The girl isn't dead—she's only asleep."

The mourners were offended by this Stranger. Some even laughed at Him. They had seen that the child was dead. Jesus had them removed from the house. Then He took the father and the mother—and Peter, James, and John—and went into the little girl's room. Stepping to the side of her bed, Jesus took the girl's hand. Softly, in the familiar language of her home, He said, "My child, stand up."

Instantly, the little body trembled. Then her eyes opened wide, as if she had been waked up from a deep sleep, and she stared with amazement at the little group around her bed. She jumped up and into her parents' arms as they cried with joy.

FAITH BRINGS HEALING

With the sick woman in the crowd, Jesus didn't give anyone a chance to claim that His coat had magically healed her. He made it clear that it was her faith connected with His divine power that allowed the healing miracle to happen.

Faith is not merely agreeing that Jesus is real and that He is the Savior of the world. That is not the kind of faith that can bring healing to a heart in need. It is not enough to believe *about* Jesus—we must believe *in* Him. True faith—faith that can heal and save us—is deciding to accept Jesus as our Savior and to begin a life-changing relationship with God.

Jesus wanted the woman to report her healing. The blessings of the gospel are not to be enjoyed in secret—they are to be shared. Our testimony—our story of finding and following Jesus—is the most effective witness we have. Our stories, along with a loving Christian life, have an irresistible power to bring others to Jesus.

When the ten lepers were healed by Jesus, only one came back to thank Him. Many today do the same thing! God heals the sick, saves us from danger, sends angels to guard us, but we act as if we were unaware of His love. This lack of gratitude can close our heart to Him. It strengthens our faith when we keep every gift from God fresh in our memory. Every day, we should think about His loving kindness.

CHAPTER 37

THE FIRST
EVANGELISTS

" 'All people will hate you because you follow me, but those people who keep their faith until the end will be saved' " (Matthew 10:22).

s the disciples walked and talked with Jesus through the land of Galilee, they learned how to reach out to humanity. As Jesus ministered to the crowds, the disciples organized the people to make His work easier. They helped bring the sick and injured to Him, and worked to comfort and help them. They watched closely for those who were truly interested in Jesus' words and explained the Scriptures to them personally. They had much to learn and still needed patience. Now, while He was still available to work with them as they learned, He sent them out.

Jesus called the twelve disciples together and sent them into the towns and villages—two by two, so they could pray and work together. His instructions to them were simple. They weren't going out to argue to convince people that Jesus was the Messiah. They were going out to heal the sick and the lepers, raise the dead, and drive out demons—all in Jesus' name.

The disciples had been confused by the teachings of the priests and Pharisees, but Jesus strengthened their confidence in God's Word. He taught them the difference between truth and tradition. After Jesus

This chapter is based on Matt. 10; Mark 6:7-11; Luke 9:1-6.

went back to heaven, every look on His face, every word from His lips came back to them. They found themselves often repeating His words to those they were trying to reach.

Jesus spent more time healing than He did preaching. His voice was the first sound that many people ever heard; His face the first one that many ever saw. As He traveled through the towns and cities, He was like a live wire, sending jolts of life and joy in every direction.

The evangelistic work that we do would be much more effective if we did the same. We should work as Jesus did—feeding the hungry, comforting those who suffer, and holding out hope to those who have given up. This will be much more effective in changing lives than will preaching or stern treatment.

THE FIRST EVANGELISTIC TRIP

On this first trip, the disciples went only to places where Jesus had already been—places where He was known and loved. They weren't to dress up like the rabbis or priests, but to wear the clothes of the common people. They weren't to call people together in great crowds but to go from home to home and share the truth with the people there.

Their prayers, their songs, and their sharing of the Scriptures would bless every home that welcomed them. But they wouldn't always be welcomed. Jesus said, "I'm sending you out like sheep to a pack of wolves. You must be as wise as snakes and as harmless as doves."

Jesus never held back a truth that needed to be said, but what He spoke was always said with love. He was never rude and never hurt a sensitive person for no reason. He understood human weaknesses. When He condemned two-faced hypocrisy and sin, He did it with tears in His voice. Every person was precious in His eyes. Only a close relationship with God and a true love for all of His children will allow us to do the same.

If we keep our eyes on Jesus, we can present the gospel with kind words no matter the circumstances. Gentle words, even when provoked, will be more effective than any argument.

PROBLEMS WILL COME

Jesus warned His disciples that many would oppose them. They would be arrested and dragged before the governors and rulers of their day. This would give them an opportunity to speak to kings and other great leaders who otherwise might never hear the gospel. These people might have heard many false things about followers of Jesus—the testimony of the disciples might be the only way they would hear the truth.

> *Jesus was like a live wire, sending jolts of life and joy in every direction.*

Jesus said, "Don't worry about what you will say. When the time comes, you'll be given the right words. The Holy Spirit will speak through you." If God's children show only the humility of Jesus when their angry accusers shout, both the rulers and the people will be able to see the difference between Satan's agents and the followers of Jesus.

There is no need for Jesus' followers to memorize their answers for these trials. The Holy Spirit will flash the scriptures we have studied into our minds at the right time. Of course, if we haven't studied the words of Jesus faithfully, we can't expect that kind of help.

WHEN PERSECUTION COMES

Jesus told them, " 'All people will hate you because you follow me, but those people who keep their faith until the end will be saved' " (Matthew 10:22). He warned that even their own families would turn against them.

Jesus didn't send them out to look for persecution. He Himself often left an area of the country to avoid those who were looking to harm Him. So while His followers shouldn't be discouraged when people are against them, they should always be looking for a place where they may continue to spread His good news.

In spite of the danger, Jesus' followers should never keep their message quiet. Jesus never kept the peace by overlooking sin. His heart overflowed with love for the whole human race, but He never accepted their sinfulness. He was too much their Friend to remain quiet while they made plans that would destroy them. As followers of Jesus, we should never value peace and harmony so much that we compromise our principles of truth. No one can hold to right principles without creating enemies. Jesus said, "Don't be afraid of people who can only kill you. They can't touch your soul." We need only be afraid of giving up the truth and betraying God's trust.

Satan works to fill people's hearts with doubt. He tempts them to sin, and then to consider themselves too wicked to approach their heavenly Father. But God understands all this. Jesus assured His disciples that every sigh of discouragement, every stab of pain, every wave of grief we feel is echoed in the heart of God.

The Bible tells us that God does not sit silent and still in His holy place. He is surrounded by thousands of angels waiting to do as He instructs. In ways we cannot comprehend, He is in touch with every part of His universe, including this speck of a planet. God is bending down from His throne to hear the cry of every person in need. To every sincere prayer He answers, "I am here."

Jesus told His disciples and tells us too: "As you speak for Me to people, I will speak for you to God and the angels. You represent Me on earth; I will represent you in heaven. And when the Father examines your life, He will not see your faults and failings—He will see you wrapped in My perfect character. And everyone who shares My sacrifice to save the lost will share the joy and the glory of having saved them."

Sharing Jesus with others is more than having the correct doctrines or beliefs. It is about sharing the love that Jesus has for others. We can misrepresent Jesus by speaking words that are untruthful or unkind, or by being lazy or rude or selfish. If we do these things on earth, then Jesus cannot stand up for us in heaven.

Jesus knew that sending out His disciples and His followers throughout history would cause battles on every side, because Satan would always oppose them. His followers would have to be willing to give up everything—and everyone they loved, if necessary—to share His mission to the world. He promised that any act of kindness shown to His followers would be rewarded as if it had been done for Him personally.

And so Jesus finished His instructions and sent out His evangelists to preach His gospel and share His love by acts of kindness.

CHAPTER 38

TAKING TIME TO REST AND PRAY

"Come away by yourselves, and we will go to a lonely place and get some rest" (Mark 6:31).

fter they returned from their missionary trips, the disciples came to Jesus to report everything they had said and done. Of course, the crowds of people, anxious to be healed and hear Jesus' words, were coming and going constantly. The disciples had little time to talk or even eat, but from their stories, Jesus saw that they needed more instruction. During their trips, they had often been confused about what to do or say. They were also in danger of giving credit to themselves for the miracles they had performed. Satan tempted them to be proud, as if the power came from them. They needed to spend time with Jesus, to open their hearts to Him in the quiet peace of nature.

It was a difficult time for Jesus also. He had recently heard the news of John the Baptist's execution. This reminded Him all too clearly where His life was leading. The priests and rabbis were constantly criticizing Him, spies followed every step He took, and every day there were more plots to destroy His ministry or kill Him.

Now people were reporting to King Herod that Jesus was "John the Baptist come back to life." There was much talk in the streets about

This chapter is based on Matt. 14:1, 2, 12, 13; Mark 6:30-32; Luke 9:7-10.

an armed rebellion against the Romans, and Herod lived in fear that the Jews would rise up and throw him off the throne. Naturally, anyone who attracted crowds like Jesus did was suspect. It was clear that Jesus couldn't continue His public ministry much longer in Galilee.

The disciples of John the Baptist had buried his body and now they joined Jesus as they searched for comfort and guidance. The whole group needed time away from the noise and confusion of the crowds, from the spies and accusations of the Pharisees. Finally Jesus said to His disciples, "Come, let's go to a quiet, secluded place and get some rest." So they headed their boat toward a lonely spot at the northern end of the lake, a spot made beautiful by the fresh green of spring.

REST AND RECONNECTION

Jesus spent the time talking with His disciples about the work they were doing. He showed them where they were taking the wrong approach to people and corrected the mistakes they had made. They were refreshed by the rest and inspired with hope and courage to go out and work again.

Although there is a great deal of work to be done, Jesus didn't give anyone the burden of endless work. His words to His disciples were for His workers today also. Those who minister to others must find their times to rest. When we work successfully for God, we are tempted to trust in human plans and methods. We tend to pray less and to have less faith. We can lose sight of our dependence on Jesus and focus on the work as if that is what will save us. It is Jesus' power that makes the work successful. We must take time for prayer, meditation, and Bible study to stay connected to Him.

> *Jesus didn't give anyone the burden of endless work.*

JESUS' EXAMPLE

No one was ever busier, no one ever carried greater burdens than Jesus. But see how often He took time out to pray! Again and again the Bible records that He got up very early, or went away into the mountains to pray.

Our Savior needed to turn away from His endlessly busy life and spend time alone with His Father. Just like us, He was totally dependent on God. In His private prayers, He asked for divine strength for the work and the trials of the coming days. He was able to leave His fears and His sorrows with God. His connection of prayer turned into a current of life that connected all humans with the God of the universe. Like Jesus, we can receive life from God and give it to the world.

Everyone needs this kind of experience in prayer. When every other voice is quiet, when the world and all its pressures are left behind, the silence in our souls allows us to hear the voice of God. This is where true rest and peace are found. When we are re-energized this way, we will have the power to reach the hearts of others.

If we take time to share our needs with Jesus, we will not be disappointed. When we ask for wisdom to deal with the pressures of life, He will give it.

CHAPTER 39

"GIVE THEM SOMETHING TO EAT"

"But Jesus answered, 'They don't need to go away. You give them something to eat'" (Matthew 14:16).

he disciples thought that their quiet time with Jesus would not be disturbed, but it was. The crowds quickly missed Jesus and began to ask, "Where is He?" Some had noticed the direction the disciples' boat had sailed, and before long people were moving in that direction. Some sailed, many walked around the lake, but all were searching for Jesus.

It was Passover time, so many people who were traveling to Jerusalem stopped to see this Jesus whom they had heard so much about. As the crowd converged, at least 5,000 men had gathered along with many of their families.

From their secluded place on a hillside, Jesus looked out over the crowd and was touched by their needs. They were like sheep without a shepherd. He moved to a spot where He could speak to them and heal those who suffered.

As the people listened to the words of the Son of God, their hearts were soothed and filled with hope. His hands touched those who were suffering and dying and suddenly they had health and joy. The whole day seemed like heaven on earth.

Before they realized it, the sun began to go down. Still no one left

This chapter is based on Matt. 14:13-21; Mark 6:32-44; Luke 9:10-17; John 6:1-13.

to go home or eat. Jesus had gone all day without food or rest, but He would not leave the people who wanted so much to hear Him. Finally, the disciples urged Jesus to send the people away for their own sakes.

The whole day seemed like heaven on earth.

Most had eaten nothing since morning. "They can find something to eat in the nearby towns."

"They don't need to go away," Jesus said. "You give them something to eat." Turning to Philip, He asked, "How much food would we need to buy for this many people?"

Philip looked out over the crowd. "Two hundred pennyworth of bread would not be enough to give everyone even a bite."*

"How much food is there among the people?" Jesus asked.

Andrew answered, "There is a boy here who has five loaves of bread and two small fishes. But what good would that do for so many people?"

Jesus asked that the bread and fishes be brought to Him, and that the disciples have everyone seated on the grass in groups of fifty or a hundred. He wanted everyone to see what He was about to do. When everyone was settled, Jesus looked up to heaven and blessed the food.

Then He broke the bread into pieces and gave them to His disciples to pass on to the crowd. Next He divided the fishes and handed those to the disciples who passed them on to the people. All ate until they were full. In fact, there were twelve baskets of leftovers!

Jesus never performed miracles without a real need and an opportunity to lead people to know God. That simple food—the daily food of most fishing families—taught many lessons. Jesus could have fed them a feast of rich foods but it wouldn't have added to what they could learn. These people enjoyed the rest and simple meal more than anyone else would enjoy a banquet of rich food.

If people today lived simpler lives in harmony with nature, there would be plenty of food for all the families of the earth. There would be fewer things we would imagine we want and need, but more opportunities to do God's work. Our selfishness has created a demand for exotic and unnatural foods and has only brought more sin and misery to the world.

To that vast crowd, tired and hungry, the simple food was evidence not only of Jesus' power but of His concern about the everyday needs of life. The Savior didn't promise riches or luxuries, but He promised that their needs would be met—and more than that, He promised to be with them.

In a very real way, God is working this same miracle every day. Farmers prepare the soil and plant the seeds, but God makes the seeds sprout and grow. Even though humans claim credit for skill and work, it is God's miracle of life that feeds millions every day from the crops harvested for food. The miracle of the bread helps us recognize this gift that God gives us every day.

LESSONS TO LEARN

After the miracle of the bread, Jesus had the leftovers gathered up so that nothing would be wasted. In addition to wasting no food that could feed the hungry, the leftover bread served another wonderful purpose—it taught a powerful spiritual lesson. The people were able to take some home to share with family and friends and to share what they had seen and learned about God.

The miracle also teaches us that we can depend on God. Jesus saw that the people were far from home and in need of food. He knew that God had placed Him there at that time to meet their needs. We can depend on God to know our needs as well. We shouldn't create problems and misuse what God provides. But if we have followed God as faithfully as we know how and find ourselves in need, He will help us. We should call on our heavenly Father in every emergency.

WE MUST PASS IT ON

This miracle of Jesus has a deep spiritual meaning for all who follow Him. From His Father, Jesus received the power to multiply the food—He passed the bread on to the disciples. They passed it on to the crowd and the people passed it to one another. Jesus didn't invite the disciples to eat what He gave them—they were to pass it on. As they did, the food multiplied in Jesus' hands. Whenever they reached for more, it was there. After the crowd was fed, Jesus and the disciples shared the miracle food together.

No matter how intelligent or spiritual we are, we can share only what we have received from Jesus.

In the same way, Jesus gives us the bread of life—the truth about God—and we must pass it on to others. Like the disciples, we are the channel from God to people. No matter how intelligent or spiritual we are, we can share only what we have received from Jesus. We can receive more only when we have shared what we have. The more we share with others, the more we can learn from God and the greater our joy can be.

Too often we fail to recognize our personal responsibility for others. It is easy to leave the work of sharing the love of God to the church or the pastor, believing that the "professionals" will do a better job. But the miracle of the bread teaches us to use what we have, to "give them something to eat" instead of sending people to someone else when they need to know about God's love. Whenever we are surrounded by people in need, Jesus is there with us. He will multiply our small talents as He did the loaves of bread. What little talents we have will be used in a great way.

Jesus said, "Give and you will receive."

---

* 200 times the daily wages of a common worker

CHAPTER 40

A NIGHT
ON THE LAKE

"But quickly Jesus spoke to them and said, 'Have courage! It is I. Do not be afraid'" (Mark 6:50).

As twilight fell that evening, the people sitting on the grassy plain grew more and more excited. The food in their hands was just like manna—the miracle food created for their ancestors in the desert many years before. This miracle erased any doubts. Voices shouted it from all sides: "This must be the Promised One—the Messiah!"

And in their minds, only one thing could happen next. The Messiah would drive the Romans out of Israel and make their land a paradise on earth. With Him at the head of the armies, the soldiers would be well fed and strong, and anyone wounded would be instantly healed. They would be a force that no one could stop! He would make Judea an earthly paradise. He would make Israel the most powerful country in the world.

The crowd was ready to crown Jesus king immediately. Since He hadn't seized the throne already, they were afraid that He never would. So the leaders among the people conspired with the disciples to take Jesus by force and announce everywhere that He was the Messiah, the new King of Israel. Then the arrogant priests and rulers would be forced to admit that Jesus was the Promised One.

This chapter is based on Matt. 14:22-33; Mark 6:45-52; John 6:14-21.

But Jesus saw what was happening. He knew it would lead only to violence and a rebellion that would keep Him from doing His real work. He called His disciples together and instructed them to take the boat and sail back across the lake to Capernaum. He would dismiss the crowd by Himself.

The crowd was ready to crown Jesus king on the spot.

The disciples protested. This was their golden opportunity to put their Master on the throne of Israel! But Jesus spoke to them with an authority they had never felt Him use before. Finally, silently, they walked to the sea and their boat.

Just as men were stepping forward to seize Him, Jesus commanded the crowd to scatter. His quiet words stopped them in their tracks. The people recognized the divine power and authority in His words and quickly began to leave.

When He was finally left alone, Jesus went up into the mountain again to pray. For hours He prayed for the power to make people understand His mission in spite of Satan's effort to confuse them. Jesus knew that His time on earth was running out rapidly. He knew that instead of seeing Him seated on the throne, His disciples would see Him hung on a cross. He knew that without the Holy Spirit, their faith would fail. In agony with tears, He prayed for them.

THE STORM

The disciples had not immediately sailed, hoping that Jesus would come with them if they waited a while. Finally, the dark night fell and they headed across the sea. As they went, they blamed themselves for not insisting that Jesus be announced as king. When were they going to be rewarded for their faith in Jesus? Why didn't He use His power to make all their lives easier and better? Their selfish thinking continued until they began to doubt Jesus Himself. Hadn't He let John the Baptist die when He could have saved him?

The events of that day should have left them filled with faith and hope, but they forgot it all. As their thoughts spiraled into doubt and depression, God did something He often does when we create trouble for ourselves—He allowed something to happen that would occupy their minds and change their focus. There was no reason for them to imagine problems—real problems were approaching fast.

A violent storm came up suddenly and caught them completely unprepared. Quickly, all of them forgot their doubts and impatience with Jesus and worked to keep the boat from sinking. Normally it only took a few hours to cross the lake, but the disciples fought the storm until well after midnight, when they finally gave up all hope. Helpless to save themselves, they prayed for help from Jesus.

From His place on the shore, Jesus watched with deep concern as they battled the storm. These men were supposed to be the light of the world someday. When they finally gave up their pride and their ambitions to be great, when they humbly prayed for help, help came.

When troubles come, we focus on the problems instead of keeping our eyes on Jesus.

At just the moment they were certain that they would be thrown into the water and drown, a gleam of light showed a mysterious figure approaching on the water. They were terrified. Their iron-strong hands dropped the oars as they forgot everything and stared. Certain that it must be some sort of phantom, some sign of certain death, they cried out in fear.

Jesus, walking on the water, looked as if He would pass by the boat. Some thought they recognized Him and cried out, asking for help. Then Jesus said, "Don't be afraid. It is I."

As soon as they were sure of His face and His voice, Peter called out, "Lord, if it is You, let me walk to You on the water."

Jesus said, "Come."

PETER STEPS OUT

So Peter locked his eyes on Jesus and stepped out onto the water. As long as he looked at Jesus, he walked safely. But Peter couldn't resist the urge to glance back and see how impressed the others were. As he did, the waves rolled up and when he looked back, Jesus was out of sight. Peter panicked, his faith vanished and he began to sink. While dark waves promised death, Peter looked up and cried, "Lord, save me!"

Instantly Jesus was there. He grabbed Peter's hand, pulled him up and said, "Why is your faith so small? Why did you doubt?" He led Peter back by the hand and together they stepped into the boat. Peter was quiet now—his pride and lack of faith had nearly cost him his life.

We are often like Peter. When troubles come, we focus on the problems instead of keeping our eyes on Jesus. Jesus hasn't called us to follow Him only to leave us. "Don't be afraid," He says. "I will be with you."

With this experience on the water, Jesus wanted to show Peter that he was safe only when he was depending on God's power. While he thought he was strong and faithful, Peter was actually weak. If he had learned the lesson on the lake, he would not have failed so miserably in the days ahead.

Every day, God is teaching us in the same way, preparing us for what lies ahead in His plans for our lives. We may think that we are strong in the faith, ready to face any temptation or situation, but Satan is working to take advantage of our weaknesses. Only by keeping our eyes on Jesus can we be safe.

As soon as Jesus was settled in the boat, the wind died. Instantly, the boat was at the shore where they had planned to go. The disciples bowed at Jesus' feet and said, "Truly You are the Son of God."

CHAPTER 41

THE CRISIS
IN GALILEE

" 'I am the bread that gives life. Whoever comes to me will never be hungry' " (John 6:35).

esus knew that His life on earth had reached a turning point. The crowds that wanted to place Him on the throne today would turn against Him tomorrow. When their selfish dreams were disappointed, their love would turn to hate, their praise would turn to curses.

But Jesus did nothing to avoid the crisis. He had always known that there would be no "earthly" benefits from His mission. Many of the crowd followed Him because they hoped for a worldly kingdom. Now they must see the truth.

Early the next morning, many people flocked back to the spot where they had left Jesus the night before. They expected to find Him there—after all, there had been no boat to take Him to the other side of the lake. But He was nowhere to be found. As other boats arrived, they crossed the lake to look for Him.

Many who had been at the scene of the miracle of the bread came to Gennesaret, where Jesus and the disciples had landed. They heard from the disciples about the storm, about Jesus' walking on the water, about Peter's adventure, and how the boat arrived at shore. They waited anxiously, hoping to hear Jesus tell more about these miracles.

This chapter is based on John 6:22-71.

But Jesus sadly said, "You're not looking for Me because of the miracles. You're looking for Me because you ate the bread and it filled you. Don't just look for regular food that spoils—look for food that can give you eternal life."

The people asked, "What do we have to do to get into heaven? What price do we have to pay for eternal life?"

Jesus had a simple answer. "Believe in the One whom God has sent to you." The price of heaven is Jesus. The way to heaven is faith in the Lamb of God.

Jesus did exactly what the prophecies said the Messiah would do. But the people were sure that the Messiah should do much more than just give manna for forty years as Moses did. Why didn't Jesus give them all health and riches, and drive out the Romans if He really was the Messiah? He claimed to be the Son of God, but He refused to be the king of Israel! Maybe He wasn't certain that He was really the Promised One.

Almost sarcastically, a rabbi asked, "What miracle will You do, so that we will believe in You? Moses gave our ancestors bread from heaven to eat in the desert."

It was Jesus Himself who had given the Hebrews manna from heaven in the desert. He answered, " 'I tell you the truth, it was not Moses who gave you bread from heaven; it is my Father who is giving you the true bread from heaven. God's bread is the One who comes down from heaven and gives life to the world' " (John 6:32, 33).

Why didn't Jesus give them all health and riches, and drive out the Romans if He really was the Messiah?

Some in the crowd still thought He was talking about food to eat. They said, "Sir, give us this bread to eat every day."

Jesus tried to make it clear. " 'I am the bread that gives life. Whoever comes to me will never be hungry, and whoever believes in me will never be thirsty' " (John 6:35). The spiritual lesson of the miracle of the bread was clear in the teachings of the prophets. If they understood the Scriptures, they would have understood His words, "I am the bread that gives life." The bread they had eaten would give them physical strength and life. Jesus wanted to give them spiritual strength and eternal life.

Jesus knew that they didn't believe. They had seen many miracles—the bread, the healings, His power over the storm—another miracle would not have changed their minds. But He reached out to them anyway. " 'I came down from heaven to do what God wants me to do . . . Those who see the Son and believe in him have eternal life, and I will raise them on the last day' " (John 6:38-40).

Now the rabbis and leaders were offended. "Isn't this Jesus, the son of Joseph? Don't we know his mother and father? How can he say, 'I came down from heaven'?" The claims of this uneducated carpenter, born in questionable circumstances, were not worth their attention.

Jesus didn't try to explain the mystery of His birth any more than He had explained how He had crossed the sea that night. He didn't need to defend His reputation. His character, His identity, were revealed by His words and His actions. And as usual, the Pharisees got even angrier when He refused to argue or strike back at them.

The Father is drawing all human hearts to Him. Only those who resist Him will refuse to accept Jesus. Those who have been touched by God's love would recognize Jesus as God's Son when they heard His message.

BREAD OF LIFE

The manna in the wilderness didn't prevent death, but the bread from heaven could. Jesus became one of us in human flesh so that we could become one with Him in spirit. Because of this union we will be resurrected. Through faith, His eternal life is ours. Through the Holy Spirit, Jesus lives in us and that is the beginning of eternal life.

Jesus wanted them to understand that He hadn't come to earth to provide bread for people to eat. He came to offer them life—eternal life, which He would pay the price for. " 'I am the living bread that came down from heaven. Anyone who eats this bread will live forever.

This bread is my flesh, which I will give up so that the world may have life' " (John 6:51). The Jews didn't understand that the Passover lamb was a symbol of Jesus. They didn't understand that this was the truth Jesus was teaching them. The rabbis got angry. "How can this man give us his flesh to eat?" They understood some of what Jesus meant, but they wanted to turn the people against Him.

He came to offer them life— eternal life, for which He would pay the price.

Jesus repeated His words with even stronger language. " 'I tell you the truth, you must eat the flesh of the Son of Man and drink his blood. Otherwise, you won't have real life in you. Those who eat my flesh and drink my blood have eternal life' " (John 6:53, 54). Jesus wanted them to understand that what food was to their bodies, He must be to their souls. When Jesus is our food and drink, He becomes a part of our being, a part of all we say and do and are.

Are we committed to following Jesus? Then we have the spiritual life He did because of our bond to Him. If our "first love" experience has grown cold, we must accept Him again—eat His flesh and drink His blood—to become one with the Father and His Son.

Most of the people in the crowd were offended by Jesus' words. Jews were forbidden by religious rules to even taste blood in meat, and they twisted Jesus' words to make it sound as if He was a law-breaker and a heretic. Even many of His followers said, "This teaching is hard. Can anyone accept these words?"

Jesus answered, "Does this teaching offend you? Then it will really offend you to see Me return to heaven! It is the spirit that gives life, not the body. My words were talking about spirit, and they can bring you life."

WORDS OF LIFE

It was Jesus' words that brought life to the world. His words drove out demons and healed diseases. His words calmed storms and raised the dead. Our whole Bible is filled with His words and those words have power. Jesus wanted to build His followers' faith in the Scriptures. When He was gone, those words would have to be their source of faith and power.

Our physical strength is nourished by food. Our spiritual strength must be nourished by the Word of God. We should study the Bible carefully, asking for the help of the Holy Spirit to understand it. Just as we must eat for ourselves, we must study for ourselves. In His promises and warnings, Jesus is speaking to us personally. God gave His Son not just for the world but for me. The experiences shared in God's Word can be my experiences. The promises and prayers found there are meant for each of us personally. Eating the bread from heaven means absorbing the words of God in the Bible—applying those words to our own lives until they change our character.

THE TEST OF FAITH IS FAILED

Jesus knew His words would test the faith of all who claimed to be His followers. They would have to surrender their ideas of power and glory. They would have to surrender to Jesus' plans. He knew that many would fail this test.

This sermon opened the eyes of those who had been planning to force Jesus to be king. They realized that there would be no power or glory, no free food or riches. They wanted Jesus' miracle-working power, but weren't interested in His self-sacrificing life. If He wasn't going to free their country from the Romans, they didn't want anything to do with Him.

Everything Jesus said and did had a purpose in His work to save us.

When Jesus said plainly to the crowd, "I know some of you don't believe," more of His followers were offended. They wanted to hurt Jesus for betraying their selfish plans, so they left, never to follow Him again. Many, in fact, joined those who fought against Jesus. They twisted their reports of His words and actions, turning every story against Him. Their words stirred up so much anger that soon Jesus' life was in danger.

People today are tested the same way. When they learn a new truth and see that they must change their lives, they sometimes refuse and walk away, offended that God would ask so much of them.

As others left, Jesus turned to His twelve disciples and asked, " 'Do you want to leave, too?' " (John 6:67).

Peter answered for all of them. "Lord, where would we go? You have the words of eternal life. We know that You are the Messiah, the Son of God." The disciples had found more peace and joy since finding Jesus than any time before in their lives. How could they turn away from the most holy and most loving Person they had ever met? To be without the Savior was to be drifting on a dark, stormy sea.

Everything Jesus said and did had a purpose in His work to save us. We may not always understand, but we can see the love in everything God does for humans. If we spend time with Jesus, we will recognize His kindness in testing us and showing us our weaknesses.

The twisted news quickly spread that Jesus had confessed that He was not the Messiah. So now in Galilee the popular feeling turned against Him as it had in Judea. Israel was rejecting its Messiah.

A LOVING SAVIOR

Jesus knew what would happen because of His words that day. He saw ahead to Gethsemane and the Cross. He knew what a terrible ordeal it would be for His disciples. Without this test, those who were following Him for selfish reasons would have turned their back on Him at that point. It would have caused a great deal more pain and confusion for the faithful disciples and possibly turned others away. But Jesus smoothed the way ahead as best He could, bringing the crisis while He was still present to strengthen the faith of His true followers.

What a loving Savior! Knowing the terrible death that was waiting for Him, He thought about His disciples and worked to make their suffering easier.

CHAPTER 42

PULLED UP
BY THE ROOTS

" 'If a blind person leads a blind person, both will
fall into a ditch' " (Matthew 15:14).

he evangelistic trips of the twelve disciples stirred up
the jealousy of the religious leaders in Jerusalem. Now new
spies were sent to watch Jesus and find some way to turn
the people against Him.

The one thing they could always accuse Jesus of was His lack
of respect for the religious traditions and laws of the rabbis. One of
the most obvious of these was the ceremonial hand washing that the
rabbis required in order for a person to be considered "clean," or sin-
free. This time, the spies did not accuse Jesus directly—they criticized
His disciples. They asked, "Why do your disciples ignore the unwrit-
ten laws of hand washing?"

Jesus didn't defend Himself or His disciples. He asked, "Why do
you insist on following your own laws and breaking God's?" He reminded
them of the commandment "Honor your father and your mother." But
the rabbis' laws allowed people to neglect their father and mother—
even if they desperately needed help—if they announced that their
money or property would be given to the temple after they died.

Jesus said, " 'You teach that person not to honor his father or his
mother. You rejected what God said for the sake of your own rules.

This chapter is based on Matt. 15:1-20; Mark 7:1-23.

You are hypocrites!' " (Matthew 15:6, 7). By showing everyone the truth about the rabbis' laws, Jesus hoped to free those who really wanted to serve God from their daily struggle to be ceremonially clean.

> *Cleanness and purity come from inside a person, not from the outside.*

Jesus declared that by making their rules more important than Scripture, the rabbis were placing themselves above God. He explained to the crowd. "It is not what people put into their mouths that makes them unclean—it is what comes out of their mouths." "Cleanness" and purity come from inside a person, not from the outside.

THE BLIND LEADING THE BLIND

The disciples saw how angry this made the spies. They wanted Jesus to make peace with the leaders and rabbis. They asked Him, "Do You know that what You're saying will make the Pharisees angry?"

Jesus answered, " 'Every plant that my Father in heaven has not planted himself will be pulled up by the roots' " (Matthew 15:13). He meant that any law or tradition that humans create has no value in God's eyes. Then He said this about the religious leaders: " 'Stay away from the Pharisees; they are blind leaders. And if a blind person leads a blind person, both will fall into a ditch' " (Matthew 15:14).

Even today some Christians and religious organizations have created institutions and traditions that they claim must be followed as closely as any Bible teaching. We can point out just like Jesus did that real truth and laws come only from the Scriptures. We must always place the Word of God above the authority of any church leader.

God's remnant people in the last days will be those who keep His commandments, not the traditions and rules of humans. Jesus urges us to follow the words of His Father instead of the traditions and rules of church leaders. Only in God's Word is the truth pure, unmixed with any errors.

CHAPTER 43

BREAKING DOWN
THE BARRIERS

" 'Woman, you have great faith! I will do what you asked' "
(Matthew 15:28).

fter the public disagreement with the Pharisees, Jesus left Capernaum and crossed the Sea of Galilee again—this time to the hill country near the ancient cities of Tyre and Sidon. Beyond those cities was the Mediterranean Sea, which His followers would someday cross to carry the gospel to the world. Jesus' work here was to prepare His disciples for that mission.

In this area lived a Canaanite woman who had heard of this new prophet who could heal any disease. She must have questioned whether a Jewish prophet would even listen to her request. But with a mother's love, she was determined to ask. She found Jesus and called out, "Lord, have mercy on me. My daughter is possessed by a demon and she is suffering."

Jesus had traveled this way just to meet this woman. He knew what she needed. By helping her, He could begin to teach His disciples how badly the rest of the world needed to hear about God's love. The walls between the Jews and the rest of the world had to be broken down. At first, Jesus ignored the woman's cries, as any other Jew would.

This chapter is based on Matt. 15:21-28; Mark 7:24-30.

But this woman was determined. She kept following them and shouting her request until the disciples finally said, "Tell her to go away." As far as they could tell, Jesus had no interest in helping a heathen woman.

Jesus said, "God sent Me only to the lost sheep—the lost people—of Israel." Although it sounded as if Jesus was as prejudiced as any other Jew, it was really meant to remind the disciples of something He had often told them—that He had come to save everyone who would accept Him.

> *Nothing but a personal choice can keep any person from heaven.*

The woman rushed up and bowed at Jesus' feet. "Lord, help me," she cried again.

Jesus' heart was breaking for her, but He kept up His lesson for the disciples. He said, "It is not right to take the children's food and give it to the dogs." He seemed to agree that the special blessings given to Israel shouldn't be shared with other peoples.

Anyone less determined would have been completely discouraged. But this woman saw Jesus' compassionate side that He could not hide. She quickly answered, "Yes, Lord, but even the dogs get to eat the crumbs that fall from the table." If they thought of her as less than a person—a dog—well, even dogs got a few blessings. It was clear she believed that Jesus could heal her child, if only He would.

Jesus had finished His lesson and tested her faith as well. He had shown that she was a child of God. As His child, she could share His gifts. Now the look of love was clear on His face. He said, " 'Woman, you have great faith! I will do what you asked' " (Matthew 15:28). And at that moment, her daughter was healed. The woman left, praising her Savior for answering her prayer.

A LESSON FOR ALL

By healing the Roman officer's servant in Capernaum and preaching to the Samaritans, Jesus had already shown that He didn't share the Jewish prejudice toward others. Now He was showing that His love wasn't restricted to any race or nation. When Jesus said, "God sent Me to the lost sheep of Israel," He was including the Canaanite woman. She was a "lost sheep" that Israel should have found by sharing the truth about God.

This miracle opened the disciples' minds. They began to understand that their mission would reach beyond Israel—that there was a world filled with people in need. After Jesus' death, this lesson was a great influence on the leaders of the new church.

Still today, prejudice divides people and causes hate and despair. Many may feel that the love of Jesus was meant only for others. But salvation is for everyone. Nothing but a personal choice can keep any person from heaven. Treating people differently because of color or race is repulsive to God. Every human being has the same Creator and the same Savior. All are invited to accept His love and His promise of eternal life.

CHAPTER 44

THE
SIGN OF JONAH

"They will not be given any sign, except the sign of Jonah"
(Matthew 16:4).

esus and the disciples sailed across the lake again, this time back to the area of Decapolis. This was where Jesus had healed the two demon-possessed men, and the people had asked Jesus to leave. But the two healed men had repeated their story many times and now a crowd gathered to hear what Jesus would say.

Some in the crowd brought a deaf man who could not speak clearly to Jesus. Jesus took the man a short distance away, put His fingers in the man's ears and touched his tongue. Then Jesus said, "Be open!" And the man could hear and speak.

As news of this miracle spread, Jesus found a good spot on the mountainside where He could teach and heal. Even though these were not Jewish people, great crowds—more than four thousand men plus their families—came to hear about the God of Israel. They brought all the sick and injured people in the whole area to Jesus—and He healed them. For three days Jesus taught and healed. At night the people slept on the ground just to see and hear Him the next day.

After three days, all their food was gone. Jesus didn't want to send them away hungry, so once again He asked His disciples to bring them food.

Even though they had seen the miracle of the bread before, the disciples weren't sure that Jesus would do the same kind of miracle for these people. After all, they weren't Jews. The disciples were still prejudiced. They said, "Where would we get enough bread for this many people?"

Finally they brought Jesus what they had—seven loaves and two fishes. Once again, Jesus prayed, then divided the food for the people. Everyone ate and there were seven large baskets of leftovers.

"SHOW US A SIGN"

Next, Jesus and the disciples sailed to Magdala. There, instead of people hoping to be healed, He found people hoping to trick Him.

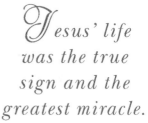

Jesus' life was the true sign and the greatest miracle.

The Pharisees and the Sadducees, the two most powerful groups of religious leaders in Israel, usually fought and argued with each other. But now they had a common enemy—Jesus. Too many people were following Jesus instead of listening to them. "Show us a miracle from God," they demanded, "then we will believe in you."

They wanted something spectacular—like commanding the sun to stand still as Joshua had. Jesus said, "You can predict the weather by watching the sky. You watch the signs and you know what they mean. But when you see the things that I am doing, you can't tell what they mean." The power of Jesus' words was a sign they had witnessed. The angels over Bethlehem, the star and the wise men, the Voice from heaven at His baptism—all these were signs and miracles they ignored.

Then He sighed and said, "Why do you insist on seeing a miracle as a sign? You will get no sign but the sign of Jonah."

Jonah's preaching was a sign to the people of Ninevah. Jesus' preaching was a sign to the Jews. But while the people of Ninevah listened and changed their ways, the Jews refused to listen. "The people of Ninevah would condemn you," Jesus told them.

Every miracle of healing that Jesus performed was a sign of His divinity—proof of His relationship with God. But these Jewish leaders didn't care about suffering people. Often they were the ones causing the suffering. So His miracles offended them. This was the strongest proof of who Jesus was and it was exactly what made the Jewish leaders reject Him.

Jesus' life was the true sign and the greatest miracle. He did God's works in healing and helping as He spoke God's words of truth. Many today ask for a sign, a miracle, to show that God is real. But isn't it a miracle that any of us can escape Satan's control and surrender to God? The change in a person—to go from a selfish lifestyle to a selfless one—is a miracle that shows the presence of Jesus in their heart. When God's Word is preached, there should always be a sign or miracle—the presence of the Holy Spirit, shown by changed lives.

BEWARE OF THE YEAST

Turning away from the critical Jewish leaders, Jesus climbed back into the boat with His disciples. In sad silence they sailed all the way back across the water. As they reached the other side, Jesus said, "Beware of the yeast of the Pharisees and Sadducees." In Jewish teachings, yeast was often a symbol for sin.

The disciples, who had forgotten to buy bread before they sailed, completely misunderstood. They thought He wanted them to buy bread, but not from the Pharisees or Sadducees.

Jesus knew what they were thinking. "Why are you talking about not having bread? Your faith is so small! Remember the five loaves of bread that fed five thousand people? I was not talking about bread. I am telling you to be careful of the clever teachings of the Pharisees and Sadducees."

The disciples still felt that Jesus should have shown them a miracle. They knew He could and they thought it would silence His enemies. But they didn't understand what hypocrites these leaders were.

SELFISHNESS IS THE CENTER OF SIN

The clever deception of the Pharisees' teachings made it hard for people to accept what Jesus taught. One good example was their law that allowed people to neglect their parents by giving to the temple. The selfish desire for wealth was at the center of this law. This deceptive kind of teaching made it hard for people to accept Jesus' words.

The same kind of deception is seen today from those who try to explain God's law in a way that allows for selfish behavior. They don't attack the law directly. Instead they suggest ideas that undermine its principles. Then they explain the law in a way that makes it seem out of touch and unnecessary.

It was selfishness—self-centeredness—that led the Pharisees to pervert the teachings of the Scripture. This selfishness influenced the disciples a great deal. In many ways, they were still seeking great things for themselves. Each one wanted to be the most important, the most powerful in Jesus' new kingdom. They didn't understand Jesus' self-sacrificing mission.

Today, this sin is just as common. Even our work for Jesus is often spoiled by a secret desire to be popular or powerful. The love of self, the desire for an easier, quicker way to do things leads us to put human ideas and traditions ahead of God's laws.

Only God's power can change us from selfishness to selflessness. That change is a real miracle and the true sign that God is working in our lives.

CHAPTER 45

THE
COMING CROSS

"On this rock I will build my church"
(Matthew 16:18).

ven before Jesus joined the human race, He saw the whole
path that He would have to travel to save them. Before
He laid down His crown and covered His divinity with
humanity He saw every injury, every insult, every struggle
He would face. His life on earth, with all its work and sacrifice, was brightened by the idea that by giving His life He was bringing
this world back to God. Even though He would bleed and suffer, carry
the weight of all the sins of the world, and live under the shadow of
unspeakable sadness—for the joy of bringing humans back to God,
Jesus chose the Cross.

Soon His friends and disciples would see the One they loved
and trusted hanging on the cross. Soon He would have to leave
them to face the world without His visible presence. Then they
would be hated and arrested. Jesus had to prepare them for His
future and for theirs.

Jesus and His disciples had traveled past Galilee to the area of
Caesarea Philippi, where most of the people did not know about God
at all. Jesus was still working to help the disciples see their mission to
the heathen, nonbelievers of the world.

This chapter is based on Matt. 16:13-28; Mark 8:27-38; Luke 9:18-27.

Before He began the discussion of His future, Jesus prayed for the disciples and gave them a chance to show their faith in Him. He asked a question: "Who do people say that I am?"

The disciples had to admit that the nation of Israel did not accept Jesus as the Messiah. Many thought He was a prophet. The crowds at Bethsaida wanted to make Him king, but they didn't believe He was the Messiah.

Jesus asked a different question. "Who do you say that I am?"

Peter answered without hesitating. "You are the Messiah—the Son of God." Many others doubted, but not Peter. He did not need to wait for Jesus to be crowned in order to be sure. And Peter spoke for the other disciples as well. They were still confused by the attitude of the priests and leaders, and by the things they had learned from the rabbis. But on this day, the voice of the Holy Spirit in their minds was clear—they were certain that although human, Jesus was also the Son of God.

Jesus said, "You are blessed, Simon Peter, son of Jonah. It wasn't a person who taught you that—it was God. You are called Peter, which means 'a rolling stone.' On this rock I will build My church. And the power of death will not defeat it."

The rock on which Jesus was building His church was not Peter, but Himself. He was the One that death could not defeat. His words and actions would be the foundation on which the Christian church would build and grow. It

Jesus wasn't setting Peter up as the leader of the new church.

was a small weak group that day, and all the powers of hell would fight against it. But there was no doubt—it would grow and become strong.

Peter's words were the foundation of the new church's faith—of every believer's faith: Jesus was the Messiah, the Savior. So for all believers, Jesus said to Peter, "I will give you the keys of the kingdom of heaven." These keys were the words of Jesus Himself, both as He walked this earth and as written in the books of Scripture. Those who share these powerful words open the doors of heaven to all who will believe.

Jesus wasn't setting Peter up as the leader of the new church. If He had, there would have been none of the arguing later among the disciples about who was the most important. The church is built on Jesus. It cannot depend on or be controlled by one person. No position in the church gives a person the right to dictate what others will believe or do.

The people had a twisted idea of what the Messiah would do. So Jesus warned the disciples not to tell anyone that He was the Promised One.

THE CROSS IS COMING

The disciples still believed that Jesus would soon become the king of Israel. They couldn't imagine that His own people would have Him condemned and crucified as a criminal. But it was time for Jesus to warn them about what was ahead. Sadly He began to talk about His future: He would go to Jerusalem, be arrested by the priests and elders, then be killed, and be raised again the third day.

At first the disciples were speechless, shocked and horrified. Jesus had just agreed that He was the Messiah—now He was telling them that He was going to suffer and die!

Peter couldn't stay quiet for long. He grabbed Jesus as if he could pull Him back from such a terrible fate. "No!" he said, "those things will never happen to You!"

Peter spoke because of his love for his Friend, but it was the wrong thing to say. His words went against God's plan to save the world and the selfless love Jesus taught and lived. The last thing Jesus wanted was for His followers to rise up to protect Him from what was coming. He quickly answered Peter with some of the strongest words that ever came from His lips. "Get away from Me, Satan! You are not helping. You are not on the side of God." Jesus knew that Satan had stepped between Him and Peter, trying to discourage Him and keep Peter focused on the dream of power and glory.

As Jesus had refused to be tempted He had refused to let Peter be led astray. His words were really spoken to Satan. "Get behind Me, Satan. Let Peter see Me face to face so I can show him more of My love." It was a hard lesson for Peter. But over time, he realized that the path of Jesus led through pain and shame. Years later, he was able to say, "Be happy when you share Jesus' sufferings. Then you will be full of joy when He comes again."

Jesus explained that His life and His suffering was an example of what theirs would be. "If people want to follow Me, they must give up the things they want, pick up their own cross every day and follow My way." The cross was the most painful and humiliating way to die. Criminals were forced to carry their own cross to the place were they would die on it. These words helped the disciples begin to understand how completely they needed to surrender themselves to Jesus.

It also helped them understand what Jesus had done for them. He left heaven for a life of insult and injury followed by a shameful death. To carry His message, His gospel to the world, they would have to share His suffering.

True followers of Jesus should see themselves as links in the chain that was lowered from heaven to save the world. Linked to Jesus they go with Him to find and save the lost. When we're linked to Jesus, we show Him to the world.

Jesus said, "Those who give up their lives for Me will have true, eternal life." Selfishness causes eternal death. If the heart refuses to pump blood through the body, it will quickly weaken and die. In the same way, Jesus' love flows through us. If we refuse to share it, our souls will weaken and die. It's worth nothing to us to have everything we want in the whole world if we lose our souls—our eternal life.

Finally, Jesus pointed the disciples to His second coming—this time in glory and power. Then He would reward all humans for their choices—those who lived and died for Him and those who rejected and killed Him. Then to encourage them, Jesus said, " 'I tell you the truth, some people standing here will see the Son of Man coming with his kingdom before they die' " (Matthew 16:28).

The disciples didn't understand. With heavy hearts, all they could see was the poverty, the shame, the suffering ahead of them. Could it be true that they wouldn't see Jesus be made king but see Him arrested and killed? Why would Jesus go to Jerusalem and face that? Why would He agree to go and die, and leave them worse off than they were before He had appeared?

True followers of Jesus should see themselves as links in the chain that was lowered down to save the world.

They were certain that Jesus could stay in Caesarea Philippi and be safe from the Jewish leaders. Why not stay and work there? How could His kingdom—so strong that no power could destroy it—ever really exist if He died?

The disciples followed Jesus back toward Jerusalem where all their hopes would be crushed. For six long days they walked, doubting and afraid, but hoping for something that would change Jesus' predecided future.

CHAPTER 46

JESUS'
TRANSFORMATION

" 'This is my Son, whom I love. Listen to him!' "
(Mark 9:7).

It was evening when Jesus called Peter, James, and John aside and led them far up a lonely mountainside. They were exhausted from a long day of traveling and teaching. As the sun went down, the darkness added to the gloom and sadness in their hearts. They didn't ask Jesus where they were going or why. He often spent whole nights in prayer in lonely places like this. But they wondered why He would lead them up so far after a long and tiring day.

Finally, Jesus asked them to stop while He went on a little farther. Then He poured His heart out in prayer, tears flowing as He asked for strength to go forward and save humanity. He prayed for His disciples, that their faith would not fail. Hours passed and the dew soaked His body, but He didn't notice. At first Peter, James, and John prayed with Jesus, but eventually they fell asleep.

Jesus knew they were discouraged after hearing what would soon happen. He wanted to lighten their sorrow and build their faith. Of the twelve disciples, only these three would witness His struggle and pain in the Garden of Gethsemane. Jesus asked His Father for a miracle that would comfort them in the difficult days

This chapter is based on Matt. 17:1-8; Mark 9:2-8; Luke 9:28-36.

ahead, a miracle that would reaffirm their belief that He was the Son of God.

Suddenly, heaven opened and a holy, radiant glow descended toward the mountain and encircled Jesus' body. Divine light from inside Jesus flashed through His human form and joined the glorious glow. Rising from the ground, Jesus stood God-like and majestic. His face shone like the sun, His clothes glowed with white light.

The disciples snapped awake and stared in fear and amazement at their Master. As their eyes adjusted to the glorious light, they saw that two heavenly beings were with Jesus—Moses, who had talked with God on Mt. Sinai and Elijah, who had never died but gone straight to heaven. Moses had died, but Jesus Himself called him back to life and to heaven.

The three beings on the mountain represented the future kingdom of glory—Jesus the King, as He would appear at the Second Coming; Moses, representing those who would be resurrected on that day; and Elijah, standing for those who would be translated and never die. But before He could wear a crown, Jesus would have to carry a cross.

As He faced the pain and suffering the months ahead would bring, Jesus needed support. His disciples didn't understand His mission. In the world He had created, Jesus was lonely. So heaven sent messengers who understood His loneliness and His desire to save humankind.

Jesus often spent whole nights in prayer in lonely places like this.

Moses and Elijah talked with Jesus and encouraged Him in His mission. They had worked with Him to save His people in their day. They shared Jesus' desire to see humans rescued from sin. Moses had shown great love for the children of Israel during the wandering after they were rescued from Egypt. Later in Israel's history, Elijah had been hated and hunted during three years of famine as he hid alone in the desert. These two men comforted Jesus and sympathized with His suffering. But most of all, the three discussed the plan to save every human.

Peter, James, and John missed most of the talking and failed to get the blessing God had intended for them. They could have understood that Jesus would suffer and die, but that a resurrection and a glorious return was promised. However, they did understand Jesus' mission better and realized that the powers of the universe recognized Him as the Messiah.

PETER SERIOUSLY MISUNDERSTANDS

The disciples were thrilled to see that Jesus, so humble and poor, was honored by these holy men from heaven. They were sure that Moses and Elijah had come to protect Jesus and announce His authority as king. Peter didn't want the experience to end. "Teacher, it's good that we are here. Let us set up three special tents—one for You, one for Moses, and one for Elijah."

While the disciples stood staring, a bright cloud covered them and a voice from the cloud said, " 'This is my Son, whom I love. Listen to him!' " (Mark 9:7). At the sound of that voice—the voice of God—the whole mountain trembled and the disciples fell on their faces. They didn't look up until Jesus came near and touched them.

"Stand up," He said. "Don't be afraid."

And when they looked, they saw that the glorious light and cloud were gone. Moses and Elijah were gone. They were alone with Jesus.

CHAPTER 47

THE
BATTLE

" 'All things are possible for the one who believes' "
(Mark 9:23).

n the light of the rising sun, Jesus and the three disciples walked back down from the mountain. The disciples were quiet, awestruck and lost in thought.

As they neared the spot where the other disciples waited, they could see that a large crowd had gathered. Before they got close, Jesus said, "Tell no one what you saw on the mountain until I have risen from the dead." He knew that sharing the story of seeing Moses and Elijah would only cause confusion and ridicule.

His words left the three disciples confused. They wondered among themselves what Jesus meant about "rising from the dead." But they didn't ask Him to explain.

When the people saw Jesus, they ran to meet Him. The faces of all four men still reflected the glory they had seen that night. But Jesus could see that something was wrong—something had happened that left His other disciples disappointed and humiliated. He could see the spies of the priests gloating as they claimed that Jesus and His disciples were frauds.

Jesus asked, "What is going on? What are you arguing about?" Sud-

This chapter is based on Matt. 17:9-21; Mark 9:9-29; Luke 9:37-45.

denly, all the voices that had been so loud and scornful were silent. Finally, a man came out of the crowd and said, "Teacher, I brought my son to You. He is possessed by an evil spirit that won't let him speak. It throws him to the ground where he foams at the mouth and grinds his teeth. I asked Your disciples to throw the evil spirit out, but they couldn't."

It was true. When the disciples had traveled out to preach and heal for Jesus, they had been given the power to throw out demons. But this time when they commanded the demon to leave in Jesus' name, the evil spirit only mocked them. The disciples felt that they were disgracing themselves and Jesus.

Jesus looked at the crowd and read their hearts—the doubts, the anger, the contempt. He said, "You people have no faith. How long must I put up with you?" Then He said to the father, "Bring the boy to Me."

As the boy was brought forward, the evil spirit saw Jesus and threw the boy to the ground, foaming and shrieking. Once again, the Prince of Life and the prince of darkness met for battle—Jesus to free the captives and Satan to hold tight to his victim. For a moment, Jesus allowed the evil spirit to show its power. He asked, "How long has this been happening?"

"Since he was young," the father answered. He shared the stories of how the spirit had tried to kill the boy. Finally, he cried out, "If You can do anything for him, please have mercy and help us!"

Jesus stared into the man's eyes. " 'You said, "If you can!" All things are possible for the one who believes' " (Mark 9:23).

Suddenly the father recognized that his own doubt might doom his son. With tears on his face, he begged for help. " 'I do believe! Help me to believe more!' " (Mark 9:24).

Then Jesus turned to where the boy lay twitching and foaming. " 'You spirit that makes people unable to hear or speak, I command you to come out of this boy and never enter him again!' " (Mark 9:25).

The evil spirit screamed, shook the boy once more, then left. As he lay there still and quiet, people began to whisper, "He must be dead." But Jesus took his hand and helped him stand up. Then the boy—looking and thinking normally now—stepped into his father's arms. Together they thanked Jesus and praised God. Meanwhile, the disappointed spies left to report what they had seen.

FAITH CONNECTS US TO HEAVEN

Through the ages, many people who carry heavy burdens of sin and guilt—ready to give up all hope—have prayed the same prayer: "If You can do anything, please help me." And the answer always is: "All things are possible for the one who believes."

It was a snapshot of the plan of salvation—God reaching down to save those who are lost.

In Jesus, God has made a way for us to resist every temptation and overcome every sinful habit. But many times we feel that we don't have enough faith to follow Jesus' way. We should turn to Jesus with the same request as the boy's father: "I believe! Help me to believe more!" We will never fall into sin when we do this—never.

During those few short hours, Peter, James, and John had seen a demonstration of salvation. Jesus as a human, changed into the likeness of God, came down to rescue a human changed into the likeness of Satan. They had seen Jesus wrapped in glory as the Son of God. Now they saw Him reach down to help a victim of Satan and return him healed to his family. It was a snapshot of the plan of salvation—God reaching down to save those who are lost.

It was also a lesson for the disciples. As amazing and joyful as their time with Jesus on the mountain was, their mission was down on the plain. People in slavery to sin and Satan were waiting for words of faith and prayer to set them free.

The nine disciples asked Jesus, "Why couldn't we throw out the demon?"

Jesus said, " 'Because your faith is too small. I tell you the truth, if your faith is as big as a mustard seed, you can say to this mountain,

"Move from here to there," and it will move. All things will be possible for you' " (Matthew 17:20).

Their casual attitude toward their mission—along with envy of the other three disciples—had made their faith so small that they could do nothing. They were too full of self-pity and selfish thoughts.

To win that battle with Satan, they needed to make their faith stronger by serious prayer, fasting, and humility. They would have to let go of their selfishness and be filled with the Holy Spirit's power. Only the kind of faith that leads to total dependence on God and complete dedication to His work can bring the Holy Spirit into the battle against the evil spirits of Satan.

Our faith will be stronger if we study God's Word, alone and with other believers. Then the barriers Satan throws across our path, which seem impossible to cross, will disappear.

CHAPTER 48

WHO WILL BE THE MOST IMPORTANT?

" 'Whoever wants to be the most important must be last of all and servant of all' " (Mark 9:35).

hey returned to Capernaum quietly since Jesus wanted to avoid the crowds and spend the rest of His time in Galilee teaching His disciples. He tried to tell them again that He was going to be put to death, then rise from the grave. But while Jesus' words filled them with sadness, the disciples didn't understand what He was saying.

Instead the disciples argued among themselves about who would be the greatest—the most important and powerful—in Jesus' new kingdom. They hid their argument from Jesus, but He read their thoughts. He wanted to discuss it, but He had to wait until they were ready to understand.

THE TEMPLE TAX

As they entered town, a temple tax collector stopped Peter and asked, "Does your teacher pay the temple tax?" The rabbis required everyone to pay this tax to support the temple—everyone except for priests and prophets. Jesus' enemies saw this as a way to trap Him, and the tax collector was happy to help. If Jesus didn't pay, they would say that He didn't support the temple. If He did, it would

This chapter is based on Matt. 17:22-27; 18:1-20; Mark 9:30-50; Luke 9:46-48.

show that the rabbis were right to reject Him as a prophet.

Peter answered quickly and incorrectly. "Yes," he said, trying to protect Jesus' reputation. He didn't realize what the rabbis were trying to do.

When Peter rejoined the others, Jesus asked, "What do you think, Peter? When kings collect taxes, who pays them—his own children or others?"

Peter answered, "Other people pay the taxes."

Jesus agreed. "The children don't pay." In Israel, the people of God paid taxes to support God's services in the temple. But Jesus, the Son of God, did not need to pay.

> *God chooses workers who are humble to fill the highest positions of power.*

If Jesus paid the tax quietly, He would have been agreeing that He should and denying that He was the Son of God. But He refused to get caught in the trap and be accused of not supporting the temple. Instead He showed His divinity in the way He obtained the money for the tax.

"Go fish in the lake," Jesus told Peter. "When you catch the first fish, you will find a coin in its mouth. Take that coin and pay the tax collector."

Jesus did not have to pay the tax, but He didn't want to offend anyone. It was a great lesson for the disciples. While they should never compromise on principles of truth, they should avoid offending or antagonizing anyone whenever possible.

LIKE A CHILD

While Peter was away fishing, Jesus asked the others, "What were you arguing about on the way here?"

They were too ashamed to answer. Their selfish ambitions didn't compare well to His selfless love. Finally, someone asked, "Teacher, who will be the greatest in Your kingdom?" Although He had spoken plainly about what was waiting for Him in Jerusalem, just the mention of the city made them hope that He was going to set Himself up as king. Jesus knew that they didn't understand His kingdom yet. But this selfish kind of thinking could destroy them and the new church. It reminded Him of Lucifer who wanted the highest place in heaven. Lucifer wanted to be the greatest, and humans who want the same are being influenced by him. Satan's kingdom is a kingdom of force: every person sees others as obstacles in their way or stones to step on as they climb higher. Those motivated by pride and power are focused on themselves. They have no place in Jesus' kingdom, for they are following Satan.

While Lucifer wanted to be equal with God, Jesus gave up His power and became a servant, a human. He lived the truth of His answer to their question: " 'Whoever wants to be the most important must be last of all and servant of all' " (Mark 9:35).

Now, even with the Cross almost in view, His own disciples were so self-centered that they couldn't understand His mission or show any sympathy for Him. Jesus tried to correct their thinking. He wanted them to see that people who are motivated by pride and power are focused only on themselves and the rewards they could get. They would have no place in heaven, because they were following Satan.

Before honor comes humility. God chooses workers who are humble to fill the highest positions of power. The most childlike follower is the best worker for God—he or she feels the need for divine help and pleads for it. This follower will succeed where more intelligent or talented workers fail, because they depend on God and follow His plan. When Christians begin to think highly of themselves and feel that their abilities are needed in order for God's work to be successful, God sets them aside. His work goes on without them.

The disciples didn't just need to understand Jesus' kingdom better—they needed a change of heart. Jesus called a child to stand in front of them. Then as He tenderly held the little one in His arms, He said, "You must change and become like this child. Otherwise, you will never be a part of the kingdom of heaven. The greatest person in My kingdom is the one who is humble like this child." The simple, self-forgetting love of a child is what heaven values. It is the mark of true greatness.

With Jesus, pride and appearances are forgotten. Rich, poor, educated, ignorant—all have been paid for with His blood, and all are equal in His eyes. God values people by their relationship with Jesus.

The disciples began to rethink some of their actions. John asked, "Teacher, we saw someone using Your name to force demons out of a person. We told him to stop, since he isn't one of us." James and John thought they were protecting Jesus when they did this. Now they saw that they were just jealous of their relationship with the Savior.

Jesus said, "Don't stop him. Anyone who uses My name to do a miracle will not be speaking against Me. Whoever is not against us is with us."

Many besides the disciples had been touched by Jesus' work and words. It was important that the disciples not discourage any of these people. Jesus is the world's Great Teacher. We sit at His feet and learn. And every person whom He has touched can be a channel by which He shows His love. We must be very careful not to criticize or discourage any of God's messengers and interrupt the light He is shining into this dark world.

Jesus compared these new believers to little children. He said that it would be better to have a large heavy stone tied around their neck and drown in the sea than to cause new believers to lose their faith. This strong language makes it clear—one of the worst sins a person can commit is to claim to be a Christian, but lead others away from God.

Jesus healed the sick and taught about God's love even though He was criticized and cursed. When we see what He went through for us at Gethsemane and on the cross, we, too, can give up our selfish ways. We will be delighted to follow His example, to be shamed, criticized, even persecuted for Him.

One cherished sin—a sinful habit we repeat and refuse to give up—is enough to weaken our characters and mislead other people. Just as a person would cut off an arm or a leg to save his or her life, we must give up anything to follow Him and save our souls.

Just as salt can save food and prevent it from going bad, Christians can have a saving influence on society. But to do so, they must reflect the love of Jesus. Then there can be no selfishness, no "me-first" attitudes, no trying to be the most important.

Each person who chooses to follow Jesus has great value. If we have the advantages of good education, a religious background, or strong personal character, then we are in debt to those who are less fortunate. Angels are always with those who have the hardest battles to fight—those who have weak personalities or flawed characters or who find themselves in discouraging situations. We can join in the work to save them.

Jesus put it this way: "If a man has a hundred sheep, and one of them gets lost, doesn't he leave the others and go to look for the lost one? If he finds it, he is happier over that sheep than the ninety-nine that never left! Your Father in heaven does not want anyone to be lost."

SOMEONE WHO SINS AGAINST YOU

If a believer sins against you, don't embarrass him or her by sharing the fault with others, and don't disgrace the followers of Jesus by making it public. Dealing with wounded souls requires a most delicate touch—handle each difficulty in private, not with a critical or judgmental attitude but with the love of Jesus for this person in your heart.

If the person refuses to listen, then take one or two others with you to express your concern. If he or she still refuses to listen, then and only then should you take the issue to the whole church. The members should pray and work with love to draw this person back. When they do, the Holy Spirit will work through them.

The simple, self-forgetting love of a child is what heaven values.

Persons who reject all these efforts have broken their tie to Jesus and the church. Jesus said that such persons should be treated like unbelievers—not despised or ignored, but treated with kindness. It is our duty as Christians to try to bring back those who have fallen away from Jesus into sinful habits. If we don't try to help, we're guilty also.

We should not discuss people's problems with others. While trying to help them and bring them back to God, we should go out of our way to shield their problems from others in the church, and of course, from the rest of the world. We should treat each other the way we would want Jesus to treat us.

But in all these efforts, we are not alone. Jesus said, " 'If two of you on earth agree about something and pray for it, it will be done for you by my Father in heaven. This is true because if two or three people come together in my name, I am there with them' " (Matthew 18:19, 20). All of the powers of heaven are working with us when we are reaching out to others with Jesus' love.

CHAPTER 49

LIVING
WATER

" 'Let anyone who is thirsty come to me and drink' "
(John 7:37).

hree times each year the Jews were expected to travel to Jerusalem for religious festivals, and it was time for the Feast of Tabernacles. This feast came at the end of the year, when the grain had been harvested, the olives had been picked, and the grapes had been gathered and squeezed into grape juice. It was a feast of thanksgiving and a time to remember that many years before the Israelites had lived in tents in the desert.

People from all over Palestine and many from other lands came to Jerusalem bearing gifts of thanksgiving for this festival that lasted seven days. During that time, many Israelites camped out in shelters built from leafy tree branches. All around the city, these shelters covered the hillsides. In the city itself, tree tents were built in the streets, in the courts of the temple, and on the rooftops.

The center of the festivities was the temple. There, choirs of Levites led songs that were joined by voices around the city. At night, the temple was lit with many lamps that shone brightly over the people who gathered for the songs and the ceremonies.

The most impressive ceremony honored an event from that journey in the desert. It began at dawn. At the sound of long blasts from

This chapter is based on John 7:1-15, 37-39.

the priests' silver trumpets and the happy shouts of the people in their tents, a priest dipped water out of the Kedron and carried it up the steps of the temple. There at the altar it was mixed with fresh wine and both were poured out again into the brook. This represented the water that God commanded to flow from a rock to satisfy the thirst of the people.

THE RIGHT TIME

Jesus had avoided Jerusalem since the healing at Bethesda in order to avoid useless conflicts with the priests. As Jesus' brothers prepared for their trip to the festival, they tried to talk Him into going as well. They—and the disciples—thought it was a mistake to always be offending the religious leaders. They were sure that the priests and leaders must be right. But they were deeply impressed with Jesus' miracles and His life.

He spoke like no one they had ever heard.

"Go to Jerusalem," his brothers urged Him. "Show the people there the miracles you do. If you really have the power to do these things, show the world!" They hoped that by showing His powers in Jerusalem He would convince the priests and rulers and then set up His kingdom. They liked the idea of being brothers to the king!

Jesus said, "The right time for Me has not yet come." He stayed in Galilee. Jesus was not going to rush into danger and cause a crisis. He knew that the world was going to hate Him. He knew that His mission would lead to His death. He would not hurry and go ahead of His Father's plan.

People from across the world came to this festival hoping to see the man they had heard so much about. Even the Pharisees searched for Jesus, hoping to trap Him. But no one knew where He was. People talked about Him all over the city. Many claimed that He was a prophet sent from God, but others declared that He was just an impostor.

Meanwhile Jesus quietly slipped into the city by the back streets. In the middle of the festival, He walked into the court of the temple, where the enormous crowd had gathered, shocking every voice to silence. Standing there, He spoke like no one they had ever heard. He explained the services of the temple and the words of the prophets with an authority that the priests never had. He would not let His people be guilty of rejecting and murdering their Messiah if He could save them from it.

While Jesus spoke, the crowd was spellbound. "How does He know these things if He never learned from the rabbis?" they asked each other. Like John the Baptist, Jesus had been taught by God.

LIVING WATER

On the last morning of the festival, the priests performed the ceremony honoring the rock in the desert. Jesus, seeing how tired everyone was, cried out, " 'Let anyone who is thirsty come to me and drink. If anyone believes in me, rivers of living water will flow out from that person's heart, as the Scripture says' " (John 7:37, 38).

Moses struck that rock in the desert to make the water flow. It was a symbol of the One who would die to make living streams of salvation flow. Now that One was here, preparing to be struck, so that the water of life would flow out.

Many of those who heard Jesus that day suddenly wanted this water that He offered. In spite of the joy and beauty of the festival, they had been unsatisfied and unhappy. The words "If anyone is thirsty" surprised them and they listened to Jesus' words with new hope. They recognized the offer of the priceless gift of salvation.

Jesus' offer to the thirsty soul is still available. Now more than ever, we need the water of life He promised that day in the temple.

CHAPTER 50

TRAPS

" 'The things I teach are not my own, but they come from him who sent me' " (John 7:17).

Spies shadowed Jesus wherever He went during the festival. Each day the priests and leaders came up with new schemes to keep Him quiet until they could have Him killed. On the first day, the Pharisees asked, "By whose authority do you teach these things?"

Jesus replied, " 'The things I teach are not my own, but they come from him who sent Me. If people choose to do what God wants, they will know that my teaching comes from God and not from Me' " (John 7:16, 17). Those who have surrendered every corner of their hearts to God will recognize God's truth. Once again, Jesus showed His divinity by revealing the rabbis' exact thoughts. He said, "Moses gave you the law, but you're not obeying it. Why are you planning to kill Me?"

Like a flash of lightning, these words helped them see that they were fighting against God. But they wouldn't admit it. Their evil plans had to be concealed. "You must be possessed by a demon," they exclaimed. "We're not trying to kill you."

Jesus ignored their taunts and explained that the healing He had done at Bethesda on Sabbath was justified by their own understanding of the law. According to their law, every boy born must be circum-

This chapter is based on John 7:16-36, 40-53; 8:1-11.

cised after eight days—even if that day was Sabbath. If that was acceptable, then Jesus asked, "Why are you angry with Me for healing a
person's whole body on Sabbath? Stop judging by the way things look
and judge by what is right."

WRONG IDEAS ABOUT THE MESSIAH

Many people in Jerusalem felt drawn to Jesus by an irresistible
power. They felt convicted that He was the Son of God. But Satan
tried to raise doubts. It was generally believed that though the Messiah would be born in Bethlehem, He would then disappear. When
He reappeared, no one would know from where He had come. Many
were sure that the Messiah would have no human relatives.

Jesus said, "You know Me and where I am from. But I didn't come
here by My own power, but by the power of the One who sent me." He
was again claiming to be the Son of God.

The Pharisees wanted to arrest Jesus right then, but He had many
supporters among the people. "When the Messiah comes," they asked,
"will He do more miracles than this man has done?" It was this kind of
thinking that caused the Pharisees to rush to the priests to make plans
to arrest Jesus when He was alone—they didn't dare do it in public.

Still, many who had been convinced that Jesus was the Son of God
began to doubt because of the priests and leaders. Repeating the prophecies that said the Messiah would rule gloriously in Jerusalem, and
from "sea to sea," they sneeringly made comparisons between the glory
described in the prophecies and the poor Jesus. If the people had
studied the prophecies for themselves, they would have found that
Isaiah had prophesied the very things Jesus was doing—as well as what
would happen to Him next.

God doesn't force people to believe Him or to give up their doubts.
He wants us to decide not from impulse, but from the weight of evidence. If the Jews had compared their prophecies with the facts before them, they would have seen the prophecies fulfilled in the life of
the Man from Galilee. Many today are deceived the same way—they
allow others to do their studying and thinking for them. The only way
to truly know truth from error is through our own study of the Bible.

PLANS TO KILL

On the last day of the festival, the priests sent officers to arrest Jesus no matter how angry this would make the crowds. But the officers returned without Him. Furious, the priests asked, "Why didn't you arrest him?"

The officers could only answer, "No one has ever said things like he does." As they had stood near Jesus they listened to Him, hoping to hear something they could use to condemn Him. But the more they heard, the more they saw the glory of Jesus' divinity flooding through His human self.

The priests had once felt that same power and had the same thought: "No one has ever said things like he does." But they had snuffed out the voice of the Holy Spirit. They said, "So Jesus has fooled you too! None of the priests or Pharisees believe in Him—only people who are cursed by God and are ignorant of the law." This type of reasoning is still used by people today. The question asked is not whether something is true, but instead how many other people have accepted it.

> "*Stop judging by the way things look and judge by what is right.*"

The leaders were still afraid that Jesus would keep pulling the people away from them, so He had to be killed. But one of the Pharisees, Nicodemus—who had visited with Jesus one night—said, "Our laws don't allow us to condemn a man without hearing him first."

The others were exasperated. "Are you from Galilee too? If you studied, you would know the Scriptures say that no prophet comes from Galilee." But because of Nicodemus's protest, the leaders gave up for the moment and went home.

A CASE OF ADULTERY

Jesus left the city that night to rest and pray in the olive groves away from the crowds. Early the next morning, He returned to the temple to speak to the people.

There He was soon interrupted by a group of Pharisees who dragged a terrified woman through the crowd to Him. With loud, harsh voices they accused her of adultery—of having sex with a man who was not her husband. This time, they were sure they had Jesus trapped. They asked, "The law of Moses says that a woman like this should be stoned to death. What do you say?"

If Jesus told them to set her free, they would accuse Him of ignoring the law of Moses. If He said to stone her, they would report to the Romans that He was claiming authority to have someone killed—the Romans didn't allow that.

Jesus looked at the scene in front of Him—the trembling, shame-faced woman and her harsh accusers who had no pity. But He looked deeper, into their hearts and lives. Without appearing to have even heard their question, He bent down and began to write in the dust with His finger.

God doesn't force people to believe Him or to give up their doubts.

Impatient and annoyed at Jesus' reaction, the accusers edged closer. When they saw what He was doing, they panicked. There in the sand were all the guilty secrets of their own lives.

The watching crowd pushed forward to find out what was going on. Jesus stood up and said, "Anyone here who has never sinned can throw the first stone." Then He bent over and continued writing. With their robes of false holiness stripped off, the Pharisees stood guilty before the One who is perfect and pure. One by one, they silently slipped away in shame.

Finally, Jesus stood up and looked at the woman. "Where are the ones who accused you? Has no one judged you guilty?"

She shook her head. "No one, sir."

Then Jesus said, "I don't judge you either. Go now, but don't sin anymore."

The woman had trembled as she stood before Jesus, certain that she was going to die. But with His words, her heart melted and she sobbed out her love and her sorrow for her sins. This was the beginning of a new life for her. She became one of Jesus' most loyal followers.

Jesus doesn't gloss over our sins or keep us from feeling guilty when we do wrong. But He has sympathy for our weaknesses and reaches out to us to save us. In the same way, His followers reach out to those who are taking a path away from God. Humans hate sinners but love sin. Jesus hates sin, but loves sinners. Jesus' followers will show the same attitude—a Christian love that is slow to condemn, quick to forgive and encourage, and eager to lead the sinner back toward God.

THE LIGHT
OF THE WORLD

"Then you will know the truth and the truth will make you free"
(John 8:32).

During the festival, the people gathered early in the morning to hear Jesus speak. As the rays of the rising sun lighted the marble palaces and shone off the gold of the temple walls, Jesus pointed up and said, "I am the Light of the world."

God is light, and with those words, Jesus declared His "oneness" with God and His relationship to the earth. He created light in the beginning. He is behind the light that shines from the sun, the moon, and the stars. Just as sunbeams touch every part of this planet, the light from Jesus—the Sun of Righteousness—touches every human heart.

Scientists whose great intelligence and massive research have changed our lives are honored for what they have contributed to humankind. But there is One who knows more and has contributed more. We can trace the line of the great teachers and thinkers as far back as human records go, but the Light was there before then. As the moon reflects the light of the sun, the world's great thinkers—when their teachings are true—reflect the light of Jesus, the Sun of Righteousness. He is the Source of all true education and knowledge.

This chapter is based on John 8:12-59; 9.

When Jesus said, "I am the Light of the world," it was clear to everyone that He was claiming to be the Messiah, the Promised One. The Pharisees and leaders were outraged that an ordinary man was making such a claim. "Who are you?" they asked, trying to force Him to say it plainly. They believed that with such a difference between what the people expected, and Jesus' actions and appearance, that if Jesus announced Himself as the Messiah plainly, the people would reject Him as an imposter.

Jesus is the Source of all true education and knowledge.

But Jesus refused to be trapped. He didn't try to prove who He was. He just talked about His relationship with God. "I do nothing on My own. I say the things that My Father tells Me to say."

To those who were interested in His message, Jesus said, "If you keep following My teachings, then you are really My followers. Then you will know the truth and the truth will make you free."

ABRAHAM'S CHILDREN

This offended the Pharisees again. "We are Abraham's children—we have never been slaves. What do you mean we will be free?"

Jesus looked at these men—slaves of their own hate—and sadly answered, " 'I tell you the truth, everyone who lives in sin is a slave to sin' " (John 8:34). People who refuse to give their hearts to God are under the control of another power. They are in complete slavery, their minds under the control of Satan. But Jesus came to break those chains and set humans free. He paid the price to give everyone the freedom to choose.

There is no greater freedom than when a person surrenders to Jesus. When we want to be set free from sin and cry out for help, our willpower is charged by the energy of the Holy Spirit and we are freed, as God wishes us to be. Sin wins by destroying a person's freedom to choose. The only way we can be free is to join with Jesus. That restores us to the true glory and dignity of being human.

The Pharisees claimed to be the children of Abraham. But being from the genetic line means nothing. If they were Abraham's children, they would recognize the truth being spoken. Being the heir of the apostles is proved the same way. It is shown in the lives of those who have the same spirit of love and who believe the same truths. It is a spiritual relationship, not one passed on by church authority.

"If you really were the children of Abraham," Jesus said, "you would act like him. You wouldn't be trying to kill Me. Your father must be someone else."

The Pharisees saw a chance to remind the people of Jesus' questionable birth. "We're not like some people who don't know who their father is," they said. "Our Father is God."

Jesus ignored their rude remark. "If God was really your Father, you would love Me because I came from Him to you. You are children of the devil—he was a murderer from the beginning and was against the truth." The fact that Jesus spoke the truth is what offended the Pharisees and leaders. It condemned what they taught and how they acted.

> *Jesus lived by God's law in full view of heaven, the unfallen worlds, and sinful humans.*

Every day for three years, these men had been trying to find some defect in Jesus' character. But there was none. "Can any of you prove that I am guilty of sin?" Jesus asked. "If I am telling you the truth, why don't you believe Me?" Satan had found no weaknesses in Him either. Even the demons saw that Jesus was holy. Jesus lived by God's law in full view of heaven, the unfallen worlds, and sinful humans. He always did the things that pleased God.

The Jews didn't recognize God's voice in the message of His Son. They thought they were judging Jesus—actually they were judging themselves. There are those today who approach the Bible the same way. They search for little things to criticize, to argue about, to question, thinking that this shows their intelligence and independent thinking. But it can lead them to lose the ability to appreciate God.

Jesus told them, "Your father Abraham was very happy to see My day." Abraham had prayed to see the Promised One before he died. And in a vision, he saw Jesus' life and death. Then Abraham better understood his experience when God asked him to place his son Isaac on the altar. God stopped Abraham from sacrificing his own son, but Abraham understood that it was God's Son who would be sacrificed to save the world.

By providing a sacrifice in the place of Abraham's son Isaac, God was declaring that no human could pay the price for sin. The pagan system of sacrificing children to pay for their sins was totally unacceptable to God. Only the Son of God can carry the guilt of the world.

The Pharisees responded to Jesus' words with a sneer, seeing them as an opportunity to claim that He was insane. "You aren't even fifty years old and you've seen Abraham?"

With quiet dignity, Jesus answered, " 'I tell you the truth, before Abraham was even born, I am!' " (John 8:58).

The crowd went silent. "I AM" was a name of God given to Moses. Now this teacher from Galilee was claiming to be the ever-existing God. Immediately, the priests and Pharisees shouted that He had committed blasphemy—the worst disrespect for God. Many of the people agreed with the priests and picked up stones to throw at Jesus.

But Jesus hid Himself and left the temple.

A BLIND MAN'S TESTIMONY

As Jesus walked away with His disciples, they saw a young man who had been born blind. The disciples asked, "Teacher, whose sin caused this man to be born blind—his own or his parents'?"

"Neither his sin nor his parents' made him blind," Jesus answered. "He was born blind so that God's power could be shown in him." Then Jesus spit on the ground, made mud from it and put the mud on the blind man's eyes. He told the man, "Go and wash in the pool of Siloam."

The man went and washed the mud off his eyes. When he opened them, he could see for the first time in his life!

Satan had led the Jews to believe that God sent diseases and death as a punishment for sin. So a person who was terribly sick was always considered a terrible sinner. Jesus answered the disciples' question in a practical way. Instead of a discussion about whether God punishes people, He showed them a God of love and mercy who gave sight to a blind man. There was no special healing power in the mud or the pool. The power came from Jesus.

When neighbors and others who had seen the young man begging saw him now, some doubted that it was the same man. But he assured them that it was he. "How did you get your sight?" they asked.

"A man named Jesus made some mud and put it on my eyes," he answered. "Then he told me to go and wash it off. When I did, I could see!"

The neighbors asked, "Where is this man?"

He could only answer, "I don't know."

When the Pharisees heard about the miracle, they were astounded. But it had happened on the Sabbath day, so they hated Jesus even more. They demanded that the young man come to their council and explain. He told them the story again. "He put mud on my eyes, and when I washed it off, I could see!"

Some of the Pharisees said, "This must not be a man of God. He doesn't keep the Sabbath day holy." They appeared to be protecting the Sabbath, though they spent the day planning a murder!

Others of the group were convinced that someone who could heal a blind person was more than an ordinary man. They said, "How can someone be a sinner and do miracles like this?"

The rabbis asked the man, "What do you think of the man who healed you?"

"He is a prophet," the man answered.

Even with the man himself telling them that he had been healed, the Pharisees refused to accept it. They thought of one last way to disprove this miracle—they would intimidate the man's parents into giving some other explanation. It was well known that anyone who declared faith in Jesus as the Messiah would be barred from the synagogue for thirty days—a major disgrace in the community. The Pharisees asked the parents, "Is this your son, whom you say was born blind? How is it that he can now see?"

After the miracle, the man's parents believed in Jesus, but they were afraid. They said, "We know that this is our son who was born blind. But we don't know how he can see now. Ask him—he's old enough to speak for himself."

The Pharisees' questions showed their prejudice against Jesus. As they refused to accept the plain facts, the watching crowds began to wonder: "If Jesus is really an imposter, a fraud, then why would God do such powerful miracles through him?"

A person who was terribly sick was always considered a terrible sinner.

The Pharisees couldn't deny that the miracle had happened. Overwhelmed with joy and gratitude, the man was telling everyone his story. So they tried to silence him again. "You should give God the glory by telling the truth. We know that Jesus couldn't have healed you—he is a sinner."

The man answered, "I don't know if he is a sinner. I only know one thing: I was blind, and now I can see."

The Pharisees asked him to tell them again how it happened, trying to trick him into changing his story. The man said, "I have already told you and you didn't listen. Why do you want to hear it again? Do you want to become his followers too?"

This made them even angrier. They insulted him and said, "You are his follower, but we follow Moses. We know that God spoke to Moses, but we don't even know where this man came from."

Now God gave the healed man words to speak. "This is strange," he said. "You don't know where he came from, but he still healed my eyes. We all know that God doesn't listen to sinners, only to those who worship and obey Him. No one has ever heard of anyone who could heal the eyes of a person who was born blind. If this man wasn't from God, he could do nothing."

For a moment the Pharisees were silent, spellbound by the man's words. They couldn't argue with his reasoning. But then they gathered their robes around themselves as if warding off some contagious disease and said, "You were born full of sin! How can you teach us?" Then they threw him out of the synagogue.

When Jesus heard what happened, He found the man and asked, "Do you believe in the Messiah, the Son of man?"

For the first time, the young man looked at the face of the One who had healed him. He had seen his parents looking confused and concerned. He had seen the angry, frowning faces of the rabbis. Now his new eyes gazed at the love and peace on Jesus' face. "Who is this Son of man, sir, so I can believe in Him?"

Jesus must have smiled as He answered. "You have seen Him. You are talking to Him!" The man fell at Jesus' feet and worshiped Him as the Messiah, the Son of God.

Some of the Pharisees were nearby, so Jesus said, "I came to this world so it could be judged. I came so the blind could see and those who could see would be blinded." People who lived in Jesus' day were shown more about God than the world had ever seen before. But because they were shown more, they were held responsible for what they knew. They were judged by how they responded to Jesus.

Some who heard Jesus asked, "Are we blind also?"

Jesus answered, "If you were blind, you wouldn't be guilty. But the truth is here for you to see." Many people opened their eyes and accepted Jesus as the Messiah. The Pharisees refused to see Him for who He was. They stayed blind and full of their own sin.

THE
GOOD SHEPHERD

" 'I have called you by name, and you are mine' "
(Isaiah 43:1).

esus reached His listeners by speaking of things they were familiar with. Nothing was more common to these people than the sight of a shepherd leading his flock across a pasture of grass. So Jesus said, " 'I am the good shepherd. The good shepherd gives his life for the sheep' " (John 10:11). After having heard this, His followers would see Him in every faithful shepherd and themselves in every helpless flock of sheep.

The Pharisees had just shown that they were not faithful shepherds. They had driven a man out of the fold because he dared to share his story about Jesus. So Jesus pointed to Himself as the real Keeper of God's flock. He said, "The person who climbs into the sheepfold by some other way than the door is a robber. The one who comes in through the door is the shepherd."

Jesus could see that the Pharisees were confused, so He said it plainly. " 'I am the door, and the person who enters through me will be saved and will be able to come in and go out and find pasture. A thief comes to steal and kill and destroy, but I came to give life—life in all its fullness' " (John 10:9, 10).

This chapter is based on John 10:1-30.

Jesus is the door to God's fold. Through Him, all of His children since the beginning of history have found God. In the symbols of the sanctuary, the words of the prophets, and the miracles and lessons the disciples witnessed, Jesus is shown to be the "Lamb of God, who takes away the sin of the world."

Humans have created ceremonies and systems to justify their lives and bring them peace. But anyone who puts a system, ritual, or person in the place of Jesus is a robber. The Jewish priests and leaders destroyed the living pastures and poisoned the springs of the well of life. The Scripture describes these false shepherds: "You have not made the weak strong. You have not healed the sick or put bandages on those that were hurt. You have not brought back those who strayed away or searched for the lost. But you have ruled the sheep with cruel force" (Ezekiel 34:4).

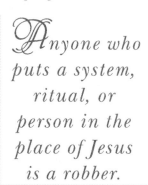

Anyone who puts a system, ritual, or person in the place of Jesus is a robber.

Every non-Christian nation has had its great teachers and religions that offer some other way to find enlightenment or peace. Millions are chained down by false religions that offer no hope or joy, just a dull fear of what happens when we die. Only the gospel—the love of God as shown in Jesus—can lift up the human heart. Anything or anyone who offers another path to God—instead of Jesus—is a robber.

A FAITHFUL SHEPHERD

In those days in the Middle East, a shepherd had to care for his flock constantly, often at the risk of his own life. Bandits, bears, or lions often lay in wait to attack and steal or kill. But the good shepherd cared about his sheep—he knew each one by name, and they would respond when he called.

In the same way, Jesus—the Divine Shepherd—knows His flock even though they are scattered around the world. Jesus knows us each as individuals. He says, " 'I have called you by name, and you are mine' "

(Isaiah 43:1). He knows where we live and the things we face each day. Jesus has on occasion directed His followers to a certain house on a certain street in a certain city to find one of His lost sheep.

Jesus knows each of us as well as He would if we were the only ones for whom He came to die. He knows our needs and our pain. He came to attract all people to Himself. He said, "My sheep hear My voice and follow Me." He cares for each of us as if there was not another person on the planet.

WHY THE SHEEP FOLLOW

A good shepherd does not drive his sheep. He doesn't try to force them or frighten them into going the right way. Instead, he goes ahead of the flock and calls them. This is what our Savior and Shepherd does with His flock. As the shepherd leads his sheep, always meeting the dangers first, Jesus leads His people. Our path to heaven is blessed by our Savior's footprints.

Jesus' disciples don't follow Him to avoid punishment or to earn eternal rewards. They see the Savior's life of flawless love, and that attracts their minds and softens their souls. Love rises in their hearts. They hear His voice, and they follow Him.

Although He now sits on the throne of the universe, Jesus hasn't lost any of His concern for His people. Each person who has given his or her heart to Jesus is more precious to Him than the whole world. Jesus would have come to earth and died on the cross for just one person. He will never abandon someone that He died for. Unless His followers choose to leave Him, He will never let them go.

Our untiring Shepherd has not left us alone to struggle with temptations and finally be crushed by our burdens. Though we cannot see Him, by faith we can hear Him saying, "Don't be afraid; I am with you. I have shared your sorrow, your struggles, your temptations. I have cried tears like yours—I know the pain that is too deep to share with anyone else. You are not alone."

Because we are a gift from His Father and the reward of His work on earth, Jesus loves humans as if they were His children. He loves you! Heaven could give you no better gift. So trust in His love.

Jesus thought about all of the others around the world who were misled by false shepherds and scattered by wolves. He said, "I have other sheep that are not in this fold. I will call them to Me also and there will be one flock and one Shepherd."

As a human, Jesus was mortal. As God, He was the Source of life for the whole world. He could have refused to die, but He gave up His life freely to bring eternal life to us. "We all have wandered away like sheep; each of us has gone his own way. But the Lord has put on him the punishment for all the evil we have done" (Isaiah 53:6).

CHAPTER 53

THE LAST JOURNEY FROM GALILEE

" 'I praise you, Father, Lord of heaven and earth' "
(Luke 10:21).

s the end of His ministry approached, Jesus changed His method of working. Always before, He tried to avoid publicity. He turned away from the people's praise and insisted that no one declare that He was the Messiah. But now all that changed. On His last trip to Jerusalem, Jesus traveled publicly with great crowds. Announcements that He was coming traveled ahead of Him to the towns He would pass. He was headed toward His own sacrifice and that demanded the attention of all the people.

The disciples would have stopped Jesus if they could. They knew how much the religious leaders hated Him. And it was painfully hard for Him to lead His beloved disciples to the distress and misery waiting for them in Jerusalem.

This was also a time that Satan stepped up his attempts to tempt Jesus. "Why should you go to Jerusalem and die? You're young and strong. Everywhere around you are suffering people just waiting to be healed. You could travel through the world, sharing your message, bringing love and healing to those who so desperately need it. Why face death now and leave your work just as it's get-

This chapter is based on Luke 9:51-56; 10:1-24.

ting started?" But Jesus was determined to go to Jerusalem.

The one law of His life was to do His Father's will. And in God's great plan, it was almost time for Jesus to offer Himself as the Sacrifice for humans. He would not fail. His enemies had been plotting to take His life—now He would give it freely.

So Jesus sent messengers ahead to a Samaritan village to announce that He was coming. But these Samaritans hated the Jews and they refused to let Jesus stay there because He was going to the Jewish people in Jerusalem. Because of their prejudice they missed out on the blessing He could have brought to their whole town.

James and John were greatly insulted at this rude treatment. Seeing Mount Carmel in the distance, they were reminded of the story of Elijah and the prophets of Baal. "Lord, do You want us to call fire down from heaven to destroy these people?" they asked.

They were surprised at Jesus' sharp answer. "You don't realize what kind of spirit you're speaking with. I didn't come to destroy people. I came to save them."

Jesus never forces people to accept Him. He accepts only the willing surrender of love. A desire to hurt others who don't agree with us or appreciate our work can only come from Satan. Nothing offends God more than when people try to harass or torment those who won't accept their religious views.

THE SEVENTY DISCIPLES

Jesus spent a good portion of the final months of His ministry in Perea, the area across the Jordan from Judea. Here, with crowds following Him at every step, He repeated many of the things He had taught in other places. He sent out seventy other disciples—ones He had been teaching and training as they followed Him—to go two-by-two to the villages He would visit. Even after His rejection at the Samaritan town, Jesus directed them to visit the cities of Samaria first.

Just before He returned to heaven, Jesus directed His disciples to Samaria as one of the first places they should preach His gospel. When they went to Samaria, the disciples found that the people there had been won over by Jesus' love. Many Samaritans joined their former enemies, the Jews, as they began the Christian church.

When Jesus sent out the seventy disciples, He told them that if the people of a city wouldn't listen to them, they should shake the dust off their sandals and remind them that God's kingdom was coming. They weren't to do this out of anger or spite, but to show how serious it was to refuse to listen to Jesus' gospel. If the people rejected Jesus' message, they also rejected their Savior.

A KNOCK AT THE DOOR

God will never leave His people as they battle with evil.

As He thought of people rejecting His message, Jesus thought of the towns in Galilee where He spent so many days. The people there had heard His words and witnessed the power of His miracles. But instead of trying to understand the Word of God for themselves, they listened to the priests and rabbis, rejected the truth, and kept their traditions. Many people were almost convinced to follow Jesus, but never did.

Every message in the Bible or from God's messengers is a knock at the door of our hearts. It is the voice of Jesus, asking to come in. Every time we ignore that knock, our will to open the door gets weaker. If we ignore the impressions of the Holy Spirit today, they will not be as strong tomorrow. Our heart will be less sensitive. Finally someday we could lose our salvation not because we are evil but because we ignored opportunities to accept truth.

POWER OF THE HOLY SPIRIT

When they finished their work, the seventy disciples came back very happy. "Lord, even the demons obeyed us when we used Your name!" Jesus said, "Of course they did. I saw Satan fall from heaven like a bolt of lightning." Jesus could see beyond the Cross to the great day when sin and Satan would finally be destroyed. He wanted His followers to see Satan as an enemy that was already defeated. "I have given you power to walk on snakes and scorpions and not be hurt. Nothing will hurt you." Satan can defeat no one who claims Jesus' protection by faith. When temptations and troubles come, ask for help from Jesus. God will never leave His people as they battle with evil.

Jesus added, "You should not be happy because spirits obey you, but because your names are written in heaven." It is too easy to be impressed with our own success. We can be safe only by remembering how Jesus has forgiven and changed us. The more we are in touch with Him, the more the Holy Spirit can use us to reach others.

As the disciples listened to Jesus, the Holy Spirit was writing these truths on their hearts. Even though a crowd surrounded them, it seemed as if they were alone with God.

Jesus saw this and praised His Father: " 'I praise you, Father, Lord of heaven and earth, because you have hidden these things from the people who are wise and smart. But you have shown them to those who are like little children. Yes, Father, this is what you really wanted' " (Luke 10:21).

The most respected, the greatest and wisest men of that time, did not understand what Jesus was. But these fishermen and tax collectors knew. From time to time, when they were most open to the Holy Spirit, the disciples realized that God—dressed in the body of a human—was really standing with them. Often when Jesus taught them from the Old Testament—especially verses that pointed to Him, the Messiah—the disciples understood better than those who had written the words.

The only way we improve our understanding of truth is to keep our hearts open to the Holy Spirit. Science is too limited to understand the plan of salvation. Philosophy cannot explain it. Salvation can be understood only by experience. Only a person who sees his or her own sinfulness can understand the precious value of the Savior.

The people of Perea listened thoughtfully to Jesus' teachings as He slowly made His way toward Jerusalem. During this time, Jesus told many of His parables. The stories and the lessons Jesus taught on this last trip strengthened the disciples later when they began their mission to the world.

CHAPTER 54

THE
GOOD SAMARITAN

"If we love each other, God lives in us, and his love is made perfect in us" (1 John 4:12).

s Jesus was teaching, an expert on the law stood up and asked, "Teacher, what must I do to have eternal life?" The priests and rabbis were using this lawyer to trap Jesus into saying something that would upset the people.

But Jesus refused to argue. He asked, "What do you read in the law?"

The lawyer answered, "Love the Lord your God with all your heart, all your soul, all your strength, and all your mind. Also, love your neighbor as you love yourself."

Jesus must have nodded approvingly. "That is right," He said. "Do those things and you will have eternal life." It isn't possible to keep one of these rules and break the other. They are tied together—the same principle runs through them both. A complete love for God and an unselfish love for others should be the guiding principles of our lives.

The lawyer had been studying the Scriptures. His answer didn't include any demand that the rabbis' traditions and rituals be kept. He knew that he did not always show love to others. His heart was touched by Jesus' words, but he tried to justify his actions. He asked, "Who is my neighbor?"

This was a question the Jews often argued about. All agreed that the heathen and Samaritans were strangers and enemies. But what about the poor, ignorant, "unclean" people in their own country? Should these count as neighbors?

Jesus didn't condemn their prejudice. Instead He told a simple story, creating such a beautiful picture of heaven-like love that it touched all their hearts. As Jesus showed here, the best way to deal with misguided thinking is to present truth.

Jesus said, "As a man was traveling from Jerusalem to Jericho, he was attacked by robbers. They ripped off his clothes, beat him senseless, and left him lying on the side of the road. Later, a Jewish priest traveled down that same road. When he saw the man, he walked by on the other side. Next, another temple worker, a Levite, came by. He went over and looked at the man, then he also walked by on the other side of the road."

This was a true story, known to have recently happened. In fact, the priest and the temple worker were in the crowd listening to Jesus. Everyone knew that the road to Jericho was dangerous. It led through a rocky canyon that seemed to be infested with bandits.

Both the priest and the temple worker were expected to help those in need in their society. Jesus Himself had given instructions that all who worked in the temple were to especially look out for the widows, the orphans, and the strangers in their land. But like the other leaders in their country, these two were selfish, prejudiced, and uncaring. The priest barely glanced at the victim. The temple worker felt that he should do something, but since he couldn't be certain that the man wasn't a Samaritan, he left him there.

Angels of heaven were watching to see if the priest and temple worker would feel compassion for the stranger and help him. Through Moses, Jesus had taught the Israelites to care for the weak and needy and to "love the stranger" among them. But in their schools of national prejudice, the priest and temple worker had learned to be selfish and narrow-minded. Since they couldn't be sure that he was a Jew, they left the wounded man to die.

Our neighbor is every person who needs our help.

Next a man from Samaria came down the road, riding a donkey. This man knew that if he were the one lying by the road, no Jewish man would help him. He knew that he was risking his own safety by lingering there. But nothing mattered to him except the man lying there suffering. The Samaritan took off his own coat to cover the man, and washed and bandaged his wounds. Then he lifted the victim onto his donkey and led it slowly and carefully to an inn where he cared for the man all night.

Before he left the next morning, the Samaritan gave the innkeeper money and said, "Take care of this man. If you spend more than this on him, I will pay it back when I return."

As He finished the story, Jesus looked into the lawyer's eyes and asked, "Which of these three men was a neighbor to the man who was attacked by robbers?"

The lawyer answered, "The one who helped him."

Jesus nodded. "Then go and do what he did."

KEEPING THE LAW

The question, "Who is my neighbor?" is clearly answered. Our neighbor is every person who needs our help, every heart wounded by Satan, everyone who is a child of God.

In this story, Jesus was sharing the story of His mission. Humankind had been robbed and left to die by Satan. But our Savior left heaven to rescue us. He healed our wounds, covered us with His coat of righteousness, and paid the way for our salvation. Pointing to His own example, He says to His followers, "As I have loved you, so you should love one another."

By obeying the demands of his kind heart, the Samaritan showed that he obeyed the law. Jesus' message to the lawyer was, "Go and do what he did."

We need the same lesson today. Selfishness threatens to extinguish the fires of love that should be in our hearts. Unless we practice self-less service for others, whatever we claim, we are not really Christians. Jesus asks us to join Him in saving humanity. Many who have made mistakes feel shame and guilt. They need encouragement. As Christians, when we see a person distressed—no matter the reason—we can never say, "They must deserve it" or "This doesn't involve me."

The story of the good Samaritan and Jesus' life show us what keeping the law and loving our neighbor as ourselves really means. When we show this kind of love, we are declaring to everyone that Jesus lives in our hearts. "If we love each other, God lives in us, and his love is made perfect in us" (1 John 4:12).

G O D ' S   K I N G D O M
I S   I N   Y O U

" 'I have many more things to say to you, but they are too much for you now' " (John 16:12).

ore than three years had gone by since John the Baptist announced: "The kingdom of heaven is here." Many of the Pharisees who spoke out against Jesus began saying that He had failed at His mission. "Where is this kingdom of heaven you keep talking about?" they asked.

Jesus answered, " 'God's kingdom is coming, but not in a way that you will be able to see with your eyes. People will not say, "Look, here it is!" or, "There it is!" because God's kingdom is within you' " (Luke 17:20, 21).

Then He turned to His disciples. " 'The time will come when you will want very much to see one of the days of the Son of Man. But you will not see it' " (Luke 17:22). Jesus wanted to tell them, "You do not realize what a great privilege you have had. You will look back and long for the days when you could walk and talk with the Son of God."

It wasn't until after Jesus returned to heaven and the Holy Spirit had come to them that the disciples really understood Jesus' life and mission. They finally began to grasp that they had spent those years in the presence of God. They began to actually understand His teach-

This chapter is based on Luke 17:20-22.

ings, His miracles, and the prophecies about Him. It was as if they were waking up from a dream.

They never got tired of repeating His words or discussing the things He did. The things He had tried to teach them now seemed new and fresh. The Scriptures seemed like a new book.

As they studied the prophecies of the Messiah again, the Holy Spirit helped them learn. They understood Jesus' work here and the work He had gone to complete in heaven. They were amazed to realize how little they had grasped of the prophecies that so clearly described Jesus and His mission. Even though they had watched Him each day walking beside them, they had not fully seen the divinity hidden behind His human form.

Oh, how they longed to see Jesus again, to listen while He explained the Scriptures and talked about the kingdom of God. What did Jesus mean when He said, " 'I have many more things to say to you, but they are too much for you now' "

The kingdom of God comes quietly and personally to human hearts.

(John 16:12)? It hurt them to realize how weak their faith was, and how much more Jesus wanted to tell them that they were not ready to hear. They often asked themselves "Why did we allow the priests and rabbis to confuse us so that we didn't fully appreciate who was teaching us?"

When they were arrested and brought before councils and kings, or thrown in prison, they felt it was a privilege to suffer as Jesus did in order to share the message He had given them.

THE CHRISTIAN AND THE WORLD

The kingdom of God comes quietly and personally to human hearts. It is not flashy and demanding like the things of this world. Today many want to make Jesus the ruler of this world's governments, courts, and marketplaces. Since He isn't here in person, they feel free to speak for Him and try to enforce laws they think are His will. This is the kind of kingdom the Jews wanted when

Jesus was here. But He said, "My kingdom does not belong to this world."

The government Jesus lived under was dishonest and cruel. People were treated unfairly—even abused. Jesus didn't try to reform or replace that government. He didn't speak out against the Romans or other national enemies. He didn't interfere with the authority of those who were in power. He kept out of government issues not because He didn't care but because the cure for those problems had to begin in the heart of each person.

Jesus' kingdom isn't established by the decisions of courts or legislatures. It is set up by the influence of the Holy Spirit changing the hearts of humans. That is the only power that can truly change our society. And it is seen as we share the Word of God and show its power in our lives.

Today, as it was in Jesus' day, God's kingdom is not with those who demand recognition and support by governments and civil laws. It is with those who live and share this spiritual truth: "I was put to death on the cross with Christ, and I do not live anymore—it is Christ who lives in me" (Galatians 2:20).

CHAPTER 56

JESUS
LOVED CHILDREN

*" 'Let the little children come to me. Don't stop them, because the
kingdom of God belongs to people who are like these children' "
(Mark 10:14).*

esus loved children. He was blessed by their simple words
of praise and joy, especially after dealing with deceitful,
hypocritical adults. Wherever He went, His kind, gentle
manner won the love of children.

It was the custom in those days for children to be brought
to a respected rabbi or teacher for his blessing. But when mothers
brought their little ones to Jesus, the disciples were annoyed. They
felt that children were too young to understand anything and that
they would bother Jesus. But it was the disciples who were bothering
Him! Jesus understood the burden of mothers who were trying to
train their children. He had drawn these mothers to Him.

On this day, several mothers together brought their little ones to
be blessed by Jesus. Jesus heard their request, but waited to see how
the disciples would react. When they tried to send the mothers away,
Jesus stopped them. " 'Let the little children come to me. Don't stop
them, because the kingdom of God belongs to people who are like
these children' " (Mark 10:14).

Then Jesus gathered the children in His arms and gave them a
blessing. He saw that some of these very children would give their

This chapter is based on Matt. 19:13-15; Mark 10:13-16; Luke 18:15-17.

lives for His kingdom. On this day, He answered their questions and simplified His most important lessons just for them.

Jesus gathered the children in His arms and gave them a blessing.

Those mothers were encouraged in their work by Jesus' words, and mothers today should be also. He cares about mothers today just as He did when He gathered the little ones in His arms in Judea.

Jesus knows the burden that mothers carry. He made a long journey to relieve the anxious heart of a Canaanite woman. He gave the widow from Nain her son again by raising him to life. Even in His suffering on the cross, Jesus remembered His own mother. He is still touched today by the sorrow of mothers. He will give them comfort and help whatever their worries or needs.

Jesus still invites mothers to bring their little ones to Him to be blessed. Even an infant in its mother's arms can come under God's influence through the mother's faith and prayer. John the Baptist was filled with the Holy Spirit when he was born. If we, as parents, maintain a close relationship with God, we can expect the Holy Spirit to mold the lives of our children, even from their earliest moments.

MOTHERS AND FATHERS

With their open hearts and simple trust, children accept the gospel more easily than adults. Fathers and mothers should see their children as young members of God's family and educate them to be ready to join Him in heaven. Each home can be a school where children learn to bring their sins to Jesus and ask forgiveness, knowing that He loves and accepts them—just as He did with children while He was on earth.

As a mother teaches her children to obey because they love her, she is teaching them their first Christian lesson. Little ones who trust and obey their mothers are learning to trust and obey their Savior. Fathers can learn from Jesus' example. His words were powerful but never unkind even to rude or selfish people. The grace of Jesus in their hearts will lead fathers and mothers to treat their children the way they themselves wish to be treated.

Parents can learn from nature how to train their children. A gardener trains a rose bush with a gentle touch. Repeating little attentions to its leaves and stem, using no violent moves that might damage it, moistening the soil around it, protecting it from strong winds and the scorching sun—this allows God to make the rose bush flourish and produce lovely flowers. By similar gentle touches, we can influence the characters of our children to be like the character of Jesus.

Encourage children to express love for each other and for God. Take them out to see Jesus in nature. Teach them to see His love in all the wonders of creation. Show them that God made laws for all living things, and help them see that His laws for us protect our happiness. Don't wear them out with long prayers and dreary sermons—use nature's object lessons to teach them the importance of obeying God's laws.

Don't keep children away from Jesus by being cold or harsh. Never let them think that heaven couldn't be a happy place if you are there. Don't speak of religion as something children can't understand. Don't make them think that religion is gloomy and that following Jesus means giving up all the joy and fun in life.

Cooperate with the Holy Spirit as God's power moves in their hearts. Jesus is calling them to be His followers. Nothing gives Him more joy than for children to give their hearts to Him. His heart goes out to children who have inherited troubling character traits and personalities. Many parents don't have the tenderness and wisdom to help solve the problems they themselves have created. But Jesus watches over these children with sympathy and understanding.

We can have a part in drawing them to the Savior. With wisdom and gentle kindness, we can give these children courage and hope. The grace of Jesus can change their characters and make them into the kind of children who are fit citizens for the kingdom of God.

CHAPTER 57

THE WEALTHY YOUNG LEADER

" 'Go and sell everything you have, and give the money to the poor' "
(Mark 10:21).

s Jesus started to leave, a man ran up and fell to his knees before Him. "Good Teacher," the man asked, "what must I do to have eternal life?"

Although he was young, this man was wealthy and already held office as a member of the Sanhedrin. He was one of the leaders of the Jewish nation. But as he saw Jesus' love for the children, he was deeply moved. He had to ask the question that was so important to him and to every human being.

Jesus wanted to find out what was behind the question. Did this man realize that he was talking to the Son of God? Jesus asked, "Why do you call Me good? Only God is good." In answer to his question, Jesus told him that a person who wants eternal life should obey the commandments.

The man nodded. "Teacher, I have obeyed all of them since I was a boy. What am I missing?" This young leader had a high opinion of his own righteousness, but he could see that Jesus had something more.

Jesus looked into the man's eyes and read his heart. He could see that this young leader was just the kind of person the new church

This chapter is based on Matt. 19:16-22; Mark 10:17-22; Luke 18:18-23.

would need. He saw what kind of man this leader could become if He would choose to follow Jesus. But most of all, Jesus loved him and wanted to give him the peace he was looking for. " 'There is one more thing you need to do,' " He said. " 'Go and sell everything you have, and give the money to the poor, and you will have treasure in heaven. Then come and follow me' " (Mark 10:21).

Jesus looked into the man's eyes and read his heart.

Jesus could see what was missing. The wealthy young man needed the love of God in his heart. Without it, his good behavior was of no value. To receive God's love, he needed to surrender his love of self. His wealth, the things he owned, and his position of power were too important to him. They were a quiet evil in his character that would become more important to him than God. He had to choose between the treasures of this world and the treasures of heaven.

Jesus watched the young man, hoping that he would listen to the Holy Spirit and choose to follow. Jesus' words may have seemed radical, but accepting and obeying them was this leader's only hope for salvation.

THE PRICE IS TOO HIGH

The young leader, quickly seeing what Jesus' words would mean to his lifestyle and his position in society, shook his head with sadness. He wanted heaven's treasure, but he didn't want to give up the life his wealth gave him. He left depressed because the price Jesus asked seemed too high.

This man may have behaved properly all his life, but he showed that he was not keeping the commandments. Wealth and power were idols he put ahead of God. He loved the gifts God had given him more than the Giver. Being with Jesus meant less to him than being seen as rich and powerful. From this point on, he treasured only worldly things.

This story is a lesson to us. Obeying God's law is more than behaving properly. It means living the kind of life that Jesus did—a life of selfless love. Only those who give all they have and all they are to God are really His children.

God gives us the money, the abilities, and the opportunities to work in His place for those who are poor or suffering. When we use our gifts as God intended, we become coworkers with Jesus. Those who have wealth or positions of power—like the rich young leader—may think that they cannot give all that up to follow Jesus. But surrendering self is the basis of what Jesus taught. The only way to save humans is to cut away the things that will weaken their characters and lead them away from God.

When Christians give back to God some of the things He has given them, they are building up treasures in heaven. The joy of seeing others saved in God's kingdom is the reward for all who put their feet in the footprints of the One who said, "Follow Me."

CHAPTER 58

LAZARUS

" 'Didn't I tell you that if you believed you would see the glory of God?' " (John 11:40)

ne of Jesus' closest friends and most faithful followers was Lazarus, who lived in Bethany, a small town close to Jerusalem. Jesus loves every person on earth, but He formed a special friendship with some while He was here. Lazarus was one of those.

Jesus often visited Lazarus's house. With no home of His own, He was glad to have a place where He could escape the endless conflicts of His public appearances. Most of the time He had to teach with parables and use lessons from nature to help the crowds understand, but here He could speak clearly.

Jesus loved Lazarus's sisters, Mary and Martha, also. Mary wanted only to sit at Jesus' feet and listen as He taught. On an earlier trip, Martha—who was working hard to care for her guests—had complained to Jesus. "Lord, don't You care that my sister is leaving all the work to me? Tell her to help me."

Jesus answered her kindly and patiently. "Martha, Martha, you are worried about many things. Mary has chosen the most important thing—it will never be taken from her." Martha needed to worry less about little things so she could concentrate on important things. The

This chapter is based on Luke 10:38-42; John 11:1-44.

truths Mary was hearing would be with her for the rest of her life, long after Jesus was gone.

One day Lazarus suddenly became ill. His sisters sent a message to Jesus: "Lord, Your friend is sick." They were worried because the sickness seemed serious. But they knew that Jesus could heal any disease. They were sure He would come quickly.

Jesus loves every person on earth, but He formed a special friendship with some while He was here.

The disciples were surprised at how Jesus took this news. He didn't seem sad or worried. But He told them, " 'This sickness will not end in death. It is for the glory of God, to bring glory to the Son of God' " (John 11:4). Then He stayed where He was for two more days. This surprised the disciples even more. They knew how He loved that family.

The sisters waited anxiously as Lazarus got weaker. The messenger returned with only Jesus' message: "This sickness will not end in death." They held on to their hope. When Lazarus died, they were bitterly disappointed, but somehow felt Jesus' peace.

As the two days passed, Jesus seemed to forget about the message. The disciples worried. They thought about John the Baptist dying in prison when Jesus could have saved him. Jesus had warned them that trials and dangers were coming. Would He leave them to suffer alone also? Then Jesus said, "Let's go back to Judea."

The disciples wondered why He waited two days if He was planning to go back to the area near Bethany. They were worried for Him and for themselves. "Teacher," they said, "You can't go there. The Jews there tried to stone You not long ago."

Jesus tried to reassure them. "Aren't there twelve hours in a day?" he asked. He was saying, "These are the last hours of My day, but while My time lasts, I am safe." He knew that as long as He followed His Father's plan, He was secure. Anyone who follows the Holy Spirit's lead will walk the path of life safely. But if we choose a path of our own, we're not safe no matter where we are.

Then Jesus told them, " 'Our friend Lazarus has fallen asleep, but I am going there to wake him' " (John 11:11).

The disciples were glad to hear that Jesus really did care about Lazarus and his sisters. They said, "But Lord, if he's sleeping, he'll get well."

So Jesus said it plainly. " 'Lazarus is dead. And I am glad for your sakes I was not there so that you may believe. But let's go to him now' " (John 11:14, 15).

The disciples were shocked by Jesus' words. Did He really avoid going to His friends to let Lazarus die? They didn't understand that Jesus had been there as His friends suffered and cried. But He had to think of more than just their feelings and their lives. His disciples were going to take His message to the world. He had allowed Lazarus to die for their sake—so their faith would grow stronger. And there was another reason Jesus waited—He didn't want to give up on His people. He wanted to give them one more reason to believe that He was the Messiah.

If Jesus had been in Bethany, Lazarus could not have died. So He had to stay away. He allowed their suffering. He felt their pain. He didn't love them less because He waited. He knew that for the sisters, for Lazarus, for Himself, and His disciples, the pain would be worthwhile.

All who have reached out for God in pain or sadness should know that God is never closer to us than at the moment of our greatest discouragement. Someday we will look back with thankfulness at this dark time in our lives. Our faith will be stronger for every trial and temptation we face.

When they reached Bethany, Jesus sent a messenger in to the sisters and waited in a quiet place along the road. Their house was filled with hired mourners, wailing and crying. Jesus knew that some of His worst enemies were there also. That's why He kept His distance.

The message was given to Martha so quietly that not even Mary heard. She slipped out to meet Jesus and saw on His face the same love and tenderness she had always known. But looking at Him, all that came out were the same words she and Mary had repeated to each other over and over. "Lord, if You had been here, my brother wouldn't have died." But then she added, "I know—even now—that God will give You anything You ask for."

God is never closer to us than at the moment of our greatest discouragement.

Jesus declared, " 'Your brother will rise and live again' " (John 11:23). He wanted her to think about the resurrection that is promised to the righteous at the end of time.

Martha answered, "I know he will, at the resurrection on the last day."

Then Jesus said to her, "I am the Resurrection and the Life. If those who believe in Me die, they will live again. Everyone who lives and believes in Me will never die. Do you believe this, Martha?" Jesus was gazing into the future, to the time of His second coming. Then His righteous followers who had died would rise up to never ending eternal life, and the righteous ones who still lived would never die. The raising of Lazarus would be a sample of that great resurrection day. By these words and His soon-coming miracle, Jesus was showing that He had the right and the power to give eternal life.

Martha answered with all the faith in her heart, "Yes, Lord. I believe You are the Messiah, the Son of God." Then she went to get Mary. "Jesus is here, asking for you," she told her sister quietly. They knew the priests were waiting to arrest Jesus if they could. Fortunately, the mourners were so loud that no one could hear their voices.

As soon as Mary heard, she jumped up and went out. Thinking that she was going to the grave to weep, the mourners followed her. When Mary found Jesus, she cried out, "Lord, if You had been here, my brother wouldn't have died."

Seeing Mary's tears—and hearing the fake sadness of the mourners who followed her—upset Jesus. He knew that some of the very people who were pretending to mourn would soon be plotting to kill Him and Lazarus. "Where did you bury Lazarus?" He asked.

"Come and we'll show You," the sisters answered. Together, they led Jesus to the gravesite in a cave closed with a giant stone. With breaking hearts, the sisters began to cry again as others of Lazarus's real friends joined them.

Seeing their pain and grief, Jesus cried with them. But His tears went deeper than just Mary and Martha's loss. He felt the pain that sin had caused since the beginning—the suffering, the sorrow, the death that had come to humans as a result of breaking God's laws of life. Jesus wept, wanting more than anything to stop that pain forever.

Finally, Jesus said, "Move the stone back."

Thinking that He just wanted to see Lazarus's body, Martha objected. "Lord, it's been four days since he died. There will be a bad smell." This was an important point to make, because Jesus' enemies had always before claimed that He tricked people with His miracles. When Jesus raised Jairus's daughter from the dead earlier, they claimed that she had only been sleeping. This time, there could be no doubt that Lazarus was dead.

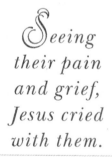

Seeing their pain and grief, Jesus cried with them.

When God is about to do something wonderful, Satan finds someone who will object. Martha's faith still hadn't grasped Jesus' promise. But He answered her gently. " 'Didn't I tell you that if you believed you would see the glory of God?' " (John 11:40)

Things that we think are impossible are not impossible to Someone who is all-powerful. Jesus could have commanded the angels who were always near Him to move the stone. But again He would show that humans are to cooperate with God in His work. What human power can do, divine power is not summoned to do.

Finally, the stone was rolled back and the cold, silent body of Lazarus could be seen. Surprised, uncertain what to expect, the crowd stood silently around the cave, waiting to see what would happen.

Jesus stepped closer to the cave opening, then looked up and said, "Father, I thank You that You heard Me. I know that You always hear Me, but I say this for the people here. I want them to believe that You sent Me." His enemies wanted to kill Him because of His claim to be the Son of God, but Jesus made it clear who He was and who had sent Him. Now they would see the truth of His claim. This prayer also showed that Jesus did not work independently of His Father. His miracles came by faith and prayer.

Then Jesus raised His voice and cried out, "Lazarus, come out!" As divine power flashed through His human form, His face glowed with the glory of God.

From Jesus' face, every eye turned to stare at the cave, waiting for evidence that Jesus really had that kind of power, that He really was the Son of God. Now His claim would be proved or the hope of His followers would be snuffed out forever.

There was a stir—then the dead man stood at the door of the cave. With the grave cloth wrapped around him, Lazarus could barely move. As the people stared, barely breathing themselves, Jesus said, "Take that cloth off of him. Let him go."

In a rush, it was done and Lazarus stood before them, not weak as he had been, but perfectly healthy and strong. With eyes full of love, he threw himself at Jesus' feet.

At first the crowd was speechless with amazement. Then, suddenly, the gravesite rang with shouts of rejoicing. With their arms wrapped around their brother's neck, Mary and Martha thanked Jesus through tears of joy.

While this wonderful reunion went on, Jesus slipped away.

CHAPTER 59

PLOTS
AND PLANS

"That day they started planning to kill Jesus"
(John 11:53).

he news about Lazarus spread across Jerusalem. Through their spies, the Jewish leaders soon learned exactly what had happened. A dead man had been brought to life in broad daylight in front of a crowd of witnesses, and nothing could explain it away as a trick. This mighty miracle was the crowning evidence that God had really sent His Son to the world to save humans. It was a demonstration of divine power that would convince anyone whose mind was still capable of clear thinking. A meeting of the Sanhedrin was called to decide what should be done.

The other strong religious group among the Jews, the Sadducees, had never been as hateful toward Jesus as the Pharisees were. But now they were worried. They taught that there was no resurrection of the dead and argued that it was impossible for a dead body to be brought to life. But a few words from Jesus had shown that they were ignorant about the Scriptures and about God's power. Now the Sadducees decided that Jesus had to die.

The Pharisees believed in the resurrection, but they refused to see this miracle as proof that Jesus was the Messiah. They hated Jesus because He ignored their traditions and rules. By exposing

This chapter is based on John 11:47-54.

their hollow, unholy lives, He had seriously cut into their influence and power. They wanted revenge for the things He said about them. Several times they tried to stone Him but Jesus always escaped.

They tried everything to discredit Jesus with the people, but nothing worked. Too many had heard His teachings and seen His miracles and they knew He was not evil. In desperation, the Pharisees finally declared that anyone who claimed to believe in Jesus would be thrown out of the synagogue.

So while they fought each other on every other point, the Pharisees and Sadducees were united against Jesus. Together on the Sanhedrin council they discussed what to do about Him. Actually, the Sanhedrin had no real power, but the Romans allowed them to meet and deal with issues that concerned the Jewish religion.

THE SANHEDRIN

As the council debated how to have Jesus killed, some members had second thoughts. Influenced by the Holy Spirit, they seemed to clearly remember events in Jesus' life, starting when He was a child teaching them in the temple. This last miracle seemed to prove that Jesus must be the Son of God. The troubled leaders didn't know what to do.

Caiaphas argued that even if Jesus was innocent, He must be disposed of.

Then Caiaphas, the high priest stood up to speak. A proud and cruel man, Caiaphas said, "Don't you people know anything? Don't you know that it is better for one man to die than for the whole country to be destroyed?" He argued that even if Jesus was innocent, He must be disposed of. He was causing people to lose confidence in their leaders. And if Jesus' followers revolted, the Romans would step in, close the temple, and destroy their nation. Was the life of one man from Galilee worth that price?

Caiaphas's suggestion was based on a heathen principle—the same principle that led to human sacrifices. Caiaphas suggested sacrificing Jesus to save their guilty nation not from their sins, but in their sins so their sinful behavior could continue.

At this meeting, the Holy Spirit had impressed them with the truth. But Satan reminded them how they had suffered because of Jesus, how little He had respected them and their rules. Now with the exception of a few who didn't dare speak up, the Sanhedrin accepted Caiaphas's thinking. They decided to have Jesus killed at the first opportunity. Completely deceived by Satan, they now saw themselves as patriots trying to save their nation.

Afraid that the people would turn violently against them if something happened to Jesus, they decided to be patient and wait. Jesus knew what must soon happen, but He refused to force the crisis and left the area with His disciples.

Jesus had given three years to teaching and healing His people. Everyone saw His selflessness, His caring spirit, His purity, and His devotion. But this short time was as long as the world could stand the presence of its Savior. The One who healed the sick, fed the hungry, and comforted those in sorrow was driven away from the people He worked to save. The One who woke the dead and held thousands captivated by His words could not reach the hearts of those who were blinded by prejudice and hate.

CHAPTER 60

POSITIONS OF POWER

"This is how we know what real love is: Jesus gave his life for us"
(1 John 3:16).

hen Passover time drew near, Jesus turned back toward Jerusalem. Even though He knew what was waiting for Him there, His heart was at peace because He was following His Father's plan. The disciples were amazed that Jesus would go there, but even though they were afraid, they followed Him.

Jesus took them aside and again explained His future. " 'Everything the prophets wrote about the Son of Man will happen. He will be turned over to those who are not Jews. They will laugh at him, insult him, spit on him, beat him with whips, and kill him. But on the third day, he will rise to life again' " (Luke 18:31-33).

But they didn't understand. Hadn't they been telling everyone, "The kingdom of heaven is here"? Hadn't Jesus promised them honor in His kingdom? Hadn't the prophets predicted the glory of the Messiah's reign? Jesus' words about betrayal and death seemed strange and vague. Whatever obstacles might stand in the way, the disciples were sure that it was almost time for the new kingdom.

John and James were among the first who left their homes to follow Jesus. John sat next to Jesus at every opportunity and James

This chapter is based on Matt. 20:20-28; Mark 10:32-45; Luke 18:31-34.

was always nearby. Their mother had given generously to support Jesus. Now the three of them came to Jesus.

He asked, "What can I do for you?"

The mother answered, "Promise me that one of my sons will sit at Your right side and one at Your left in Your kingdom."

Jesus read their hearts. He knew that their love for Him was real, just clouded by ambition. He said, " 'You don't understand what you are asking. Can you drink the cup that I am about to drink?' " (Matthew 20:22).

John and James sensed a connection to His words about suffering, but still they said, "Yes, we can."

Jesus nodded. "You will drink from it." James would be the first of the disciples to be killed for his faith. John would live and suffer longest for his. Then He added, "But I can't choose who will sit at My right and left. My

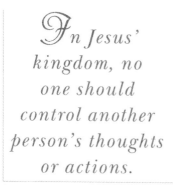

In Jesus' kingdom, no one should control another person's thoughts or actions.

Father will make that decision." In God's kingdom, positions are not given to favorites. The one who stands next to Jesus will be the person who most closely followed His example of self-sacrificing love. This love will be shown as that disciple gives everything—even his or her life—to save his fellow humans.

The other ten disciples were angry when they heard this. Each of them hoped for the position of highest honor, and John and James seemed to be getting an unfair advantage.

A NEW KIND OF KINGDOM

Jesus called them together and said; "You know that rulers in this world love to show their power over people. But it should not be that way with you." In the governments of this world, a high position means having power and privileges. In many cases, the common people serve their rulers. Wealth and education are seen as ways of controlling others. Those in control decide how everyone else will think and act. Like everything else, those in authority dictate religion.

Jesus' kingdom would use different principles. He called leaders to be servants, not masters. "Whoever wants to be great must serve the others like a servant. Whoever wants to be first, must be last." Those with talent, education, or positions of power are more obligated to serve their fellow humans. Jesus didn't come to be served but to serve others. This is the principle His church should follow. In God's kingdom, this is what defines who is greatest.

In Jesus' kingdom, no one should control another person's thoughts or actions. God gave every person the freedom to think and to choose. Even angels don't come to earth to rule and be honored—they come as messengers of mercy and to help humans work for others.

The words of Jesus stayed with John all of his life. Later, he would write, "This is how we know what real love is: Jesus gave his life for us. So we should give our lives for our brothers and sisters" (1 John 3:16). This was the spirit in the early church. And after the Holy Spirit was poured out on them, they were able to preach with great power that Jesus had risen from the dead.

CHAPTER 61

ZACCHAEUS

" 'God can do things that are not possible for people to do' "
(Luke 18:27).

*T*he city of Jericho gleamed like an emerald among the limestone hills and ravines. Watered year around by gushing springs, it was a regular stopping point for traders and travelers. Because of the traffic, many tax collectors made their homes there.

The chief tax collector, Zacchaeus, was a Jew. He was wealthy and powerful, but was despised by his countrymen. Zacchaeus had heard of Jesus. The reports of Jesus' kindness even to those that society shunned had spread far and wide. Zacchaeus had listened to John the Baptist call sinners to repent. Now, hearing the stories of Jesus, he had hope that even someone like himself could repent and change his ways. Wasn't one of Jesus' closest followers also a tax collector?

Zacchaeus acted on his changed ways and began to repay those whom he had overcharged or wronged in some way. From then on, he treated everyone fairly and honestly.

When news came that Jesus was coming to Jericho, Zacchaeus was determined to see Him. He wanted to see the face of the One who had given him the hope of a changed life. Being a short person,

This chapter is based on Luke 19:1-10.

Zacchaeus found that he couldn't see over the heads of the people in the crowded streets. So he ran ahead of the crowd and climbed a fig tree. From his perch on the branches, he searched for the One he so much wanted to see.

As Jesus and His group approached, they suddenly stopped right under the fig tree. The One whose mere glance seemed to read his innermost soul was looking right up at him. Almost doubting his own senses, he heard the words, "Zacchaeus, hurry and come down! I am staying at your house today."

Walking as if in a dream, Zacchaeus led the way to his home. The rabbis scowled and said, "Jesus is staying with a sinner!"

Zacchaeus was so overwhelmed by Jesus' kindness, he felt compelled to respond. Stopping in the middle of the crowd, he said to Jesus, "I will give half of all I own to the poor. If I have cheated anyone, I will pay back four times as much."

Jesus must have smiled. "Today, salvation has come to this man's house." Now the disciples saw that Jesus' words were true. " 'God can do things that are not possible for people to do' " (Luke 18:27). They could see how through the life-changing grace of God, a rich man could enter God's kingdom.

No repentance is real if there are not changes in a person's life.

Before Zacchaeus ever saw Jesus, he had repented and changed his ways. His first response when he learned about Jesus' love was to care for the poor and needy around him. No repentance is real if there are not changes in a person's life. The righteousness of Jesus does not cover unconfessed and unforsaken sin—it changes a person's character and behavior. Holiness is measured by the complete surrender of our hearts and lives to the principles of heaven.

Christians should handle their business transactions the same way Jesus would. Any unfair or dishonest dealings should end when a person surrenders his or her heart to Jesus. If we have in any way damaged another person—even if it was legal—we need to confess that wrong and make it right as far as possible, not only repaying what they lost but also what that money could have earned for them.

Jesus went to Zacchaeus's home to teach him and his family about the kingdom of heaven. They had been shut out of the synagogue because of the rabbis' hate for them. But now they learned from heaven's Teacher in their own home.

When a person accepts Jesus as Savior, as Zacchaeus did, he or she is saved. The rabbis and Pharisees saw Zacchaeus as a sinner, but God saw him as a child of Abraham—a true believer.

CHAPTER 62

MARY ANOINTS JESUS

"Why are you troubling this woman? She did an excellent thing for me" (Matthew 26:10).

imon of Bethany was one of the few Pharisees who was known to be a follower of Jesus. He hoped that Jesus might be the Messiah, but he hadn't accepted Him as the Savior. Jesus had healed Simon of leprosy, and to show his gratitude, he held a dinner for the Savior and His disciples.

As usual, Jesus was staying at the home of Lazarus during this visit to Bethany. Many people crowded into the small town, some to be near Jesus, others to see the man who had been raised from the dead. To all of them, Lazarus declared that Jesus was indeed the Son of God. The people were anxious to see if Lazarus would travel with Jesus to Jerusalem and if Jesus would be crowned king during the Passover.

The priests and leaders could hardly wait for the chance to do away with Jesus. Remembering how often He had escaped them before, they were afraid that He would stay away from the Passover. At another meeting of the Sanhedrin, they agreed that it would be dangerous to arrest Jesus publicly. Since the raising of Lazarus, Jesus had become wildly popular with the people. So they planned to arrest Him secretly and keep the trial as quiet as possible. They hoped

This chapter is based on Matt. 26:6-13; Mark 14:3-11; Luke 7:36-50; John 11:55-57; 12:1-11.

that after Jesus was condemned to die, the people would begin to doubt Him. But as long as Lazarus was alive, the people would remember Jesus' power. They might plan revenge on their leaders for taking the life of someone who could perform that kind of miracle. It was agreed that Lazarus must die also.

While this plotting was going on, Jesus and His friends were sitting down at Simon's dinner. At the table, Simon sat on one side of Jesus while Lazarus sat on the other. Martha helped serve the meal, while Mary stood nearby, listening to every word Jesus said.

Jesus had forgiven her sins and had brought her brother back from death. So Mary wanted to do something to show her gratitude. She had heard Jesus say that He would soon die, so she bought a very expensive alabaster jar of fragrant lotion to prepare His body for burial—as was the custom at the time.

But now everyone was saying that Jesus was going to be crowned king. Her sorrow turned to joy and she was eager to be the first to honor Him. Slipping into the room, she broke open her jar of lotion and applied it to His head and feet. Her gratitude flowed out in tears as she knelt beside Him, kissing His feet and wiping them dry with her long hair.

Mary might not have been noticed in the busy room, but the fragrance of her lotion caught everyone's attention. When Judas saw what she had done, he was greatly annoyed. He began to whisper, "Why would Jesus allow such a waste? That lotion should have been sold and the money given to the poor."

Judas said this because Mary's act of love made him ashamed. He held the moneybag for Jesus and the disciples. From this bag, money was given to those in need. But often, money from the bag slipped into Judas's pocket. If Mary's money had been given to the poor, they would never have received it. Judas would have stolen it for himself.

Still, the disciples didn't know that, and Judas was one of the most influential members of their group. Soon his whisper of complaint was being repeated around the table. Mary heard the whispers and her heart trembled. She was afraid of what her sister would say about the money. And would Jesus also think that her gift was wasteful? She was about to slip out when she heard Jesus say, "Leave her alone."

Jesus knew what was in Mary's heart. Speaking above the murmuring, He said, "She did an excellent thing for Me. You will always have the poor, but you won't always have Me. She did the only thing she could for Me. She poured her fragrant lotion on Me to prepare Me for burial."

Until the end of time, that broken alabaster jar will tell the story of God's love for fallen humanity.

By pouring out her love while He was still alive, Mary brought great joy to Jesus. As He went down the dark road to His trials and death, He carried the memory of her gift. It was a taste of the love and gratitude He would someday receive from all who are forgiven and saved. Mary didn't understand the full meaning of what she had done. She couldn't explain why she had chosen that time to give her gift. The Holy Spirit had influenced her heart. Jesus told Mary that she had prepared His body for burial. Because the alabaster jar was broken, it filled the house with fragrance. Because Jesus' body would be broken, He would rise from the grave and fill the earth with the fragrance of His life.

Jesus said, "I tell you the truth, wherever the gospel is preached in all the world, what this woman has done will be told, and people will remember her." Kings and kingdoms would rise up, and then be forgotten. But this woman's gift would be written down in the Holy Scriptures and remembered. Until the end of time, that broken alabaster jar will tell the story of God's love for fallen humanity.

JUDAS SELLS OUT JESUS

Jesus could have exposed Judas's lies and stealing. But if He had, some would later see this as the reason Judas betrayed Him. Jesus would not give Judas an excuse for his disloyalty.

Even though Jesus didn't reprimand him directly, Judas was angry and embarrassed. By praising Mary's gift, Jesus had made him look bad. The look in Jesus' eyes told him that He knew all about his stealing and hypocrisy. When the dinner was over, Judas went directly to the high priest's palace and offered to betray Jesus—to tell them when and where He could be arrested privately. After complaining that Mary's gift was wasted money, he sold out the Savior for only thirty pieces of silver.

The other disciples weren't like Judas. They loved Jesus, but didn't fully understand who He was. The wise men from the East, who barely knew about Jesus, showed more appreciation and honor for Him. Jesus appreciated acts of heartfelt kindness. He never refused the smallest flower from the hand of a child. These acts of love and respect—like Mary's—showed faith in Him as the Son of God.

By praising Mary's gift, Jesus had made Judas look bad.

Jesus accepted Mary's act of love even though His disciples did not understand it. That lotion was a symbol of her heart, a demonstration of love that responded to His words and grew until it overflowed. The disciples never understood how lonely and sad Jesus often was, so they couldn't appreciate how much Mary's gift meant to Him. Only when Jesus was gone did they begin to understand how they had neglected and hurt Him. As they took His bruised body down from the cross, they remembered their words of criticism that night and regretted them greatly. Too few of us today appreciate all that Jesus did and does for us. If we did, nothing would be too much to give or to endure for His sake.

From a human point of view, the plan of salvation is a tragic waste of mercy and resources. Angels stand amazed that humans can refuse to be blessed by the love Jesus offers. They must often ask, "Why this great waste?"

But Jesus' payment for this lost world would be in full—enough for every soul. Not everyone will be saved, but that won't mean that the plan of salvation was wasted.

SIMON'S SECRET

Simon was surprised at Jesus' reaction to Mary. He thought to himself, "If he was really a prophet, he would have known that a sinful woman was touching him." But Simon didn't know what God and Jesus are really like—kind and merciful. Simon thought that sinners should be pointed out and avoided.

Jesus knew what Simon was thinking. He said, "Simon, I have a story for you. A certain man had two debtors. One owed 500 pence* and the other 50 pence. When neither of them could pay the money back, he forgave them both. So tell me, which one of them will love him the most?"

Simon replied. "I suppose the one that was forgiven the most."

Jesus said, "You are right." Using a story as the prophet Nathan had done with King David, Jesus let Simon condemn himself. Simon had led Mary into sin. She had been deeply mistreated by him. The two debtors in the story represented Simon and Mary. Jesus wasn't teaching that they owed different debts of gratitude to God. They each owed more than could be repaid. Jesus wanted to show Simon that his sin was as much greater than Mary's as a 500-pence debt is greater than a 50-pence debt.

Simon began to see himself differently. As shame seized him, he realized that he was in the presence of Someone greater than any human.

Jesus went on. "When I came into your house, you gave Me no water to wash My feet. You did not greet Me with a kiss, but this woman has kissed My feet over and over." Then He responded to what Simon had been thinking. "See this woman? Her many sins are forgiven, so she loves very much. Someone who is forgiven for only a few sins loves only a little."

Simon thought He was honoring Jesus with a dinner. Now he saw that he was not honoring Him at all. He saw that his own religion was a farce, and that while Mary was a sinner, she was forgiven. Simon was a sinner, but was not forgiven.

Simon was touched by Jesus' kindness in not exposing his sins to the others. He had not been treated as he wanted Mary to be treated.

A stern rebuke would have hardened him against repenting, but Jesus was trying to win his heart by love. As he finally understood his great debt, he confessed his sins. The proud Pharisee became a humble follower.

Jesus knew what had happened to shape Mary's life. He could have destroyed her last hopes, but He didn't. He lifted her up, casting demons out of her seven times. When others saw her as a hopeless case, Jesus saw the good in her. By His grace, she became a different person. Mary sat at His feet and listened. Mary spread lotion on His head and washed His feet with her tears. Mary stood beside the cross and followed His body to the tomb. Mary was the first to announce that He had risen.

Jesus knows all about every person. You may think you are very sinful, but the worse you are, the more you need Jesus. He won't turn any sincerely sorrowful person away. He freely pardons all who come to Him for forgiveness and bonds them to His own divine-human nature where no human or evil angel can tear them away. They stand beside Him, the great Sin Bearer, in the light from the throne of God. He died to take the blame and the pain for their sins. And He lives to represent them before the Father.

---

*At that time, a pence was equal to a day's wage for a common laborer.

CHAPTER 63

JESUS ANNOUNCED AS ISRAEL'S KING

"God bless the king who comes in the name of the Lord"
(Psalm 118:26).

ive hundred years before Jesus was born, the prophet Zechariah foretold the day the King would come to Israel: "Rejoice greatly, people of Jerusalem! Shout for joy, people of Jerusalem! Your king is coming to you. He does what is right, and he saves. He is gentle and riding on a donkey, on the colt of a donkey" (Zechariah 9:9).

It was the first day of the week, the day Jesus would make His glorious trip into Jerusalem. The crowds that had gathered to see Him in Bethany walked with Him. Many more who were on their way to the Passover festival joined them. On a day when even nature seemed to be rejoicing, there was great hope for a new kingdom.

Jesus sent two disciples to bring Him a donkey on which to ride. He had to depend on a stranger's kindness even for this. But it happened as He predicted—when His disciples told the owner, "The Lord needs it," the donkey was freely lent. They spread their coats on the donkey's back and seated Jesus on it. Jesus had always walked before, and they were amazed that He wanted to ride now. But it gave them hope that He was finally ready to enter the capital city and proclaim Himself king.

Jesus was following the Jewish custom for a royal visit. The people

This chapter is based on Matt. 21:1-11; Mark 11:1-10; Luke 19:29-44; John 12:12-19.

were familiar with the prophecy about how the Messiah would come to His kingdom. As soon as Jesus was seated on the donkey, the crowd hailed Him as the Messiah, their King. As they imagined the Romans driven from their city and Israel once more a powerful nation, each one fought to honor Him. Since they had no gifts, many people spread their coats to carpet the path in front of Him. Others cut palm and leafy olive tree branches and laid them along the road. With no royal banners to wave, they waved palm branches over their heads.

Thousands who had gathered for Passover lined the road, waving palm branches and singing holy songs.

Spectators mingled with the crowds asking, "Who is this? What does it mean?" They were amazed to learn it was Jesus, since He had discouraged all plans to put Him on the throne. Thousands who had gathered for Passover lined the road, waving palm branches and singing holy songs. When the priests at the temple blew the trumpet for the evening service, only a few people responded. "The whole world is following Him," they said to one another.

WHY JESUS ALLOWED IT

Jesus had never allowed a demonstration like this one before. He knew what it would lead to—the Cross. But it was time to call the people's attention to His mission and His sacrifice. In the future, His church would want to study and understand what He had done, so there must be no confusion about the events. This glorious ride would be the talk of the whole city. Now every person would follow the rapid events that led to the Cross. After His death, many would remember, study the words of Scripture, and be convinced that Jesus really was the Messiah.

The disciples thought that this was the brightest, most wonderful day of their lives, but it would have been shadowed with clouds if they had known that it would lead to their Master's death. He had told them over and over that He would be a sacrifice, but in the triumph of the day, they forgot His sad words.

THE STONES WOULD SHOUT

With few exceptions, the thousands of people who joined the procession were caught up in the hopeful joy. Their shouts filled the air: "Hosanna to the Son of David! Blessed is He who comes in the name of the Lord!"

The world had never seen a parade like this one. Jesus rode surrounded by the trophies of His works of love—men and women, boys and girls, who had been rescued from Satan's power. The blind to whom He had given sight led the way. Those who had been given the ability to speak shouted the loudest praises. Those who had been physically handicapped now leaped for joy. Those who had been healed of leprosy laid their clean coats in His path. Lazarus, freshly back from the grave, led the donkey on which Jesus rode.

Many envious Pharisees tried to silence the people, but their threats only increased the enthusiasm. As a last resort, they stepped up to Jesus and demanded, "Tell your followers not to say these things!"

Jesus' answer silenced them. "I tell you, if My followers were quiet, the stones around them would shout." God's prophets had foretold this event. If humans had failed to shout praises, God would have caused the stones to do it.

When the procession reached the top of the hill, Jesus stopped. Spread out before them was the city of Jerusalem, bathed in the light of the setting sun. The light gleamed from the pure white marble of the temple walls and sparkled on its gold-capped pillars. From the hill where Jesus watched, the temple seemed to glow with the glory of heaven.

JESUS CRIES FOR HIS PEOPLE

The crowd was spellbound by this vision of beauty. But when they turned to watch Jesus' reaction to the sight, they were shocked to see tears in His eyes. With a cry of grief, Jesus rocked back and forth like a tree in a windstorm. What a sight for the angels to see! What a sight for the excited crowd that thought they were escorting Him to His throne! Israel's king was in tears of agony. A cloud of sadness covered the whole crowd. Many of the people cried with Jesus without understanding why.

From where He was, Jesus could see Gethsemane, where He would face the darkest hours of His life. Nearby was Calvary where He would suffer and die. Just in front of Him was the sheep gate, through which sheep for the sacrifices had been led for hundreds of years. But these things didn't cause Jesus' sorrow. It was the sight of Jerusalem that broke His heart—the city that had rejected the Son of God and was about to take His life. He saw what Jerusalem could have been—how could He give up on her?

God had favored the people of Israel. Their temple had been His home on earth. But all the symbols and ceremonies must now end. Jesus reached out toward the city and said, " 'I wish you knew today what would bring you peace. But now it is hidden from you' " (Luke 19:42). What Jesus didn't say was what could have happened if Jerusalem had accepted God's Gift. She could have been free and prosperous, a mighty city, the world's crown of peace and glory.

But Jesus knew that the city was doomed. He saw the time when enemies would surround the city and the people would starve and die. He saw crosses standing as thick as forests on Calvary. He saw the palaces destroyed, the temple demolished, the very stones of the walls scattered, and the ground left plowed like a garden. He said, " 'All this will happen because you did not recognize the time when God came to save you' " (Luke 19:44).

But God's Holy Spirit would speak to Jerusalem one more time. Before the day ended, Jesus would appeal to her again. If He was accepted, Jerusalem might still be saved!

But the city's leaders had no welcome for the Son of God. As the procession started down the hill, they demanded to know, "Who is this?"

The disciples, inspired by the Holy Spirit, repeated all the prophecies pointing to Jesus. Then they declared their own testimony: "This is Jesus, the Messiah, the Prince of life, the Savior of the world."

CHAPTER 64

DOOMED

" 'May no one ever eat fruit from you again' "
(Mark 11:14).

he last appeal to the leaders of Israel was wasted. The priests and leaders refused to listen to the words of the prophets or the people. First they tried to silence the people. When that failed, they turned to the Roman military officers who were watching the procession. "This Jesus is the leader of a revolt against Rome. He is going to take the temple, and try to reign as king in Jerusalem."

In a sad, but powerful voice, Jesus repeated that He had not come to set up an earthly kingdom. He said that soon He would return to His Father and when He returned in glory, they would recognize Him—but it would be too late.

The Romans could read the love and dignity on Jesus' face. Their hearts were touched with sympathy. They turned on the priests and leaders and accused them of causing the disturbance.

Meanwhile, Jesus slipped away unnoticed to the temple. Since the crowds of people were still outside the city, it was quiet there. For a few moments, Jesus looked at the temple sadly, and then He returned to Bethany. When the crowds looked for Him—to crown Him king—He was nowhere to be found.

This chapter is based on Mark 11:11-14, 20, 21; Matt. 21:17-19.

THE FIG TREE

After praying through the night, the next morning Jesus headed again to the temple. As He and His disciples walked through an orchard of fig trees, Jesus felt hungry. One fig tree was in full leaf, so He stopped to pick some figs. But He found no figs—only leaves. It wasn't time for ripe figs yet. But this tree appeared to be maturing more quickly than the others. Its leafy appearance promised ripe fruit. But it was a lie. So Jesus cursed the tree. He said, " 'May no one ever eat fruit from you again' " (Mark 11:14).

The following morning, on their way to the city again, Jesus and His disciples passed the tree. Now its leaves were withered and its branches were drooping. Having never seen Jesus kill anything, the disciples were shocked and confused.

God takes no pleasure in death, not even the death of the wicked. His plan to judge and destroy them is called a "strange work." But in mercy and love, He gives us a glimpse of the future so we can see the final results of sin.

Jesus was using the barren tree as a symbol of the Jewish nation. Like the tree, the Jewish religion with the magnificent temple and impressive ceremonies appeared beautiful. But there was nothing in its heart—no love, no humility, no concern for others.

The other leafless trees in the orchard represented the non-Jewish nations. They didn't mislead anyone. Knowing nothing about love or selflessness, they didn't pretend to be holy. Instead they were still waiting to learn about God.

Much more was expected from the Jews, since they knew God. Jesus had come to Israel, hoping to find in them the fruits of their knowledge of God—selflessness, kindness, and a desire to share God with the world. But their pride and selfishness eclipsed their love for God and others. The cursed tree illustrated both their sin and their punishment. It showed what the Jewish nation would be when God's grace was removed—withered and dried up. Since they refused to share God's blessings, they would no longer receive them.

By cursing this tree that He created, Jesus sends a warning to all churches and all Christians. There are many who claim to be followers of Jesus who don't live His kind, unselfish life. They spend all their time getting money and things for themselves. God designed them to help their fellow humans in any way that they could. But "self" is so large that they can see no one else.

Like the fig tree, they live only for show—attending church, going through the motions of a good life, but without the love that comes from a heart that belongs to Jesus. The open sinner is less guilty than someone who claims to be a Christian but doesn't live like one.

> *Jesus was using the tree as a symbol of the Jewish nation.*

For more than a thousand years, the Jewish nation had rejected God's messages and killed His prophets. By doing the same thing, the people of Jesus' day made themselves responsible for the sins of their ancestors. The time comes when the sweet voice of the Holy Spirit no longer pleads with a sinner. That time had come for Jerusalem. Jesus had done everything He could to rescue her, but by rejecting God's Spirit, Israel rejected their only hope.

As He wept for Jerusalem, Jesus cried for the sins of all who would turn away from His love. Many today are walking the same path the unfaithful Jews walked. The Holy Spirit has spoken to their hearts, but they are not willing to confess their errors. They reject God's message and His messenger.

In the world today, Jesus' followers struggle against a strong current of moral impurity and prejudice. The truth from God's Word doesn't harmonize with the natural thinking of humans. Many reject the Bible and live by their own judgment. But they do this at the risk of their souls. Those who questioned Jesus' words found more and more reasons to question until they turned away from His truth and light completely. God has not promised to remove every possible doubt from human hearts. To those who refuse truth, His Word remains a mystery.

Jesus is shedding tears over you who have no tears to shed for yourself. Every evidence of God's love, every ray of truth from the Bible, is either melting your heart to accept Jesus or confirming that you have totally rejected Him. Just like Jerusalem and the Jews, those who reject Jesus are to blame for their own misery, pain and eternal loss.

CHAPTER 65

CLEANSING THE TEMPLE AGAIN

"It is written in the Scriptures, 'My Temple will be a house for prayer.' But you have changed it into 'a hideout for robbers!' " (Luke 19:46).

t the beginning of His ministry, Jesus drove the traders and merchants out of the temple because they were defiling it with their unholy business activities. Now, near the end, He found that it was just as desecrated as before. The services were interrupted by the cries of animals, the clinking of coins, and the shouted arguments. The priests and leaders were directing the business being done. Controlled by greed, they were as bad as thieves themselves.

At every Passover and Festival of Tabernacles, thousands of animals were sacrificed. The Jews had almost forgotten that all this was necessary because of sin. And they didn't understand at all that the sacrifices represented the Lamb of God, the world's Savior. They had turned these festivals into times of bloodshed and cruelty, with more and more sacrifices, as if this would please God more.

The priests and rulers had twisted the symbols of the Lamb of God into a way of making money. The sacredness of the services was destroyed. And Jesus knew that His blood—soon to be shed for the sins of the world—would be just as misunderstood and unappreciated.

This chapter is based on Matt. 21:12-16, 23-46; Mark 11:15-19, 27-33; 12:1-12; Luke 19:45-48; 20:1-19.

Jesus had earlier spoken through His prophets against this problem of overdoing sacrifices and ignoring people's needs. Now He repeated the same warning Himself. The people had declared that Jesus was their King. He had accepted their homage. So as a King He must now act. Jesus knew that the dishonest priests wouldn't change, but He could show the people more evidence that He was the Messiah.

Once again, Jesus' piercing look swept over the desecrated courtyard. Silence fell as every eye was on Him. Divinity flashed through His human form, giving Jesus a majestic glory He had never shown before. Those closest to Him stepped away as far as they could. Except for a few of the disciples, Jesus stood alone. After a moment of almost painful silence, Jesus spoke with a power that rocked the people. "It is written in the Scriptures, 'My Temple will be a house for prayer.' But you have changed it into 'a hideout for robbers!' " (Luke 19:46). With a voice like a trumpet, He commanded, "Take these things out of here!"

Three years before, the priests had been ashamed of running from Jesus' voice. Certain that it could never happen again, they found that they were now even more terrified than before. The priests and traders raced out, chasing their cattle as they went.

The children shouted their praises the loudest.

On the way out, they ran into a large crowd bringing their sick and injured to find Jesus. When they heard why the priests were running, some turned back. But many people pushed forward, anxious to see Jesus. Once again, the temple court was filled with sick and dying people. And once again, Jesus healed them all.

After a time, the priests and leaders crept back into the temple, expecting to see Jesus crowned as king. Instead, to their astonishment, the court was filled with joy and laughter as those who had been sick, blind, and injured shouted praises to God.

The children shouted their praises the loudest. Jesus had held them in His arms and healed them. Now they repeated what they had heard the day before, "Hosanna to the King!" and waved palm branches.

The sound of such happy voices offended the priests. They were sure that God's house was dishonored by children and loud praises. They wanted Jesus to quiet the children. "Don't you hear the things those children are saying?" they asked.

Jesus answered, "Haven't you ever read in the Scriptures, 'You have taught children and babies to sing praises'?" Prophecy had foretold that Jesus would be proclaimed King. God inspired the children to speak for Him. If they were silenced, the pillars of the temple itself would have shouted the words.

"ANSWER MY QUESTION"

The priests and Pharisees were completely frustrated. Jesus had done amazing miracles before, but never had He acted like a king. They gave up trying to arrest Him that day. But the Sanhedrin met the next morning to come up with another plan—they would try to trick Him into saying something for which He could be condemned.

In the temple, they asked, "Who gave you the authority to do the things you do?"

Jesus said, "I will ask you a question. If you can answer it, I'll answer yours. Where did John the Baptist get his authority to baptize? From heaven or from humans?"

Quickly, the priest saw that they were the ones who were trapped. If they said that John's authority was from heaven, Jesus would say, "Then why don't you believe what he said?" They knew that John had pointed to Jesus as the Messiah, the Lamb of God. If they claimed to believe John, how could they reject Jesus?

They knew that John had pointed to Jesus as the Messiah, the Lamb of God.

If they answered what they really believed—that John's authority came only from himself—it would outrage the people since they believed that John was a prophet. The people remembered that the priests had claimed to believe John. Consequently they expected the priests to say that John's authority had come from God.

After a quick whispered discussion, the priests decided not to commit themselves. "We do not know," they said finally.

Jesus replied, "Then I won't tell you where I get the authority to do what I do."

The priests and leaders could only stand there confused and disappointed. They didn't dare ask any more questions. The people who watched this exchange were amused to see these proud men defeated.

All these things that Jesus said and did were important. After His death and resurrection, many of the people who watched and listened that day became His followers. But the more the people listened to Him, the more the priests hated Him.

Jesus didn't set out to humiliate the priests, but He had an important lesson to teach. Since they brought up John the Baptist, He asked, "Tell me what you think about this:

"A man had two sons. He told the first one, 'Son, work today in my vineyard.'

"The son answered, 'No, I won't.' But later he changed his mind and went and worked.

"The man told his second son, 'Son, work today in my vineyard.'

"The son answered, 'Yes, sir, I will.' But he never went and worked."

Then Jesus asked, "Now, which son obeyed his father?"

Caught by surprise, the priests answered immediately. "The first son."

Jesus looked them straight in the eyes and said solemnly, "Tax collectors and prostitutes will get into God's kingdom before you do." It was clear that the first son in the story was like the sinners of the land who had not been doing what God wanted—but when John the Baptist preached, they changed, repented, and were baptized. The second son was like the priests and leaders who claimed that they obeyed God, but they really didn't.

The priests and leaders didn't say a word. Then Jesus told another story:

"A man who owned a vineyard built a hedge around it, a wine press, and a tower. Then he rented it to some farmers while he went on a trip. When it was time for the harvest, he sent some servants to the farmers to collect his rent—a portion of the harvested grapes. But the farmers didn't pay. They beat one servant and had the others killed. The man sent more servants and they too were beaten or killed.

"Finally, the man said, 'They will respect my son. I will send him.'

"When the farmers saw that the man's son was coming, they said, 'This is the heir of the property. Let's kill him and keep the vineyard for ourselves.' So they caught the son and killed him."

Then Jesus asked, "When the man returns to his vineyard, what will he do to those farmers?"

The priests and leaders answered, "He will destroy those evil men and rent his vineyard to others who will pay." They quickly saw that they had condemmed themselves. Just as the farmers should have paid rent, the Jews should have honored God by living by His principles. Just as the farmers killed the servants, the Jews had killed God's prophets. The meaning of the rest of the story was clear—the man's son who was sent to the farmers and killed was Jesus. The doom of the ungrateful farmers would be theirs.

THE CORNERSTONE

Looking at them with pity and sadness, Jesus said, "Haven't you read in the Scriptures that the stone rejected by the builders became the cornerstone? God's kingdom will be taken from you and given to others who will do the things God wants. Whoever falls on this stone will be broken; whoever this stone falls on will be crushed."

Jesus was trying to make as clear as possible what the results would be of what they were planning to do. The priests and leaders saw that Jesus was warning them about their plans, but they wanted to kill Him anyway. They would have arrested Him right then and there, but they were afraid of the crowd.

When Jesus quoted the prophecy of the rejected cornerstone, He was referring to an actual incident that happened when Solomon's temple was being built. The enormous stones were cut and finished at the quarry. After they were carried to the building site, the workers only had to place them in position. But one stone of an unusual size and shape was brought and no one could find a place for it.

When they were ready to lay the cornerstone, they needed a special stone of the right size and shape, one that would hold up under all the weight of the building without cracking. Several stones were tested with heavy weights, but each one crumbled.

By faith and obedience, we build on Jesus, our Foundation.

Finally, the strange stone that had been rejected was tested. It held the weight without cracking and when it was put in place, it was a perfect fit. This stone was a symbol of Jesus. The whole world can pile their burdens and sorrows on Him. Those who trust Him are never disappointed.

To "fall on this stone and be broken" means to give up our selfish ways, to repent, and to believe in Jesus' forgiving love. By faith and obedience, we build on Jesus, our Foundation. Those who are crushed are the ones who reject Jesus. The Jewish leaders would see their city and their nation destroyed. They rejected the Stone that could have protected them. By crucifying Jesus, they destroyed their city and themselves.

On the last day, Jesus will return to judge the whole world. The glory of His face will mean eternal life to His followers and will be a white-hot fire to the wicked. Sinners will be destroyed because they rejected the One who could have saved them. Unless they repent, they will be as doomed as ancient Jerusalem.

CHAPTER 66

JESUS CONFUSES
HIS ENEMIES

"Love the Lord your God with all your heart, all your soul, and all your mind" (Matthew 22:37).

The priests and leaders couldn't disprove anything Jesus said, which only made them more determined to trap Him. They sent spies—young men who pretended to be true followers—to ask trick questions. Acting as if they simply wanted to do what was right, they came to Jesus and asked, "Teacher, we know that you only teach the true way of God. Is it right to pay taxes to Caesar or not?" The Pharisees resented having to pay Roman taxes, and they had declared that it was against God's law.

The spies thought their real purpose was disguised, but Jesus read them like a book. "Why are you trying to trap Me?" He asked. While they were still reeling from that, He said, "Show me a coin." When they held one up, Jesus asked, "Whose picture and name are on it?"

"Caesar's," they answered.

Pointing to the coin, Jesus said, " 'Give to Caesar the things that are Caesar's, and give to God the things that are God's' " (Matthew 22:21).

The spies felt defeated. The way Jesus had answered left them with nothing to say. Jesus didn't dodge the question. He declared that since they were being protected by Rome, they should pay taxes to support

This chapter is based on Matt. 22:15-46; Mark 12:13-40; Luke 20:20-47.

it. But although subject to the laws of the land, their first loyalty should always be to God.

Jesus' answer impressed even the Pharisees. He had not only escaped their trap, He had given a principle that shows the boundary between our duty to civil governments and our duty to God.

As soon as the Pharisees were silenced, the Sadducees stepped up with their clever questions. As a group most of them were prejudiced, but some were sincere believers who accepted Jesus' teachings.

RESURRECTION

One subject that the Pharisees and the Sadducees disagreed on was the resurrection. The Pharisees believed in the resurrection, but they were confused about the after life. To them, death was an unexplainable mystery.

The Sadducees believed that God created humans and then left them alone. That meant that humans were free to direct their own lives and shape their world as they saw fit. Their ideas about God molded their own characters. Since God had no interest in humans, they had little respect for others. They weren't concerned with the needs of others—they lived for themselves. Since they didn't believe in the Holy Spirit, they lacked God's power in their lives.

The Sadducees were confident that they could trip Jesus up.

By His teachings and actions, Jesus disagreed with the Sadducees. He showed that a divine power is involved in human lives. He taught that God cares for humans like a father cares for his children. He taught that God works through the Holy Spirit.

The Sadducees were confident that they could trip Jesus up. They chose to question Him about the resurrection. If He agreed with them, He would offend the Pharisees. If He didn't, they would show that His teachings were illogical and ridiculous.

The Sadducees reasoned that if a resurrected body is made of the same particles of matter as a normal human body, then people who were resurrected would have the same lives they had had before—and the same marriages. So they asked a trick question. "What about a woman who had married—and then had been widowed—by seven brothers during her life? When they are resurrected, whose wife will she be?" To them, this question showed how illogical the idea of a resurrection was.

Jesus answered their question with a peek at life in heaven. He said, "When people rise from the dead, they don't marry at all, but are like the angels in heaven. You are wrong," He told the Sadducees, "because you don't know the Scriptures or the power of God."

This ignorance was the cause of their confusion between having faith and understanding the mysteries of God. Jesus challenged them to open their minds to the sacred truths that would increase their understanding. Many give up believing in God because they cannot find answers to every question or understand every mystery. All we can do to understand those things is to recognize God as the Creator of the universe, the One who controls and directs all things.

Jesus declared that if there was no resurrection, then the Scriptures were worthless. He reminded them that " 'God said, "I am the God of Abraham, the God of Isaac, and the God of Jacob." God is the God of the living, not the dead' " (Matthew 22:32). Those who have died in the faith will hear the voice of the Son of God and rise up to live forever. There will be a close, tender relationship between God and these saints. To God, this relationship has already begun. The dead are alive in His mind.

The shocked Sadducees had no response. They didn't know what to say. But the Pharisees were ready with a new question. They found an expert on the law to question Jesus about the Ten Commandments. They taught that the first four—which show our duty to God—are by far the most important. They accused Jesus of teaching that the last six—which show our duty to others—are more important.

The lawyer asked, "Which commandment is the most important?"

Jesus answered, " ' "Love the Lord your God with all your heart, all your soul, and all your mind." This is the first and most important command. And the second command is like the first: "Love your neighbor as you love yourself" ' " (Matthew 22:37-39).

Jesus taught them that all of the law centers in the principle of love. You can't keep the first four while you break the others. And you can't keep the last six while you are breaking the first four. Only as we love God supremely can we sincerely love those around us. Jesus taught that God's law is one unit, not a collection of laws of varying importance. When we love God, we obey all His commandments.

Many give up believing in God because they cannot find answers to every question or understand every mystery.

The lawyer who asked the question was astonished. In front of everyone, he agreed that Jesus was correct. He began to understand what Jesus had been teaching. Love, obedience to God, and unselfish service seemed more valuable to him than the rituals and traditions of the priests.

Jesus recognized the man's honesty. "You are close to the kingdom of God," Jesus told him.

Now, with the Pharisees gathered around, Jesus asked them a question, "What do you think about the Messiah? Whose Son is He?" He wanted to know if they thought the Messiah would be the Son of God or just another human.

They answered, "The Messiah is the Son of David."

Many who called Jesus the Son of David didn't see Him as the Son of God. So Jesus said, " 'Then why did David call him "Lord"? David, speaking by the power of the Holy Spirit, said, "The Lord said to my Lord: 'Sit by me at my right side, until I put your enemies under your control' " ' " (Matthew 22:43, 44).

Jesus finished with a question none of them could answer. "David calls the Messiah, 'Lord,' so how can the Messiah be his Son?"

No one could say a word to answer that question. After that day, no one had enough courage to ask Jesus other questions.

CHAPTER 67

JESUS' LAST VISIT TO THE TEMPLE

"Love the Lord your God with all your heart, all your soul, and all your mind" (Matthew 22:37).

his was the last day Jesus would teach in the temple. He stood there calmly, surrounded by priests and leaders in their rich robes and lawyers holding scrolls. Their plans to trap Him had all failed. He had met every argument they raised, showing the difference between the pure light of truth and the darkness of their errors. Now there was only one thing left for Jesus to accomplish.

The people were charmed with Jesus' teaching, but very confused. They respected the priests and rabbis, but they could see that these men were trying to harm Jesus' reputation. They were amazed that their leaders didn't accept Jesus when His teachings were so plain and simple. They weren't sure what to do.

Jesus had been warning the leaders and teaching the people by using parables. Now it was time to speak plainly. These leaders taught the people the laws of Moses, but often they did not practice what they taught. Because of their blind faith in these dishonest priests, the people were in slavery. Jesus had to break their chains. He said to them, " 'So you should obey and follow whatever they tell you, but their lives are not good examples for you to follow' " (Matthew 23:3). Also, they taught

This chapter is based on Matt. 23; Mark 12:41-44; Luke 20:45-47; 21:1-4.

things that were not part of the Scriptures. They burdened the people with keeping laws that they themselves didn't keep.

Jesus revealed their selfishness and fake humility. " 'They do good things so that other people will see them' " (Matthew 23:5). The Pharisees and priests were always scheming to get the most attention and special favors. Jesus reproved them for this and for insisting on being called "rabbi" (teacher) or "master." Priests, leaders, rabbis, or common people are all brothers, children of one Father. The people were to give no one a title that suggested some control of their faith or thinking.

The people were charmed with Jesus' teaching, but very confused.

If Jesus were on earth today, He would have the same things to say about those who carry the title of "Reverend" or "Father." Only God should carry these titles. How many times have ambition, pride, and the worst kinds of sin been hidden under the garb of a high and holy office!

Jesus said, " 'Whoever is your servant is the greatest among you. Whoever makes himself great will be made humble. Whoever makes himself humble will be made great' " (Matthew 23:11, 12). Again and again, Jesus taught that true greatness is measured by whether we live to help others. Jesus—the King of glory—was a servant to fallen humans.

By perverting the Scriptures, the priests and Pharisees blinded the minds of many who would have learned about God's kingdom. They often convinced devout widows to donate their property to the temple, and then used its value for themselves. To cover this kind of dishonesty, they offered long prayers in public, appearing to be very holy.

Many today operate the same way. They cover their selfishness and greed with a layer of holiness for all to see.

THE GIFT OF THE POOR WIDOW

Jesus condemned the misuse of gifts, but He never removed our obligation to give. God blessed the giver even when the priests stole the money for themselves.

While Jesus was in the temple court, He watched those who came to give their gifts. As rich people made a great show of dropping their donations into the money box, Jesus just watched sadly and said nothing. But His face lighted up when He saw a poor widow approach quietly, as if she were afraid someone might notice her. She glanced down at her gift, small compared to the others, but all she had to give. Then she dropped in two small copper coins and turned to leave.

But Jesus caught her eye. Looking right at her, He said, " 'I tell you the truth, this poor widow gave more than all those rich people' " (Mark 12:43). The rich did not sacrifice anything to make their donations, but this woman gave money she needed to live on. Others might have suggested that she keep her money, that it would mean nothing compared to other gifts. But she believed that God had set up the temple services and that she must help support them. Tears filled her eyes as she realized that her gift was appreciated. She did what she could, and her gift would be a monument to her memory for all time, and her joy in heaven.

Our motives are what determine the value of our actions. Small tasks cheerfully done, small gifts no one knows about—these are the things God values most. The poor widow went hungry in order to give those two coins. She did it in faith, believing that God would watch over her needs. Her unselfish giving and childlike faith brought her praise from Jesus.

Even if we are poor, we can show our thanks to God by giving from a heart full of love. Our small gifts can become priceless offerings as God smiles on and blesses them.

Jesus said those two coins were a greater gift than the rich had given. Through the centuries, the widow's gift has brought vast amounts of money into God's treasury. Her example of self-sacrifice has touched thousands of lives in every land and in every age. No human can measure the real value of a gift given for God's glory.

ISRAEL'S DIVORCE FROM GOD

Jesus turned His attention to the rabbis and Pharisees. "You hypocrites! You give God one-tenth of everything you earn—even the spices from your gardens. But you don't obey the important teachings of the law—justice, mercy, and truth." Jesus didn't speak against tithing. The tithing system had been established by God as a fair and equal way of funding the work of His church. But the priests and rabbis had made it a real burden.

They were very exact to tithe things like garden herbs since this didn't cost much and it made them appear to be deeply spiritual. But at the same time, they ignored things like justice, mercy, and truth. Jesus taught that both should be done.

> *The holiness that the priests showed to others concealed their sinfulness.*

Other laws had been perverted as well. Through Moses, the Jews had been taught not to eat meat from pigs and certain other "unclean" animals, since the danger of diseases was higher. But the Pharisees required everyone to go as far as to strain their drinking water to avoid the possibility of consuming some tiny unclean insect. Comparing this to their actual sins, Jesus said, " 'You are like a person who picks a fly out of a drink and then swallows a camel!' " (Matthew 23:24).

Jesus compared them to tombs that are painted white. Outside, the tombs look fine, but inside, they are full of bones. The exterior holiness that the priests showed to others concealed their inward sinfulness. They also spent great amounts of money building tombs at the gravesites of prophets and righteous people. To God, this was like worshipping idols. They neglected the living needy people in order to build these monuments to the dead.

It showed that they did not love God or their neighbors. Many today do the same—they neglect the poor, sick, and needy while they build monuments to remember those who have died.

The Pharisees said to each other, "If we had lived long ago, we would not have helped our ancestors kill God's messengers." But at the same time, they were plotting to kill Jesus! This should make us aware of the power Satan has to deceive. Many of us wonder how the Jews could have rejected Jesus—we are sure we would never have done such a thing. But when obeying God means giving up what we want as well as being humble, we find ourselves as unwilling to obey as the Pharisees were.

Little did the Jews realize the price of rejecting Jesus. By doing this, they were taking responsibility for the death of all of His messengers through the ages from Adam's son, Abel, to the prophet Zechariah. They all knew the story of Zechariah. Long centuries before, as Zechariah spoke God's words of warning, the evil king commanded that the prophet be killed where he stood. His blood stained the stones of the temple court permanently and was a constant reminder of this terrible sin. Just hearing Jesus speak about this event sent a shudder of horror through the crowd.

In a glow of divine light, Jesus saw that the Jews would do the same again. Speaking as a judge, He said, "I am sending you prophets and teachers. Some of them you will kill, some you will beat and chase from town to town."

Jesus' righteous anger was focused on the sins by which these people were destroying their own souls, deceiving the people and dishonoring God. But He did not speak in anger or irritation. Divine pity showed on His face as He looked once more around the temple and on the people listening. Then with a voice choked by grief and bitter tears, He cried out, " 'Jerusalem, Jerusalem! You kill the prophets and stone to death those who are sent to you. Many times I wanted to gather your people as a hen gathers her chicks under her wings, but you did not let me' " (Matthew 23:37). This cry from the heart of God marked the end of His longsuffering love for His special nation.

The Pharisees and the Sadducees stood silent as Jesus called His disciples to leave the temple. He did not leave defeated, but left because His work there was finished. On this day, many people began to think about what Jesus said. And after His death and resurrection, those people accepted His words and began to share His message—a message that changed hearts and exposed human theories as fables.

As a nation, Israel had divorced herself from God. Looking around one last time, Jesus said sadly, " 'Now your house will be left completely empty. I tell you, you will not see me again until that time when you will say, "God bless the One who comes in the name of the Lord" ' " (Matthew 23:38, 39).

As the Son of God walked out, God's presence left His temple forever. From this point on, its ceremonies and services were meaningless.

CHAPTER 68

"WE WANT
TO SEE JESUS"

" 'Whoever serves me must follow me,' "
(John 12:26).

ome people from Greece came to Jerusalem for the Passover festival. They came to Philip and said, "Sir, we want
to see Jesus." Philip told Andrew, and together they found
Jesus and told Him.

This was a discouraging time in Jesus' ministry. He had
certainly won His arguments with the priests and Pharisees, but it was
clear that they would never accept Him as the Messiah. When He heard
the words, "We want to see Jesus," His face lighted up and He said, "It
is time for the Son of man to receive His glory."

At the beginning of His life, wise men had come from the East to
find Jesus. Now near the end of His life, men came from the West to
find Him. These men from Greece represented the people of all the
nations and ages of the earth who would be drawn to the Savior on the
cross.

When He heard their request, Jesus was in the inner court of the
temple where only Jews could go. So He came out to the outer court
to personally answer their questions about His mission.

Their questions showed Jesus that His sacrifice would bring many
sons and daughters to God. He knew that these men would soon be

This chapter is based on John 12:20-43.

shocked to see Him standing beside a robber, accused and condemned to die. But Jesus knew that by paying the price for sin, His kingdom would one day spread throughout the world. For a moment, Jesus heard voices all over the world announcing, " 'Look, the Lamb of God, who takes away the sin of the world!' " (John 1:29). In these strangers, Jesus saw the promise of a great harvest of believers.

A SEED MUST BE PLANTED

Only by Jesus' death could the world be saved. He explained, "A grain of wheat must fall to the ground and die to create more seeds." When a grain of wheat is buried in the soil, it dies. But the new seed grows into a stalk of wheat and creates many more grains. The harvest is multiplied as those grains are planted also.

In the same way, Jesus' death on the cross would create more believers, more followers of His Father. Those believers will have the joy forever of studying the love behind His sacrifice. Jesus could have saved Himself from death. But He alone would have been saved.

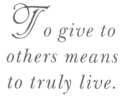

To give to others means to truly live.

Only by dying could He become the seed of a great harvest of all who would be saved by God.

All should learn the law of self-sacrifice. "Those who love their own lives more than others will lose them. Whoever sacrifices his life for others will have life that lasts forever." The law of self-sacrifice is the law of self-preservation. To give to others means to truly live.

A selfish life is like a grain of wheat that is eaten. When it is gone, it is gone forever. The law of self-serving is the law of self-destruction.

" 'Whoever serves me must follow me,' " Jesus said. " 'Then my servant will be with me everywhere I am. My Father will honor anyone who serves me' " (John 12:26). All who share Jesus' mission and His sacrifice will share in His glory one day. The Father will honor them as He honors His Son.

These words with the Greeks left Jesus quiet. A mysterious cloud seemed to form over Him as He thought about the plan to save humans—from the time the plan was formed in heaven to His death so soon to come. In a sorrow-filled voice He said, "Now I am very troubled. Should I say, 'Father, save Me from this time'?"

Jesus' human self backed away from what He knew was coming—being treated like a criminal, and dying a shameful death. He was almost overwhelmed by a sense of the burden of human guilt and of His Father's anger toward sin.

Jesus again submitted to His Father's will, to the plan They had created together. " 'No, I came to this time so I could suffer. Father, bring glory to your name!' " (John 12:27, 28). Only by Jesus' death could Satan's kingdom be destroyed, humans be saved, and God be glorified. Jesus accepted His role as the Sin Bearer.

THE FATHER SPEAKS

A voice was heard from the cloud over Jesus. " 'I have brought glory to it, and I will do it again' " (John 12:28). As the Voice spoke, a light surrounded Jesus as if His Father's arms were wrapped around Him, guarding Him like a wall of fire.

Everyone stood frozen, eyes locked on Jesus. No one spoke. Then with the Father's testimony given, the cloud lifted and dissipated. The Greek men saw the cloud, heard the Voice, and understood it. It was clear to them that Jesus was the Messiah, the Son of God.

The voice of God had been heard at Jesus' baptism and again at His transformation with Moses and Elijah. This third time it was heard by a larger group of people. Jesus had just made His last appeal to the Jewish people and had announced their tragic future. Now God spoke to show His approval of the One they had rejected.

Jesus told them, "The Voice spoke for your sake, not for Mine." God's voice should have been proof that Jesus had spoken the truth and really was the Son of God. "Now is the time for the world to be judged," Jesus continued. " 'If I am lifted up from the earth, I will draw all people toward me' " (John 12:32).

Jesus knew that His payment for human sins would light up the whole world and break Satan's grip on humans. The disfigured image of God would be restored in humans, and a family of believers would finally inherit the heavenly home God had always intended for His children. Jesus saw the cross—the cruel, shameful, horrible cross—shining with glory.

But the Cross did more than just save humans. It displayed God's love to the whole universe and removed the doubts Satan had raised in heaven. Angels as well as humans were drawn to the Savior.

Many people heard Jesus say these things. And though many had also seen His miracles, they still didn't believe in Him. Countless signs had been given to show them that Jesus was the Messiah, but they closed their eyes and hardened their hearts. Now God the Father had spoken from heaven. They could not ask for a more convincing sign. But they still refused to believe.

Some among the leaders did believe, but because they were afraid of what the Pharisees would do, they said nothing. To save themselves from embarrassment and criticism, they denied Jesus and rejected His offer of eternal life.

Slowly and sadly, Jesus left the temple for the last time.

SIGNS OF THE SECOND COMING

" 'When the Son of Man comes, he will be seen by everyone, like lightning flashing from the east to the west' " (Matthew 24:27).

esus' words to the priests and the leaders—"Now your house will be left completely empty"—struck terror in their hearts. Could what He said be true? Could their magnificent temple soon be destroyed?

The disciples had the same unsettled feeling. As they walked out of the temple with Jesus, they pointed out its beauty and strength. The stones of the temple were carved from the purest marble—some of an incredible size. A few of the stones had stood against the armies of Nebuchadnezzar.

Jesus saw their beauty, but He said sadly, "You think these walls are indestructible, but listen: The day is coming when not one of these stones will be left stacked upon another. They will all be knocked down."

Later Peter, James, John, and Andrew came to Jesus and asked, "When will these things happen? What will be the sign that it is time for You to come again and for this world to end?"

If Jesus had shown them the future as He saw it, they would not have been able to bear it. So He mingled the descriptions of the destruction of Jerusalem and the day of His second coming, leaving it to them to study the meaning for themselves. In fact, His answer was not

This chapter is based on Matt. 24; Mark 13; Luke 21:5-38.

just for those four disciples, but for all Jesus' followers to the end of time. His prophetic words about the destruction of Jerusalem would have a second meaning—they also refer to the end of time when the Lord punishes the wicked world for its iniquity.

"Many false messiahs will appear," Jesus said. And they did. Between the time of His death and the destruction of Jerusalem, many men claimed to be the Messiah and claimed that it was time for the nation of Israel to be freed. As the end of time approaches, again false messiahs will appear.

"When will these things happen?"

Jesus told them that wars, famines, diseases, and earthquakes would come. The rabbis would point to them as signs that the Messiah was coming. Instead these disasters were signs that destruction was coming for them.

" 'Then people will arrest you, hand you over to be hurt, and kill you. They will hate you because you believe in me. At that time, many will lose their faith, and they will turn against each other' " (Matthew 24:9,10). The first Christians suffered all of these things. Families and friends betrayed those they should have loved. Stephen, James, and many others were tried and killed. Through these witnesses, Jesus gave the Jewish leaders one last chance to repent. But by killing His followers, in effect they crucified the Son of God once more.

These things will happen again. Those in authority will make laws to restrict religious beliefs. They will continue their efforts to control or destroy people until God steps in to save His commandment-keeping followers. When this persecution happens, many will give up their faith. To save themselves, they will betray other church members. With Jesus' warning, we can be prepared to face these trials.

Jesus told His disciples how to escape the destruction of Jerusalem. "When you see Jerusalem surrounded by armies, then you will know that the time of destruction is near. That is the time for the people of Judea to run to the mountains." Forty years later, Christians remembered Jesus' words and fled out of Jerusalem when armies came to surround it. Not one Christian died when the city was taken.

"Pray that your escape won't be in winter or on the Sabbath day," Jesus added. By indicating that the Sabbath would still be kept forty years later, Jesus showed that it did not end with His death.

THE DARK AGES OF PERSECUTION

From His warning about Jerusalem, Jesus moved quickly to the last link in the chain of this earth's history—His return in majesty and glory. Between these two events, Jesus saw the long centuries of darkness, centuries when the true church suffered with blood and tears. But He mentioned them only briefly: " 'There will be more trouble than there has ever been since the beginning of the world until now, and nothing as bad will ever happen again' " (Matthew 24:21).

For more than a thousand years, the worst persecution ever recorded would fall on Jesus' followers. Millions would be killed, and if God hadn't stepped in to protect them, every faithful follower would have died.

Then Jesus spoke clearly about His second coming. He warned His followers about false messiahs and false prophets who would do great miracles. There is no reason to believe people who claim that the Messiah has returned in secret. " 'When the Son of Man comes, he will be seen by everyone, like lightning flashing from the east to the west' " (Matthew 24:27).

Many today claim to speak with the dead or with other spirits. Spiritualism may claim that Jesus has returned quietly and secretly. But we have been warned not to believe it.

SIGNS IN THE HEAVENS

Jesus gave specific signs of His coming: the sun and moon will be darkened, the stars will fall from the sky, and the powers of the heavens will be shaken. " 'At that time, the sign of the Son of Man will appear in the sky. Then all the peoples of the world will cry. They will see the Son of Man coming on clouds in the sky with great power and glory' " (Matthew 24:30). At the sound of a trumpet, Jesus will send His angels to gather His people from every part of the world.

These events would follow quickly at the end of the great religious persecution. Jesus said, "When you see these things happening, you will know that the time is near. All these things will happen while the people of that time are still living." Since those signs have occurred, we can be sure that Jesus' return is very near.

His return will be glorious. With a massive number of shining angels, Jesus will return to raise the dead to life and give His living followers immortal bodies. He will come back to honor those who have loved Him and kept His commandments, and to take them home with Him.

Whenever we feel the pain of losing a loved one to death, we can think of that day when they will be raised to live forever. Jesus Himself will wipe the tears from our eyes.

Jesus made it clear that He could not tell humans the day or time of His return. The exact time of the Second Coming is the Father's mystery, His secret to keep.

JUST LIKE NOAH'S DAY

Jesus compared the time of His return to Noah's day. People were going on with their normal lives—eating, drinking, marrying and having children—until the day Noah went into the ark. " 'They knew nothing about what was happening until the flood came and destroyed them. It will be the same when the Son of Man comes' " (Matthew 24:39).

The Flood came in Noah's time because of the great wickedness of those humans. But today, many are following in their wicked footsteps. As they ignore God's laws, they are filling the world with pain, lust, and violence. Jesus said, "Because evil is everywhere, many will lose their love for God. But the ones who endure to the end will be saved."

Then Jesus added, "When the gospel is preached all over the world to the people of every nation, then the end will come." So in this way we can do more than just wait anxiously for Jesus' return—we can hurry it by sharing the gospel. If the church had done the work as Jesus directed, the whole world would have already been reached and Jesus could already have returned.

A SURPRISE RETURN

We cannot know the exact time of Jesus' return, so we must watch and wait. But there is much to be done as we wait. We can purify our souls by obeying Jesus' teachings. We can cooperate with angels in reaching out to others with the good news about Jesus. Like Enoch, Noah, Abraham, and Moses in their times, we have a special warning for our generation.

Jesus told His disciples a story of an evil servant who tells himself, "My master will not come back soon." This servant then beats his fellow servants and gets drunk. When the master returns unexpectedly, the servant is thrown out with the hypocrites.

The evil servant represents the supposedly faithful believers who claim that Jesus' return is delayed, that He is not coming back soon. They influence others to forget about focusing on God, to just think about the pleasures of the day. They cause pain for their fellow believers, accusing them of being unfaithful.

We cannot know the exact time of Jesus' return, so we must watch and wait.

Jesus' return will surprise many unfaithful, false believers. Many pursue only pleasure and wealth, eagerly searching to know more about everything except the truths found in the Bible. To these people, Jesus will return like a thief in the night—completely unexpected.

The signs of the end all around us are frightening. As God's Spirit withdraws from the world, tragedy after tragedy occurs in every land. Earthquakes, fires, floods, crimes, and murder touch every family. Who can feel secure about the future?

The end-time crisis is creeping up on us gradually. The sun rises and shines each day, people build houses, and eat and drink. Merchants buy and sell as people struggle to get more money and more power. People search for pleasure and amusement at theaters, sporting events, and casinos. But in the middle of all this excitement, the close of probation is rapidly approaching. Every person's eternal fate will soon be decided. Satan is working overtime to keep us deceived, amused, and busy until the door of heaven is closed forever.

" 'So be ready all the time. Pray that you will be strong enough to escape all these things that will happen and that you will be able to stand before the Son of Man' " (Luke 21:36).

CHAPTER 70

THE POOR
AND SUFFERING

" 'Do to others what you want them to do to you' "
(Matthew 7:12).

he Son of Man will come again in his great glory, with all his angels. . . . All the nations of the world will be gathered before him, and he will separate them into two groups" (Matthew 25:31, 32).

Jesus described the day of judgment in a way that His disciples could easily picture. In the judgment, people will be divided into two groups. But what separates them must have really surprised the disciples. Their eternal destiny will be determined by how they have treated people in need—the poor and suffering.

HELPERS OF THE POOR

On that Judgment Day, Jesus doesn't proclaim the great things He has done for humans by giving His life for them. He announces the faithful works of love that humans have done for Him. "My Father blesses you; inherit the kingdom," Jesus says. "I was hungry and you gave me food. I was thirsty, and you gave me something to drink. I was alone and away from home, and you invited me into your house. I was without clothes, and you gave me something to wear. I was sick,

This chapter is based on Matt. 25:31-46.

and you cared for me. I was in prison, and you visited me" (Matthew 25:35, 36).

Those whom God praises don't know they have been ministering to Jesus. To their perplexed questions, Jesus answers, "Whenever you helped any of My people here—even the weakest or the poorest—you helped Me."

The judgment divides people into two groups.

We can see Jesus in the faces of each of His children who suffer. And as we help them, it is like helping Jesus personally. All who have accepted Jesus as their Savior are in a special sense His brothers and sisters. His love binds us all together as members of His heavenly family.

The people Jesus praises in the judgment may not know much theology, but they understand and love His principles. Many who have never heard of Christianity live with a spirit of kindness. Those who worship God without knowing Him, never contacted by Christian missionaries, will not be lost. They may have been ignorant about God's written laws, but the Holy Spirit has touched their hearts and it shows in their actions. They may be surprised to hear it, but they are God's children!

As the Son of Man, Jesus is a brother to every descendant of Adam. His followers are part of the great web of humanity and we should feel like brothers and sisters to all. Jesus' love reaches out to the fallen, sinful people around us, and every act of kindness done for them is accepted as if it were done for Jesus Himself.

The angels of heaven join us in helping others. They are sent to minister to all who need and choose to be saved, and when we open our doors to help the poor and suffering, they join us, bringing a holy atmosphere of joy and peace. Every helpful act of mercy makes music in heaven. Unselfish workers are among God's most precious treasures.

NEGLECTORS OF THE POOR

Those on the left side of Jesus in the judgment are those who—with their self-focused approach to life, not caring about the needs of others—are guilty of ignoring Jesus. No matter what they claim to believe or what church they belong to, they are lost forever.

God gives wealth to the rich so that they can help the needy and suffering. But too often, they are don't care about others. They don't understand the struggles poor people face, and mercy in their hearts dies out. The poor are robbed of what they could have learned about God's love and of what they could have been with the proper help. Their difficult lives tempt them to be jealous and think all kinds of evil thoughts.

Jesus sees it all. He says, "While you were partying with your beautiful table settings, I was starving in a shack. While you were relaxing in your elegant home, I was homeless on the street. While you were choosing your entertainment for the evening, I was wasting away in prison. When you did give a little money or a few morsels of food to the hungry, when you did donate a worn out coat or blanket to the homeless, did you remember that you were giving those things to Me—the King of heaven? Every day of your life I was near you in the person of these needy ones, but you didn't look for Me. You refused to have any relationship with Me. So I don't know you."

> *Jesus gave His life to create a church that could care for others.*

JESUS' FOOTSTEPS

Many people travel to the Holy Land to see the places where Jesus lived and worked and did His miracles. But we don't need to go to Nazareth or Jerusalem to walk in the steps of Jesus. We can find His footprints beside hospital beds, in homeless shelters, in inner-city ghettos, in every place where human hearts need help and hope.

There is much for each of us to do. Millions have never heard of Jesus' love. Jesus' rule of life—the rule we will each be measured by in the judgment—is " 'Do to others what you want them to do to you' " (Matthew 7:12).

Jesus gave His life to create a church that could care for others. Individually, we may be poor, uneducated, and unknown, but in Jesus we can do things in our communities and around the world that will have eternal results. When this kind of work is neglected, young Christians never learn the true joy of helping others. When their restless energy is focused on blessing other people, they'll have little interest in the wasteful, dangerous entertainments of the world.

To make all of us children of one family, the King of heaven became one of us. When we love the world as He does, then His mission will be accomplished. And we will be ready for heaven, because heaven will already be in our hearts.

On the great day of judgment, those who have done nothing for Jesus, who have drifted along thinking only of themselves, will be placed in the same group as those who were evil.

In the judgment, the Chief Shepherd will ask each person, "Where are the sheep I gave you to watch over and care for?" What will we answer?

CHAPTER 71

SERVANT
OF SERVANTS

" 'Do you understand what I have just done for you?' "
(John 13:12).

esus met with His disciples to share the Passover Feast. He knew that His time had come—He was the true Lamb and on this Passover, He would be sacrificed. He had only a few quiet hours left to teach His disciples.

Throughout His ministry Jesus had lived a life of unselfish service. But His disciples still hadn't learned that lesson. On this night, He was quiet and troubled. The disciples could tell that something was weighing on His mind. As they gathered around the table, He said, " 'I wanted very much to eat this Passover meal with you before I suffer. I will not eat another Passover meal until it is given its true meaning in the kingdom of God' " (Luke 22:15, 16).

Jesus lifted a cup of grape juice, gave thanks to His Father, and said, " 'Take this cup and share it among yourselves. I will not drink again from the fruit of the vine until God's kingdom comes' " (Luke 22:17, 18).

The shadow of the Cross had fallen over Jesus and its pain was torturing His heart. He knew His friends would desert Him. He knew He would be put to death in a most humiliating, painful way. Those He had come to save would respond with cruelty. For many, His sacri-

This chapter is based on Luke 22:7-18, 24; John 13:1-17.

fice would be wasted. Knowing this, He should have been overwhelmed at the thought of His own suffering. But care for His disciples was His chief concern.

On this last evening, Jesus had much to tell them. But as He looked into their eyes, He said nothing. They weren't ready to hear what He had to say. As the silent moments passed, they shifted uncomfortably, shooting jealous glances at one another.

Once again they were arguing over who would be the most powerful and important in the new kingdom. James and John's request for the highest offices still rankled the others and threatened to cause a real split among them. Judas was the harshest critic of the two brothers.

Judas had forced his way to the left side of Jesus as they entered the room. John had taken the right side. Whatever the most important office would be in the new kingdom, Judas was determined to have it.

THE CRISIS OF FOOTWASHING

All of this led to another crisis—it was the custom at a meal like this for a servant to come in and wash the feet of the guests. A pitcher of water, a pan, and a towel had all been provided with the room, but there was no servant. With their Teacher present, it fell to the disciples to offer this service. But they sat silently, each one refusing to be seen as a servant doing this humble job.

How could Jesus make them understand that claiming to be disciples did not make them true followers? How could He awaken the love in their hearts that would make them understand His words? How could He save them from Satan's temptations?

On this last evening, Jesus had much to tell them.

For a time, Jesus waited to see what they would do. Then He stood, took off His cloak, and picked up the towel. In shocked silence, the disciples could only watch as He poured water into the pan. One by one, Jesus began to wash their feet and wipe them dry with the towel. This opened their eyes, and with bitter shame they realized how they had been behaving. This example Jesus gave was something they would never forget. His love for them was so strong that He was willing to lay aside His royal holiness and be their servant.

Judas had already agreed to betray Jesus to the priests, although the disciples knew nothing about it. Jesus knew, but He didn't expose Judas's plans. When the Savior's hands were washing his feet and tenderly wiping them, Judas almost confessed his plans. But in the end, his pride was too strong—he couldn't admit that he was wrong. He hardened his heart against ever repenting.

As his heart hardened, Judas became offended that Jesus would wash His disciples' feet. "Anyone who would do this," he said to himself, "could not be Israel's true king." Satisfied that he would gain nothing by following Jesus, he felt sure that betraying Him was the right thing to do. Under the influence of demons, Judas was determined to go ahead with his plan.

THE MIRACLE OF CHANGED HEARTS

Judas had tried to place himself first by sitting at Jesus' left side, and Jesus had served him first. This left John for the last, but like Peter, John was ashamed of himself and didn't feel slighted. When Peter's turn came, he still couldn't believe what Jesus was doing. "Lord, are You really going to wash *my* feet?"

Jesus said, "You don't understand what I am doing now, but you will understand later."

Peter couldn't stand to see his Lord, the Son of God, acting as a servant. Filled with shame, his whole heart rose up against this humiliation for Jesus. He cried, "You will never wash my feet."

"If I don't wash your feet," Jesus said, "then you will not be one of My people."

That was not something Peter could accept. "Lord, then don't just wash my feet, but my hands and head also."

Jesus must have smiled at Peter's enthusiasm. "A person who has bathed needs only to have his feet washed to be clean." But Jesus was speaking of more than just being washed. Peter and the others had been forgiven—washed clean of sin—when they accepted Jesus as the Savior. But having been led into sinful jealousy, they still needed Jesus' cleansing grace—they needed to repent and be forgiven again.

Jesus wanted to wash the jealousy and pride out of their hearts. Without an attitude of humility and love, they were not ready to share the memorial service Jesus was about to create. But by washing their feet, Jesus created this change. Except for Judas, their hearts were united with love for each other and each one was ready for someone else to have the most important position. Now they were ready to listen and learn.

We also have been washed clean of sin by accepting Jesus and His sacrifice for us. But often we find our hearts dirtied by sin. We need to be washed again by Jesus' grace. Our temper, our anger, our pride cause Him pain like the disciples' did. But we must come to Jesus, because only He can wash us clean again.

THE PURPOSE OF THE SERVICE

When Jesus finished washing their feet, He said, " 'Do you understand what I have just done for you? You call me "Teacher" and "Lord," and you are right, because that is what I am. If I, your Lord and Teacher, have washed your feet, you also should wash each other's feet . . . a servant is not greater than his master' " (John 13:12-16).

Under the influence of demons, Judas was determined to go ahead with his plan.

Knowing the selfishness that lives in the human heart, Jesus set this example of humility and selflessness. Jesus—equal with God, Ruler of the universe—bent down to wash the feet of those who followed Him. He washed the feet of the one who had already agreed to betray Him to His death.

God does not live for Himself—He lives for others. Jesus came as a human and lived as an example of that. He reached out to help every person with whom He came in contact. He lived the law of God and showed us how to obey it.

Jesus told His disciples, "I did this as an example so that you should do the same." With these words, He began a religious service, a ceremony that should be repeated by His disciples to help them remember the lesson of humility and service.

This ceremony was Jesus' way to prepare the human heart for the service we call "the Lord's Supper" or "Communion." While pride or any kind of selfish thinking is dominating our hearts, we are not ready to receive the symbols of Jesus' body and blood. So Jesus declared that the foot-washing service should take place first.

As humans we just naturally work to put ourselves ahead of others, to work for what we want at the expense of others. The foot-washing ceremony calls us out of our selfishness to humility and service. The Holy Spirit is always present at this service to convict us of sin, and to assure us that we are forgiven. Jesus is there with the power to change our selfish thoughts if we ask.

This service can bring up a chain of memories for each of us—memories of God's goodness and the loving kindness of friends and family. Memories of our own failings—our impatience and selfishness—come to mind. This is the time to confess sins and be forgiven as the grace of Jesus draws us closer together. Now we are ready to celebrate Communion with the sunshine of Jesus' righteousness filling our souls.

When the foot-washing ceremony is celebrated properly, the children of God go out dedicated to unselfish ministry for one another. As it was in Jesus' day, the world is full of people in need. When we have felt His presence in our foot-washing ceremony, we will go out to minister as He did.

CHAPTER 72

THE LORD'S SUPPER

"Look into your own hearts before you eat the bread and drink the cup" (1 Corinthians 11:28, 29).

On the night when the Lord Jesus was handed over to be killed, he took bread and gave thanks for it. Then he broke the bread and said, 'This is my body; it is for you. Do this to remember me.' In the same way, after they ate, Jesus took the cup. He said, 'This cup is the new agreement that is sealed with the blood of my death. When you drink this, do it to remember me' " (1 Corinthians 11:23-25).

Jesus, the Lamb of God, was about to bring an end to the Passover service and all the Jewish ceremonies pointing to the Messiah. In its place, He created a new ceremony that could be celebrated by His followers in all lands for all time. The Passover was celebrated to remember Israel's rescue from Egyptian slavery; the Lord's Supper would be celebrated to remember the rescue of all humans from slavery to sin. This ceremony would keep Jesus' sacrifice on the cross fresh in our hearts and minds.

In Jesus' day, the Passover supper was eaten as the guests lay on couches placed around a low table. In this position, the guests' heads were close together while their feet could be washed by someone passing around the outside of the circle.

This chapter is based on Matt. 26:20-29; Mark 14:17-25; Luke 22:14-23; John 13:18-30.

As they lay around the table where the Passover meal was served, Jesus took some of the unleavened bread, thanked God for it, then broke it into pieces. As He handed it to them, Jesus said, "Take this bread and eat it; this is My body."

Next Jesus picked up a cup of Passover wine—unfermented grape juice—and thanked God for it. Then He handed it to them to pass around. " 'Every one of you drink this. This is my blood which is the new agreement that God makes with his people. This blood is poured out for many to forgive their sins' " (Matthew 26:27, 28).

Jesus handed Judas the symbols of His blood and broken body. As he sat there before the Lamb of God, Judas cherished his thoughts of revenge. During the footwashing earlier, Jesus had shown that He knew Judas's plan when He said, "Not all of you are clean." Now He spoke more clearly. " 'I am not talking about all of you. I know those I have chosen. But this is to bring about what the Scripture said: "The man who ate at my table has turned against me" ' " (John 13:18).

The others still didn't suspect Judas, but they could tell that something was terribly wrong. They ate in silence until Jesus said, "One of you will betray Me." The group was dismayed. How could any of them turn against their beloved Teacher?

But as they remembered how true Jesus' statements always were, they began to doubt themselves. One after another, they turned to Jesus and asked, "Lord, I'm not the one, am I?" Only Judas was silent.

Finally, John asked, "Lord, who is it?"

Jesus answered, "The one I give this bread to is the man who will betray Me." Then He gave the bread to Judas.

In all the questions and confusion, Judas hadn't heard Jesus' answer to John. Now with everyone staring, he asked, "Certainly I am not the one, am I?"

Jesus could only answer sadly, "Yes, you are."

The Lord's Supper would be celebrated to remember the rescue of all humans from slavery to sin.

Shocked and confused to have his plan exposed, Judas jumped up to leave. Jesus called after him, "Do what you are going to do quickly." Then Judas went out into the darkness. By reading his heart, Jesus gave Judas one more evidence that He really was the Son of God. Until he left the room, Judas could have repented and been saved. But now he was set on the path to betray Jesus and destroy himself.

Jesus had earlier told all the disciples, Judas included, the fate of the one who would betray him—it would be better if that person had never been born. But now to build the faith of the remaining disciples, Jesus says, "I am telling you this before it happens so that when it does, you will believe who I am." If Jesus had said nothing, the disciples might have doubted His divine power, thinking He had been surprised. Now as the terrible events began, they would remember His words.

JESUS' EXAMPLE INCLUDES ALL

Jesus was also teaching His disciples about the patience and mercy of God toward the most terrible of sinners. Even Judas was allowed to be with Jesus and share the Passover supper. This shows us that we should not avoid others simply because we think they may be living in a sinful way. All the disciples came into the meal with jealous, sinful thinking. But Jesus' actions led all but one to repent.

Open, public sin should exclude a person from celebrating the Lord's Supper. But since no one can read hearts, we should not judge others. We should judge ourselves. "Look into your own hearts before you eat the bread and drink the cup, because all who eat the bread and drink the cup without recognizing the body eat and drink judgment against themselves" (1 Corinthians 11:28, 29).

When believers gather today to celebrate the Lord's Supper, there may be people like Judas present. Others may be there who are not following God. Dark agents of Satan will be with them as they are with all who aren't surrendered to the Holy Spirit, but these people should be welcomed to the service if they wish to take part. Heavenly angels will be there also, and Jesus will speak through the Holy Spirit to soften hearts and convict of sin. The One who washed the feet of Judas longs to wash the sin from the hearts of all who come in repentance.

No one should avoid Communion services because unworthy individuals may be there. These are Jesus' appointments and He will meet His people there and energize them with His presence. Even if those who lead out in the service are unworthy in some way, those who come with their faith fixed on Jesus will be blessed. Those who miss these celebrations will lose the blessing Jesus offers.

REASONS FOR CELEBRATING THE LORD'S SUPPER

When believers gather for the Lord's Supper, it is not a time to focus on their shortcomings or on the differences between them. The foot-washing ceremony dealt with those issues. Now they are meeting with Jesus, not in the shadow of the Cross, but in its saving light. They can open their souls to the bright beams of Jesus, the Sun of Righteousness.

At these services the Lord speaks to us saying, "If you feel oppressed or distressed because of Me or the gospel, remember that My love is so strong that I gave My life for you. When your work is too hard or your burdens are too heavy, remember that I suffered the shame of the cross for you. And I now live to stand and speak for you in heaven."

The Communion service was designed to keep the hope of Jesus' second coming alive in our minds. "Every time you eat this bread and drink this cup you are telling others about the Lord's death until he comes" (1 Corinthians 11:26).

This service reminds us of God's love. It reminds us that Jesus' death on the cross created a permanent connection between God and humans. It can help us understand what Jesus suffered to pay for our sins and save us. It reminds us that because of Jesus' death, we can look forward to His second coming with real joy.

Jesus' death allows humans to live on, filled with hope. We owe even our everyday lives to His sacrifice. The cross of Calvary is stamped on every loaf of bread and reflected in every well of water. His blood paid for our bread and water.

Eating Jesus' body and drinking His blood means accepting His words and doing the things He commands us to do. Jesus lived by His Father's will; when we accept Jesus, we live by His will. Every Communion service forms a living connection from us to Jesus and by Him to the Father.

Any person who sees the Savior's matchless love will be changed.

When we share the bread and wine that represents Jesus' broken body and spilled blood, we can in our imagination relive the sacrifice He made. The thought of what happened on Calvary will create holy emotions—selfless love—in our hearts. Pride and self-centeredness cannot exist in a heart that remembers the Cross. Any person who sees the Savior's matchless love will be changed. That person will go out to be a light to the world, a reflection of that mysterious love.

CHAPTER 73

WORDS
OF HOPE

" *'I give you a new command: Love each other'* "
(John 13:34).

fter Judas left, Jesus wanted to talk to the other
disciples about what was coming, to explain how
He would be separated from them. To hear Jesus—
their Teacher and Friend—say, "I will be with you only
a little longer," left the disciples troubled and worried. But
His next words were full of hope. Jesus knew that Satan is most successful when people are depressed. So He turned their thoughts to
heaven.

Jesus said, " 'Don't let your hearts be troubled. . . . There are many
rooms in my Father's house; I would not tell you this if it were not
true. I am going there to prepare a place for you. After I go and prepare a place for you, I will come back and take you to be with me so
that you may be where I am. You know the way to the place where I am
going' " (John 14:1-4).

Jesus' leaving meant just the opposite of what the disciples
feared—it was not a permanent separation. He was going to build
mansions for them so they could come and be with Him. While He
was building mansions for them, they should be building characters
like His.

This chapter is based on John 13:31-38; 14-17.

Thomas was worried and doubtful. "Lord, we don't know where You are going. How can we know the way?"

Jesus tried hard to prepare His disciples for the coming storm of temptation.

Jesus answered, " 'I am the way, and the truth, and the life. The only way to the Father is through me. If you really knew me, you would know my Father, too. But now you do know him, and you have seen him' " (John 14:6, 7). There is only one way to heaven—Jesus. He is the way the kings and prophets of long ago were saved and He is the only way we can be saved today.

But the disciples still didn't understand. Philip said, "Lord, show us the Father."

Jesus answered in pained surprise, "I have been with you a long time, Philip. Do you still not know Me? Is it possible that you do not see the Father in the things He does through Me? Whoever has seen Me has seen the Father." Jesus hadn't stopped being God when He became human. His work showed His divinity and showed His Father.

If the disciples understood this connection, they wouldn't lose their faith when they saw Jesus suffer and die. Jesus tried hard to prepare them for the coming storm of temptation. As they listened with sacred awe that evening, the disciples were drawn closer to Jesus and to each other. Heaven seemed very close.

The Savior was anxious for His disciples to understand why His divinity was joined to His humanity. He came to the world to show God's glory and lift humans up by its power, but He didn't show any abilities or use any power that humans can't have through faith in Him. His followers can have the same perfect humanity that He did if they will give themselves to God as He did.

Jesus said that the disciples would do even greater things than He had done. They would have the help of the Holy Spirit to reach more people. After Jesus returned to heaven, they saw His promise fulfilled. When they spoke about God's love, people's hearts were changed— thousands became followers of Jesus.

THE PRIVILEGE OF PRAYER

Jesus explained that the secret of their success would come in asking for strength and power in His name. Jesus presents the prayer requests of His followers to His Father as if they were His own. Sincere prayers might be said awkwardly or simply, but Jesus presents them to His Father with the fragrance of His own perfection.

Following Jesus' way does not give us a path that is free from obstacles or pain. But every difficulty can be an invitation to pray. Jesus said, "If you ask Me for anything in My name, I will do it." In Jesus' name, His followers are to stand before God. Because of Jesus' righteousness, God will not see a sinner. Instead, He sees in them the image of His Son.

The Lord is disappointed when His people think they are not worth much. How much God values them is shown by the fact that He sent His Son to rescue them. He is pleased when they make great demands in prayer so that they can praise His name. If they have faith in His promises, they can expect great things.

To pray in Jesus' name means that we accept His character, show His spirit, and do the things that He would do. The Savior doesn't save people in sin—He saves them from sin. And those who love Him show it in their obedience to His words.

True obedience comes from a person's heart. If we ask, Jesus will blend our hearts and minds to His will so that in acting on our own impulses we will be obeying Him. The more we know God, the more our lives will reflect the perfect obedience of His Son. As we spend time with God, sin will become something we hate.

Jesus lived God's law as a human, and we can live it also if we learn to depend on Him. We cannot rely on others to tell us what God wants in our lives. If we decide to do nothing that will displease God, we can come to Him with our concerns and know which direction to take. God will give us more than just the wisdom to decide—He will give us the strength to do the right thing.

HOW THE HOLY SPIRIT WORKS

Before offering Himself as a sacrifice, Jesus asked for the best and most important gift for His followers. " 'I will ask the Father, and he will give you another Helper to be with you forever—the Spirit of truth' " (John 14:16, 17). While Jesus was with them, the disciples wanted no other helper. After Jesus was gone, they would feel the need for the Holy Spirit and He would come.

When believers stand up for their faith, Jesus stands with them.

The Holy Spirit represents Jesus on earth now. With His human body, Jesus could not be everywhere personally. But through the Holy Spirit, He is available to every person on the planet at the same time.

Jesus could see the trials and persecution in His disciples' future—one disciple would be hung, one killed on a cross, one exiled to a lonely island. But He would be with each of them in their trials. When believers stand up for their faith, Jesus stands with them. When they are in prison, Jesus fills their hearts with love.

Anywhere and anytime we feel helpless and alone, the Holy Spirit will come to comfort us if we pray, asking in faith. Even if we are separated from every friend on earth, nothing can separate us from our heavenly Comforter.

Jesus explained it again. " 'The Helper will teach you everything and will cause you to remember all that I told you. This Helper is the Holy Spirit whom the Father will send in my name' " (John 14:26). Through these disciples, Jesus would speak to the people of the whole world. They would be devastated by the Savior's death, but the Holy Spirit would bring back to their minds everything Jesus had taught them.

More than that, the Holy Spirit would help them understand Jesus' words. The disciples had been educated to accept the teachings of the rabbis as the voice of God, and it was hard for them to change their thinking. Now through the work of the Holy Spirit, the truths of Jesus' kingdom would be understood and appreciated.

The Helper or Comforter is called the Spirit of Truth. Satan gains power over our minds through false teachings, and his false standards warp our characters. The Holy Spirit exposes error—false teachings—and expels it from our hearts by filling our minds with truth. The Spirit of Truth—working through the Bible—leads people to follow Jesus and obey Him.

THE PURPOSE OF THE SPIRIT

Jesus wanted to share His joy at being able to give them the best gift He could ask of His Father. The power of evil had been growing stronger through the centuries, and humans were more and more easily controlled by it. Only the power and the presence of the Holy Spirit would make it possible for people to turn to God and escape sin. The Holy Spirit would make Jesus' sacrifice accomplish its purpose. Its power is the only way humans can overcome their inherited and learned tendency to do evil. God's image is to be reproduced in people. Both God's and Jesus' honor is involved in the perfection of character in the people of God.

Peter meant what he said, but he didn't know his own heart.

Jesus promised that the Holy Spirit would teach the people of the world about sin and righteousness and judgment. Preaching the Word or sharing the gospel is of no use without the Holy Spirit's influence in the hearts of those who hear it. No amount of education or talent will make a person a channel of God's life-changing light without the cooperation of the Holy Spirit.

Jesus promised this gift to His church and the promise was meant for us as much as it was for the first disciples. But like every other promise, it has conditions. We will receive no help if all we do is talk about Jesus and about the Holy Spirit. We must surrender our will. We cannot use the Holy Spirit—the Spirit must use us.

PREDICTION OF PETER'S DENIAL

Before they left the upper room, Jesus led His disciples in a song of praise. There was no sadness in His voice, but the joy of the traditional Passover song:

> All you nations, praise the Lord.
> All you people, praise him
> because the Lord loves us very much,
> and his truth is everlasting.
> Praise the Lord! (Psalm 117).

As they walked slowly out through the city gate toward the Mount of Olives, each one was busy with his own thoughts. Then Jesus said, "Tonight you will all stumble in your faith because of what happens to Me."

Peter protested. "Everyone else may stumble but I will not."

Jesus warned him again. "Peter, I tell you the truth: before the rooster crows twice in the morning, you will say three times that you don't know Me."

Peter almost shouted, "I will never say that I don't know You. I will even die with You!" And the others all said the same.

Peter meant what he said, but he didn't know his own heart. Jesus could see in Peter a love for himself that was stronger than his love for his Savior. Peter needed to learn to stop trusting himself and have more faith in Jesus. When he was sinking on the Sea of Galilee, Peter had cried, "Lord, save me!" If he had said the same thing now, he would have been safe. Instead Peter thought it was cruel of Jesus not to trust him, and his confidence in himself increased.

Jesus couldn't protect His disciples from what was coming, but He didn't leave them without hope. Even before they abandoned Him, they had assurance of His forgiveness. After His death and resurrection, they knew they were loved and forgiven.

THE TRUE VINE

As they walked toward the Garden of Gethsemane through the bright moonlight, Jesus noticed a grapevine and drew the disciples' attention to it. "I am the True Vine," He said, "and My Father is the Gardener." Unlike the strong palm and oak trees, the grapevine needs support to grow toward heaven. And like the vine, Jesus depended on His Father's power.

"I am the Vine," Jesus said, "and you are the branches." Like branches that are grafted onto the vine, Jesus' followers must grow into a relationship with Him. Then like the branch, we will receive life through our connection to Him. Our weaknesses are united with His strengths. This is how we can have the mind of Jesus—how we can think and act like Jesus did.

But this cannot be an on-again, off-again relationship. Jesus said, " 'Remain in me, and I will remain in you. A branch cannot produce fruit alone but must remain in the vine. In the same way, you cannot produce fruit alone but must remain in me' " (John 15:4). Our relationship with Jesus must be constant—every moment of every day—in order to stay strong. Without Him, we cannot overcome temptations. We must hold on tight to Jesus, then by faith we can receive His perfect character.

When we live by faith in Jesus, our lives will be changed—the fruits of the Spirit will be seen. Many act like Christians, and claim to be Christians, but their characters will show if they have any real connection to Jesus. If they produce no fruit—no kindness or love for others—they are false branches. Branches that produce no fruit are cut off and burned.

Branches that produce fruit are pruned—trimmed so that they can produce even more and better fruit. Of the twelve disciples, one was a false branch about to be cut off and the others were soon to be pruned by a terrible ordeal. Pruning can be painful, but it's our Father the Gardener who does the pruning. He works to make us stronger, wiser, better followers of Jesus.

Jesus said, " 'You should produce much fruit and show that you are my followers, which brings glory to my Father' " (John 15:8). God wants to show His holiness, kindness, and compassion through humans. But Jesus didn't teach His disciples to work hard to bear this fruit. He told them to remain in Him, to keep their connection to Him. Living in Jesus, following Jesus, supported by Jesus, we will produce fruit like His.

A NEW COMMANDMENT

Jesus' first words when He was alone with His disciples in the upper room that night was: " 'I give you a new command: Love each other. You must love each other as I have loved you' " (John 13:34). To the disciples, this was new. They had not had much love for each other. But they were developing a new understanding of love. This command to love each other had a new meaning after they witnessed Jesus' sacrifice.

When people take care of each other—not because they are forced to or because of some personal benefit—they are showing the influence of heaven. It is evidence that the image of God is being recreated in humans. And this kind of love in the church will stir Satan's anger. Jesus told His disciples, "If the world hates you, remember that it hated Me first. If they did wrong to Me, they will do wrong to you too." Showing the kind of love Jesus did will get the same response from those controlled by Satan—hate.

Like branches that are grafted onto the vine, Jesus' followers must grow into a relationship with Him.

As the Savior of the world, most of the time Jesus didn't seem to have much success. He was not able to do much of the work He wanted to do. Satan and those he influenced were always working against Him. But He would be not discouraged. He knew that when He cried out, "It is finished," all heaven would claim victory. He knew that His triumph would be trumpeted from world to world throughout the universe. He knew that truth—

armed with the power of the Holy Spirit—would win the battle with evil.

He knew that His disciples' lives would be like His—a string of successful battles that might not seem like victories when they happened. But in eternity, they would be recognized as the triumphs they really were.

We should live as Jesus lived, work as He worked, and have the same faithful endurance that He had. Instead of being discouraged with difficulties, we can overcome the problems we face.

Jesus expects the order and harmony of heaven to be seen in His church on earth. He receives glory when His church displays the riches of His love and grace. Finally, He will see His people with their pure hearts and perfect lives as His reward for His sacrifice.

And so Jesus ended His last talk with His disciples with strong, hopeful words. He had finished the work He had been given—He had shared the truth about His Father and trained those who would continue His work among humans.

Then as a high priest, Jesus prayed for His people. " 'Holy Father, keep them safe by the power of your name, the name you gave me, so that they will be one, just as you and I are one' " (John 17:11). " 'I pray for these followers, but I am also praying for all those who will believe in me because of their teaching. Father, I pray that they can be one. . . . Then the world will know that you sent me and that you loved them just as much as you loved me' " (John 17:20, 21, 23).

Jesus left His followers, His church in His Father's hands. Then He went out to face His final battle with Satan.

CHAPTER 74

THE STRUGGLE
IN GETHSEMANE

" 'My Father, if it is possible, do not give me this cup of suffering. But do what you want, not what I want' " (Matthew 26:39).

ith the Passover moon shining brightly in the night sky, the group walked on toward Gethsemane. As they neared the Garden, Jesus became strangely quiet. Every day of His life on earth, Jesus had lived in the light of God's presence. But the time had come for Him to be considered a sinner, so that He could carry the guilt of fallen humans. That guilt was so heavy that Jesus was tempted to fear that it would cut Him off forever from His Father's love. He cried out, "My heart is full of sorrow, to the point of death."

The disciples had never seen their Master so utterly sad. The disciples looked anxiously for Jesus' usual place of resting. Twice Jesus would have fallen down if they hadn't supported Him.

Jesus left all but three of the disciples near the Garden entrance, asking them to pray. Then with Peter, James, and John, He walked on a little further. They had often prayed with Him in this garden. After a time of prayer, they would sleep until Jesus woke them in the morning. Now He wanted them to spend the night in prayer with Him.

Not wanting them to witness His great struggle, Jesus went to a

This chapter is based on Matt. 26:36-56; Mark 14:32-50; Luke 22:39-53; John 18:1-12.

hidden area, where He fell to the ground. He could feel that sin was separating Him from His Father. That separation seemed so wide and so deep, His heart shuddered to think of it. He couldn't use His divine power to escape it. As a human, Jesus had to suffer the results of human sin. As a human, He had to endure God's anger against sin.

THE TERRIBLE TEMPTATION

Taking the place of sinful humankind, Jesus was suffering divine justice. As He felt the bond with His Father breaking up, Jesus feared that in His human nature He would fail. Satan brought all of his power into the terrible struggle. If he failed here, his destruction was certain and the world would finally belong to Jesus. But if Jesus could be overwhelmed, earth and the human race would be Satan's forever.

Satan told Jesus that if He accepted the guilt of the sinful world, He would be seen as part of Satan's kingdom and never be with His Father again. "And for what?" Satan asked. "The people who claim to know God's plans best want to kill you. One of your own disciples will betray you. One of your most dedicated followers will deny that he knows you, and all of them will leave you."

The eternal fate of the world hung in the balance.

It hurt Jesus deeply that the ones He loved so much would be used as Satan's traps. The struggle in His heart was terrible. The sins of every human being weighed heavily on Jesus, and His sense of God's anger against sin was crushing out His life. In His agony, Jesus clutched at the cold ground as if that could keep Him from being pulled further from God. From His pale lips came the cry, " 'My Father, if it is possible, do not give me this cup of suffering. But do what you want, not what I want' " (Matthew 26:39).

JESUS NEEDED HUMAN ENCOURAGEMENT

Like all humans, Jesus longed for sympathy and encouragement in His time of suffering. He struggled back to the three disciples, hoping for some words of comfort. He wanted so much to know that they were praying for Him and for themselves. It was a terrible temptation to let the human race bear its own guilt, instead of Him. If only He could be sure that His disciples appreciated this, He would feel stronger.

But they were asleep. They hadn't heard His warning to "Watch and pray." The three had not intended to leave Jesus alone. They could have shaken off their daze if they had only kept praying. Now when Jesus needed them most, they slept.

The disciples woke up but Jesus' face was so changed by the suffering that they barely recognized Him. He said to Peter, " 'You men could not stay awake with me for one hour? Stay awake and pray for strength against temptation' " (Matthew 26:40, 41). Jesus was afraid that they would not endure when He was arrested and killed.

Then the Son of God was overwhelmed again with terrible agony. He staggered back to the spot where He had prayed. His suffering was so great that He began to sweat large drops of blood. The cypress and palm trees that silently witnessed His torture dropped heavy dew from their branches as if nature itself was weeping over its Creator.

A short time before, Jesus had stood like a mighty cedar tree against the storm of danger and criticism. Now He was like a bent and tattered reed. His voice was heard again in the evening air, full of human pain. " 'My Father, if it is not possible for this painful thing to be taken from me, and if I must do it, I pray that what you want will be done' " (Matthew 26:42).

Again Jesus turned to His disciples for encouragement. But their heavy eyes had overtaken them again and they were asleep. They awoke to see His face streaked with the bloody sweat of His pain. It frightened them, but they couldn't understand His mental suffering.

THE WORLD HUNG IN THE BALANCE

Jesus turned away and fell once more to the ground. The awful moment had come. The eternal fate of the world hung in the balance. Even then, Jesus could have refused to drink the cup that belonged to guilty humans. He could have wiped the bloody sweat from His face and left humans to die in their own sin. He might have said, "Let the lawbreakers pay the price for sin and I will go back to My Father." Instead He said for the third time, "My Father . . . I pray that what You want will be done."

Three times Jesus pulled back from making the final decision. But He could see that the human race if left to itself, was helpless, that sin was too powerful. He saw the misery of a doomed world and the fate its people would suffer. His decision was made. He would save humanity at any cost to Himself. He left heaven to save the one world that had fallen to sin and He would not turn away from His mission now.

With the decision made, Jesus collapsed, dying, to the ground. But God suffered with His Son. Heaven was silent as the angels watched the Father separate His beams of light, love, and glory from His beloved Son. Satan and his demons watched as well. What would be the answer to Jesus' prayer?

The answer came when the mightiest angel of heaven rushed to Jesus' side. The angel didn't come to take the cup of suffering away from Jesus, but to strengthen Him with the assurance of His Father's love. He assured Jesus that His death would destroy Satan's kingdom and give this world back to those who followed God. He told Jesus that He would see many of the human race saved eternally.

Jesus' pain did not go away, but the depression and discouragement did. His bloodstained face now reflected the peace of heaven. He had done what no human could ever do—He had tasted the sufferings of death for every person.

The sleeping disciples suddenly woke up. They saw the angel and heard the words of encouragement and hope he spoke to Jesus. Now they no longer worried for their Master—God was taking care of Him. But again the strange daze came over them, and when Jesus was strong enough to walk to where they were, He found them sleeping again.

Looking at them sadly, Jesus said, "Are you still sleeping? The time has come for the Son of man to be handed over to sinful people." Even as He spoke, He heard the footsteps of the mob that was searching for Him. He called out to the three disciples, " 'Get up, we must go. Look, here comes the man who has turned against me' " (Matthew 26:46).

With no sign of His recent struggle on His face, Jesus stepped out to the crowd and asked, "Who are you looking for?"

They answered, "Jesus of Nazareth."

"I am He," Jesus replied. As He spoke, the angel who had come to help Him stepped between Jesus and the mob. A divine light shone on Jesus' face. This flash of glory staggered the mob and they fell back.

The answer came when the mightiest angel of heaven rushed to Jesus' side.

Even Judas fell to the ground. Then the angel backed away and the light faded. Jesus could have escaped, but He stood still as the soldiers and priests lay helpless at His feet.

Their fear, however, didn't last long. Quickly they jumped up and surrounded Jesus, afraid that He would escape. In spite of further glorious evidence that Jesus was the Son of God, they would not believe. Jesus asked again, "Who are you looking for?"

They said again, "Jesus of Nazareth."

" 'I told you that I am he,' " Jesus said. " 'So if you are looking for me, let the others go' " (John 18:8). He was ready to sacrifice Himself to save His disciples.

Judas had arranged a signal with the priests to avoid any tricks—he would kiss the person they should arrest. So now he played his part. With the words, "Greetings, Teacher," he took Jesus by the hand like a friend, and kissed Him, pretending to weep as if he sympathized with Jesus' situation.

Jesus said, "Friend, do what you came to do." With sadness He asked, "Judas, are you betraying the Son of man with a kiss?" This should have touched Judas's conscience, but he had no honor or kindness left. Judas had surrendered his will to Satan and could no longer resist him.

Then the mob took hold of Jesus, tying those hands that had only done good things. The disciples, shocked to see their Master's hands bound like a criminal's, became indignant. In anger, Peter pulled out his sword and attacked, slicing off the right ear of a servant.

When Jesus saw this, He freed His hands and said, "Stop! No more of this." Then He touched the man's ear, and it was instantly healed. Jesus said to Peter, " 'Put your sword back in its place. All who use swords will be killed with swords. Surely you know I could ask my Father, and he would give me more than twelve legions of angels' " (Matthew 26:52, 53)—a legion* for each of the disciples.

The disciples thought, "Why doesn't He save Himself and us?" But Jesus answered the question they didn't ask aloud. "It must happen this way to bring about what the scriptures say. Shouldn't I drink the cup My Father gave Me?"

Turning to the priests and leaders who had joined the mob armed as if they were hunting wild animals, Jesus spoke words they would never forget. "You come after Me with swords and clubs as if I were a criminal. But every day I sat in the temple teaching and you did nothing. Your work is better done in darkness."

The disciples were terrified when they saw that Jesus was allowing Himself to be arrested. They were offended that He and they would be humiliated like that. They couldn't understand and they blamed Jesus for allowing it. In their shock and fear, Peter suggested that they save themselves. So they all left Jesus and ran.

---

*Legion—in Roman times, a military division varying from 3,000 to 6,000 foot soldiers.

CHAPTER 75

THE
ILLEGAL TRIAL

"If what I said is true, why do you hit me?"
(John 18:23).

he guards hurried Jesus through the quiet streets of the sleeping city. It was past midnight. With His hands still tied, the Savior moved painfully to the palace of Annas, a former high priest. Annas was the oldest member of the ruling family of Jewish priests. Because of his age, the people respected him as if he were still the high priest. To many, his advice was like the opinion of God.

The Jewish leaders made certain that Annas was in charge when the prisoner was questioned. They were afraid that the younger Caiaphas—the actual high priest—might not have the force of will and trickery to push Jesus' death sentence through.

Before Jesus was tried officially in front of the Jewish court—the Sanhedrin—Annas was going to question Him. Under Roman law, the Sanhedrin could make judgments about prisoners, but the Roman authorities had to approve them. So they had to press criminal charges against Jesus that both the Romans and the Jews would accept.

A number of the priests and leaders had been touched by Jesus' teachings. Since everyone knew they supported Jesus, Joseph of Arimathea and Nicodemus were not called to the meeting. But others

This chapter is based on Matt. 26:57-75; 27:1; Mark 14:53-72; 15:1; Luke 22:54-71; John 18:13-27.

might insist on a fair trial. The evidence had to convince the council that Jesus was guilty.

They needed to charge Jesus with two crimes. If they proved that He blasphemed against God (falsely claiming to be God or be as powerful as God), the Jews would condemn Him. If they proved that He was leading a rebellion, the Romans would condemn Him.

Annas tried to prove the second charge first. He questioned Jesus, hoping to trick Him into saying something that would prove He was trying to create a secret plan to set up a new kingdom.

Jesus knew what Annas was trying to do. " 'I have spoken openly to everyone,' " He said. " 'I have always taught in the synagogues and in the temple, where all the Jews come together. I never said anything in secret' " (John 18:20). It was obvious that Jesus was comparing His way of working to theirs. They had hunted Him down and brought Him to a secret trial, allowing Him to be abused along the way. They broke their own law that said a person was innocent until proved guilty.

Then Jesus turned the question on Annas. "Why are you questioning Me?" The priests' spies had listened to Him every day. "Ask the ones who heard Me teach. They know what I said."

Annas was too angry to speak. But one of his guards hit Jesus in the face. "Is that any way to answer the high priest?" he shouted.

The angels of heaven wanted so much to rescue Jesus.

Jesus answered calmly, " 'If I said something wrong, then show what it was. But if what I said is true, why do you hit me?' " (John 18:23) His answer came from a patient, sinless heart that would not be pushed to anger.

Jesus was shamed in every way by those for whom He was making the ultimate sacrifice. His holiness and hatred of sin made His suffering worse because being surrounded by people under Satan's control was revolting to Him. His trial was even harder to bear because He knew that with His divine power He could destroy His tormentors in a flash.

The Jews were expecting a Messiah who would change people's thoughts and force them to recognize him as their leader. Jesus was strongly tempted to do just that—to force these priests into admitting that He was their Messiah. It was difficult for Him to set aside His divine power and take their abuse as a human.

The angels of heaven wanted so much to rescue Jesus. As they witnessed the shameful actions of the priests, they were ready to sweep down and destroy them. But they were commanded not to. It was part of Jesus' mission to suffer as a human all the abuse that humans could throw at Him.

ON TO CAIAPHAS AND THE SANHEDRIN

Although Jesus stood with His hands tied, indicating that He had already been condemned, the Jewish leaders needed to make it look like a legal trial. But they had to do it quickly. They knew how much the people loved Jesus and were afraid that there might be an attempt to rescue Him. If they couldn't force the execution immediately, there would be a week's delay because of Passover. With that much time, thousands of people would come forward to testify about the mighty miracles Jesus had done. The Sanhedrin's actions would be thrown out and Jesus would be freed. Knowing all this, the Jewish leaders were determined to hand Jesus over to the Romans as a criminal who deserved to die, before anyone else learned of their plans.

But first, they had to find some crime to charge Jesus with. Annas ordered Jesus to be taken to Caiaphas. With torches and lanterns, the armed guards led their prisoner through the dark early morning hours to the high priest's palace. Although not as forceful as Annas, Caiaphas was just as cruel and deceitful. While the members of the Sanhedrin gathered, Annas and Caiaphas questioned Jesus again. But Jesus said nothing.

When they gathered in the judgment hall of the Sanhedrin, Caiaphas sat on a throne as the presiding officer. On either side of him were judges and leaders. Roman soldiers were stationed on the platform below the throne. At the foot of the throne stood Jesus. In the intense excitement, only Jesus was calm and quiet.

Caiaphas had seen Jesus as his rival, his chief competitor for the attention and respect of the people. He was bitterly jealous of their eagerness to see and hear Jesus. But now as he looked at the prisoner, Caiaphas admired the noble, dignified way Jesus stood. It struck him that this man was somehow like God. But in the next instant, he banished that thought and demanded that Jesus work one of His mighty miracles. Jesus showed no sign of even hearing his words.

The Jewish leaders were stuck, not sure how to get Jesus condemned. There were plenty of witnesses to prove that Jesus had called the priests hypocrites and murderers, but they didn't want to bring that out. The Romans wouldn't be interested. There was much evidence that Jesus spoke irreverently about the Jewish ceremonies. But the Romans would see no crime in that either. They didn't dare accuse Jesus of breaking the Sabbath, or the stories of His healing miracles would come out.

They called the false witnesses who had been bribed to accuse Jesus of trying to start a rebellion against Rome. But their testimony was weak and with only a few questions they contradicted themselves.

Early in His ministry, Jesus had said, "Destroy this temple and I will build it again in three days." He was talking about His death and resurrection. But of all the things Jesus had said, these were the only words they could find to use against Him. The Romans had rebuilt the temple and took great pride in it. They would not like to hear someone talking about destroying it. On this, the Jews and Romans agreed.

One bribed witness declared, "I heard this man say 'I can destroy God's temple and rebuild it in three days.'" If Jesus' words had been reported exactly as He said them, the Sanhedrin wouldn't have found them strong enough to convict Him. But even as much as the witness had twisted them, Jesus' words weren't a crime worthy of death in the Romans' eyes.

By now, Jesus' accusers were confused, enraged, and desperate. Their last chance was that Jesus would somehow condemn Himself. Caiaphas leaned down from the judgment throne and demanded, "Aren't you going to answer any of these charges against you?" But Jesus said nothing.

Finally Caiaphas asked in a solemn oath, "I command you by the power of the living God: Tell us if you are the Messiah, the Son of God."

Jesus knew that to answer this question would be His death sentence. But this was asked in the name of God by the highest authority in the nation. He had taught His disciples to stand up and tell others who He was. Now He repeated the lesson by His example.

Every eye was locked on Jesus' face as He answered. "Those are your words," Jesus said. A heavenly light seemed to illuminate His pale face as He went on. " 'But I tell you, in the future you will see the Son of Man sitting at the right hand of God, the Powerful One, and coming on clouds in the sky' " (Matthew 26:64).

> *Jesus knew that to answer this question would be His death sentence.*

CAIAPHAS IS ALMOST CONVINCED

For a frozen moment in time, Caiaphas trembled before the penetrating eyes of the Savior. For the rest of his life, he never forgot that look from the Son of God.

The thought that everyone would stand before God and be rewarded for their deeds terrified Caiaphas. In his mind, he saw the final Judgment Day with the dead rising to share secrets he hoped were hidden forever. He felt as if the Eternal Judge was reading his soul and the secrets there.

But in an instant, Caiaphas snapped back. He didn't believe in the resurrection or a judgment day anyway. Now, with satanic fury, he ripped his robe and demanded that the prisoner be condemned for blasphemy. "This man has said things that are against God! We don't need any more witnesses. How shall we judge him?"

His fellow priests and leaders agreed. "He must die!" they shouted.

Caiaphas was furious with himself for momentarily believing Jesus. Instead of opening his heart and confessing that Jesus was the Messiah, he ripped open his priestly robes. By trying to cover his horror at

Jesus' words, Caiaphas had condemned himself and shown that he was not qualified to be a priest.

According to the laws given through Moses, a high priest must never tear his robe. Their service in the sanctuary demanded that their robes be in perfect condition. Later rabbis had created a law that allowed the high priest to rip his robe in horror at sin, but this was never God's law. When Caiaphas ripped his robe, his act symbolized the Jewish nation's rejection of the Messiah. Now Israel was divorced from God.

> *No criminal was ever treated as badly as was the Son of God.*

THE ILLEGAL TRIAL

The Sanhedrin condemned Jesus to die even though it was against Jewish law to try a prisoner at night. Legally, nothing could be done except during daylight in front of a full meeting of the council. In spite of this, the Savior was now treated as a condemned criminal.

As Jesus was taken to a guardroom, every person along the way mocked Him and His claim to be the Son of God. His own words— "coming on clouds in the sky"—were repeated as a joke to make fun of Him. While He waited there for His legal trial, Jesus was not protected as even a normal criminal might be. The ignorant mob, made up of some of the cruelest, most degraded people in the city, was allowed to abuse Him verbally and physically. They were controlled by demons, and Jesus' calm, godlike attitude drove them mad. No criminal was ever treated as badly as was the Son of God.

But the deepest pain Jesus felt didn't come from an enemy's hand. While He was being tried before Caiaphas, one of His own disciples had denied knowing Him.

BEFORE THE ROOSTER CROWS TWICE

Peter and John had followed at a distance the mob that arrested Jesus. When they came to the Sanhedrin hall of judgment, the priests recognized John and let him inside. They hoped that when John witnessed what happened to Jesus, he would stop believing that this could be the Son of God. John asked them to allow Peter in as well, and they did.

A fire was burning in the courtyard outside the hall, and Peter joined the people huddled around it trying to keep warm. By mingling with them, Peter hoped to be mistaken for one of the crowd who had arrested Jesus.

But the woman who watched the door saw the sadness in Peter's face and asked, "Aren't you one of his disciples?" Peter was startled and confused. He pretended not to understand her. But she kept asking.

Finally, Peter had to answer. "I don't know him," he said. At that moment, a rooster crowed. A short time later, someone else accused him of being a follower of Jesus. This time Peter swore, "I do not know the man!"

An hour later, a relative of the man whose ear Peter had cut off confronted him. "Didn't I see you in the Garden with him? You must be one of them—you're obviously from Galilee."

Trying to deceive them, Peter acted angry, cursing and swearing that he didn't know Jesus at all. As the words left his mouth, the rooster crowed again. Suddenly, Peter remembered Jesus' words: "Before the rooster crows twice, you will say three times that you don't know Me."

With the curses still on his lips and the sound of the rooster still in his ears, Peter's eyes were drawn to where Jesus stood in the hall. At that moment, Jesus turned and looked at Peter—not with anger, but with pity and deep sadness.

The sadness on Jesus' face pierced Peter's heart like an arrow. He remembered his promise given only a few hours before. Now he realized how well Jesus had read his heart and seen the weakness there. A tide of memories washed over him—memories of Jesus' love and patience and his own lies and pride. As he stared, another evil hand rose up and struck his Master in the face again. Heartbroken, unable to watch for even another second, Peter rushed out of the courtyard into the darkness.

Peter ran without thinking or caring where he was going until he found himself back in Gethsemane. He replayed his bitter memories of Jesus suffering alone, of not being able to stay awake and pray, of ignoring Jesus' appeal that he pray to avoid falling into sin. It tortured him to know that he had given Jesus the most pain that night by denying Him. Peter fell to the ground and wished that he could die.

If those hours in the Garden had been spent in prayer, Peter wouldn't have been left to depend on his own strength—and he wouldn't have denied knowing Jesus. If the disciples had witnessed Jesus' agony in the Garden, they would have been prepared for His suffering on the cross. They would have had hope in the dark hours ahead.

CONDEMNING JESUS ONE MORE TIME

As soon as it was daylight, the Sanhedrin met again and Jesus was brought back before them. They couldn't condemn Him immediately, because many of those now present had not heard His words at the night meeting. And they knew the Roman authorities would not consider Jesus' words serious enough for a death sentence. But if they could get Jesus to claim to be the Messiah, they might be able to twist His words to sound like a plan to lead a rebellion.

"If you are the Messiah, tell us," they demanded. But Jesus said nothing. They kept badgering Him until He finally said, "If I tell you, you will not believe Me. And if I ask you, you will not answer." Then He added a solemn warning. " 'But from now on, the Son of Man will sit at the right hand of the powerful God' " (Luke 22:69).

This was the opening they had hoped for. "Then are you the Son of God?" they asked.

Jesus answered, "You say that I am."

This was all they needed. They cried out, "Why do we need any other witnesses? We heard him say it himself." So once again, Jesus was condemned to die. All they needed now was for the Roman authorities to agree.

Once again, this time in the presence of the Jewish priests and leaders, Jesus was beaten and abused. When the judges announced the death sentence, a satanic fury took possession of the people watching, and they rushed toward Jesus. If armed Roman soldiers hadn't stepped in, Jesus would not have lived to be nailed to the cross—He would have been torn to pieces.

These Roman officers—even though they knew nothing about God—were angry at the brutal treatment of someone who had not been proved guilty of anything. They pointed out that it was against Jewish law to condemn a man to death based on his own testimony. But the Jewish leaders had no shame or pity.

Priests and leaders forgot the dignity of their offices as they shouted curses at the Son of God. They said that claiming to be the Messiah meant that He should die in the most horrible way. An old coat was thrown over His head and people struck Him in the face, shouting, "Prove that you are a prophet, you Messiah. Tell us who hit you!"

> *If armed Roman soldiers hadn't stepped in, Jesus would not have lived to be nailed to the cross.*

Angels recorded every blow, every word, every look of these evil men against their beloved Commander. One day the same men who shouted and spit at the face of Jesus will see it shining with glory brighter than the sun.

CHAPTER 76

JUDAS

"I sinned; I handed over to you an innocent man"
(Matthew 27:4).

udas's story is the sad ending of a life that could have been honored by God. If Judas had died before his last journey to Jerusalem, he would have been remembered as a good member of the Twelve, one who would be greatly missed. The loathing that followed him through the centuries would never have existed. As it happened, his true character was put on display as a warning to anyone who would betray a sacred trust.

Since the night of the dinner at Simon's, Judas had had time to think about what he had agreed to do. But he hadn't changed his mind. For the price of a slave, he sold the Lord of the universe.

Judas had always had a strong love for money, but he had not always been dishonest enough to do a thing like this. He had fed his greedy spirit until it outweighed his love for Jesus. Through this one weakness, he ended up being controlled by Satan.

Judas had joined the disciples when crowds were already following Jesus. He saw the Savior's mighty miracles—healing the sick, throwing out demons, and raising the dead. Jesus' teaching was better than any other he had ever heard. He wanted to become a better person and he hoped this would happen when he joined Jesus.

Jesus didn't push Judas away. He gave him a place among His twelve closest disciples, and along with them gave him the power to heal the sick and throw out demons. But Judas didn't surrender his life to Jesus. He didn't give up his love of power or money. Instead of becoming more like Jesus, he became more critical of others.

> *For the price of a slave, Judas sold the Lord of the universe.*

Judas had a strong influence on the other disciples. He had a high opinion of himself and thought the others were inferior to him. Judas flattered himself that the new church would often be embarrassed if it weren't for his skill as a money manager. In his thinking, the group was lucky to have him.

Jesus gave Judas the opportunity to see and correct his weakness of greed, but he didn't. He was constantly tempted by the small amounts of money that came to him for the group. Whenever he did something for Jesus, he paid himself. In his own eyes, this served as an excuse to take money. In God's eyes, Judas was a thief.

In his mind, Judas had a plan for Jesus to follow. He planned for John the Baptist to be rescued from prison, but John was killed. Instead of taking revenge, Jesus retreated into the countryside. Judas was sure that their work could have been more successful if Jesus hadn't stopped the disciples from carrying out their own schemes. When the Jewish leaders demanded a sign from heaven, Judas saw it as a challenge that should be answered. But Jesus did not. Judas began to doubt. Why did Jesus keep predicting trials and persecution for Himself and His disciples? Was he ever going to get that powerful position in the new kingdom?

WORKING AGAINST JESUS

Judas was always pushing the idea that Jesus would rule as king in Jerusalem. At the miracle of the loaves and fishes, Judas was the one behind the plan to take Jesus by force and make Him king. His hopes were high and he was bitterly disappointed when Jesus refused.

Jesus' teaching about the bread of life was the turning point for Judas. He finally saw that Jesus was offering spiritual, not earthly, riches. He began to see that Jesus wasn't looking for fame or power and that His followers wouldn't be given those things either. He decided not to work so closely with Jesus that he couldn't pull away. And then he would watch and see how things worked out.

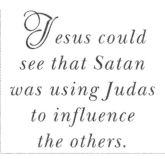

Jesus could see that Satan was using Judas to influence the others.

From that time, Judas shared doubts that confused the other disciples. He brought up texts of Scripture that had nothing to do with the truths Jesus was teaching. In a very religious and seemingly wise way, Judas was giving Jesus' words meanings that Jesus hadn't intended. He usually started the ongoing argument about which disciple would be the greatest.

When Jesus' response turned away the wealthy young leader, Judas thought it was a mistake. Jesus' cause needed men like that one. Judas had many ideas he thought would improve their mission. In things like this, he thought he was wiser than Jesus.

JUDAS'S LAST CHANCE

Judas began to find something to disagree with in everything Jesus taught His disciples. He was influencing the others to be unhappy with their situation. Jesus could see that Satan was using Judas to influence the others. But Judas said nothing publicly until the dinner in Simon's house. When Mary bathed Jesus' feet with the expensive oils, Judas showed his greed. After Jesus quietly corrected him, Judas's wounded pride and desire for revenge broke down his last resistance to betraying Jesus.

Still, Judas's heart was not completely hardened. Even after he had contracted twice to sell Jesus out, he could still have repented.

At the Passover supper, Jesus tenderly washed Judas's feet along with the others. But Judas turned away from the last appeal of love.

Judas had it all figured out. If Jesus was destined to be killed, it would happen no matter what—his betrayal wouldn't change that. If Jesus was not destined to die, then this would force Him to save Himself. Judas was sure that he had been very clever.

However he didn't think that Jesus would allow Himself to be arrested. Judas wanted to teach Jesus a lesson. He wanted Jesus to treat him with more respect. After all, the Pharisees and priests had tried to stone Jesus several times and He had escaped. Certainly, He wouldn't allow Himself to be arrested now.

So Judas decided to push Jesus. If He was really the Messiah, the people would make Him king. And Judas would be the one who forced Him onto the throne. This would give Judas the highest office next to Jesus in the new kingdom.

In the Garden, Judas had told the leaders of the mob to arrest Jesus and hold Him firmly. He fully believed that Jesus would escape. Then if the leaders blamed him, he could say, "Didn't I tell you to hold Him firmly?"

Judas was astounded to see Jesus allow Himself to be arrested, tied, and led away. He kept watching, certain that at any moment Jesus would surprise them and show Himself with power as the Son of God. But as the hours passed, Judas began to fear that he had sold his Master to die.

As Jesus' trial was ending, Judas could no longer take his guilty conscience. His harsh voice rang out in the judgment hall: "Caiaphas, release Him. He is innocent!" Judas pushed his way through the crowd; sweat standing out on his pale face. He rushed to the throne of judgment and threw the silver coins down in front of the high priest. Grabbing Caiaphas's robe, he cried, "I sinned and handed an innocent man over to you."

Caiaphas shook him off, but didn't know what to say. It was clear that the priests had bribed the disciple to betray Jesus. Finally he answered, "That's your problem, not ours." The priests were willing to use Judas, but they despised his greediness.

JUDAS'S SAD END

Judas then threw himself at Jesus' feet, admitting to all that He was the Son of God and begging Him to save Himself.

The Savior knew that Judas didn't feel any deep, heartbreaking sorrow because he had betrayed the Son of God. But He didn't condemn Judas. He looked at him with pity and said, "This is why I came to this world."

The watching crowd was amazed at how Jesus treated this traitor. They were sure that He must be more than human! But why didn't He free Himself and punish the ones who arrested Him?

When Jesus wouldn't listen, Judas ran from the hall shouting, "It's too late! Too late!" He just couldn't bear to see Jesus crucified. In his hopeless misery, Judas went out and hanged himself.

Later that day, the crowd that led Jesus to the place of crucifixion saw Judas's body under a dead tree. His weight had broken the rope around his neck. Dogs were now feeding on his mangled body. Justice was already coming to those who were guilty of shedding Jesus' blood.

CHAPTER 77

THE
ROMAN TRIAL

" 'This is why I was born and came into the world: to tell people the truth' " (John 18:37).

*J*esus stood—tied like a prisoner, surrounded by guards—in the judgment hall of Pilate, the Roman governor. The hall was filling with spectators. Just outside were the priests, others of the Sanhedrin, and the mob.

After condemning Jesus, the Sanhedrin came to Pilate to have the death sentence confirmed and carried out. But these Jewish leaders would not enter the hall. According to their ceremonial laws, entering would have made them unclean and forced them to miss Passover. They couldn't see that their hate had already made them unclean or that since they had rejected the true Passover Lamb, the festival no longer had any purpose.

Pilate was not feeling friendly. He had been called from his bed and was determined to get his work done quickly and return to it. Putting on his most stern expression, he turned to see what kind of man he was to question.

Pilate had dealt with many criminals, but never had someone who seemed so noble and good been brought to him. He saw no sign of guilt or fear or angry defiance on Jesus' face. He saw a man whose face

This chapter is based on Matt. 27:2, 11-31; Mark 15:1-20; Luke 23:1-25; John 18:28-40; 19:1-16.

showed the mark of heaven. Pilate's wife had told him about the prophet from Galilee who could heal the sick and raise the dead. Remembering rumors he had heard from other sources, Pilate turned to the Jews and asked, "Who is this man and why have you brought him here?"

"He is a liar called Jesus of Nazareth," they answered.

So Pilate asked again, "What charges do you have against this man?"

The priests were offended that he would question their decision. They said, " 'If he were not a criminal, we wouldn't have brought him to you' "(John 18:30). They hoped that Pilate would give them what they wanted without any delay.

Pilate had quickly condemned innocent men before. In his mind, a prisoner's guilt or innocence was not really important—he did whatever was politically helpful. The priests hoped that Pilate would pass the death sentence on Jesus without even a hearing.

> *Something about Jesus held Pilate back.*

But something about Jesus held Pilate back. He remembered that Jesus had raised Lazarus from the grave after four days. He wanted to know what crimes Jesus was charged with before he would agree to have Him killed. "If your decision is all that is needed, why bring him to me? Judge him by your own laws," Pilate told them.

They explained that they had judged Him and sentenced Him to death. But they needed Pilate to enforce the sentence. As morally weak as he was, this time Pilate refused to condemn Jesus until he heard some criminal charge against Him.

The priests were trapped. They couldn't allow it to seem that Jesus had been arrested on religious charges, because Pilate wouldn't care about that. What really worried the Romans were signs of a rebellion against them. So they called false witnesses to say, "We caught this man misleading the people, telling them not to pay taxes to Rome, and calling himself the Messiah, a king." They had no evidence for any of these charges, but the priests were willing to lie to get what they wanted.

PILATE RECOGNIZES A PLOT

Pilate didn't believe that this prisoner schemed against the Roman government. He knew a plot to destroy an innocent man when he heard one. Turning to Jesus, he asked, "Are you the King of the Jews?"

Jesus answered, "Those are your words." As He spoke, His face lighted up as if touched by a beam of sunlight.

Hearing Jesus' words, Caiaphas insisted that Pilate himself had heard Jesus admit to the crimes. Pilate turned to Jesus. "Don't you hear them accusing you of these things? What do you say?" But Jesus said nothing. He stood untouched by the waves of anger and abuse that broke around Him.

Pilate was astonished. "Doesn't this man want to save his own life?" he wondered. He couldn't believe that Jesus was as evil as the shouting priests. To escape the roar of the angry crowd, he pulled Jesus off to one side and asked again, "Are you the King of the Jews?"

Jesus could see that the Holy Spirit was working on Pilate's heart and gave him a chance to respond. "Is that your own question, or did others tell you about Me?"

Pilate understood what Jesus was asking, but he wouldn't admit to a personal interest in the Savior. "I am not Jewish," he answered. "Your own people and your leaders and priests handed you over to me. What have you done wrong?"

Jesus still tried to teach Pilate. He said, "My kingdom does not belong to this world. If it did, My servants would fight to free Me from the Jews. But My kingdom is from another place."

Pilate nodded. "So you are a king!"

Jesus answered, " 'You are the one saying I am a king. This is why I was born and came into the world: to tell people the truth. And everyone who belongs to the truth listens to me' " (John 18:37). Jesus wanted Pilate to know that only by accepting truth could his twisted character be repaired.

Pilate was confused. In his heart, he longed to know what this truth really was and how he could find it. "What is truth?" he asked. But he didn't wait for an answer. He went back out to where the screaming priests wanted some immediate action and declared, "I find no guilt in this man at all."

When the priests heard this, they nearly went mad with disappointment and rage. Rather than see Jesus released, they seemed ready to tear Him to pieces with their own hands. They shouted criticisms of Pilate, threatening to report him to Rome since he refused to condemn a man who claimed to be king instead of Caesar. Angry voices declared, "He stirs up people to rebel across the land, from Galilee to here."

At this point, Pilate didn't even consider condemning Jesus. He knew that the Jews accused Jesus because of their hate and jealousy. The right thing to do would be to release Jesus. But Pilate knew that if he did, the Jews would create problems for him. When he heard that Jesus was from Galilee, he decided to send Him to Herod, who was king of that province. This would put the responsibility for what happened on Herod and maybe end an old quarrel between himself and Herod.

TRIAL AT HEROD'S PALACE

Followed by the jeering mob, Jesus was rushed through the streets of Jerusalem to the palace where Herod was staying. Herod, the same king who had put John the Baptist to death, was delighted to see Jesus. He had heard much about Him and wanted to see one of His miracles. When Herod first heard about Jesus, he had been afraid that it was John the Baptist come back to life. But now he had the chance to save the life of a prophet and silence the memory of John's death. Herod was sure that Jesus would do whatever he asked in order to be released.

When the Savior was brought in, the priests quickly began explaining their charges against Him. But Herod commanded them to be silent. He ordered Jesus to be untied and accused the Jews of mistreating the prisoner. He was as quickly convinced as Pilate that Jesus was being falsely accused. Herod began to ask Jesus questions, but Jesus kept silent. At the king's command, sick and lame people were brought in and Jesus was commanded to prove who He was by healing them.

Jesus did not respond. Herod kept urging, "Show us that you have the power we've heard about."

But the Son of God had taken human nature, and He would do only what any human could have done under those circumstances. He would not perform a miracle to save Himself from pain and humiliation.

Herod promised that if Jesus would perform a miracle, He would be released. The Jewish leaders were terrified that Jesus would do it—certainly they knew that He could. If He did, their plans would be ruined and likely they themselves would be killed. They began to shout, "He is a traitor and a blasphemer! He works his miracles by the power of the devil!"

Herod's conscience had been dulled since the days when he trembled at Herodias's request for John the Baptist's head. His loose lifestyle had degraded his morals so badly that he even boasted about killing John. Now he threatened to have Jesus killed if He didn't respond. But Jesus gave no indication that He even heard the words.

Jesus' silence irritated Herod. He seemed to have no respect for Herod's authority. Once again, Herod threatened Jesus with death, but again Jesus was silent.

> *Herod promised that if Jesus would perform a miracle, He would be released.*

Jesus' mission did not include amusing the curious. If His words would have healed souls sick from sin, He would have spoken. But He had no words for someone who trampled truth as Herod had done with John the Baptist. Herod had rejected John's words and he would be given no more messages. Jesus had no words for this arrogant king who felt no need of a Savior.

So angry that his face was red, Herod declared that Jesus was an impostor. "If you won't prove who you claim to be, I will hand you over to the soldiers and the mob. If you are an impostor, you deserve to die. If you are the Son of God, save yourself by working a miracle."

At that instant, the crowd leaped at Jesus like wild animals attacking their prey. Jesus was dragged back and forth as Herod joined in trying to humiliate the Son of God. Once again, if the Roman soldiers hadn't stepped in, Jesus would have been torn to pieces. Then Herod had his soldiers wrap a kingly robe around Jesus' shoulders and they joined the Jewish leaders in the worst abuse they could manage. But Jesus still said nothing.

A few people who came up to mock Jesus turned back, silent and afraid. Even Herod had to step back, suddenly concerned. The last rays of mercy were shining into his sin-hardened heart. Divinity flashed through the human form of Jesus and Herod felt like he was seeing God on His throne. As calloused as he was, he suddenly didn't dare send Jesus to His death. Instead Herod sent Him back to the Roman judgment hall.

THE LAST TRIAL BEFORE PILATE

Pilate was disappointed to find the Jews bringing Jesus back. He reminded them that he had already found Jesus innocent. And Herod, a king of their own country, had not agreed to sentence Him. "I will punish him and let him go free," he announced.

But this showed Pilate's weakness. Jesus was innocent, but he was willing to have Him whipped to try to please the Jewish leaders. If Pilate had stood firm, refusing to condemn a man who was innocent, he would have escaped the chains of regret that haunted him the rest of his life. Jesus would have been killed anyway, but the guilt would not have rested on Pilate. But Pilate, having ignored his conscience so many times before, was almost helpless in the face of the pressure from the priests and leaders.

Pilate was still given help from heaven. An angel had given his wife a dream in which she spoke with Jesus. Pilate's wife was not a Jew, but seeing Jesus in her dream, she knew He was the Son of God. She saw Pilate have Jesus whipped, then declare, "I find Him innocent." She saw him give Jesus to His murderers. She saw the cross, the strange darkness, and heard the mysterious cry, "It is finished." Then she saw Jesus seated on a white cloud and His murderers trying to escape His glory. With a cry of horror, she woke up and immediately wrote a message to Pilate.

The note rushed to him by messenger said, "Don't do anything to that innocent Man. Today I had a very troubling dream about Him."

Pilate's face paled. He was confused by his own conflicting emotions. And while he delayed, the priests were stirring up the anger of the crowd. Then he remembered a custom the Jews cherished that he might use to free Jesus. At Passover time, the Jewish people were often allowed to choose one prisoner to be released from jail. The Romans were holding a prisoner named Barabbas who was already sentenced to die. Barabbas pretended to be a religious revolutionary who was trying to overthrow the Romans. But in reality, he was just a common criminal trying to get rich by robbing others.

> *The answer was like the bellow of wild beasts: "Give us Barabbas!"*

By giving the people a choice between this thief and the clearly innocent Jesus, Pilate was appealing to their sense of justice. He shouted out his question. "Who do you want me to set free? Barabbas or Jesus, who is called the Messiah?"

The answer was like the bellow of wild beasts: "Give us Barabbas!"

Thinking that they couldn't have understood his question, Pilate asked again, "Do you want me to free the King of the Jews?"

The crowd roared even louder. "Take this man away and set Barabbas free!"

Pilate cried out, "Then what should I do with Jesus the Messiah?"

Demons in human form stood in the crowd and led out in the answering shout: "Crucify him!"

Pilate never thought it would come to that. He cringed at the thought of sending an innocent man to that most cruel death. "Why? What has he done wrong?" he asked. But it was too late for a logical argument. Pilate tried once more to save Jesus. He asked again, "What has he done wrong?"

But this only stirred the mob up more. They cried out louder and louder. "Crucify him! Crucify him!"

Pilate finally commanded that Jesus be beaten with whips. Already weak and covered with cuts and bruises, Jesus was whipped and led into a room where the soldiers gathered. They shaped a crown out of thorny branches and put it on Jesus' head. Then they wrapped a purple robe around Him and mocked Him. "Hail the King of the Jews!" they called out as they struck Him in the face and spit on Him. Every now and then someone struck the crown, forcing the thorns into His scalp and sending blood trickling down His face.

An enraged mob surrounded the Savior of the world. Mocking and jeering laughs were mixed with cursing and blasphemy. Satan himself led this mob. His plan was to provoke Jesus into striking back or performing a miracle to save Himself. Just one sin, one failure to stand the

Satan himself led this mob.

test, and the plan to save humans would have failed. But Jesus endured it all, peacefully and calmly.

Jesus' enemies had demanded a miracle to prove His divinity. Before them was the greatest evidence they could have asked for. His patience and humility in these circumstances proved His relationship with God. Satan was greatly enraged when he saw that Jesus remained faithful to His Father's will.

When Pilate sent Jesus to be beaten, he hoped that this punishment would satisfy the crowd. But the Jews saw the weakness of claiming that He was innocent and then punishing Him anyway. They pressed even harder, determined to see Jesus die.

Pilate had Barabbas brought to the court to stand side-by-side with Jesus. Pointing to the Savior, he said, "Look at this man!" There stood the Son of God, stripped to the waist, blood flowing freely from the long gashes in His back. His face was strained and bruised, but never more beautiful. Every feature on His face communicated tender pity for His enemies. He showed strength and dignity in spite of His pain.

The prisoner beside Him seemed the very opposite. Every line on Barabbas's face said that he was a tough thug. The difference between them was clear to everyone. Some in the crowd wept with sympathy as they looked at Jesus. Even the priests and leaders were persuaded that Jesus was all He claimed to be.

The Roman soldiers who surrounded Jesus were not all hardhearted. As they watched Jesus with pity, His silent surrender was stamped in their hearts. This scene never faded from their minds until they decided to follow this Savior or reject Him forever.

Pilate was sure that the sight of Jesus next to Barabbas would find sympathy with the Jews. But he didn't understand the fanatical hate of the priests. Once again, the priests and leaders led the crowd in that awful chant: "Crucify him! Crucify him!"

Finally, Pilate lost his patience with their unreasonable cruelty and cried out sadly, "Take him then, and crucify him. I find nothing against him."

The priests answered, "We have a law that says he should die, because he claimed to be the Son of God."

This startled Pilate. He began to wonder whether this might be a divine being standing before him. He turned back to Jesus and asked, "Where are you from?" But Jesus didn't answer. He had spoken to Pilate before and explained His mission. Pilate had ignored the truth. He had abused the power of his office by caving in to the demands of the mob. Jesus had nothing else to say.

Annoyed at Jesus' silence, Pilate spoke arrogantly. "You refuse to speak to me? Don't you know I have the power to set you free or to have you crucified?"

This Jesus answered. " 'The only power you have over me is the power given to you by God. The man who turned me in to you is guilty of a greater sin' " (John 19:11). Jesus was talking about Caiaphas who represented the Jewish nation. They had the prophecies of the Messiah and the unmistakable evidence of Jesus' divinity. The leaders had the greatest responsibility for what the Jews did to Jesus. Pilate, Herod, and the Roman soldiers were mostly ignorant about Jesus. If they had had the light the Jews had, the soldiers would not have treated Jesus as they did.

Once again, Pilate suggested letting Jesus go free. But the Jews cried out, "If you let this man go, you are no friend of Caesar's." No country hated the domination of the Roman power more than the Jews. But to get rid of Jesus, the Jewish leaders would swear loyalty to the foreign power they hated. "Anyone who makes himself a king is against Caesar," they added.

Pilate was already under suspicion from Rome. A report that he was allowing people to call themselves king would ruin him. And he knew the Jews would stop at nothing for revenge if he stopped their plans. But Pilate presented Jesus to the crowd one more time, saying, "Here is your king!"

And again the mad cry rang out: "Take him away! Crucify him!"

In a voice that rang through the courtyard, Pilate asked, "Do you want me to crucify your king?"

From the unholy lips of the crowd came the answer: "The only king we have is Caesar!" By choosing a heathen king, the Jews rejected God as their King. From then on, Caesar was their king. The priests and rabbis had led the people to this, and they were responsible for the terrible things that would soon follow.

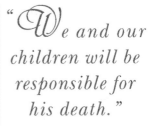

"*We and our children will be responsible for his death.*"

When Pilate saw that he could do nothing and that a riot was starting, he called for a basin of water and washed his hands in front of them all. Then he said, "I am not guilty of this man's death. You are responsible for it."

Pilate looked at Jesus, sure in his heart that He was a God. Turning again to the crowd, he said, "I am innocent of His blood. Crucify Him if you must, but I declare that He is innocent. May the One He claims is His Father judge you and not me for this." Then he said to Jesus, "Forgive me for this. I cannot save You." Then he had Jesus beaten with whips once more and sent Him to be crucified.

Pilate wanted to save Jesus, but he couldn't do it and save his own position. He chose to sacrifice an innocent Person rather than lose his power. Many today sacrifice their principles for the same reasons. Our conscience and duty point one way while our looking out for ourselves point in another.

In spite of his efforts, the very thing Pilate feared happened. He was soon thrown out of office. Hurt by regrets and wounded pride, not long after the Crucifixion, Pilate ended his own life.

When Pilate declared that he was innocent of Jesus' blood, Caiaphas answered defiantly, "We and our children will be responsible for his death." Those awful words were echoed by the people. The whole crowd roared, "We and our children will be responsible for his death."

The people of Israel chose Barabbas, the murderer and thief, and rejected their Messiah. In making this choice, they accepted Satan as their leader. Now they would live under his rules. When they cried, "We and our children will be responsible for his death," their prayer was heard. They were responsible for the destruction of Jerusalem in a few short years and for the fate of the Jewish nation for the next two thousand years.

And that prayer will be answered again on the great Judgment Day. Jesus will return in glory with thousands of angels as an escort. In the place of thorns, He will wear a crown of glory. On His robe will be the words, "King of kings and Lord of lords."

The same priests and leaders will see again the scenes in those judgment halls. Every thing that happened will be written out in letters of fire. Then those who prayed, "We and our children will be responsible for his death" will see what they asked for. In their shame and horror, they will beg the rocks and mountains to fall on them.

CHAPTER 78

JESUS DIES ON THE CROSS

"Jesus cried out, 'Father, I give you my life' "
(Luke 23:46).

The news that Jesus had been condemned to die spread quickly, and people of all types flocked toward the place of crucifixion. The priests had agreed not to harass Jesus' disciples when Judas agreed to betray Him, so many disciples and followers of Jesus joined the crowds.

Three crosses had been prepared for Barabbas and two of his thieves who were scheduled to die that day. The cross that had been ready for Barabbas was placed on Jesus' bleeding shoulders. Since the Passover supper, Jesus had had nothing to eat or drink. He had suffered the pain of being betrayed and abandoned. He had been rushed from Annas to Caiaphas to Pilate to Herod and back to Pilate. The night had been filled with events that would test the heart of any human. Jesus hadn't failed. He had taken it all with dignity. But after the second beating with the whip, when the cross was laid on His shoulders, His human body could take no more. Jesus collapsed.

The crowd showed no mercy, taunting Jesus because He couldn't carry the cross. The soldiers lifted the cross up and placed it on Him again. Again Jesus fell to the ground. When it was clear that Jesus could not carry the cross, they began to search for someone who could. No

This chapter is based on Matt. 27:31-53; Mark 15:20-38; Luke 23:26-46; John 19:16-30.

Jew would carry it because this would make them unclean for Passover.

Then Simon, a stranger from Cyrene, met the crowd as he came into the city. Simon, astonished at what he saw, expressed pity for the poor Man. So the soldiers seized him and forced him to carry the cross for Jesus. Simon's sons were followers of Jesus, but Simon was not. Carrying the cross to Calvary turned out to be a real blessing for Simon, because he became a believer in the Messiah that day.

The cross that had been ready for Barabbas was placed on Jesus' bleeding shoulders.

Many women were in the crowd that followed the Savior. Some had brought their sick loved ones to Him to be healed—others had been healed themselves. They were shocked at how the crowd hated Jesus. When Jesus fell under the cross, these women ignored the angry priests and began wailing with sorrow.

Even in His pain and exhaustion, Jesus noticed. He knew that they didn't understand who He was or His sacrifice for them, but He appreciated their sympathy. He said, " 'Women of Jerusalem, don't cry for me. Cry for yourselves and for your children' " (Luke 23:28). He looked ahead to the time when Jerusalem would be destroyed and some of these same women would die along with their children.

In the destruction of Jerusalem Jesus saw a symbol of the end of the world. He said, " 'Then people will say to the mountains, "Fall on us!" And they will say to the hills, "Cover us!" If they act like this now when life is good, what will happen when bad times come?' " (Luke 23:30, 31). God's anger against sin was now focused on His Son. What would the suffering be like at the end for someone who refused to give up sin?

In the crowd that followed Jesus to Calvary were many who had shouted the hosannas and waved palm branches when He rode into Jerusalem. More than a few who had shouted praises that day with everyone else now joined in screaming, "Crucify him!" When Jesus rode into Jerusalem, His disciples pressed close around Him and felt the honor. Now they followed Him at a distance to escape the humiliation.

JESUS' MOTHER

When they reached the place of execution, the two thieves fought those who forced them onto their crosses. Jesus did not resist. Mary, His mother, supported by John, had followed her Son's steps to Calvary. She wanted so much to put her hand under His head and comfort Him but this was not permitted. She still held on to the hope that Jesus would save Himself. But in her heart she remembered that He had predicted these events.

As the thieves were bound to their crosses, Mary held her breath. Would the One who could bring the dead to life allow Himself to be crucified? Must she give up her faith that He was the Messiah? She saw His hands stretched out on the rough wood and the hammer raised up. When the spikes were driven through His tender flesh, Mary fainted. The disciples carried her away.

THE SAVIOR IS SACRIFICED

Jesus did not cry out, but great drops of sweat formed on His forehead. No caring hands wiped His face, no words of comfort or sympathy were spoken to sooth His human heart. While the soldiers went about their dreadful work, Jesus prayed, "Father, forgive them, because they don't know what they are doing."

Jesus didn't call down curses on these soldiers who handled Him so roughly. He didn't call for revenge on the priests and leaders. He only breathed a prayer for their forgiveness because they didn't understand what they were doing. But this ignorance didn't take away their guilt. They could have learned about Jesus and accepted Him as their Savior. Some of them would see their sins, repent, and change. Others, by not repenting, would make it impossible for Jesus' prayer to be answered. But God's plan was being completed—Jesus was earning the right to represent all humans to His Father.

Jesus' prayer for His enemies included every sinner from the beginning of the world to the end of time. All of us are guilty of crucifying the Son of God. But all are offered forgiveness.

As soon as Jesus was nailed to the cross, it was lifted up by strong men and dropped into its hole in the rock—causing intense pain for

Jesus. Then Pilate had a board inscribed with the words "Jesus of Nazareth, King of the Jews" nailed to the cross above Jesus' head.

This irritated the Jews. But they had claimed Caesar as their true king. The sign declared that whoever else claimed to be king in Israel would be killed. In order to have Jesus killed, the priests had sacrificed their national identity. But they asked Pilate to change the words to "This man said, 'I am the King of the Jews.'"

All of us are guilty of crucifying the Son of God. But all are offered forgiveness.

Pilate, already angry with himself, replied coldly, "What I have written, I have written."

God guided the hand that wrote the inscription. People from many lands were in Jerusalem, and that sign declaring that Jesus was the Messiah was noticed. Many people went back to the Scriptures to study the prophecies.

Many prophecies were fulfilled as Jesus suffered on the cross. From the Psalms came predictions that the Messiah's hands and feet would be pierced, and that others would gamble for His clothes. The soldiers at the Crucifixion were given the prisoners' clothes to destroy or keep. Since Jesus' cloak was one seamless piece of woven cloth, the soldiers gambled to decide which of them would keep it.

Another prediction from Psalms said that the suffering Messiah would be offered vinegar to drink. Those who suffered death on the cross were allowed to have a drink that would dull the pain. But when Jesus tasted it, He refused to drink it. He needed a clear mind to keep focused on God, His only strength. Clouding His senses would only give Satan an advantage.

The Jewish priests and leaders joined the mob in mocking the dying Savior. "If you are the Son of God, come down from there," they shouted. "If he is the Messiah, let him save himself." Satan and his angels—in human form—were there encouraging the priests and stirring up the mob.

The Father's voice from heaven was silent and no one else spoke up for Jesus. He suffered alone. He heard the priests declare, "If he really is the Messiah, let him come down from the cross. Then we will believe in him." Jesus could have come down from the cross. But because He didn't save Himself, sinners have the hope of forgiveness.

ONE THIEF BELIEVES

Jesus felt one gleam of comfort on the cross—the prayer of the repentant thief. Both of the men crucified with Jesus had mocked Him at first, and one only became more desperate and defiant as he suffered. But the other was not a hardened criminal. He was less guilty than many who stood beside the cross cursing the Savior. He had seen Jesus and heard Him teach, but had been convinced by the priests not to listen. Trying to quiet his conscience, he plunged into a criminal life until he was arrested and condemned.

On the cross he saw the religious teachers ridicule Jesus. He heard his fellow thief shout, "If you are the Messiah, save yourself and us." Among the crowd he heard many telling stories of what Jesus had done and said. Once again, he felt sure that this was the Messiah. He turned to the other thief and said, "You should fear God! You are getting the same punishment He is." The thieves were be-

From that moment John cared for Mary in his own home.

yond fearing humans, but one of them realized that there was a God to fear. To the other thief he said, "We are getting what we deserve, but this Man has done nothing wrong."

When he was condemned for his crime, the thief had given up all hope. But now strange, gentle thoughts were stirring in his mind. The Holy Spirit led his thinking step by step until it all made sense to him. In spite of being mocked and hanging on a cross, he saw Jesus as the Lamb of God. Hope mingled with the pain in his voice as he said, "Lord, remember me when You come into Your kingdom."

Quickly the answer came in a voice full of love and power: "Today I tell you the truth—you will be with Me in paradise."

Jesus had listened with a longing heart for some words of faith from His disciples. Instead He had only heard sad doubts: "We believed that He was the One who would save Israel." The dying thief's words of faith encouraged Jesus when no one else would even acknowledge Him.

Those words of faith also got the attention of bystanders. The soldiers gambling over Jesus' clothes stopped to listen. As Jesus spoke His promise, a ray of living light pierced the dark cloud that seemed to cover the cross. Jesus, hanging there in shame, was bathed in glory. Heaven recognized Him as the Bearer of sin. Humans could strip Him of His clothing, but they could not take His power to forgive sins and save all who came to God through Him.

Jesus did not promise that the thief would be with Him in paradise that same day. He Himself did not go to heaven that day. On the morning of the Resurrection, He said, "I have not yet gone up to My Father." But the promise was given "today"—right then as He hung dying on the cross—and the forgiven thief will be with Jesus in heaven.

Jesus was placed in the middle between the two thieves at the request of the priests to show that He was the worst of the criminals. But in the same way, His cross was placed in the middle of a dying world trapped in sin. And His words of forgiveness to the thief are a light that shines hope to the farthest parts of the world. During His suffering, Jesus spoke as a prophet to the women of Jerusalem. As a priest or representative, He asked His Father to forgive His murderers. As the Savior, He forgave the sins of a repentant thief.

Mary, His mother, returned to the foot of the cross, supported by John. She couldn't bear to be away from her Son, and John, knowing that the end was near, brought her back. Looking into her grief-filled eyes, Jesus said, "Dear woman, here is your son." Then He said to John, "Here is your mother."

John understood and accepted the responsibility. From that moment he cared for Mary in his own home. Jesus had no money to leave for His mother's care, but He gave her what she needed most—a friend who loved her because she loved Jesus. John was greatly blessed as well—Mary was a constant reminder of his beloved Master. Those who follow Jesus will never leave their parents without care or respect.

THE DEATH OF JESUS

Now the Lord of glory was near death, feeling agony of both body and soul. It wasn't the fear of death or the pain of the cross that caused His suffering. It was a sense of the horrible wickedness of sin. Jesus saw how few humans would be willing to break their addiction to it. Without help from God, all humans would be exterminated.

The guilt of every human since Adam was placed on Jesus—our Substitute—and it pressed heavily on His heart. All of His life, Jesus had been sharing the good news of the Father's forgiving love. But now with this terrible weight of sin on Him, He could not see the Father's face. This tore at His heart in a way that humans will never fully understand. The agony was so overwhelming that He hardly felt the physical pain.

Satan pressed Jesus' heart with fierce temptations. All hope seemed to be gone that He would rise from the grave or that the Father would accept His sacrifice. Jesus felt the anguish a sinner will feel when no One pleads for mercy for the guilty. It was this sense of sin—the sense that the Father's anger was focused on Him as the one taking the place of sinful humans—that broke His heart.

The sun refused to look on this awful scene. Its bright rays had been lighting the earth at noon when suddenly it seemed to be blotted out. The whole land was dark until three o'clock in the afternoon. This unnatural darkness was as deep as midnight without moon or stars. It was a miraculous sign given by God to strengthen our faith.

God and the holy angels were there beside the cross, hidden in the thick darkness. The Father was with His Son. But His presence had to be hidden. In that terrible hour, Jesus could not be comforted by His Father's presence.

God created the darkness to cover the last human suffering of His Son. All who had seen Jesus suffer that day had been convicted of His divinity. His long hours of torture had been accompanied by the stares and jeers of the mob. Now, mercifully, God hid Him.

When the darkness came, an unexplainable terror came over the crowd gathered around the cross. The cursing and shouting stopped. Brilliant lightning occasionally flashed through the clouds and revealed the crucified Savior. Priests, leaders, soldiers, and the mob thought their payback was coming. Some whispered that Jesus would now come down from the cross.

At three o'clock the darkness lifted from the crowd but still covered Jesus. No one could see through the gloom that shrouded His suffering soul. But Jesus' voice was heard crying, " 'My God, my God, why have you rejected me?' " (Matthew 27:46).

> *The Father was with His Son. But His presence had to be hidden.*

Many voices suggested that Jesus was being punished for claiming to be God. Many of His followers who heard His despairing cry gave up all hope. If God had rejected Jesus, in what could His followers trust?

Then the darkness lifted and Jesus revived enough to feel the physical pain. He said, "I am thirsty." One of the Roman soldiers felt pity and offered Jesus a sponge soaked in vinegar. But the priests mocked Jesus again. They misinterpreted Jesus' cry to mean that He was calling for the prophet Elijah. They refused to relieve His thirst. "No," they said, "we want to see if Elijah will come and save him."

HE DID IT FOR YOU

The perfect Son of God hung on the cross, His skin slashed by whips. His hands that had so often reached out to bless others were nailed to the wooden boards. His feet, so tireless on missions of love, were spiked to the beam. His royal head was pierced by the crown of thorns; His trembling lips twisted in a cry of pain.

All that He suffered—the blood that dripped from His head, His hands, and His feet, the agony that tore His body with every breath, and the unspeakable anguish in His heart from being separated from His Father—speaks to each of us, saying, "For you the Son of God agrees to carry this guilt; for you He battles death and wins; for you He opens the gates of heaven; for you He offers Himself as a sacrifice. All of this He does because of His love for you."

JESUS DIES TRIUMPHANTLY

Suddenly the darkness lifted from the cross. In a voice that seemed to ring through all creation like a trumpet, Jesus cried, "It is finished. Father, I give You My life." A light surrounded the cross and the Savior's face shone like the glory of the sun. Then He bowed His head and died.

In the darkness, Jesus drank the cup of human suffering and sin. During those dreadful hours, He was sustained by what He had known all His life. By faith, He rested in His Father's love even though He could no longer feel it. As He surrendered His life to God, the sense of having lost His Father's love vanished. By faith, Jesus won the battle.

Now darkness covered the land again and there was a violent earthquake. In the surrounding mountains, rocks split into pieces and crashed to the plains below. Graves were ripped open and the dead were thrown out. Priests, soldiers, and the others in the crowd fell to the ground in fear.

The moment Jesus cried, "It is finished," was the time of the evening sacrifice at the temple. The lamb that represented the Messiah had been brought in to be killed. The priest stood with the knife in his hand as the people watched. Then the ground trembled, because the Lord Himself was approaching. With a loud ripping sound, the inner curtain of the temple was torn from top to bottom. People stared right into the place that was once filled with the presence of God. The Most Holy Place of the temple was no longer sacred.

There was terror and confusion everywhere. The knife fell from the priest's suddenly numb hand and the lamb escaped. The symbolic intersected with reality. The great sacrifice had been made. A new, living path to salvation was available to everyone. Jesus would now become our Priest, our Representative in heaven.

CHAPTER 79

THE DEFEAT OF SATAN

"God was in Christ, making peace between the world and himself"
(2 Corinthians 5:19).

esus had finished the work He came to do. When with His dying breath He proclaimed, "It is finished," the battle was over. All of heaven celebrated His victory.

At the same moment, Satan was defeated. His kingdom was lost. Until Jesus' death, Satan had disguised his rebellion so well that even the angels had not clearly understood his plans and character. So Jesus' great plan of salvation was for the angels and unfallen worlds as well as for humans.

Before he sinned, Lucifer stood next to God, the highest of all created beings. He announced and explained God's plans to the universe. After he rebelled against God, he took advantage of that position to raise questions in the minds of many. Because of who he was, it was difficult to expose the truth about him or his rebellion.

God could have destroyed Satan and his fellow rebels, but that was not His way. Only those under Satan's power use force to control others. God's power comes from His goodness, His mercy, and His love. These are the principles He uses to deal with others. In God's government, truth and love are the power that prevails.

In heaven, it was decided that Satan would be given time to work out his rules of life, which he claimed were superior to God's. This would allow the whole universe to see the truth about him. For 4,000 years, Jesus had worked to lift humans up while Satan worked to destroy them. And the universe watched it all.

From the moment Jesus was born as a baby in Bethlehem, Satan was on the attack. He tried to keep Jesus from being a perfect child, a faultless man, from having a holy ministry, and from being a flawless sacrifice. But he failed. He could not lead Jesus into sin. All of Satan's efforts just brought out more clearly Jesus' perfect character.

HEAVEN WATCHES THE DRAMA ON EARTH

Heaven and the unfallen worlds followed the closing scenes of the battle with intense interest. They heard Jesus' bitter cry in the Garden, "My Father, if it is possible, do not give me this cup of suffering." They saw that His sorrow and pain were worse than death. After His third prayer begging to be spared from the agony, heaven could take no more and an angel was sent to comfort the Son of God.

Heaven watched astounded as Jesus hung on the cross.

Heaven watched as Jesus was betrayed and violently rushed from one trial to another. It heard the sneers of the accusers and Peter's cursing denial. It saw the Savior dragged back and forth from palaces to judgment halls, accused twice before the Jewish high priests, twice before the Sanhedrin, twice before Pilate, and once before Herod. It saw Jesus mocked, beaten, condemned, and taken out to be crucified.

Heaven watched astounded as Jesus hung on the cross, blood flowing from His head, His feet, and especially His hands, as those wounds were ripped wider by the weight of His body. With amazement, they heard Jesus' prayer as He suffered: "Father, forgive them, because they don't know what they are doing."

The powers of darkness had gathered around the cross. They cast a hellish shadow of doubt into the hearts of the humans there. Satanic forces led the people to believe that Jesus was the worst of sinners. These same forces inspired the taunting and cursing. But even with all this, Satan failed. If Jesus had given in to Satan even in the smallest way, the enemy would have won. Jesus bowed His head and died, but He held on to His faith.

Satan's disguise was torn away and he was shown to be a murderer. When he killed the Son of God, the last link of sympathy between Satan and the heavenly world was broken.

But still, the angels did not fully understand all that was involved in the great controversy. The principles at stake would have to become clearer. Humans would also have to see the difference between the Prince of light and the prince of darkness. Then all must choose whom they will serve.

At the beginning of this great battle, Satan had declared that God's law could not be obeyed, that justice was incompatible with mercy, and that if the law was broken, the sinner could not be pardoned. If God did not punish sin, then He could not be a God of justice. When humans broke God's law, Satan declared that this proved that the law could not be obeyed and that humans could not be forgiven. Because he had been thrown out of heaven after his rebellion, Satan claimed that the human race must also be shut out of God's favor—it would not be right for God to show mercy to sinners.

But humans were in a different situation from that of Satan. Lucifer sinned in the light of God's glory. Even though he knew God and understood His character, Satan chose to follow his own selfish way. There was nothing else God could do to save him. But humans were deceived, their minds clouded by Satan's lies. They did not know the height and depth of God's love. By learning about God, humans could be drawn back to Him.

JUSTICE COULD BE BLENDED WITH MERCY.

God showed mercy to humans through Jesus, but this mercy did not override justice and fairness. The law could not be changed, but God sacrificed Himself in Jesus to save humankind.

The law demands a righteous life, a perfect character, and this humans do not have to give. But Jesus as a human lived a holy life and developed a perfect character. And He offers these as a gift to all who accept Him as their Savior. His life then stands in the place of their lives, and their sins are forgiven. More than this, Jesus gives humans the qualities of God. He builds human character to be like the character of God. This is how those who believe in Jesus live out the righteousness that the law requires. God can both uphold the law and save those who believe in His Son.

Satan worked to separate mercy from truth and justice. But Jesus showed that in God's plan they are tied together, that one couldn't exist without the other. By His life and His death, Jesus proved that God's justice did not destroy His mercy, that sin could be forgiven, and that the law is righteous and can be obeyed. Satan's charges were proved wrong.

So Satan tried another deception. He declared that Jesus' death repealed the Father's law. If it were possible for the law to be changed or repealed, then Jesus did not need to die. But repealing the law would give Satan control of the world and allow sin to exist forever. Satan claimed that the Cross—where Jesus showed the law's unchangeable importance—actually destroyed the law. The last battle of the great controversy between Jesus and Satan will be fought over this issue.

SATAN'S NEW LIE

Satan's claim is that some parts of the law—the Ten Commandments spoken by God Himself—are no longer in effect. He doesn't need to attack all ten commandments. If he can lead people to disregard just one, he has succeeded. When we agree to break even one law, we separate ourselves from God and come under Satan's power.

Prophecy tells us that a great fallen power will speak for Satan. It will speak out against God, will persecute God's followers, and will appear to change God's laws. Humans will set up their own laws to take the place of God's, and they will enforce them with violence.

The war against God's law will continue until the end of time. Everyone will have to choose between God's law and the laws of humans. Every person's character will show which side has his or her loyalty.

Then the end will come. God will vindicate His law and save His people. Satan and all who have joined his rebellion will be cut off. Sin and sinners will be destroyed forever.

God is the Source of life, and if we choose sin, we cut ourselves off from life.

This is not a heartless, random act by God. Those who have rejected His offers of mercy will harvest what they have planted. God is the Source of life, and if we choose sin, we cut ourselves off from life. God gives all humans a time to live and develop their characters and show what is in their hearts. Then they receive what they have chosen. Satan and all who have joined him are so out of harmony with God—the Source of love and life—that His very presence will destroy them.

At the beginning of this great battle, the angels didn't understand this. If Satan and his angels had been destroyed then, doubts about God's goodness would have remained in their minds. These seeds of doubt could have grown into sin.

But this will not be the case when this great controversy is over. Then, with the plan of salvation completed, God's character will be clear to all created intelligent beings. His law will be seen as perfect and unchangeable. The results of sin will also be clear, and so will Satan's character. The extermination of sin will prove God's love and His honor before the universe.

This, then, is why the angels could celebrate as they saw Jesus on the cross. They did not yet understand it all, but they knew that Satan and sin would be destroyed, that humankind would be saved, and that the universe would be safe forever.

Jesus fully understood the results of His sacrifice on Calvary. This is why He could look forward and cry, "It is finished."

CHAPTER 80

JESUS
RESTS

"He took the body down from the cross, wrapped it in cloth, and put it in a tomb" (Luke 23:53).

t last the long day of shame and torture was over. As the sun was setting, the Son of God rested, His work complete.

In the beginning, the Father and the Son rested on the Sabbath after Their work of creation. All of heaven rejoiced to see what They had done. Now Jesus rested after His work of redemption, and though those who loved Him on earth were weeping, there was joy in heaven. God and the angels saw the results of Jesus' work—a redeemed people, who having overcome sin, would throughout eternity never fall again.

When sin is gone forever and all is made new again, the Sabbath of Creation—the day that Jesus rested in the tomb—will still be a day of rest and rejoicing. From one Sabbath to the next, the saved peoples of earth will bow in joyful worship of God and of their Savior.

At Jesus' dying words, there was another witness to who He really was. The Roman centurion, who had seen Jesus' patience in suffering and heard His cry of victory as He died, said, "This Man was truly the Son of God." On the very day that Jesus died, three people declared their faith in Him—this Roman centurion,

Simon, who carried His cross, and the thief who hung next to Him.

As evening drew closer, an unearthly stillness hung over Calvary. Many people had flocked to the Crucifixion out of curiosity, not out of hate for Jesus, even though they did see Him as a criminal. Influenced by satanic powers, they had joined in the shouting and mocking. But when the unnatural darkness fell, they felt guilty for what they had done. When the darkness lifted, these people silently and solemnly headed home, convinced that the charges against Jesus were false and that Jesus really was the Messiah. A few weeks later, when Peter preached on the Day of Pentecost, these people were among the thousands who were converted and became followers of Jesus.

As evening drew closer, an unearthly stillness hung over Calvary.

The Jewish leaders hadn't changed their minds—their hate for Jesus was stronger than ever. The darkness in their minds was thicker than the darkness around the cross. But in their hour of triumph, they were plagued by doubts. What would happen next? The earthquake shook their confidence. They feared Jesus dead more than they feared Him alive. They didn't want any more attention drawn to His crucifixion. They certainly didn't want His body to stay on the cross during the Sabbath. Using the excuse that it would violate their Sabbath for the bodies to stay there, the Jewish leaders asked Pilate to hurry the death of the victims so they could be removed before the sun set.

With Pilate's permission, the soldiers broke the legs of the two thieves so they would die faster. But Jesus was already dead. The rough soldiers, moved by what they had seen and heard from Jesus, held back from breaking His legs. In this way, they lived by the law of the Passover lamb, which required that its bones not be broken.

The priests and leaders were amazed to find that Jesus was dead. It was unheard of for someone to die after just six hours on a cross. Wanting to make sure Jesus was really dead, they asked a soldier to stick a spear into the Savior's side. Blood and water flowed out from the cut.

After the Resurrection, the priests started rumors that Jesus hadn't died on the cross, that He only fainted and was later revived. But the

Roman spear proved that Jesus had died. If He hadn't been dead already, the spear would have killed Him.

It wasn't the spear or the pain of the cross that killed Jesus. He died of a broken heart, a heart broken by the sins of the world.

DISCOURAGED DISCIPLES

When Jesus died, the hopes of His disciples died as well. Until the last, they refused to believe that He would die. Now they could hardly convince themselves that He was dead. Overwhelmed by sadness, nothing they could remember Jesus saying comforted them. Their faith in Jesus died, but they had never loved Him as much as they did now—and never needed Him so much.

The disciples longed to give Jesus an honorable burial, but they didn't know how. People who were executed for treason against the Roman government were buried as criminals. John and the women from Galilee were unwilling to leave Jesus' body to be handled by uncaring soldiers and be buried in a shameful grave. But they couldn't get help from the Jewish leaders, and they had no influence with Pilate to get him to give them the body.

UNEXPECTED HELP

Help came from an unexpected place. Joseph from Arimathea and Nicodemus, both members of the Sanhedrin, wealthy and powerful, were determined that Jesus would have an honorable burial.

Joseph went straight to Pilate and begged him for permission to take Jesus' body. Since the priests had purposely not informed Pilate, this was the first he heard that Jesus was dead. He sent for the Roman officer in charge at the cross and got his report of what had happened. This confirmed Joseph's story and Pilate granted his request.

Joseph came to the disciples with permission to take Jesus' body, and Nicodemus brought expensive spices to embalm the body. The most honored man in Jerusalem could not have been given more respect in death. The disciples were astonished.

Neither Joseph nor Nicodemus had publicly accepted Jesus while He was living. They would have been thrown out of the Sanhedrin if they had, and they had worked to protect Him there. But the crafty priests had ruined their plans by having Jesus' trial without them. Now, no longer concealing their true beliefs, the two men boldly stepped out to help the poor disciples.

When Jesus died, the hopes of His disciples died as well.

With their own hands, they gently removed Jesus' body from the cross. Through tear-filled eyes, they looked at His bruised and battered form. Joseph owned a new tomb in a garden not far from Calvary. It had been cut into a stone hillside for him personally. But now he prepared it for Jesus. There the disciples folded Jesus' hands over His unmoving chest as they laid Him on the cold rock. A heavy stone was rolled across the entrance and the Savior was left at rest.

As the evening shadows lengthened, Mary Magdalene and the other women lingered near the resting place of their Savior, weeping in sorrow. Finally they went home to rest on the Sabbath day.

A SENSE OF STRANGENESS

It was an unforgettable Sabbath for the disciples, the priests and leaders, and the people of Jerusalem. The Passover was observed as it had been for centuries while the One it pointed to lay in Joseph's tomb. The courts of the temple were filled with people. The high priest was there in his fine robe; the other priests performed their duties.

But there was a sense of strangeness to everything. The people were not aware that Jesus' death had fulfilled the prophecies and the symbols of the Passover service. But they had conflicting feelings as they witnessed the service this time. The Most Holy Place—the heart of the temple that only the high priests had ever seen—was now open to be seen by anyone. No longer considered a holy place by God, its curtain had been ripped from top to bottom. This worried the priests greatly—they were sure that something terrible was going to happen.

During these hours between the Crucifixion and the Resurrection many sleepless people studied the prophecies. Some searched for evidence that Jesus was not who He claimed to be. Others searched for proof that He was the Messiah. Regardless of where they started, they all arrived at the same conclusion: the One who had been crucified was the Savior of the world. Many of them never again celebrated Passover. Even among the priests, many searched the prophecies, and after His resurrection they followed Jesus as the Son of God.

Nicodemus remembered Jesus' words spoken that night on the Mount of Olives: " 'Just as Moses lifted up the snake in the desert, the Son of Man must also be lifted up. So that everyone who believes can have eternal life in him' " (John 3:14,15). The meaning of these words was no longer a mystery to him. Nicodemus regretted not becoming a follower of Jesus while He was still alive. He had heard Jesus' words for His murderers and to the dying thief and they touched his heart. When Jesus called out, "It is finished," in a triumphant voice, Nicodemus's faith was settled. The Cross destroyed the hopes of the disciples, but it convinced Joseph and Nicodemus that Jesus truly was the Son of God.

Jesus was sealed in His tomb as securely as if He would be there for all time.

Jesus was never more popular with the crowds than He was now that He was dead. People brought their sick loved ones to the temple courts, calling out, "We want Jesus, the Healer!" But His healing hands were folded on His chest. So many people were asking loudly for Jesus, that the priests finally had them driven out of the temple courts. Then they stationed soldiers at the gates to keep out the crowds. Those who were looking for help were crushed with disappointment. The sick were dying without Jesus' healing touch.

Thousands were convinced that a great light in the world had gone out. Without Jesus, the earth was dark. Many who had shouted "Crucify him, crucify him" now realized what a terrible thing they had done.

When the people learned that Jesus had been executed, they started asking questions. In spite of their attempts to keep it private, reports of how Jesus was treated during His trial spread everywhere.

Respected thinkers asked the priests and leaders to explain the prophecies of the Messiah. Of course, the priests couldn't explain the prophecies that pointed to the Messiah's suffering and death. They nearly went mad trying to create a lie for an answer.

The priests knew they were being severely criticized by the people. The ones they had influenced to shout out against Jesus were now horrified by their shameful behavior. But worse than that, the priests were terrified that Jesus would rise from His grave and appear to them again. They remembered His words: "Destroy this temple and I will raise it up again in three days." Judas had told them Jesus' prediction that He would be betrayed and condemned by the priests, that He would be killed and would rise again on the third day. They remembered that Jesus' predictions had always been fulfilled before. Who could say that this wouldn't happen also?

As much as the priests wanted to shut out these thoughts, they could not. In their minds they could see Jesus, calm and quiet before them, suffering their taunts and abuse without a word. They were struck with the overwhelming thought that He really was the Son of God. At any moment He might appear, accusing them, demanding justice, and demanding the death of His murderers.

Even though it broke their Sabbath rules, they held a council meeting to discuss what to do about Jesus' body. Then the Pharisees and priests went to Pilate with a request. "When that liar was still alive, he said, 'I will rise again in three days.' Command your soldiers to seal and guard his tomb for at least three days so his disciples don't steal his body away and tell everyone that he is alive again."

Pilate agreed, and the soldiers did as the priests directed. Ropes were stretched across the stone that covered the tomb, and they were sealed with a Roman seal. Then one hundred soldiers were stationed around the tomb. Now no one could move the stone without the permission of Rome. Jesus was sealed in His tomb as securely as if He would be there for all time.

But the efforts made to prevent Jesus' resurrection became the most convincing arguments to prove it. The more soldiers stationed around His tomb, the greater the story would be. Roman weapons were powerless to keep the Lord of life in the tomb. The time of His release was near.

CHAPTER 81

RESURRECTION MORNING

"He is not here. He has risen from the dead as he said he would"
(Matthew 28:6).

The night before the first day of the week had worn slowly away. Jesus was still a prisoner in His tomb. The Roman guards were still on watch. Their seal was unbroken. If it were possible, the prince of darkness would have kept that tomb sealed forever. But powerful angels from heaven were waiting to welcome their Prince back to life.

As dawn lighted up the eastern sky, a great earthquake shook the world. A flash of glory split the sky as heaven's mightiest angel came down and rolled the stone away from the tomb as if it were a pebble. As the rest of the angel armies surrounded the tomb, Satan's hosts fled. The normally brave Roman soldiers trembled, acting like they had been captured without so much as a fight.

Then the angel cried, "Son of God, come out! Your Father is calling You!"

Out of the darkness of the tomb stepped Jesus, the Messiah, the Savior, the glorified Son of God. In a mighty voice that could no longer be silent, He proclaimed, "I am the Resurrection and the Life!" As He stepped out, clothed in His divine majesty and glory, the angel army greeted Him with songs of praise.

This chapter is based on Matt. 28:2-4, 11-15.

The Roman soldiers fainted away like dead men.

Pilate had already heard a report of Jesus' resurrection.

When the heavenly beings vanished, the soldiers rose up and staggered as drunk men to the city, telling everyone they met what they had seen. They were headed to Pilate to report, but the priests and leaders intercepted them and insisted on hearing their story first. Still trembling with fear, their faces as white as sheets, the soldiers told everything just as they had seen it. They said, "It was the Son of God who was crucified! We heard the angel announce Him as the King of heaven!"

Panicked, Caiaphas tried to speak. His lips moved, but no sounds came out. The soldiers were about to leave when finally he found his voice. "Wait, wait!" he cried. "Tell no one what you saw."

The other priests joined in. "Tell everyone that His disciples stole the body while you were sleeping." The priests had outsmarted themselves here. If the soldiers were asleep, how could they know what happened? And if the disciples had stolen the body, wouldn't the priests be demanding their arrest? And wouldn't they also be demanding that the soldiers be arrested for sleeping?

The soldiers were horrified at the suggestion. Sleeping on duty was punishable by death. Why should they lie and risk their lives?

The priests promised that they would not be punished. After all, Pilate would not want their story spread any more than the priests did. So the Roman soldiers sold out. They went to the priests carrying only a shocking but true report; they left carrying money and lies.

Pilate had already heard a report of Jesus' resurrection. Although he had sentenced Jesus to death unwillingly, it hadn't really bothered him until now. Terrified, he shut himself away in his house. The priests managed to get in to see him and urged him not to punish the soldiers. Pilate questioned the soldiers privately and they told him the true story. He didn't punish them, but he never felt peace again.

In putting Jesus to death, the priests had become tools of Satan. Now they were entirely in his power, trapped into continuing their war against Jesus. Their only hope was to prove that Jesus was not the Messiah, by denying that He had risen. All they could do was bribe the soldiers and count on Pilate's silence. But there were witnesses who would not be silent.

Many people had heard the soldiers' story before the priests bribed them. And others had been resurrected with Jesus. These saints appeared to many people to declare that Jesus was alive. The priests and leaders were in constant fear that somewhere on the streets or in their homes, they would come face to face with Jesus. Doors and locks are poor protection against the Son of God. Night and day, they re-

> *To the Christian, death is just a sleep, a moment of silence and darkness.*

played that awful scene when they had cried out, "We and our children will be responsible for his death."

OUR RESURRECTION GUARANTEED

When the mighty angel at Jesus' tomb said, "Your Father is calling You," Jesus came out of the grave through His own divine power. The words Jesus spoke, "I am the Resurrection and the Life," could be spoken only by God. All created beings depend on God for life. Only God could say, " 'I have the right to give my life, and I have the right to take it back' " (John 10:18).

The Passover celebration included waving before God in the temple a sample of the first grains to ripen. This was an offering of thanks to God. It represented the harvest, and no grain could be cut until this offering was given.

Jesus' resurrection happened on the day that offering was given to God. Jesus was a sample of all who would be resurrected, a guarantee that all who died believing in Jesus would be raised to life on the great resurrection day. "We believe that Jesus died and that he rose again. So, because of him, God will raise with Jesus those who have died" (1 Thessalonians 4:14).

MANY OTHERS RESURRECTED WITH JESUS

When Jesus rose, He brought many others from the grave with Him. These people had shared the truth at the cost of their lives. Now they would be witnesses for Jesus again, sharing the good news that He had risen from the grave.

Jesus had raised several people from the dead during His ministry. Those resurrected people had not been given immortality—they would age and die again. But the ones who came out of their graves with Jesus were raised to live forever. They would return with Him to heaven as trophies of His victory over death and the grave. These saints went into Jerusalem and appeared to many people, declaring, "Jesus has risen from the dead and we rose with Him."

In Jesus, the eternal life that we lost because of sin can be restored. He has the right and the power to give immortality. Jesus said, " 'I came to give life—life in all its fullness' " (John 10:10), and " 'Those who eat my flesh and drink my blood have eternal life, and I will raise them up on the last day' " (John 6:54). To the Christian, death is just a sleep, a moment of silence and darkness.

The Voice that cried from the cross, "It is finished" will penetrate graves and tombs, and those who died believing in Jesus will rise. At the Savior's resurrection a few graves were opened, but at His second coming all of His children who have died will hear His voice and come out to a glorious life that never ends. The same power that raised Jesus from the dead will glorify and raise His church—His followers—above every name and power in this world and in the world to come.

CHAPTER 82

"WHY ARE YOU CRYING?"

" 'I am going back to my Father and your Father, to my God and your God' " (John 20:17).

ery early that same morning—the first day of the week—the women who had been at the cross made their way to the tomb to place oils and fragrances on the Savior's body. They did not think about His rising from the dead. They had forgotten His words, " 'I will see you again' " (John 16:22).

With no idea what was happening, they arrived at the gardens where the tomb was, asking, "Who will roll the stone away from the tomb for us?" Suddenly the ground shook and the sky blazed with glory. Up ahead, they could see that the stone had been rolled back!

Mary Magdalene reached the tomb first. Seeing the stone moved back, she rushed away to tell the disciples. As the other women arrived, they saw a glow around the tomb, but Jesus' body was gone.

As they lingered, they suddenly noticed that they were not alone. A young man in shining clothes was sitting nearby. It was the angel who had rolled away the stone. He had put on the appearance of a human so he wouldn't frighten these friends of Jesus. But the light of heaven was still around him and the women were frightened.

This chapter is based on Matt. 28:1, 5-8; Mark 16:1-8; Luke 24:1-12; John 20:1-18.

"Don't be afraid," the angel said. "I know you are looking for Jesus, who was crucified. He's not here. He has risen from the dead just as He said He would. Come, see where His body was laid. Then go quickly and tell His disciples—Jesus is risen from the dead!"

A young man in shining clothes was sitting nearby.

They looked into the tomb and saw another angel in human form. "Why are you looking for a living person in this place for the dead? He is not here—He is alive! Remember what He said in Galilee, that the Son of man would be handed over and crucified, then He would rise from the dead on the third day."

The women remembered now—Jesus said He would rise again! They left quickly to tell the disciples. They were afraid, but they were very happy!

Mary had left before they heard that good news. She took a sad message to Peter and John. "They have taken Jesus' body from the tomb and I don't know where they put Him."

Peter and John hurried to the tomb to find out what they could. They found Jesus' grave clothes—the clothes used to wrap a dead person—but not His body. But even this was evidence that Jesus was alive. The grave clothes were not tossed carelessly aside, but folded neatly. John saw and believed. He now remembered Jesus' words about His resurrection.

Jesus Himself folded those grave clothes. As one mighty angel from heaven rolled back the stone, another entered the tomb and took the wrappings from Jesus' body. But it was Jesus who folded those grave clothes with such care. In the sight of the One who guides the stars and the atoms, nothing is unimportant.

Mary followed Peter and John back to the tomb. When they returned to Jerusalem, she stayed. With a grief-stricken heart, she stared into the tomb, only to see the two angels. "Woman, why are you crying?" they asked.

"Because someone has taken my Lord away," she said through her tears, "and I don't know where He is." Then she turned away to look for someone who could tell her what they had done with the body.

She stopped as another voice asked, "Why are you crying? Who are you looking for?"

Through her tears, Mary only saw a man who she thought must be the caretaker. "Did you take Him away, sir?" she asked. "Tell me where you put Him and I will take care of Him." If this rich man's tomb was too honorable for Jesus, she would find a place for His body.

"Mary." The man only said her name. But no one said her name like that except Jesus! She turned and saw Jesus standing before her—alive!

"Teacher!" she cried, springing toward Him to embrace Him.

But Jesus held up His hand, saying, " 'Don't hold on to me, because I have not yet gone up to the Father. But go to my brothers and tell them, "I am going back to my Father and your Father, to my God and your God" ' " (John 20:17). So Mary rushed back to share her joyful news.

Jesus refused the worship of His people until He went up to the heavenly courts and from God Himself heard that His sacrifice for the sins of humans had been enough, that through His blood all of them could have eternal life. The Father confirmed His agreement that He would accept all humans who repented and obeyed His laws, and love them just as He loves His own Son.

While the Savior was in God's presence, receiving gifts for His church, the disciples were mourning and crying. This day of great rejoicing in heaven had been a day of confusion and sadness for them. Their faith had sunk so low that they would not believe the reports of Mary or the other women. It was too good to be true, they thought. They had heard so much of the "scientific theories" of the Sadducees that they hardly knew what a resurrection from the dead would mean.

The angels had told the women, " 'Now go and tell his followers and Peter, "Jesus is going into Galilee ahead of you, and you will see him there as he told you before" ' " (Mark 16:7). This message from angels should have convinced the disciples. Words like these could only come from messengers of their Master.

Since Jesus' death, Peter had been beside himself with remorse for having denied the Savior. Of all the desiples, he was suffering the most. In mentioning Peter by name, Jesus wanted to assure him that his repentence was accepted.

When Mary told the disciples that she had seen Jesus, she repeated this call to a meeting in Galilee. And the message was sent a third time

> *Jesus is right beside them, but their tear-filled eyes do not see Him.*

when Jesus appeared to other women saying, "Tell My brothers to go to Galilee and they will see Me there."

Jesus' first work after His resurrection was to convince His disciples that His love for them had not changed. He wanted to draw them even closer. That's why He planned to meet them in Galilee.

But the disciples still doubted. When the women claimed that they had seen Jesus, the disciples thought they were seeing things. In their minds, troubles were piling onto troubles. They had seen their Master die, His body was missing, and they were being accused of stealing it to deceive the crowds. They felt they could never straighten out the lies that were being spread. They were afraid of the priests and of the crowds. They longed for the presence of Jesus.

They kept repeating the words, " 'We were hoping that he would free Israel' " (Luke 24:21). Lonely and heartbroken, they met together in an upstairs room with the doors closed and locked, knowing that the fate of their beloved Teacher might be theirs at any moment. And all the time they could have been celebrating the news that Jesus was alive.

Many today do the same thing. Jesus is right beside them, but their tear-filled eyes do not see Him. He speaks to them, but they do not understand.

We should listen and do what the angel told Jesus' disciples: "Go quickly and tell His followers that He is alive!" Don't bother looking at the empty grave. Let the song ring out across the world: "Jesus is risen!" He lives and represents us in heaven before the Father!

CHAPTER 83

THE
ROAD TO EMMAUS

" 'What are these things you are talking about while you walk?' "
(Luke 24:17).

ate in the afternoon on the day of the Resurrection, two disciples were walking to Emmaus, a small town not too far from Jerusalem. They had come to the Passover and were greatly troubled by what had happened.

Both had heard the news that Jesus' body was missing and the reports of the women who had seen angels and talked to Jesus. Now as they headed home, they could talk about nothing else. Never had they been so confused and discouraged.

As they walked, a stranger joined them. It was Jesus Himself, but they were so absorbed in their depression that they didn't look at Him closely. They continued their discussion, wondering about the lessons Jesus taught that they didn't understand. Could this Man, who had allowed Himself to be so shamed, really be the Messiah? Tears flowed as they spoke.

Jesus wanted so much to comfort them, to wipe away their tears and fill their hearts with joy. But first He was going to give them a lesson they would never forget. He asked, " 'What are these things you are talking about while you walk?' " (Luke 24:17).

The two men stopped, looking very sad. The one named Cleopas answered, "You must be the only person in Jerusalem that doesn't know

This chapter is based on Luke 24:13-33.

what's been happening." Then they told Him about their Master. "He was a prophet who did many powerful things. Our leaders handed Him over to the Romans to be killed." With quivering lips, they added, "We were hoping that He would free Israel. And this is the third day since it happened." It is strange that they didn't remember Jesus' words about rising on the third day—the priests and leaders couldn't forget them!

JESUS EXPLAINS THE SCRIPTURES

Then Jesus said, " 'You are foolish and slow to believe everything the prophets said. They said that the Christ must suffer these things before he enters his glory' " (Luke 24:25, 26).

The men were amazed. Who could this person be who spoke with such kindness and intensity? For the first time, they started to feel hope. Now they looked at their traveling Companion often, thinking that those were just the kind of things Jesus would have said.

Starting with Moses and the beginning of Bible history, Jesus discussed all the Scriptures that pointed to Himself. If He had told the two men who He was first, they would have heard nothing else He said. But to build their faith, they needed to understand the symbols of the Old Testament prophecies. Jesus didn't perform any miracles to convince them—He convinced them from the Scriptures. He showed from the writings of the prophets that His death was the strongest evidence for their faith in Him as the Messiah.

> "*You must be the only person in Jerusalem that doesn't know what's been happening.*"

Jesus showed us how important the Old Testament is in describing the mission of the Messiah. He is shown in the Old Testament as clearly as He is in the New Testament. Light from the prophets in the distant past shines on the life and teachings of Jesus and helps us understand the New Testament better. Comparing the prophecies of the Old Testament with the history of the New Testament gives us stronger proof of the Messiah than all of the miracles Jesus performed.

Like the others, these two disciples had been misled to expect a Messiah who would take the throne and rule like a king. They needed to understand the suffering that the Messiah must endure. Jesus showed them that the terrible events they had witnessed were

the fulfillment of an agreement made before the world was created. The Messiah had to die, like every lawbreaker would die if he or she continued to sin. All of this had to happen, but it would not end in defeat. It would end in glorious victory. Jesus told them that every

The disciples stared in astonishment.

possible effort must be made to save humans from sin. His followers needed to live as He lived and work as He worked, never giving up.

This is how Jesus spoke to those disciples, to help them understand Scripture. But they still had no idea who their traveling Companion was, because Jesus referred to Himself as if He were another person. He walked as carefully as they did over the rough mountainous road, and rested with them now and then along the way.

A FAMILIAR STRANGER

As they walked, the sun had gone down and workers in the fields had gone home. When they arrived in Emmaus, Jesus acted as if He would be traveling on down the road. But the two disciples wanted to hear more. "Come in and stay with us," they urged. Jesus didn't seem ready to accept their offer, so they pressed Him harder. "Come on, the day is gone and evening has come. Stay with us." So Jesus did.

If they had not pressed their invitation to Him, they would never have known that their traveling Companion was their risen Savior. Jesus never forces Himself on anyone. He will gladly enter the most humble home, but if people are too busy or too uninterested to ask Him to stay with them, He moves on.

The Guest sat at the end of the table and when the simple meal was ready, He put out His hands to bless it—exactly as Jesus had always done. The disciples stared in astonishment. They looked again and saw the prints of nails in His hands. Both of them shouted, "It is Jesus!"

They jumped up to throw themselves at His feet, but He had vanished. Looking at the empty chair, they said to each other, "We should have known! Didn't our hearts burn like fire as He talked to us along the road and explained the Scriptures?"

They forgot about being tired and hungry. They left their meal on the table and hurried back along the same path they had traveled earlier to share this wonderful news with the disciples in Jerusalem. They climbed down the steep trails and slipped on the smooth rocks, always moving as fast as they dared to in the darkness. As they rushed along, sometimes running, sometimes stumbling, their Companion traveled with them again, this time hidden from their eyes.

The night was dark, but the Sun of Righteousness was shining on them. The world seemed new and fresh and full of promise. "Jesus is alive"—over and over they repeated it. They had to tell the others the wonderful news of their walk to Emmaus. They carried the greatest message ever given—the happy news that holds the hopes of the human family for all time. Jesus is alive!

CHAPTER 84

JESUS APPEARS TO HIS DISCIPLES

" 'Why do you doubt what you see? Look at my hands and my feet. It is I myself!' " (Luke 24:38, 39).

hen the two disciples reached Jerusalem, they raced through the narrow streets to the upstairs room where Jesus had spent the last evening before His death. This is where the other disciples were hiding. They knocked on the locked door, but there was no answer. Finally, they called out their names, and the door was opened. As they entered, their unseen Companion entered with them. Then the door was locked again to keep out spies.

The two men found the room in an uproar. Voices cried out, "The Lord really has risen! He appeared to Peter!" Still panting from their journey, the two travelers told how Jesus had appeared to them. Some were saying they could not believe it, others were saying it was too good to be true when suddenly another Person was standing there with them. No one had knocked, there had been no footsteps, but there He stood.

The disciples were startled, not sure what to think. Then they heard the voice they recognized, the voice of their Master, their Teacher, their Friend. "Peace be with you," Jesus said. But they were afraid. Some were terrified, thinking it was a ghost.

This chapter is based on Luke 24:33-48; John 20:19-29.

Jesus said, " 'Why are you troubled? Why do you doubt what you see? Look at my hands and my feet. It is I myself!' " (Luke 24:38, 39). Then He showed them the scars on His hands and feet. While they could still hardly believe it because they were so amazed and happy, Jesus asked, "Is there any food here?" Someone brought Him a piece of broiled fish, and as they watched, Jesus ate it.

No one had knocked; there had been no footsteps, but there He stood.

Now, finally, the disciples could believe that it was true. Faith took over the doubt in their hearts. Jesus was alive! He had really risen from the dead!

The disciples recognized Jesus' appearance, His voice, and His mannerisms. When the dead who followed Him are resurrected at His second coming, we will recognize our friends and loved ones the same way. Even with their glorified bodies, their appearance and personalities will be the same.

Jesus reminded His disciples of His words before He died. Then he opened their minds so they could understand what He had shown them from the Scriptures. " 'It is written that the Christ would suffer and rise from the dead on the third day and that a change of hearts and lives and forgiveness of sins would be preached in his name to all nations, starting at Jerusalem. You are witnesses of these things' " (Luke 24:46-48).

The disciples had much to share with the world: the stories of Jesus' life, death, and resurrection, the prophecies that pointed to these events, the holiness of God's law, the mystery of the plan of salvation, and Jesus' power to forgive sins.

"After he said this, he breathed on them and said, 'Receive the Holy Spirit. If you forgive anyone his sins, they are forgiven. If you don't forgive them, they are not forgiven' " (John 20:22, 23). The massive out pouring of the Holy Spirit would come later after Jesus returned to heaven. For now Jesus breathed His Spirit on them to illustrate how much they would need the Holy Spirit's power to do their work for His church.

Giving us the Holy Spirit is giving us Jesus' life. It gives us His characteristics. Only those who have the Holy Spirit in their hearts and whose lives reveal Jesus are qualified to lead His church.

Jesus was not giving anyone the right to judge others and forgive sins. That is God's right. But His church as an organization is responsible for its members as individuals. The church has a duty to protect its family, and if people fall into sinful habits, to warn and teach them and if possible bring them back to a strong relationship with Jesus. As a church, evil must be confronted and sin pointed out no matter how it is disguised. The church must declare what God has said about lying, Sabbath breaking, stealing, and every other type of evil. If members continue to sin, then the penalties described in

"Stop doubting and believe!"

God's Word will be recorded against them in heaven. The church must show that their actions are unacceptable or else it brings shame on God.

But only in that sense does the church have anything to do with forgiving sinners. Sins can be forgiven only through Jesus. No human and no organization has been given the power to take away a person's guilt—only Jesus can. " 'His name is the only power in the world that has been given to save people' " (Acts 4:12).

DOUBTING THOMAS

When Jesus met the disciples in that upstairs room, Thomas was not with them. He heard the stories from the others about Jesus, but his heart was still filled with gloom and doubt. Even if Jesus had really risen, there was no longer any hope of seeing His kingdom on earth. And he was hurt to think that Jesus would show Himself to everyone else except him. Thomas decided not to believe and for a whole week he sulked sadly.

Over and over Thomas declared, "I will not believe it until I see the nail marks in His hands for myself, until I can touch those scars and the scar on His side." He had no faith in what the others told him. Thomas loved his Lord, but he allowed jealousy and doubt to control his heart.

One evening Thomas agreed to meet with the others in the usual room for supper. He still had a faint hope that the good news was true. As they ate, the disciples talked about the things Jesus had shown them from the prophecies. Suddenly, even though the door was locked, Jesus appeared in the room and said, "Peace be with you."

Then He turned to Thomas. "Look at My hands. Touch them with your finger. Put your hand on the scar on My side. Stop doubting and believe!"

Thomas knew that none of the others had told Jesus about his words of doubt. Clearly Jesus knew even his thoughts. He didn't need any other proof. His heart leaped with joy as he fell down at Jesus' feet and said, "My Lord and my God."

Jesus accepted Thomas's words, but He gently scolded him for his doubts. " 'You believe because you see me. Those who believe without seeing me will be truly happy' " (John 20:29). If we followed Thomas's example, no one would believe, because we all must learn about Jesus from someone else. Many who—like Thomas—insist on having all their doubts removed will never find the answers they seek. Doubting will eventually become what they believe in most. Then when they urgently need faith and confidence in God, they will find themselves unable to hope and believe.

The way Jesus treated Thomas also shows us how to treat those who express their doubts publicly. In spite of Thomas's unreasonable demands, Jesus showed him what he asked for. Doubt rarely can be argued away. What any doubter needs is to see Jesus, the crucified Savior, in all His love and mercy.

CHAPTER 85

BY THE LAKE
ONCE MORE

"Jesus said, 'Take care of my sheep' "
(John 20:16).

esus planned to meet His disciples in Galilee. If they had left Jerusalem during the Passover week, they would have been accused of giving up their Jewish faith. But when the week ended, they gladly headed toward home to meet Jesus as He had asked.

Seven of the disciples traveled together. For three years they had learned from the greatest Educator the world has ever known. They had become intelligent and sophisticated teachers who would lead others to understand the truth.

The disciples gathered at a place where they would not be disturbed. From here they could see the beach where thousands had been fed from a few small loaves of bread and fishes. Not far away was Capernaum, the site of many of Jesus' miracles.

They were rich in experiences and in their knowledge of truth, but otherwise very poor. Peter, who still loved boats and fishing, suggested that they go out on the lake and lower their old nets in the water. A successful night's fishing would pay for the food and clothing they needed. So they went and fished through the night, but caught nothing. Through the long tiring hours they talked about Jesus. Their

This chapter is based on John 21:1-22.

Peter himself felt that he would no longer be trusted.

own future seemed sad and confusing.

As the morning dawned, the boat was near the shore. A stranger called out to the disciples from the beach. "Friends, did you catch any fish?"

"No," they answered.

"Throw your nets out on the right side," He called back. "Then you will catch some." So they did and suddenly the net was so full that they couldn't pull it back into the boat.

Then John recognized the Stranger. "It is the Lord," he exclaimed to Peter. Peter was so happy he jumped into the water and waded to where Jesus stood. The others brought the boat in, pulling the net that was full of fish. When they got to shore, they found a fire of hot coals. Beside the fish on the fire, there was bread also.

Jesus said, "Bring some of the fish you caught." Peter rushed out into the water to help drag the net to shore. After the work was done, Jesus served the cooked food to each of them. All seven recognized Him, but they were quiet as they ate.

The disciples were reminded of the day when Jesus had asked them to follow Him. He called them from their fishing boats and promised to make them fish for people. To bring these things to their minds, Jesus performed the same fishing miracle again. His death had not changed their responsibility to do the work He had given them. The risen Savior would still provide for their needs. If they worked for Him, they could not fail.

PETER IS REINSTATED

Jesus had another lesson to teach. When Peter denied knowing Jesus, he had disgraced himself and dishonored his Savior. The others thought that he would not be allowed to keep his standing as one of the new church's leaders—the apostles. Peter himself felt that he would no longer be trusted.

Now Peter needed to show some evidence that he had truly repented and changed. If he didn't, his sin might destroy his influence as a leader for the new church. Jesus was going to give Peter a chance to regain the confidence of the others, and as far as possible repair the damage done to Jesus' cause.

This is a lesson for all Christians. Secret sins should be confessed only to God, but public sins should be confessed in public. Peter's sin gave Satan a victory and caused others to reconsider their loyalty to Jesus. By showing that he had repented and changed, Peter could repair the damage.

As the group were eating together, Jesus said to Peter, "Simon, do you love Me more than these others do?"

Peter answered quietly, "Yes, Lord. You know that I love You." This time, there was no insisting that he loved Jesus more than anyone else.

Jesus responded, "Feed My lambs." Then, He asked again, "Simon, do you love Me?"

Peter's answer again was a simple, "Yes, Lord. You know I love You."

Jesus instructed him, "Take care of My sheep." Then one more time, He asked the question. "Simon, do you love Me?"

Peter was hurt that Jesus kept asking him the same question. He answered, "Lord, You know everything. You know that I love You."

To build his faith for that final test, Jesus talked to Peter about his future.

Once again Jesus responded, "Feed My sheep."

Peter had publicly denied Jesus three times. Now Jesus publicly pressed the same question three times. In front of the other disciples, Jesus showed how sorry Peter was and how much he had changed. Because he had become humble and had repented, Peter was more prepared to act as a shepherd to the flock Jesus was leaving behind.

The first work Jesus gave Peter was to feed the "lambs"—to work with those who were new believers, to open the Scriptures and educate them. His own mistakes and repentance had prepared him especially for this work. Before his fall, Peter was always quick to correct others and to speak his mind. But the humble, converted Peter was very different. He had the same passion, but now his enthusiasm was under Jesus' control. He was ready to feed the lambs as well as the sheep of Jesus' flock.

The way Jesus treated Peter taught the disciples to handle sinners with patience, sympathy, and forgiving love. Remembering his own weakness, Peter would treat his flock the way Jesus had treated him.

PETER'S FUTURE

Before Jesus' arrest, Peter had sworn to die for Him if necessary. But he failed even to stand up for Jesus. Someday he would have another opportunity to prove his love. To build his faith for that final test, Jesus talked to Peter about his future. After a life of working for his Savior, Peter would indeed have the chance to die for Him. Jesus told Peter, " 'When you are old, you will put out your hands and someone else will tie you and take you where you don't want to go' " (John 21:18). Jesus saw that Peter's hands would be spread out on a cross. Once again, He told His disciple, "Follow Me."

Peter wasn't discouraged to know this. He felt willing to suffer anything for his Lord. Before, Peter had loved Jesus as a man; now he loved Him as God. When he was led to a cross at the end of his life, Peter asked that he be crucified upside down. He thought it was too great an honor to die the same way his Master had.

Always before, Peter had tried to plan God's work instead of waiting to follow God's plan. Jesus told him, "Follow Me. Don't run ahead of Me. Let Me go ahead of you and you won't be defeated by the enemy."

As Peter walked beside Jesus along the shore, he glanced back to see John following them. Suddenly curious, he asked, "Lord, what will happen to him?"

Jesus shook His head and answered, "If I want him to live until I come back, that isn't your concern. Just follow Me." Jesus didn't say that John would live until the Second Coming. He said that even if that happened, it wouldn't affect Peter's work. Personal duty was what was required of each of them.

Many people today are more interested in other people's business than their own. We should each be sure to look only at Jesus and follow Him. By watching Him, our lives will be changed.

John lived to see Jerusalem destroyed and the temple demolished. To the end of his life, he followed Jesus faithfully.

Peter was reinstated as an apostle, but Jesus did not give him any authority over the others. This was clear in His answer to Peter's question about John—"That isn't your concern. Just follow Me." Peter was not placed in charge of the new church. He was a very influential leader, but the lesson Jesus taught him by the lake that day stayed with him the rest of his life.

Later, in a letter to the churches, Peter reminded the leaders and elders that he had learned from Jesus how to care for His sheep. He said, "Do not be like a ruler over people you are responsible for, but be good examples to them. Then when Christ, the Chief Shepherd, comes, you will get a glorious crown that will never lose its beauty" (1 Peter 5:3, 4).

CHAPTER 86

PROMISES
IN GALILEE

*" 'Go everywhere in the world, and tell the Good News
to everyone' " (Mark 16:15).*

ust before Jesus returned to His throne in heaven, He
gave His disciples an assignment: " 'All power in heaven
and on earth is given to me. So go and make followers of
all people in the world' " (Matthew 28:18, 19). Again and
again He repeated the words so no one could mistake their importance. " 'Go everywhere in the world, and tell the Good News to
everyone' " (Mark 16:15). The light of heaven was to shine brightly on
all the people of the earth.

This assignment had first been given to the Twelve in the upstairs room, but now it was given to a much larger group. This gathering on a hillside in Galilee included all the believers who could be
called together. The angel at the tomb reminded the disciples of
Jesus' promise to meet them in Galilee. This promise was passed on
to many others who were still mourning His death. They came from
every direction.

When the announced time arrived, about five hundred believers
were standing around in small groups on the hillside, eager to learn
all they could from those who had seen Jesus since His resurrection.
The disciples moved from group to group, sharing what they had seen

This chapter is based on Matt. 28:16-20.

and heard of Jesus, and sharing what He had taught them from the Scriptures.

Suddenly Jesus was standing in the middle of the crowd. No one could tell how He got there or where He came from. Many of the people had never seen Jesus before, but when they saw the scars from the Crucifixion on His hands and feet, they accepted Him as the Savior and worshiped Him.

Still some doubted that it was Him. There will always be some people who find it hard to show faith and find it easy to doubt.

This is the only talk Jesus had with most of His believers after His resurrection. His words, coming from lips that had been still in death, thrilled their hearts. As He declared that all the power of heaven and earth was His, their minds were lifted up to see His true nobility and glory.

Jesus' words announced that His sacrifice for humans was complete—His work on this earth was finished. He was on His way to God's throne. His work as our Mediator had begun. With His unlimited power and authority, He gave the assignment: " 'So go and make followers of all people in the world. Baptize them in the name of the Father, and the Son, and the Holy Spirit. Teach them to obey everything that I have taught you, and I will be with you always, even until the end of this age' " (Matthew 28:19, 20). His disciples were commissioned to offer the world a faith that was for all people in all nations.

As they preached to people of many nations, the disciples would be given the ability to speak other languages.

Jesus made it clear that He was building a spiritual kingdom, not a national or political kingdom on earth. He reminded them that everything He had told them about the Messiah's being rejected, killed, and raised to life on the third day had come to pass just as the prophecies had indicated.

Jesus assigned His disciples to do the work He left for them, beginning in Jerusalem. Jerusalem had been the scene of His amazing sacrifice for humans. Very few had seen how near heaven was to earth while Jesus was among them there. Jerusalem was where the disciples' work would begin.

There may have been more promising places to begin the work, but the disciples didn't ask for that. Jesus had scattered the seeds of truth in Jerusalem and there would be a great harvest from that city. The first offer of forgiveness and mercy would be made to the ones who had murdered Jesus.

Many people in Jerusalem secretly believed in Jesus and many had been misled by the priests and leaders. All of these needed to hear an invitation to repent and follow Jesus. While the city was still stirred over the events of the past few weeks, the gospel would make its greatest impression.

But the work wouldn't stop there. It would spread to the farthest areas of the planet. Jesus told them, "Although Israel rejected Me as the Scriptures said they would, they will have another opportunity to accept the Son of God. I give you this message of mercy to take to Israel first, then to all nations and people. All who accept it will be gathered into one church."

THE HOLY SPIRIT

By the power of the Holy Spirit, the disciples' words would be confirmed by signs and miracles. Miracles would be performed not only by the apostles, but by those who accepted their message. " 'And those who believe will be able to do these things as proof: They will use my name to force out demons. They will speak in new languages. They will pick up snakes and drink poison without being hurt. They will touch the sick, and the sick will be healed' " (Mark 16:17, 18).

At that time, evil men thought nothing of removing those in the way of their plans by poisoning them. Jesus knew that many would think they were doing God's work by killing His followers, so He promised protection from this danger.

And with these words a new gift was given. As they preached to people of many nations, the disciples would be given the ability to speak other languages. The apostles and their fellow disciples were uneducated men, but when the Holy Spirit flooded over them on the Day of Pentecost, their speaking—in their own language or a foreign one—became clear and correct, both in the words and the accent.

So Jesus gave His disciples the gifts they would need to do His work. "Go to all the nations of the earth," He told them. "Go to the most distant lands, but know that I will be there with you. Work with confidence and faith."

The Savior's assignment includes all believers until the end of time. It is fatal to think that the work of reaching others with God's saving message belongs only to ministers. The church was started for this purpose and all who join it are pledging to become co-workers with Jesus. Whatever people do in life, their first job should be to bring others to Jesus. Not everyone can preach to large groups, but everyone can speak to individuals. It is not hard times or poverty that tears down humans—it is guilt. Jesus sends us to reach out to these sin-sick souls.

The church's life depends on faithfully following God's plan for it.

All can begin work where they are. There may be members of our own families who are starving for the bread of life. There may be friends or neighbors who know nothing about God or who do not believe He exists. If done in faith, this work will be felt all over the world. God often uses the simplest methods to get the greatest results.

The gifts of the Spirit are promised to every believer, and are given when needed to do the Lord's work. The promise is just as real today as it was in the days of the apostles.

Jesus came to heal the sick and to release the prisoners of Satan. He gave His life for them. He knew that many who begged Him for help brought their disease on themselves by their life style. But He helped them anyway. And many found healing for their spiritual problems as well as their physical illness.

His gospel still has the same power. Jesus feels the pain of every person who suffers. When one of His children is burning up with a fever, He feels the agony. He is just as willing to heal today as He was when He was here on earth. And He wants His followers to be channels for His healing power.

HEALTHFUL LIVING

In Jesus' healing there were lessons for His followers. The cure could come only by His power, but Jesus used simple and natural remedies. He taught that violating God's natural and spiritual laws caused disease. The pain and misery in this world would not exist if people lived in harmony with the Creator's plan. Jesus taught that health is the reward of obeying God's laws.

We should use the remedies God has provided in nature and point the sick to the One who can heal them and restore their health. We should teach them to believe in the Great Healer.

Life-giving energy can flow from us to others if we are receiving Jesus' love through our faith in Him. There were places where Jesus Himself could not do miracles because the people didn't believe in Him. Today, doubt often separates God's church from the Holy Spirit He sent. Our lack of faith disappoints God and robs Him of His glory. The church's life depends on faithfully following God's plan for it. When we are not working to reach others, our love weakens and our faith fades.

Angels are amazed to see how little humans appreciate God's love. How would a mother or father feel if they knew that their child died in a snowstorm while someone who could have saved the child did nothing? God sees every suffering human as His child and He is angry with those who do not reach out to help.

THE GOSPEL HAS POWER

Jesus instructed His disciples to teach people to obey what He taught them. This includes what He taught through the prophets in the Old Testament. But it leaves no room for teaching traditions, human theories, or church laws. The Bible, the record of His own words and deeds, is the treasure we are to share with the world.

The gospel should not be shared as a theory, but as a living force that changes lives. Jesus accepts even the most evil and hateful humans, then the gospel changes them. When they repent, He gives them His Holy Spirit and sends them back to their friends and acquaintances to show His life-changing love. Through His grace, humans can form a character like that of Jesus.

Jesus' followers should present the story of His gift—His love and sacrifice for us—in the most attractive way possible. The story of Jesus' wonderful love will melt hearts that will never respond to presentations of doctrine. Words alone cannot tell the story of that love—the storyteller's life must show it as well. Jesus is sitting for a portrait in every one of His followers. His love and His truth are being sketched onto each of our faces and hearts. In each of us, His patient love, His mercy, and His truth should shine out to the world.

Those first disciples prepared themselves for their work. Before the Feast of Pentecost, they met together and settled all their arguments and worries. With single purpose and mind, they prayed in faith for those in the world around them. Then the Holy Spirit was given them without measure. As they preached with power, thousands were converted to Jesus in a single day.

It can be the same way now. We should put away our disagreements and give ourselves to God's plan for saving those who are lost. We should ask with faith for the same blessing of the Holy Spirit, and it will come. The outpouring of the Holy Spirit on the apostles was called the "early rain," and the results were amazing. But when the "later rain" falls in the last days, it will be even more glorious.

Those who dedicate their body, soul, and mind to God will constantly receive new gifts of physical and mental power. By cooperating with Jesus, even weak humans will be allowed to do the works of God.

The Savior longs to show His grace and stamp His character on the whole world. He wants to make humans free and pure and holy. Through His power, we will have victories over sin that will bring glory to God and to the Lamb. Jesus will see the results of His sacrifice and be satisfied.

CHAPTER 87

THE TRIUMPHANT
RETURN TO HEAVEN

" 'I will be with you always, even until the end of this age' "
(Matthew 28:19, 20).

t was time for Jesus to return to His Father's throne as a conquering King. After His resurrection, He stayed on earth for a time so that His disciples could become familiar with Him in His glorified body. No longer did they think of the tomb when they looked at Him. Now they saw Him as glorified before the heavenly universe. So now it was time for Him to leave.

For His last meeting with the eleven disciples, Jesus chose a place they had often visited together—the Mount of Olives. His prayers and His tears had blessed its groves and gardens. He had prayed and agonized alone in the Garden of Gethsemane at the mountain's base. His feet will stand on its peak when He returns as a glorious King.

As they passed through the gate in Jerusalem, many people saw the little group, led by Someone whom their leaders had crucified only a few weeks before. The disciples didn't know that this was their last talk with their Master. Jesus spent the time discussing and repeating things He had taught them before. As they approached Gethsemane, He paused. Once more He pointed out the vine He had

This chapter is based on Luke 24:50-53; Acts 1:9-12.

used to illustrate the relationship between His Father, Himself, and His church. Again He repeated those truths.

For thirty-three years, Jesus had suffered contempt, insults, and mocking laughter. He had been rejected by His people and crucified. Now as He considered the thankless people He came to save, would He reject them and pull away His love? No. Instead, He promised, " 'I will be with you always, even until the end of this age' " (Matthew 28:20).

All of heaven was waiting to welcome the Savior home.

Jesus led the way across the top of the Mount of Olives to the area of Bethany. There He stopped and the eleven gathered around Him. Jesus looked into their faces with love. He didn't remind them of their faults and failures. His last words were words of tender love. Then with His arms stretched out to bless them, assuring them of His loving protection, He slowly rose up from among them, drawn toward heaven by a power stronger than gravity.

As Jesus rose higher, the disciples strained for the last glimpse of their Lord and Friend. As a cloud of angels met Him, His last words floated down to their ears; "I am with you always." At the same time, they heard the sweetest and most joyful music of an angel choir.

"WHY ARE YOU STANDING THERE?"

While the disciples were still staring into the sky, two angels in human form appeared beside them and said, " 'Men of Galilee, why are you standing here looking into the sky? Jesus, whom you saw taken up from you into heaven, will come back in the same way you saw him go' " (Acts 1:11).

These angels—the same powerful angels who had come to the tomb at Jesus' resurrection—longed to join the heavenly crowds who were welcoming Jesus home. But out of sympathy for those He left behind, they waited to give them comfort and encouragement.

Jesus rose as a human—the same Human who ate with them and who that very day had walked with them up the Mount of Olives. The angels assured them that this same Person would return just as He had gone. He would come back in the clouds, and every person would see Him. As He had said, " 'The Son of Man will come again in his great glory, with all his angels. He will be King and sit on his great throne' " (Matthew 25:31).

Then Jesus' own promise to them would be fulfilled: " 'After I go and prepare a place for you, I will come back and take you to be with me so that you may be where I am' " (John 14:3).

After Jesus' trial and crucifixion, His enemies expected to see the disciples depressed and defeated. Instead, their faces glowed with happiness that could come only from heaven. They were thrilled to share the wonderful story of Jesus' resurrection and return to heaven, and many people accepted Jesus and believed because of it.

The disciples no longer feared for the future. They knew that Jesus was in heaven and that He cared about them still. They knew they had a Friend at God's throne, and could hardly wait to present their requests in Jesus' name. As they prayed, they repeated Jesus' promise: " 'My Father will give you anything you ask for in my name. . . . Ask and you will receive, so that your joy will be the fullest possible joy' " (John 16:23, 24). And the Holy Spirit—the Comforter—brought them greater joy, just as Jesus had promised.

THE GLORIOUS KING COMES HOME

All of heaven was waiting to welcome the Savior home. As He rose, He led the large group of prisoners set free from death and sin at His resurrection. When they came near the city of God, the angel escort called out a challenge:

> "Gates of heaven, open wide!
> Open wide, ancient doors
> So the glorious King can come in!"

With great joy the waiting angel guards responded: "Who is this glorious King?" They knew who was coming—they just wanted to hear the answer of praise:

"The Lord, strong and mighty,
The Lord, our Mighty Warrior!
Gates of heaven, open wide!
Open wide, ancient doors
So the glorious King can come home!"

Then the mighty gates of the city opened wide and the angel throng swept through with a burst of heavenly music. The commanders of the angel armies and the sons of God from other worlds had gathered to welcome home the Savior and to celebrate His victory.

But Jesus waved them back. First He stepped up to His Father. He pointed to the healed wounds on His head, His side, and His feet. He lifted His hands, which still showed the marks of the nails. Then He presented the ones who had come to life with Him as representatives of the great numbers who will come from the grave at His second coming.

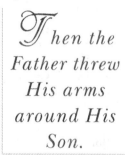

Then the Father threw His arms around His Son.

Before the earth was created, Father and Son had joined hands in a solemn pledge that Jesus would become the Guarantor for the human race. When Jesus cried out from the cross, "It is finished," He was speaking to His Father. Their agreement had been carried out. Now He declared, "Father, I have completed the work of redemption. I want the people that You gave Me to be with Me here."

The voice of God proclaimed that justice had been met, that Satan was defeated, that Jesus' struggling loved ones on earth were accepted. Then the Father threw His arms around His Son. The announcement was made, " 'Let all God's angels worship him' " (Hebrews 1:6).

With those words, heaven seemed to overflow with joy and praise. Love had conquered evil. Those who had been lost were now found. Heaven rang with choruses of voices proclaiming, " 'To the One who sits on the throne and to the Lamb be praise and honor and glory and power forever and ever' " (Revelation 5:13).

From that scene of joy in heaven, we hear the echo of Jesus' words, "I am going back to my Father and your Father, to my God and your God" (John 20:17). The family of heaven and the family of earth are now joined together forever. For us, Jesus—our Lord—our Messiah—rose, and for us He lives. "So he is able always to save those who come to God through him because he always lives, asking God to help them" (Hebrews 7:25).